Online Learning Communities

a volume in
Perspectives in Instructional Technology and Distance Education

Series Editors:
Charles Schlosser and Michael Simonson
Nova Southeastern University

Perspectives in Instructional Technology and Distance Education

Charles Schlosser and Michael Simonson, Series Editors

Research on Enhancing the Interactivity of Online Learning (2006)
edited by Vivian H. Wright, Cynthia Szymanski Sunal,
and Elizabeth K. Wilson

*Trends and Issues in Distance Education:
An International Perspective* (2005)
edited by Yusra Laila Visser, Lya Visser,
Michael Simonson, and Ray Amirault

*Toward the Virtual University:
International On-Line Learning Perspectives* (2003)
edited by Nicolae Nistor, Susan English,
Steve Wheeler, and Mihai Jalobeanu

Learning From Media: Arguments, Analysis, and Evidence (2001)
edited by Richard E. Clark

Online Learning Communities

edited by

Rocci Luppicini
University of Ottawa

Information Age Publishing, Inc.
Charlotte, North Carolina • www.infoagepub.com

Library of Congress Cataloging-in-Publication Data

Online learning communities / edited by Rocci Luppicini.
    p. cm. — (Perspectives in instructional technology and distance
education series)
  Includes bibliographical references.
  ISBN 978-1-59311-678-1 (pbk.) — ISBN 978-1-59311-679-8 (hardcover)
1. Distance education. 2. Computer-assisted instruction. 3.
Education—Computer network resources. 4. Educational technology. I.
Luppicini, Rocci.
  LC5800.L445 2007
  371.3'58—dc22

                                              2007006801

ISBN 13: 978-1-59311-678-1 (pbk.)
ISBN 13: 978-1-59311-679-8 (hardcover)
ISBN 10:   1-59311-678-0 (pbk.)
ISBN 10:   1-59311-679-9 (hardcover)

CONTENTS

Foreword
Sir John Daniel   *ix*

A Focus on Online Learning Communities
Rocci Luppicini   *xiii*

PART I:
PERSPECTIVES ON ONLINE LEARNING COMMUNITIES

1. Online Learning Communities in Perspective
   Rena M. Palloff and Keith Pratt   *3*

2. A Typology of Catalysts, Emphases, and Elements of
   Virtual Learning Communities
   Richard A. Schwier   *17*

3. Online Learning Communities With Online Mentors:
   A Conceptual Framework
   Shujen L. Chang   *41*

4. Foundations and Practice for Web-Enhanced Science Inquiry:
   Grounded Design Perspectives
   Minchi C. Kim and Michael J. Hannafin   *53*

PART II: DESIGN AND INSTRUCTION
FOR ONLINE LEARNING COMMUNITIES

5. Designing Effective Online Instruction
   Gary Morrision and Steven Ross   *75*

6. The Use of Discussion Forums in Learning Communities
    Stephen Corich, Kinshuk and L.M. Jeffrey   87

7. Engaging and Supporting Problem Solving in Online Learning
    David H. Jonassen   109

8. Laying the Groundwork for the Development of
    Learning Communities Within Online Courses
    Jennifer V. Lock   129

PART III:
RESEARCH ON ONLINE LEARNING COMMUNITIES

9. Connections in Web-Based Learning Environments:
    A Research-Based Model for Community Building
    Janette R. Hill, Arjan Raven, and Seungyeon Han   153

10. Identifying Factors That Effect Learning Community
    Development and Performance in Asynchronous
    Distance Education
    *Douglas Harvey, Leslie A. Moller, Jason Bond Huett,
    Veronica M. Godshalk, and Margaret Downs*   169

11. Examining the Use of Learning Communities to
    Increase Motivation
    *Jason Bond Huett, Leslie A. Moller, Douglas Harvey,
    and Mary E. Engstrom*   189

12. Linking Community Partners: Utilizing Videoconferencing
    *Pamela A. Havice, William L. Havice, Clint Isbell,
    and Larry Grimes*   205

PART IV:
INTERNATIONAL PERSPECTIVES
ON ONLINE LEARNING COMMUNITIES

13. Exploring Elements for Creating an Online Community of
    Learners Within a Distance Education Course at the
    University Of Southern Queensland
    P. A. Danaher, Andrew Hickey,alice Brown, and Joan M. Conway   219

14. Building Learning Communities Around New Partnership for
    Africa's Development (NEPAD) E-Schools Initiative
    Peter E. Kinyanjui   241

15. International Perspectives on Distance Education and Learning
    Communities Within Anglophone Commonwealth Countries
    Badri N. Koul   257

16. Orchestrating Ethics for Distance Education and Online Learning
   Ugur Demiray   *277*

PART V:
TRENDS IN ONLINE LEARNING COMMUNITIES

17. Online Self-Organizing Social Systems: Four Years Later
   David Wiley   *289*

18. Exploring Qualitative Methodologies in Online
   Learning Environments
   Mary Beth Bianco and Alison A. Carr-Chellman   *299*

19. Revisiting Categories of Virtual Learning Communities for
   Educational Design
   Rocci Luppicini   *319*

20. Contrasting Forces Affecting the Practice of Distance Education
   Brent G. Wilson, Patrick Parrish, Nathan Balasubramanian,
   and Scott Switzer   *333*

About the Authors   *347*

FOREWORD

Sir John Daniel

I welcome this collection of papers on online learning communities and commend the contributors for the serious and sober tone of their articles. As its name implies, distance education requires the bridging of distances that separate learners from the source of their learning. The separation may be caused by physical distance, by scheduling conflicts, or by more subtle social and psychological barriers. For this reason, distance educators have always welcomed new technologies that hold the promise of overcoming these obstacles.

Somewhere in my slide collection I have a set of quotations about the tremendous potential of each of the new learning technologies that have appeared since the industrial revolution. These statements, contemporary with the appearance of each new medium, start with the blackboard in the mid nineteenth century and continue through radio, film, television, computing, programed learning, and the Internet. Two things are notable about these quotations. First, they all claim that this new technology will revolutionise education. Second, the revolutionary potential of each innovation is compared not to the previous new technology but usually to Gutenberg's printing press.

In presenting experiences of teaching and learning online, this collection is refreshingly free from such hype. The Internet may still be rela-

Online Learning Communities
pp. ix–xii

tively new, but it so compresses time that to talk of an Internet revolution
in education is already passé. Indeed, some educators are already disillu-
sioned because e-learning has underperformed relative to the high
expectations it generated. By tracing a well-researched path between
overexcitement and unjustified cynicism, the authors have contributed
significantly to the maturing discourse about networked learning.

The most useful feature of the book is that it stimulates reflection on
the nature of learning communities. Because many of the authors are
from North America, the classroom community is usually the norm with
which comparisons are made. This is a strength—because it provides a
known reference point—but also a weakness because we ought to have
higher aspirations for educational technology than merely producing
learning outcomes that show "no significant difference" with "conventional" methods.

Why do we need learning communities? At the simplest level, they simply express the social nature of human beings. I remember one community college in which the same group of women enrolled in the Chinese
cooking course every year. Their aim was not to develop enough expertise to open Chinese restaurants, but simply to have a congenial place to
meet for social interchange while engaging in a common task. Networked
learning can provide elements of such an environment.

We should not assume, however, that all students wish to use their
course for social exchange. As a student in my first Web-based course in
the late 1990s, I resented the compulsion to take part in online discussions because I derived nothing useful from them. If the purpose of a
course is to instruct, then creating the possibility of online interaction
with the teacher and within the student group may be a useful palliative
to weaknesses in instructional clarity—but it should not be compulsory for
those who can find their way without it.

The examples explored in this book show that creating a learning
community as a team with a task is a more fruitful approach. To be faith-
ful to a commitment to constructivist learning, we must get away from the
notion of instruction and genuinely involve students in the construction
of their own learning. This can be done on an individual basis, as it was
through the weekly essay that I had to write as an undergraduate at
Oxford University.

To justify doing it through a group means bringing individual contributions to bear on a common task. I think, for example, of an online
course at the United Kingdom's Open University in which each student
group has to develop a negotiating position for a United Nations environmental conference with each member of the group contributing to
that negotiating position from the perspective of a country other than
their own. Such an exercise can be extremely engaging for both students

and teachers, although both parties usually complain that the workload involved is far beyond what it normally expected!

This is an example of a key conclusion that emerges from this book: for best results, new technologies require new pedagogies. This was true for the early media of distance education and is an even greater imperative for today's sophisticated online systems. A generation ago, the world's open universities took the pedagogy of print, exemplified by the textbook, and transformed it into a more effective vehicle for learning with objectives, self-assessment questions, and attractive layouts. Textbook publishers are now following their example. Some open universities effected similar advances in the pedagogy of television broadcasting and, later, realizing that it was a different medium, in the use of videocassettes.

Today, networked learning incorporates the media of print and video and offers much else besides. In particular, it can be a vehicle for the interactive components of learning that most students require in order to succeed. The studies of learning communities reported here show that developing an effective pedagogy of interaction must begin from an appreciation of what constitutes genuine interaction. Having something new come up on the computer screen when I click the mouse or type on the keyboard is not real interaction. Effective interaction requires a response tailored to my particular situation as a learner such as would come from another human being.

Despite considerable expenditure, automated tutorial systems are still in their infancy. As many examples in this book show, online learning communities can supply genuine and useful interaction at much lower cost—and usually in more interesting ways. One simple but important principle is that getting students to do things for themselves is more effective than pushing information at them. I learn more from having a tutor comment extensively on my own essay than from reading a model essay by an expert.

Online systems allow students to do many things for themselves. Because some in higher education have highlighted the risks of plagiarism in the online world, software to detect plagiarism is now available. One Malaysian university, instead of having its teachers use such software when they mark students' work, require the students to run a check using the software before submitting their assignments. This is surely much more effective in promoting the sense of responsibility and ethical behavior that is another theme of this book.

In summary, this book demonstrates that developing online learning systems is a work in progress. By exploring the functioning of online learning communities from various angles in a thoughtful manner, these

papers will speed up that progress and enrich the community of practice
that is emerging around networked learning.

—October 2006

A FOCUS ON ONLINE LEARNING COMMUNITIES

Rocci Luppicini

The notion of community is far from new. The roots of community are as old as history itself, for history, among other things, is about telling stories of past developments in society involving individuals and communities in various places and at various periods. Early cave drawings from thousand of years ago depict the experiences of people hunting animals and living together with one another in communities. Today, the idea of community continues to play a key role in defining who we are and what we do within society. Thus, the importance of community is part of our history and the society we live in today.

Although the conceptualization of community is deeply entrenched within society, the contemporary idea of learning communities is quite recent, particularly in the field of distance education where learning communities are most often discussed in the context of online and blended environments. The what, why, and how of learning communities has spurred a great deal of interest within distance education over the last decade. Some scholars see learning communities as an ideal solution to many challenges in education and work. Others view learning communities as a valuable add-on to instruction in online and blended learning

Online Learning Communities
pp. xiii–xviii
Copyright © 2007 by Information Age Publishing

environments. Many of the lessons gained from learning community research and practice have been applied to a variety of distance education systems around the world. Because of this widespread interest in learning communities within distance education, there is a pressing need to integrate current work in the area, including current trends and issues that affect the field of distance education.

Online Learning Communities contributes to the field of distance education by presenting key perspectives and examining and discussing specific current trends and issues faced by the distance learning community. To this end, the book brings together respected authors and internationally known experts in the field of distance education to provide insight into a wide array of themes revolving around current work on communities of learning in distance education.

ABOUT THIS BOOK

Online Learning Communities is a volume in the series Perspectives in Instructional Technology and Distance Education, from Information Age Publishing. The purpose of the book is to delve into important themes connected to current work on communities of learning in distance education. The book begins with a foreword by Sir John Daniel and is divided into five sections: Part I: Perspectives on Online Learning Communities, Part II: Design and Instruction for Online Learning Communities, Part III: Research on Online Learning Communities, Part IV: International Perspectives on Online Learning Communities, and Part V: Trends in Online Learning Communities.

Part I: Perspectives on Online Learning Communities begins with a chapter from Rena Palloff and Keith Pratt, authors of the 1999 Frandson Award-winning book *Building Learning Communities in Cyberspace: Effective Strategies for the Online Classroom* (Jossey-Bass, 1999). Palloff and Pratt discuss how the development of online environments can leverage successful learning outcomes while promoting collaboration and a sense of community among learners. This chapter reviews previous work and explores current applications of online learning communities for distance learning environments. In chapter 2, Richard Schwier examines conceptual issues concerning the development of virtual learning communities (VLCs). This chapter considers key issues surrounding the general use of communication technologies in formal and informal learning environments. Chapter 3 and chapter 4 explore specific areas of online learning. In chapter 3, Shujen Chang presents a model of online learning communities with online mentors and applies it to online degree programs at a large southeastern state university. Chapter 4, by Minchi Kim and

Michael Hannafin, investigates the foundations and practice of science learning in Web-enhanced learning environments (WELEs) to support scientific inquiry. Collectively, these chapters are conceptual in nature, integrating theory and research to address fundamental themes connected to online learning communities.

Because many of the authors are from North America, a section from international experts in distance education and online learning communities helps to broaden the focus on online learning communities by situating it within an international context of distance education and online learning community initiatives. To this end, Part II: Design and Instruction for Online Learning Communities presents a fascinating array of chapters exploring instructional design issues. In chapter 5, Gary Morrison and Steven Ross present models that describe learning in a distance education environment and explore how an instructional design model can be used to design distance education instruction. Chapter 6 extends the discussion of instructional design aspects by examining the use of discussion forums in social constructivist learning communities. This chapter introduces new discussion forum tools and explores how these tools can leverage knowledge construction and collaboration in a virtual classroom. Chapter 7 reproduces a seminal position paper from David Jonasssen. It focuses on pervasive struggles in designing online instruction and how to transcend these struggles to support problem solving in online learning. Building on this, chapter 8 provides conceptual grounding for the development of online learning communities by exploring their meaning, their defining characteristics, and practices. Overall, chapters in this section address important issues and trends related to design and instruction in online learning communities.

Part III: Research on Online Learning Communities focuses on research in distance education and online learning communities. Chapter 9 is a case study exploring best practices for community building in Web-based learning environments (WBLEs). The study uses multiple sources of evidence (e.g., chat and bulletin board transcripts, interviews, and surveys) to inform findings and offers a provocative research-based model for community building. In chapter 10, a qualitative study is presented concerning learning communities within the context of asynchronous distance education. The chapter examines how community influences learning achievement in a graduate-level asynchronous distance education class. Findings suggest a relationship between learning achievement and strength of the community. Building on this, chapter 11 examines the motivational influence of learning communities on learners and how this links to attitudinal change. Findings indicate a positive influence of motivation on learners. The section concludes with a chapter focusing on participants' reactions to the use of videoconferencing facilities to provide learning opportunities to communities and nonprofit organizations. Findings suggest that participants' reactions are negatively affected by the use of videoconferencing as a delivery method. Taken together, the research studies in this section reflect a growing trend in research on diverse aspects of online learning communities.

Part IV: International Perspectives on Online Learning Communities contains a series of chapters from international experts in distance education and online learning communities. Chapter 13 presents a study exploring elements for creating an online community of learners within a distance education course at the University of Southern Queensland. Chapter 14 highlights the New Partnership for Africa's Development (NEPAD) aimed at building information and communication technology (ICT) skills in the African population. In chapter 15, Badri Koul draws on professional experiences and explores issues related to distance education and online learning communities within the Anglophone Commonwealth currently comprising 54 countries. The section finishes with a chapter from Ugur Demiray from Anadolu University focusing on issues of ethics and how they affect teaching and learning over online distance modes in Turkey. The chapter calls for a code of ethics constructed by online universities to help nurture distance education and guard against ethical problems that often arise. The chapters in this section provided a look at international perspectives on distance education and learning communities in countries around the world.

Part V: Trends in Online Learning Communities concludes the book with a look at where trends in distance education and online learning communities are heading. Chapter 17, from David Wiley and Brent Brewer, provides a review and update on the growth of online self-organizing social systems (OSOSS). Based on ideas on biological self-organization, this chapter explores emerging forms of informal online learning juxtaposed with the evolution of the Internet. Chapter 18 explores specialized qualitative methodologies in online learning environments. This chapter addresses strategies for testing online qualitative inquires and implications for data collection in online environments. Chapter 19 posits an extended topology of virtual learning communities within formal and informal learning environments and explores key elements of virtual learning communities pertaining to educational design. The final chapter, by Brent Wilson and Scott Switzer, takes a sober look at the current state of distance education with an eye to the future. It provides a review of key forces affecting current practices of distance education (conservative, progressive) and explores technologies to help shape best practices in the field. Overall, this section reviews the current state of distance education and online learning community trends in order to look forward at possible future developments.

In a work such as this, it is impossible to do justice to the diversity of academic scholarship on online learning communities that continues to expand each year. Like most publications connected to a specific academic field or discipline, this book is limited in that it is written from the perspective of experts working in the field of educational technology and distance education. There are other publications that are useful supplementary resources for the interested reader, such as the *Encyclopedia of Virtual Communities and Technologies* (2006), which provides a broad base of information about virtual communities and supporting technologies. The intention of this book was to bring together experts to highlight important developments and new trends in online learning communities within formal and informal distance education environments. As the editor for the book, I am deeply grateful to Sir John Daniel and all contributing chapter authors for their many ideas and insights represented in this book.

PART I

PERSPECTIVES ON ONLINE LEARNING COMMUNITIES

CHAPTER 1

ONLINE LEARNING COMMUNITIES IN PERSPECTIVE

Rena M. Palloff and Keith Pratt

The concept of the online learning community has been extensively researched over the last 10 years and, as a result, our thinking about community continues to evolve as we teach online courses, follow the growing body of research on this important topic, and observe the concept in action. We continue to believe that the online learning community is the vehicle through which education is effectively delivered online. This chapter reviews the evolution in working with the concept of community and how that evolution is supporting the development of effective online courses. We also explore current expanded applications of online learning communities in the distance learning environment.

INTRODUCTION

Wenger (1999) notes that issues of education should be addressed first and foremost in terms of the identities of the participants and the ways in which we create a sense of belonging, two elements that are critical factors in the creation of community, whether it is face to face or online. In other words, it is the social aspects of education that are the most important.

Online Learning Communities
pp. 3–15
Copyright © 2007 by Information Age Publishing

Wenger feels that after these important issues are addressed in an educational setting, the instructor can then turn to the transfer of skills, knowledge, and information. The value of education, according to Wenger, is in social participation and the active involvement in community. Social identity drives learning. Research shows that communities today, whether face to face or online, are formed around issues of identity and shared values (Palloff, 1996). It is through the creation of a sense of shared values and shared identity that we feel a sense of belonging—a sense of community. We have been discussing these issues in relationship to the development of online learning communities for several years (Palloff & Pratt, 1999, 2003, 2004), continuing to believe that community is the vehicle through which online courses are most effectively delivered regardless of content. Our thinking about community, however, continues to evolve as we teach online courses, follow the growing body of research on this important topic, and observe the concept in action. Given that as a backdrop, we will now review our own evolution in working with the concept of community and how that evolution is supporting the development of effective online courses. We will also explore current applications of online learning communities in the distance learning environment that extend the community beyond the classroom.

THE ONGOING DEBATE: CAN COMMUNITY BE FORMED ONLINE?

One of the issues that fuels the debate about whether online learning communities truly exist is in the way we define them, or do not define them as the case may be. Shapiro and Hughes (2002) note that "there is no value-neutral or purely administrative or technical way of building culture and community" (p. 94) and believe that this is the weakness of the literature regarding online community that already exists. How, then, are we and others defining community in the context of an online class or the larger academic institution? Has our definition of online learning communities changed since the writing of *Building Learning Communities in Cyberspace* (Palloff & Pratt, 1999)? Is there a value-neutral way to contextualize community when discussing online learning?

Descriptions of online community have moved a long way from Howard Rheingold's (1993) definition of online community, which states: "virtual communities are cultural aggregations that emerge when enough people bump into each other often enough in cyberspace" (p. 57), to a place of knowing that certain features must be present in order to help the people who are seeing one another frequently in cyberspace coalesce into a community. Our belief in the ability to form online community as well as our own definition of online community and how it plays out in an online course has not varied significantly since we first presented it, although our concepts of what constitutes community have significantly expanded. Online community has been defined in the literature in many ways, but these definitions often include several common elements or themes that we have previously discussed, including such things as the ability to build mutual trust, a connection of the spirit, a sense of belonging, a sense of membership, a sense of support, and an ability to share in the educational journey together (Shea, Swan, & Pickett, 2004). Moore and Brooks (2000) further note that learning communities are characterized by member willingness to share resources, regular communication, systematic problem solving, and sharing in the success of individual members. Charalambos, Michalinos, and Chamberlain (2004) combine much of what has been presented by others when they note what they believe to be common characteristics of learning communities and include:

> A common sense of responsibility exists among participants toward assigned task and peers; A joint vision, control of ownership of the community, its goals and artifacts are equally shared among the members of the community; A safe environment where participants can freely express their opinions and ask questions without the fear of being "attacked" by others; A certain degree of structural dependence that establishes the need for members to interact and share resources; Mutual support among its members and sub-groups. (p. 138)

In our early writing on learning communities (Palloff & Pratt, 1999), we provided a list describing the indicators that tell us when community has formed. The indicators align closely with the elements described by Charalambos et al. (2004) and include evidence of the following:

- Active interaction involving both course content and personal communication
- Collaborative learning evidenced by comments directed primarily student to student rather than student to instructor
- Socially constructed meaning evidenced by agreement or questioning, with the intent to achieve agreement on issues of meaning
- Sharing of resources among students
- Expressions of support and encouragement exchanged between students, as well as willingness to critically evaluate the work of others (p. 32).

More than simply a common meeting space online, then, the learning community in an online course allows for mutual exploration of ideas, a safe place to reflect on and develop those ideas, and a collaborative, supportive approach to academic work.

We believe that there are two components, however, that are not included in these lists that distinguish the online learning community from an online community, such as a listserv or online group, where people meet due to a common interest. Engaging in collaborative learning and the resultant reflective practice involved in transformative learning differentiate the online learning community and lend it its power in the learning process. Gunawardena, Lowe, and Anderson (1997) believe that the process through which the online learning community socially constructs knowledge, using collaboration and reflection, goes through five phases. The first phase involves sharing and comparing information. This is the time early in the formation of the group where participants test each other out, as it were, to determine what strengths and knowledge each brings to the group. The second phase involves the discovery of areas of potential disagreement, dissonance, or inconsistency of ideas. It is at this phase that members of a group might enter into conflict with one another. As we have noted previously (Palloff & Pratt, 2003), the conflict phase is not to be feared, but welcomed as it helps to further develop the group and allows for the give-and-take necessary to the meaningful creation of knowledge. Based on the testing of ideas that goes on the first phase and the disagreement that may occur in the second, Gunawardena et al. propose that the group moves into a third phase in which the negotiation of meaning begins to occur. Phase four sees the group testing their new synthesis of ideas against fact—fact, in this case, may be what is being presented in the text and readings for the course or may be what the participants have experienced in their daily lives. Phases one through four create the "disorienting dilemma" that Mezirow (1990) describes in his theory of transformative learning. By comparing current knowledge against what has always been known, a door opens to the development of new knowledge and meaning. Phase five, then, is illustrated by the emergence of metacognitive statements on the part of students that illustrate that their thinking on the topic has changed. We often see these types of statements in the final reflections of a course and may take the form of statements like, "I didn't think studying social systems was important at all when I came into this class. I thought the content would be boring and that I would have to force myself to read. However, now that the class is ending, I am seeing systems and their interrelationships everywhere! I appreciated the lively discussions and even the arguments—it all helped me get to where I am now!"

Consequently, when designing online courses, the inclusion of collaborative activity and the ability to reflect help to form community and also to sustain it in addition to promoting positive learning outcomes and student satisfaction. Paying attention to and facilitating the group's move-ment through the five phases discussed can help the group achieve learning outcomes, attain higher levels of thinking, promote satisfaction with the learning experience, and solidify the sense of community the group has formed.

COMMUNITY AND SOCIAL PRESENCE

Recent studies of the online learning environment have noted that involvement or "social presence," better known as the degree to which a person is perceived as "real" in communication, has also contributed pos-itively to learning outcomes and learner satisfaction with online courses. Tu and Corry (2002) identified three dimensions of social presence: social context, online communication, and interaction. Picciano (2002) found a consistently strong relationship among learner perceptions of interaction, social presence, and learning. Gunawardena and Zittle (1997) linked social presence to student satisfaction with online courses. Kazmer (2000) noted that building a learning community is necessary for a sense of social presence and, ultimately, for successful learner-to-learner interac-tion. In an earlier study, Murphy, Drabier, and Epps (1998) noted that the use of asynchronous online collaboration increased learner interaction, satisfaction, and learning. It is participant behavior online that appears to have great impact on the development of presence. When there is a high degree of interaction between the participants, the degree of social pres-ence is also high and vice versa (Stein & Wanstreet, 2003). The inclusion of collaborative activity, then, can increase not only the degree to which community forms online, but also the degree to which social presence emerges.

Beyond learner satisfaction, however, is the more important belief that social presence supported by collaboration enhances learning outcomes and reduces the potential for learner isolation that can occur in the online environment. By learning together in a learning community, students have the opportunity to extend and deepen their learning experience, test out new ideas by sharing them with a supportive group, and receive critical and constructive feedback. The likelihood of successful achieve-ment of learning objectives and achieving course competencies increases through collaborative engagement. Conrad and Donaldson (2004) state, "[The] collaborative acquisition of knowledge is one key to the success of creating an online learning environment. Activities that require student interaction and encourage a sharing of ideas promote a deeper level of thought" (p. 5).

Garrison, Anderson, and Archer (2000), in their model of online communities of inquiry, describe two additional forms of presence—cognitive presence and teaching presence—which they feel can be found in online communities of inquiry, classroom online communities being one form, and are also necessary elements for teaching and learning. They contend that the three forms of presence overlap to create the educational experience. They describe cognitive presence as the element most often associated with success in education and can be defined as "the extent to which the participants in any particular configuration of a community of inquiry are able to construct meaning through sustained communication ... [it] is a vital element in critical thinking, a process and outcome that is frequently presented as the ostensible goal of all higher education" (p. 4). They note that teaching presence is generally the role and function of the instructor, although this role may be shared among the participants. Teaching presence is further divided into two major functions—first, the selection, organization, and design of content, activities, and assessment and, second, the facilitation of the course. Although Garrison et al. attribute teaching presence predominantly to the instructor, when collaborative learning processes are used online, students also develop teaching presence. In fact, it is not unusual for us to see students describe this process and note that they "taught each other" in a particular course. They do not say this as a means of complaining that the instructor was not present or did not do enough "teaching," but it is said with a sense of wonder and empowerment that indicates that other forms of learning, beyond the content, occurred in the course.

Figure 1.1 represents the evolved model of online community that that we have been discussing which relies on a cycle of collaboration and community-building and is constructed around the notions of social presence, constructivism, and the use of an online learning community to achieve successful outcomes in an online course.

The advancing study of online community, then, informs us that community is made up of more than what we originally thought. The elements of community, as we previously identified them (Palloff & Pratt, 1999, 2003) included:

- People—the students, faculty, and staff involved in an online course;
- Shared Purpose—coming together to take an online course, including the sharing of information, interests, and resources;
- Guidelines—create the structure for the online course, by providing the ground rules for interaction and participation;

Source: Palloff and Pratt (2004, p. 9).

Figure 1.1.   Evolved model of online community.

- Technology—serves as a vehicle for delivery of the course and a place where everyone involved can meet;
- Collaborative learning—promotes student-to-student interaction as the primary mode of learning and also supports socially constructed meaning and knowledge creation; and
- Reflective practice—promotes transformative learning.

In our current thinking, we now organize these elements into four groupings:

- People, including clearly the students and faculty, but also their ability to promote themselves as real people. Consequently, social presence becomes an important "people" element in the online community;
- Purpose and policies, which includes not only the class itself, but also the guidelines established for participation and how information will be shared, the shared goals for learning and, most importantly, an agreement to abide by the guidelines;
- Interactivity, which includes interaction and communication, teamwork and collaboration, as well as attention to the technology in use as it facilitates the ability to interact; and, probably most important,
- Reflective/transformative learning, involving the development of a social constructivist context that allows for reflection and the active creation of knowledge and meaning.

We particularly note that social presence is a critical element of the online community and one that is essential to collaborative work and undergirds the ability to establish the other components.

CREATING AND SUSTAINING COMMUNITY

Clearly, simple participation in an online course is not enough to create and sustain an online learning community. Certainly, the creation of minimum participation guidelines assists in getting and keeping students online. However, just checking in on a regular basis and not contributing something substantive to the discussion does little to support the development of the learning community. Designing a course with collaboration and reflection in mind helps to move the group through the phases of knowledge development described by Gunawardena et al. (2000) and solidifies the sense of community. Courses need to be designed with community in mind. Some techniques for doing so include beginning the course with what we call a "Week Zero," during which students post introductions, engage in an ice breaker activity, review and discuss course guidelines, and discuss what they hope to learn in the course. This helps to kick off what Gunawardena et al. would refer to as Phase One.

Once the course begins in earnest, other means of continuing to support and sustain the developing community include collaborative learning activities, such as WebQuests, fishbowls, jigsaw activities, small group activities, and the like, as well as the use of good questioning techniques that support reflection. Newer additions to the repertoire of activities that help to develop and sustain the online learning community include the use of "blogs," or Web logs, which are collaborative journals, or the use of "wikis," which is software that allows for the collaborative development of Web pages. The use of blogging in an online course can assist in moving students through the phases of development that Gunawardena et al. describe. The instructor can keep a blog in the course and also encourage the students to blog. There are minimal limits placed on what is said in a journal or blog posting, and students have the ability to comment on the reflections of others—sometimes they will agree, but disagreement with ideas is also possible and creates a platform for dialogue that allows the group to engage in give-and-take, rather than all agreeing with the instructor or another student. It can lessen the incidence of the "I agree" or "Good Job!" postings that are often seen in online discussions.

Although asynchronous discussion remains a major community-building tool, some students enjoy the addition of synchronous discussion, or chats, as a means of building community. When used judiciously, chat can be a good supplement to the course. Often, what occurs in a chat session is that students will wander into social discourse in addition to discussing the topic at hand. This can serve to foster community as people get to know one another in real time. In addition, the use of virtual classroom programs in which students can ask questions of the instructor in real time, perhaps share a PowerPoint presentation or some other graphic display, and discuss together either through audio (with the use of headsets and microphones) or via simultaneous chat discussion, can also be useful in creating a sense of presence and, thus, a sense of community (Finkelstein, 2006).

Synchronous discussion, blogs, and wikis should not be the only means by which students engage with one another, however. Promoting active asynchronous discussion is the best means to support interactivity and the development of community in the online course. The instructor, rather than responding to every student post, should strategically respond with the purpose of prodding so that the discussion can deepen, to question assumptions, or to extend the dialogue. Once students establish a rhythm and begin to actively interact with one another online, they will take on the responsibility to sustain it in an ongoing manner, either through social interaction or response to discussion questions posted by the instructor. Collison, Elbaum, Haavind, and Tinker (2000) believe that the learners will "internalize [the instructor's] internal monologue as commentator, clarifier, and questioner of thoughts" (p. 204). It is important, then, that the questions posted regarding course material are created with an eye toward developing and maintaining a high degree of interaction and the building of community.

The key is to employ a number of means by which community can be formed, developed, and sustained. The creation of community in the online class is not an "if we build it, they will come" situation. Students need to be invited and encouraged to join the community and then, through good modeling by the instructor about what it means to learn in community, be encouraged to gradually take on the responsibility for sustaining it.

EXTENDING COMMUNITY BEYOND THE CLASSROOM

As the research continues to show that the online learning community is an effective approach to online learning, new applications of the concept have emerged. We discuss four such examples—first, emerging models of online student services; a multilayered approach to community; the use of the learning community as part of disaster response and recovery efforts; and, finally, the use of learning communities in faculty development.

Academic institutions, wrestling with the issue of persistence in online courses and programs, have realized the need to reach out to students at a distance in ways that may not be necessary on campus. In other words, student services programs are expanding online and various means by which a sense of community and a connection to the university can be achieved are being attempted. Some of those include the creation of university-wide discussion forums to enable distance students to engage in conversation about issues that impact them or that are of interest to them. Through such forums, colleges and universities are able to offer what are known as "push and pull" choices or selections; in other words, institutions are "pushing" reminders, relevant information, and other services as appropriate out to students based on "pulled" information gathered from the students who participate in the discussions or who respond to posted surveys and the like. This allows institutions to create interactive information exchanges and create just-in-time services based on expressed need. In so doing, students feel much more engaged with their institution and are much more likely to stay enrolled.

In another example of expanding community beyond the classroom, Unisinos, a university in southern Brazil, has created a multilevel learning platform for its online program that allows both students and faculty to create communities of inquiry at multiple levels. Not unlike residential campus-based learning communities, these online communities are formed based on common interests or needs. Students or faculty can create such a space and invite others to join. The community has available to it resource such as the ability to conduct asynchronous discussions, develop its own library of resources, hold synchronous chats, or use virtual classroom space if desired. The same types of resources are also available within each online class, but instead of needing to register for a class in order to take advantage of the learning community concept, one only needs to be a registered student or a faculty member. Universities within the United States are also experimenting with this concept of taking the residential learning community online, thus extending the learning community beyond the confines of the classroom.

The extended learning community concept has also been applied in troubled times. In the wake of Hurricane Katrina, several academic institutions in the Gulf States were forced to utilize online means to connect with their students and to continue the mission of delivering education. For some, like Delgado Community College in New Orleans, the significant destruction of their physical plant has pushed them to re-emerge as a predominantly online institution. An extended online learning community approach through the college's main Web site has been used to reach both students and faculty who have been displaced all over the United

States, allowing them to support one another through this difficult time and to continue delivering education.

Finally, the learning community approach is proving to be an effective means by which to provide faculty development and training regarding online teaching. By putting cohorts of faculty into online training courses with the goal of building a faculty learning community, not only can faculty learn the techniques of building community that can be taken into the classroom, but they develop their own support network and community that is likely to extend beyond the training period. Through this extended approach, we have seen faculty use one another as resources as they develop their online courses and invite their peers to review their work as they develop syllabi and activities for online delivery.

FINAL THOUGHTS

This brief discussion has served to illustrate that community, along with the student's roles and responsibilities within it, are critical to the outcome of the online learning process. We still contend that it is the online learning community that is the vehicle through which learning occurs in the online course. The extended learning community that can be developed as the result of online work can also assist with student persistence in online courses and programs and can help faculty become better instructors.

Brook and Oliver (2003) note, based on their extensive review of the literature on the topic, "There is strong support for the supposition that the social phenomenon of community may be put to good use in the support of online learning. This is well supported by theories of learning that highlight the role of social interaction in the construction of knowledge" (p. 150). Some may continue to refer to community-building as "fluff" or too much effort for the outcome. Despite some of the criticism leveled toward the formation of a learning community in an online course and beyond, however, we remain committed to its importance in promoting the outcomes we seek and feel that the development of learning communities online distinguishes this form of learning from a simple correspondence course delivered via electronic means.

REFERENCES

Brook, C., & Oliver, R. (2003). Online learning communities: Investigating a design framework. *Australian Journal of Educational Technology, 19*(2), 139-160.

Charalambos, V., Mechalinos, Z., & Chamberlain, R. (2004). The design of online learning communities: Critical issues. *Educational Media International, 41*, 135-143.

Collison, G., Elbaum, B., Haavind, S., & Tinker, R. (2000). *Facilitating online learning: Effective strategies for moderators.* Madison, WI: Atwood.

Conrad, R. M., & Donaldson, A. (2004). *Engaging the online learner: Activities and resources for creative instruction.* San Francisco: Jossey-Bass.

Finkelstein, J. (2006). *Learning in real time.* San Francisco: Jossy-Bass.

Garrison, D. R., Anderson, T., & Archer, W. (2000). Critical inquiry in a text-based environment: Computer conferencing in higher education. *The Internet and Higher Education, 2*(2-3), 87-105.

Gunawardena, C. L., Lowe, C. A., & Anderson, T. (1997). Analysis of a global online debate and the development of an interaction analysis model for examining social construction of knowledge in computer conferencing. *Journal of Educational Computing Research, 17*(4), 397-431.

Gunawardena, C. L., & Zittle, F. J. (1997). Social presence as a predictor of satisfaction with a computer-mediated conferencing environment. *American Journal of Distance Education, 11*(3), 8-26.

Kazmer, M. M. (2000, August 29). Coping in a distance environment: Sitcoms, chocolate cake, and dinner with a friend. *First Monday.* Retrieved April 6, 2004 from http://www.firstmonday.dk/issues/issue5_9/kazmer/index.html.

Mezirow, J. (1990). *Fostering critical reflection in adulthood: A guide to transformative and emancipatory learning.* San Francisco: Jossey-Bass.

Moore, A. B., & Brooks, R. (2000, November). Learning communities and community development: Describing the process. *Learning Communities: International Journal of Adult and Vocational Learning, 1*, 1-15. Retrieved on June 22, 2006 from, http://www.crlra.utas.edu.au/Pages/files/journal/articles/iss1/1Moore&B.pdf.

Murphy, K., Drabier, R., & Epps, M. (1998), Interaction and collaboration via computer conferencing. *Proceedings of the National Convention for Education Communication and Technology.* (ERIC Document Reproduction Service No. ED 423852).

Palloff, R. (1996). *Confronting ghosts: Lessons in empowerment and action.* Unpublished dissertation, Human and Organizational Systems, Fielding Graduate Institute.

Palloff, R., & Pratt, K. (1999). Building learning communities in cyberspace: Effective strategies for the online classroom. San Francisco: Jossey-Bass.

Palloff, R., & Pratt, K. (2003). The virtual student: A profile and guide to working with online learners. San Francisco: Jossey-Bass.

Palloff, R., & Pratt, K. (2004). *Collaborating online: Learning together in community.* San Francisco: Jossey-Bass.

Picciano, A. G. (2002). Beyond student perception: Issues of interaction, presence, and performance in an online course. *Journal of Asynchronous Learning Networks, 6*(1), 21-40.

Rheingold, H. (1993). *The virtual community.* Reading, MA: Addison-Wesley.

Shapiro, J. J., & Hughes, S. K. (2002). The case of the inflammatory e-mail: Building culture and community in online academic environments. In K. Rudestam & J. Schoenholtz-Read (Eds.), *Handbook of online learning*. Thousand Oaks, CA: Sage.

Shea, P., Swan, K., & Pickett, A. (2004). *Teaching presence and establishment of community in online learning environments*. Sloan Consortium Summer Workshops 2004. Retrieved May 10, 2006, from http://www.sloanconsortium.org/summerworkshop2004/draftpapers/shea_090104.doc.

Stein, D., & Wanstreet, C. (2003). *Role of social presence, choice of online or face-to-face group format, and satisfaction with perceived knowledge gained in a distance environment*. 2003 Midwest Research to Practice Conference in Adult, Continuing, and Community Education. Retrieved 5/10/06 from   http://www.alumni-osu.org/midwest/midwest%20papers/Stein%20&%20Wanstreet--Done.pdf.

Tu, C., & Corry, M. (2002). *Research in online learning community*. Retrieved April 6, 2004 from http://www.usq.edu.au/electpub/e-jist/docs/html2002/pdf/chtu.pdf.

Wenger, E. (1999). *Communities of practice: Learning, meaning, and identity*. Cambridge, England: Cambridge University Press.

CHAPTER 2

A TYPOLOGY OF CATALYSTS, EMPHASES, AND ELEMENTS OF VIRTUAL LEARNING COMMUNITIES

Richard A. Schwier

Educators emphatically, and sometimes justifiably, criticize educational technology for concentrating too often on products and hardware, and too seldom on learners. Emerging approaches to developing rich learning environments use computer mediated communication, and a host of interactive strategies to connect people in varied and robust ways, and writers such as Kozma (2000) challenge educational technologists to think beyond the design of instruction and consider the design of learning environments. But traditional understandings of learning environments and interaction usually stop short of the kind of engagement that will allow learning communities to form. This chapter examines theoretical and conceptual issues around promoting the growth of virtual learning communities (VLCs), and it considers issues around using communication technologies in formal and informal learning environments.

Online Learning Communities
pp. 17–39
Copyright © 2007 by Information Age Publishing
All rights of reproduction in any form reserved.

INTRODUCTION

The metaphor of community has been used to describe a wide range of contexts, from communities of practice in the corporate world (Wenger, 1998) to virtual community networks (Horn, 1997). In the simplest sense, communities are collections of individuals who are bound together for some reason, and these reasons define the boundaries of the communities. When one considers the fundamental notion of community, it is apparent that the language of communities can be used to inform our understanding of virtual learning communities and how they operate (Palloff & Pratt, 1999).

Communities are Resilient

Communities seem to spring up everywhere. They are a natural extension of who we are as social animals. They are organic, and they resist being confined by the constraints that social engineers would place on them. As such, communities cannot be created; rather, they emerge when conditions nurture them. When boundaries are drawn around a community, the community seems to find a way to redefine itself—to mutate. This is not to suggest that communities are disorganized; on the contrary, they can be highly organized. But creating a community is not a matter of laying out a set of rules and providing a structure; it is an act of supporting the natural development of relationships.

This is particularly important in virtual learning communities, where the idea of community is used as a rallying point for discussion and interaction among learners. Often courses provide a structure for interaction such as requiring students to post a set number of messages on each topic under discussion. This type of protocol may be useful to engage students purposefully, but it can sometimes serve to promote trivial discussion, and consequently mitigate the natural flow of communication. There are circumstances where rigid communication protocols may be useful or necessary, but they do not necessarily contribute to the development of a sense of community.

Communities are Hospitable

Hospitality is an important moral dimension of communities that work well. People in communities are bound together, and they maintain that cohesion by practicing hospitality and courtesy to members. Is everyone in every community hospitable? Of course they are not. But community members need to feel that they are in a hospitable environment generally, or they will limit their participation. This is significant for virtual learning communities, where people are invited to test ideas and expose their level of understanding to the group. Uncertainty is prized, because it invites curiosity and intellectual growth. But uncertain learners are also vulnerable, and a learning environment has to be hospitable to support the kind of risk-taking and experimentation with ideas that results in learning.

Communities Have Life Cycles

Stages of life seem to apply to almost everything, and communities are no exception. It is reasonable to think of communities as having lives that go through fairly predictable stages. An organic view of learning communities considers ways in which the communities evolve. Misanchuk, Anderson, Craner, Eddy, and Smith (2000) suggested that learning communities evolve from simple cohorts by employing "increasing levels of student interaction and commitment" (p. 1). In learning communities, this interaction is characterized by different ways of working together, and students move through discussion to cooperation and collaboration as the learning community emerges.

The formative stage in the life of a virtual learning community is characterized by the attraction of new members. The identity of the community is malleable, and participants are typically somewhat tentative as they try out communicating and making connections with other community members. This stage of development requires a great deal of leadership. The leader at this stage is trying to set the tone of the community, attract and welcome new members to the community, and lay out the purpose and guidelines for participation with the group as it forms. At this point, the virtual learning community will be evolving from what its creators first imagined into what it will ultimately become. The purpose may change, expand, or constrict, and it is the first place in which the members will either successfully or unsuccessfully impose their will on the makeup of the community. Users will test the boundaries of the community and determine whether they will remain as members. If required to be members, they will be deciding how significant the community will be to them, or how they can shape it into something they can use. In all, it is a time of testing, negotiating, and shaping, and the match between the purpose of the community and the importance of that purpose to members will determine the length of its survival and the strength of its influence.

The mature stage of life in the virtual community is ultimately achieved once the purpose, shape, and operation of the community are settled. At this point, the leader doesn't have to play as central a role in negotiating the purpose and monitoring the activities of members. The purpose and codes of conduct are known, and the members of the community exercise their control over the community by doing much of the monitoring. A common indicator that a virtual community has reached a stage of maturity is when the members of the community tell a new member what the boundaries of acceptable behavior are, and describe the purpose of the community to the novitiate. In later stages of maturity, the community is more institutionalized and entrenched. Codes of conduct are more rigid, as are the boundaries around acceptable topics and modes of expression. A mature community may start to take on the trappings of terrestrial communities, and become much more formal in its operation. This may be characterized by the introduction of some form of governing body or fund-raising activities, for example.

Ultimately, most virtual communities will be challenged to change, to undertake a metamorphosis and become a new entity with a focus that is different from the original conception of what the virtual learning community would become. It is likely that one feature of this stage will be resistance to change by some members of the community—those who most closely identify with the virtual community may fight for its preservation; the focus may turn to maintaining the organization rather than extending its purpose or mission. One of the possibilities at this stage of life is that the virtual learning community enters a period of natural decline. Ultimately, the death of a virtual learning community, or other similar organizations, may be good thing for everyone involved. It can allow organizers and members to move on to something else. The death of a virtual community is different from the death of a physical community. Despite the sense of loss and failure that some people inevitably feel, when a virtual learning community dies people are free to move without uprooting the rest of their lives as they do when physical communities perish. This is not to suggest that virtual communities are unimportant to individuals; they may in fact become as important as geographic communities to some members. But is the message for community architects "learn to adapt or prepare to die"? In most cases, yes. There may be the rare virtual community that becomes so entrenched that it will survive without significant change, but most virtual communities will face periods of volatility. The important message is that we need to plan to address the stages of life in learning communities when we create them.

Communities are Multifaceted

It is possible to categorize communities in a host of ways— social, political, spiritual, intellectual, educational, cultural, or geographic. The focus of any particular community may emphasize one of these dimensions, but in most cases, any single community will encompass a combination of several dimensions. It is not likely that a community will draw its boundaries around a single focus to the exclusion of all others. For example, a spiritual community may have an educational mission that is accomplished primarily through social intervention. An intellectual community may focus primarily on ideas, but it may also have a political agenda. So, even when we talk about virtual learning communities, it is important to realize that they exist as a subset within a dynamic set of dimensions.

Given the right circumstances, any community can act as a learning community, typically when it engages in the acquisition, transformation or creation of knowledge (Daniel, Schwier, & Ross, 2005; McCalla, 2000). But most learning communities do not focus exclusively on learning. For example, a human resources division of a company may try to develop sense of community but may be most interested in knowledge management and organizational culture (Schütt, 2003; Schwen, Kalman, Hara, & Kisling, 1998). Similarly, a community of practice in a corporate setting may devote much of its energy to identifying tacit knowledge and making the tacit knowledge explicit for the good of the company (Wenger, 1998). By contrast, online community networks may devote their resources to connecting people in new ways, sharing information, and building interpersonal relationships, but attend to learning only peripherally.

Regardless of their focus, little is actually known about how people participating in virtual environments are influenced by those environments. We might easily suppose that people who are connected electronically are enriching their interpersonal network of relationships, whereas some emerging research suggests that electronic saturation may actually contribute to a sense of isolation among participants (Kraut, Paterson, Lundmark, Kiesler, Mukophadhyay, & Scherlia, 1998). Social critics of technology have long voiced concerns that the values and strengths of communities are undermined by the very technology that promotes new ways of interacting with others (Selznik, 1996). With equal force, critics of distance learning have warned that technology-based courses often emphasize transmission of information and isolate learners by placing technological barriers between learners and real people (Farrow, 1999; Kessell, 1999).

What may be most restricting about electronic types of learning environments is that they fail to promote a sense of community, that they remain interactive, yet fall short of becoming communities of learners. When technology is introduced to learning communities, there is a risk of promoting interaction without the concomitant elements needed to turn a virtual learning environment into a virtual learning community. This chapter uses the language of community as a window to understanding ways to construct electronic learning environments that are consistent with emerging thought in education and training.

In formal learning environments, the emphasis placed on community may be partly attributed to the epistemological assumptions driving course design. Courses are often bounded by prescribed content, and that content is defined externally in formal learning environments. Learning might manifest itself differently depending on the context of the community in which it is created, such as whether communities are bounded or unbounded. Wilson, Ludwig-Hardman, Thornam, and Dunlap (2004) distinguished between bounded and unbounded learning communities, and suggested that bounded learning communities are created across courses in higher education or corporate settings. Instructional designers, brought up in the traditions of cognitive psychology and systematic ID, often emphasize bounded environments—the structure, sequence, and control of the learning environment—over the serendipitous, untidy, and unreliable aspects of social engagement, constructivist pedagogy, and authentic contexts for learning (Kenny, Zhang, Schwier, & Campbell, 2004).

At the same time, it should be acknowledged that many learning environments do not require a community of learners—that it would be inappropriate to impose this type of engagement in cases where the learner has no need or desire to engage other learners. But, in most cases, intimate engagement with others is important for rich learning to happen, and in those cases we can learn a great deal from community development literature about how to satisfy the learner's need for additional communication.

CATEGORIES FOR EXAMINING VIRTUAL LEARNING COMMUNITIES

In order to frame the discussion of virtual learning communities, this paper considers the elements of virtual learning communities, the different purposes served by learning communities, and the events that act as catalysts to stimulate the growth of virtual learning communities (see Figure 2.1). This typology was elaborated from an earlier model following five years of research on the constituent elements of virtual learning communities in graduate level seminars (cf. Schwier, 2001).[1]

When the categories are elaborated, a number of useful topics emerge for examining the structure of communities (see Figure 2.2). The remainder of this paper will explore the categories in some detail.

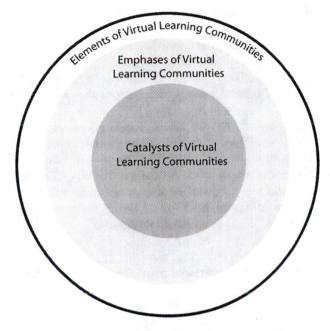

Figure 2.1.   Aspects of virtual learning communities.

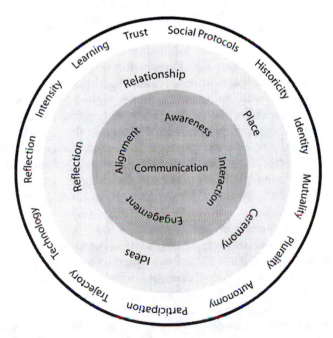

Figure 2.2.   Catalysts, Emphases and Elements of Virtual Learning Communities

Catalysts of Virtual Learning Communities

Communication is at the heart of any community, but especially virtual communities. Communication acts as the most important catalyst in virtual learning communities, where it spawns awareness, interaction, engagement, and alignment among members of the community (see Figure 2.2).

In terrestrial (physical) communities, communication is one of several necessary ingredients. When communication ends in a terrestrial community, the community slowly dissolves. By contrast, in virtual communities communication is the actual brick and mortar of the community. When communication ends in a virtual community, that community abruptly ends. Virtual communities are built out of words and language; communication literally holds virtual communities together.

The Presumed Ideal of Interpersonal Communication

The most identifiable form of participation in any community is interpersonal communication, so when we impose an idealized notion of community on a virtual learning environment, many of us compare the idea of virtual communication with a perceived ideal of "face-to-face," or interpersonal communication.[2] We attempt to build computer mediated communication systems that approximate face-to-face communication because we assume that face to face communication must be superior to mediated communication in some way. This assumption is worth examining.

First, a comparison of features reveals that many of the features of interpersonal and virtual communication are shared (see Table 2.1). But this does not assume that the quality of the experience is the same. One might argue that technology is currently available that has the capability of approximating interpersonal communication characteristics, or at least to overcome most of the deficiencies associated with virtual communication. While this is no doubt true, such technology is not ubiquitous, or even typical of the majority of virtual communications systems used by learners.

Fostering communication in a virtual learning community is not merely a matter of making virtual communication as good as face-to-face communication (See Table 2.2). Interpersonal communication is not adequate for some things, despite its reputation as an ideal form of communication. For example, in settings that are highly charged emotionally, the barrier of a virtual medium can serve as a protective screen for those trying to communicate. Consider court cases that include the testimony of children. Often, such testimony is provided on videotape rather than in

**Table 2.1. Comparison of Characteristics of
Interpersonal Communication and Virtual Communication**

	Interpersonal Communication	*Virtual Communication*
Immediacy	*Synchronous*	*Synchronous or Asynchronous*
Requisite skills	Interpersonal skills Social skills	Interpersonal skills Social skills Technological skills
Media	Multisensory Multidimensional	Limited sensory Electronic Unidimensional or multidimensional*
Flexibility	Fluid	Variable Technologically constrained
Protocols	Established Culturally bound Highly contextualized	Emerging Contextualized
Cost	Essentially free	Relatively costly
Level of intimacy	Potentially high—typically not anonymous	Variable—very intimate to anonymous

Note: *Unidimensional in typical cases, but more than one medium or sensory input may
be used simultaneously in some cases to create a multidimensional message.

person to protect the child. Similarly, a student might want to challenge a
teacher's judgment from the relatively safe position behind the keyboard
of a computer. In both of these examples, interpersonal communication is
perceived as threatening, and virtual communication provides a more
comfortable context.

On the other hand, I can not imagine preferring mediated communication for counseling a student in crisis. Yes, telephones or even video
conferencing might be the best available option at a particular time, and
indeed might be equal to the task. But my preference would be for face-
to-face communication, so that I could take advantage of the spontaneity
and nuances available in a more intimate setting.

Similar pros and cons existed for earlier communication technologies
in precisely the same way as they do for computer technologies. Telephones made it possible for people to communicate over vast distances
very easily, but telephony requires one to enter into a contract with a telephone company, pay charges for calls, learn how to use the machinery
and, most importantly, learn how to overcome its limitations and communicate effectively with someone else. Lest this seems like a trivial comparison because of its familiarity, the point is easily made if one convenes a
telephone conference call with several people who have never used teleconferencing technology. It is challenging to use technology to convene a
conference, but dealing with the people at the other end of the phone is

Table 2.2.   Summary of Positive and Negative Features of Interpersonal and Virtual Communication

	Interpersonal Communication	Virtual Communication
Positive features	• Ready access to nonverbal elements of communication (body language, gestures, facial expressions) • Misconceptions can be corrected fluidly and quickly • No barrier between communicators—no gatekeeper • Synchronicity—communication happens in real time and is effervescent	• Availability, accessibility of the receiver • Medium acts as buffer between communicators • Increased access for synchronous and asynchronous communication • Time to reflect privately and to compose thoughts • Those with sensory disabilities have additional mode for communicating • Synchronous and asynchronous communication possible
Negative features	• Dependent upon interpersonal communication skills • Reflection is done publicly • Body language and expressions may be misinterpreted • No buffer or gatekeeper between communicators • Individuals with sensory disabilities may be excluded from communication • Limited opportunity for asynchronous communication	• Requires literacy skills, technological skills • Quality of communication is medium-dependent. • Socioeconomic factors: communication among the privileged or wealthy? • Difficult to avoid communication • Barrier between communicators • Synchronous communication more expensive/technology dependent than asynchronous communication

even more challenging. Participants have to learn new conventions for setting agendas, being courteous, taking turns, and for making points forcefully but not intrusively. Teleconferencing technology offers opportunities and liberation from the tyranny of travel, and at the same time, it imposes significant barriers.

Perhaps it is a matter of understanding and acknowledging that mediated communication, as an entity, is useful but fundamentally different from face-to-face communication. However useful it might be to try to mimic interpersonal communication with virtual communication for some things, we should question whether it is useful to think of universal ideals for any type of communication.

Awareness, Interaction, Engagement, and Alignment

Four notions act as catalysts and orbit communication in a virtual learning community: awareness, interaction, engagement, and alignment

(Daniel, McCalla, & Schwier 2005; Wenger, 1998). These are the prerequisites and products of communication, and to understand the influence of communication, it is necessary to consider its constituent variables.

Awareness is a prerequisite variable to communication and it is drawn from theoretical discussions of social presence and social capital (Daniel, Schwier, & McCalla, 2003). Without awareness, purposeful communication is unlikely to occur, and co-coordinated and cooperative work is almost impossible. Gutwin and Greenberg (1998) suggested four types of awareness: social awareness, task awareness, concept awareness, and workspace awareness. Social awareness is the awareness that people have about the social connections within the group. Task awareness is the awareness of how a shared task will be completed. Concept awareness refers to the awareness of how a particular activity or piece of knowledge fits into an individual's existing knowledge. Workplace awareness is sensitivity to the context, and what is appropriate or inappropriate in a particular work setting.

The notion of interaction (interplay or activity) is also central to the idea of community. Full membership in a community requires social participation, and a community cannot exist in an inert state. Certainly individuals may identify themselves as members of communities in which they do not actively participate. For example, a fourth-generation Canadian may identify herself as Scottish, and in fact feel a very strong allegiance to that identity. But is she a member of the Scottish community? This chapter argues that she is not; she may identify closely with the Scottish community but cannot claim membership in it unless she participates in that community meaningfully. A similar issue arises with virtual learning communities. People who choose to remain as spectators (aka lurkers, voyeurs) may identify closely with the virtual learning community they observe, but they cannot claim membership in it until they participate in it in some manner.

Interaction in a community usually results in engagement of ideas, people, and processes. An individual must go beyond interaction to achieve engagement in a virtual learning community. It is important to recognize that in a virtual learning community engagement may vary among members but, at some level, participants must engage the community to be considered members. An individual can operate on the periphery of a virtual learning community and still be a part of the group, and can even learn a great deal by engaging the ideas and observing the interactions of other members. Knowledge in a learning community is not necessarily concentrated at its core. People operating on the margins of a virtual learning community comprise a great deal of what can be considered the knowledge of the community. But to become a contributing member of a community, engagement has to happen, and ultimately it is important for the tacit knowledge held by community members on the periphery of the community to be made explicit. If this does not happen, then it mitigates the effectiveness of the community and erodes its structure.

When individuals engage a virtual community, some measure of alignment occurs. Individuals align personal, private purposes with the collective, public purposes of the community. In this way, alignment coordinates personal and communal intentions. But personal and community alignment is a dynamic process. An individual's personal intentions alter the community, and the community massages the personal intentions of individuals. So, the term "alignment" describes the constant negotiation and repositioning of the individual with the community as the two work to shape each other.

EMPHASES OF VIRTUAL LEARNING COMMUNITIES

Virtual learning communities are learning communities based on shared purpose rather than geography. Through technology, learners can be drawn together from almost anywhere, and they can construct their own formal or informal groups. People in virtual learning communities are separated by space, but not necessarily time, as communication can be facilitated by technology in real time, thereby partially overcoming physical barriers. Extending the work of Kowch and Schwier (1997), it is possible to classify at least five emphases of virtual learning communities: communities of relationship communities of place, communities of intent, communities of reflection, and communities of ceremony (see Figure 2.2).

Virtual Learning Communities of Relationship

A community built on relationships emphasizes connections among people that might be based on a shared concern, issue, or learning problem. In every case, the emphasis is on the relationships built among participants (Kowch & Schwier, 1997; Schwier, in press). Issues of commitment, trust, and values are inherent in any relationships that emerge in the community. Learning in a community of relationship places an emphasis on social aspects, sometimes at the expense of content or substance; process is often valued over product or achievement. There are a number of examples of communities of relationship and, arguably, these most closely embrace the kinds of interactions one finds in terrestrial communities. Some examples of this type of community are virtual support groups such as Al-Anon or AA, "big sister or brother" sites, and virtual home study chat rooms.

Virtual Learning Communities of Place

Individuals in this type of community enjoy a common habitat or locale. This sharing of place with others can offer a sense of security, commonality, and heritage. There are a number of examples of place-based virtual communities, among them the Blacksburg Electronic Village, one of the better-known community network initiatives in the United States (http://www.bev.net/). The Blacksburg Electronic Village was built to enhance the physical community of Blacksburg, Virginia and it offers a wide range of electronic communication services and information to residents.

The place need not be terrestrial, however, and in virtual communities, places are by definition not physical. People from several countries can gather in one virtual place on the Internet, for example, as easily as people can gather for a meeting in a school building. Nevertheless, the location can be as real as the imagination and technology allow. The Internet houses thousands of virtual storefronts, for example, each of which exists metaphorically as a place.

Virtual Learning Communities of Ideas

Communities of ideas reinforce people's commitment to common interests and shared values. This could be as modest as an interest in comic books, or as intricate as a shared interest in gender politics. The two most distinguishable features of a community of ideas are sharing and common interests, and they are most often characterized as purposeful or focused, and they often adopt an achievement or product orientation. An established place to visit on the Web to see virtual communities of ideas is "the Well," which is also one of the longest-operating and successful such sites on the Web (www.well.com). It is actually a collection of communities, based on the interests of the participants.

Virtual Learning Communities of Reflection

A virtual learning community of reflection is based on a shared past or a common sense of history. Its purpose is to collectively examine events that had common significance for the community members, ponder the past, raise questions, discuss values, and examine the event. For example, groups of war veterans have created virtual communities to share thoughts, ideas, and memories. This community connects people who might otherwise feel isolated, and also provides a focal point for interpreting and understanding commonly experienced events. Generally speaking, a virtual learning community of reflection is very process oriented, and deliberately focused on making sense of shared events. One such Web site is the Vietnam Veterans home page, which has as its stated goal: "To provide an interactive, on-line forum for Vietnam Veterans and their families and friends to exchange information, stories, poems, songs, art, pictures, and experiences in any publishable form" (http://grunt.space.swri.edu/).

Virtual Learning Communities of Ceremony

A virtual learning community of ceremony is based on ritual and celebration. Often, the celebration is based on an event or the ritual practice of a group and has an element of tradition associated with it, such as religion, sports, or university affiliation. Members identify strongly with the group or the event. For example, the communities page available through Excite (http://www.excite.com/communities/) offers a wide range of communities based on various world religions. Some examples include communities named Angelic Interest, New Age Spirituality, New Age Philosophy, Muslim, Today's Islam, Christian Singles Forum, Tibetan Buddhism, Chevrah, and Harkham Hillel Friends. The same page offers sports communities, such as the St. Croix Soccer Club and Miami University Sports. For a subscription fee, Irish Online is available to all alumni of the University of Notre Dame, and it includes an e-mail address for members, access to an online directory of alumni, and e-mail lists and discussion groups. These communities are ceremonial, in that their purposes are linked to larger entities that have an element of ritual or high degree of personal identification associated with them.

The five types of communities are not mutually exclusive. Often, any particular virtual learning community will exhibit features of several of these types. The types overlap and may shift in importance within a single virtual community based on the interests of community members. For example, creators of the Buddhism community Website may have chosen to emphasize ceremony in the community, but it will also have elements of intent, relationship, and reflection. Various members of the Buddhism community will determine which categories will be prominent, and the emphasis will be different for each member.

THIRTEEN ELEMENTS OF VLCS

Once the purpose of a group is identified, what turns the group into a community rather than merely a collection of people with a common purpose? Several features seem to be manifest when a virtual gathering place of people turns into a community. Selznick (1996), in a discussion of terrestrial communities, identified six elements that were found in our own analysis of VLCs: historicity, identity, mutuality, plurality, autonomy, and participation. We have added seven features to this list based on our research: trust, trajectory, technology, social protocols, reflection, intensity, and learning (see Figure 2.2). The 13 elements were identified in a series of grounded theory studies of online graduate-level seminars and subjected to social network and modeling analyses (Schwier & Daniel, 2007). These elements underscore the idea that communities are complex. Any adequate understanding of virtual learning communities needs to recognize that these variables interact multi-dimensionally.

Historicity.   Communities are stronger when they share history and culture. Conversely, they are weak when they are based on general interests and abstract ideas. The quality of participation depends on individual and shared commitment or relevance of the substance of the community. Commitment depends on shared values in the community. At minimum, the strength of the commitment need only be sufficient to maintain participation in the group, but stronger commitment generally leads to the development of stronger communities.

Identity.   Communities foster a sense of shared identity. Successful virtual learning communities need to have boundaries—an identity or recognized focus.

Mutuality.   Communities spring from—and are maintained by—interdependence and reciprocity. While virtual communities are built around central themes, ideas, or purposes, the organizing principles are not externally imposed. Participants construct purposes, intentions, and the protocol for interaction.

Plurality.   Communities draw much of their vitality from "intermediate associations" such as families, churches, and other peripheral groups.

Autonomy.   Within the emphasis on group identity, it is important that communities respect and protect individual identity. Individuals interact with each other and have the capacity to conduct discourse freely and meaningfully, or withdraw from discourse without penalty. Interaction must be based on influence among participants rather than power relationships.

Participation.   Social participation in the community, especially participation that promotes self-determination, supports autonomy and sustains the community. Participants can select the level of intimacy appropriate for any relationship with another participant or with the group. Anonymity is possible, but as the sense of community develops, it is unlikely that a participant would choose to remain anonymous.

Trajectory.   Learning communities are not static; they create movement in a direction. Learning communities "open trajectories of participation that place engagement in its practice in the context of a valued future" (Wenger, 1998, p. 215).

Technology.   In virtual learning communities, technology facilitates the development of community, but also inhibits its growth. It brings together individuals who might otherwise not engage one another. It acts as the conduit for discourse among participants, and it is the medium of engagement that binds the community together. At the same time, technology can be a barrier to communication and can exclude some people from the community who cannot afford or use communications technology.

Social Protocols.   Conventions and rules of engagement are usually prescribed in formal learning environments, but even in informal learning environments, participants follow conventional patterns of interaction. We suspect these conventions are culturally-bound, and that students engage each other online in ways they have become used to in other parts of their lives. This introduces potential for conflict in communities when different cultural traditions (e.g., age-related traditions of communication) are brought into a single learning environment.

Reflection.   Communities exhibit conversational "flow," and later conversations often make reference to earlier conversations and interactions. Reflection is evidenced when participants ground current discussions in previous events, discussions or experiences.

Intensity.   Strong communities exude a sense of urgency, that involvement in the community is purposeful and meaningful. Intensity in VLCs is manifest by active engagement, open discourse, and a sense of importance in discussion, critique and argumentation.

Trust.   The level of certainty or confidence that one community member uses to assess the action of another member of the community. When people build communities, they commit themselves to each other through trusting social relationships. A sense of belonging and the concrete experience of social networks can produce trust, but trust is reciprocal and complex, and it shares variance with other intermediate variables, such as understanding, awareness, reputation and co-reliance. Trust reinforces an expectation of reciprocity.

Learning.   Learning is a central element of virtual learning communities, although the nature of the learning can be broadly defined and contextual. For the purpose of defining elements of community, it isn't really important whether learning is focused, lasting, substantial, educationally sound, associated with any particular curricula, or entirely serendipitous. The point is that people in a virtual learning community want to learn, and the purposes to which that learning may be put are irrelevant to the legitimacy of the community. That is not to say that learning in a virtual learning community is not purposeful; it should be, but users can define the purposes and the purposes may not fit traditional ideas of what constitutes acceptable learning. In a recent work, we have elaborated our understanding of learning in the context of VLCs (Daniel, Schwier, & Ross, in press); however, the gross granularity of learning as a key element of VLCs is sufficient for this presentation of the typology.

This list of elements begs the question of whether all of them are necessary for a community to exist, particularly a virtual learning community. Is it necessary, for example, for a virtual learning community to exhibit plurality? Depending on their focus and membership, it might be argued that some virtual learning communities can flourish in isolation. In fact, one measure of community strength might be the degree to which members create a cloister, a safe haven separated from the plurality of associations we expect to find in terrestrial communities. At least, the peripheral associations of community members might have little relevance to the success or strength of the virtual learning community in these instances. At the same time, these elements inform our understanding of how communities work, and depending on the nature and intent of a particular virtual learning community, they may apply. The interaction and importance of various elements may be different for different virtual learning communities, but they are still useful for helping us understand how communities can be grown and maintained.

It is probably apparent that these 13 elements are not realized by chance. Communities do not just happen; but neither are they created. What we are attempting to do as educators is promote the development of virtual learning communities by nurturing the conditions under which they can arise. We can wheedle, cajole, beg, whine and nag learners to become involved, but ultimately it is the learners who will determine whether a virtual learning community springs from the ooze. Still, there is much that can be done to support these elements. An important principle to growing a virtual learning community is to be deliberate, to think about and do things purposefully to foster community growth. A sampling of ideas is presented in Table 2.3.

RESEARCH ISSUES RAISED BY VIRTUAL LEARNING COMMUNITIES

If educators choose to support the development of virtual learning communities, a number of issues emerge. Some issues are financial and logistic—how does one assemble the technological and personal systems

Table 2.3. Representative Pedagogical Applications of Elements for Virtual Learning Communities

Element	Example of a Pedagogical Application
Historicity	Incorporate what members have done in the past, and make their stories part of the community culture. Explicit mention of the culture, value and context of the virtual community. Make public the history of the community.
Identity	Use team-building exercises, develop community logos, and publicly acknowledge accomplishments by the group and individual members within the community. Articulate the focus or purpose of the community, and outline the requirements and rituals accompanying membership in the community.
Mutuality	Include group exercises, assignments, activities that require each member to contribute to the final product. Ask leading questions that encourage members of the community to invest in concerns held by other members, and to share ideas and possible solutions.
Plurality	Encourage membership and participation from and association with groups related to the learning focus. These might include businesses, professional associations, or groups in other countries exploring similar issues.
Autonomy	Foster individual expression and comment explicitly on its value. Set up protocol for respectful communication and reach consensus in the group. Create strategies for settling disputes or inappropriate behavior.
Participation	Allow members of the group to shape learning agendas. Give guidance to new community members, and promote opportunities for established members to go outside the boundaries of the learning event or focus. Encourage lurkers and voyeurs.
Trajectory	Identify direction of learning. Ask participants to describe ways they will use what they have learned in the community in the future. Conduct "visioning" exercises to determine new initiatives to be undertaken by the community.
Technology	Employ technology that allows meaningful communication, and which is easy for participants to use. Promote communication approaches that are compatible with older, less costly equipment where communities intend to be inclusive.
Learning	A community moderator should remind participants of learning intentions, and intervene when interaction drifts too far away from the learning focus. Encourage individuals on the periphery of the community to contribute their tacit knowledge to the explicit knowledge of the community.
Reflection	A moderator can look for linkages in conversations over time, and ask participants to comment on how a current conversation relates to something previously mentioned.

(Table continues on next page)

Table 2.3.   (Continued)

Element	Example of a Pedagogical Application
Intensity	Introduce provocative or significant social issues related to topics of conversation to provide context and authenticity for online conversations, and to ignite controversy and debate in the community.
Trust	Provide opportunities for participants to collaborate on small activities in the community. Simple, noncompetitive activities, such as co-moderating discussions, can promote the development of trust among individuals. As part of these activities, an element of coreliance is important, such that the success of the pair or team depends on the participation of everyone in the group.
Social Protocols	Establish clear rules and expectations for engagement, especially for setting the acceptable and unacceptable ways of behaving in a community. As the sense of community grows, the group can review existing protocols and be given responsibility for monitoring engagement in the community.

Source: Adapted from Schwier (in press).

necessary to construct and maintain a communication system? But the more important questions center on the design, implementation, pedagogy and effects of virtual learning communities, the socioeducational aspects of learning through this means of communication. A few of the issues that invite investigation are listed below, although many more seem to arise every day:

- How do people select virtual learning communities and how do they make use of them for learning?
- How do voluntary members of virtual learning communities differ from those who are assigned to learning communities in formal educational contexts?
- What are the characteristics of successful and unsuccessful virtual learning communities?
- How do virtual communities recruit and maintain members?
- Are there rules of engagement or particular protocols for insinuating an individual into the fabric of a virtual learning community, and is the process contextually or culturally bound? Does the process mirror interpersonal group learning contexts?
- How does a new member of a community join discussions of established community members and develop a persona or reputation? Are there power relationships in virtual learning communities, and how do they interact with learning variables?

- In virtual learning communities that permit members to remain anonymous, how does the anonymity of participants influence the tenor of interactions and the satisfaction of the participants?
- Do elements of community exhibit themselves in virtual learning communities, and do they inform our understanding of how these communities contribute to learning environments?
- What is the nature of learning in virtual contexts, and how do architects, active members, and lurkers describe their experiences?
- What value do administrators, educators and learners place on virtual learning communities? How do political, social, educational and personal agendas interact in the development maintenance and alteration of virtual learning communities?
- Do virtual learning communities exhibit lifecycles, and what significance does this have for their design?
- What are the pedagogical issues involved in virtual learning communities? How can we use them for teaching?

This chapter does not pretend that using technology to support the development of virtual learning communities will address the many challenges faced by schools and other institutionalized learning communities. In fact, it is quite possible that virtual learning communities will remain largely irrelevant to formal, institution-based education, but will flourish in informal e-learning environments. Many people are already technologically literate, and many already participate in informal virtual learning communities. Nevertheless, this chapter proposes a way of using technology that is consistent with constructivist changes underway in education, and suggests that virtual learning communities can contribute to the way we respond to those changes.

ACKNOWLEDGMENT

This research is supported by a grant from the Social Sciences and Humanities Research Council of Canada.

NOTES

1. This chapter updates and extends a paper originally published as: Schwier, R. A. (2001). Catalysts, emphases and elements of virtual learning communities: Implications for research and practice. *Quarterly Review of Distance Education, 2*(1), 5-18.

2. It is beyond the scope of this chapter to fully describe the research program that informs the ideas in chapter but the reader is directed to Daniel, McCalla, & Schwier (2005); Daniel, Schwier, & McCalla (2003); Daniel, Schwier, & Ross (2005; in press); Daniel, Zapata-Rivera, Schwier, & McCalla (2006); Dykes & Schwier (2003); Schwier & Balbar (2002); Schwier & Daniel (2007); and Schwier & Dykes (2007) for a comprehensive treatment of the research methodologies and findings.

3. The use of interpersonal communication as a synonym for "face-to-face" communication is taking license with conventional language used in communication theory. In communication theory, interpersonal communication could include any communication between people that does not pass through a gatekeeper and that allows for immediate feedback. Interpersonal communication can embrace a number of types of communication other than face to face, but it is used here for convenience, and recognizing that face-to-face communication is always interpersonal.

REFERENCES

Daniel, B. K., McCalla, G. I., & Schwier, R. A. (2005). Mining data and modeling social capital in virtual learning communities. In C. K. Looi, G. I. McCalla, B. Bredeweg, & J. Breuker (Eds.), *Proceedings of AI-ED 2005: Supporting learning through intelligent and socially informed technology* (pp. 200-208). Amsterdam: IOS Press.

Daniel, B., Schwier, R., & McCalla, G. (2003). Social capital in virtual learning communities and distributed communities of practice. *Canadian Journal of Learning and Technology, 29*(3), 113-139.

Daniel, B. K., Schwier, R. A., & Ross, H. (2005). Intentional and incidental discourse variables in a virtual learning community. *Proceedings of E-Learn 2005*, Vancouver, British Columbia.

Daniel. B., Schwier, R. A., & Ross, H. (in press). Synthesis of the process of learning through discourse in a formal virtual learning community. *Journal of Interactive Learning Research.*

Daniel, B., Zapata-Rivera, J. D., Schwier, R., & McCalla, G. (2006). *Bayesian belief network models of trust and social capital for social software systems design. Reinventing trust, collaboration and compliance in social systems.* Workshop exploring novel insights and solutions for social systems design. CHI 2006, Montreal.

Dykes, M. E., & Schwier, R. A. (2003). Content and community redux: Instructor and student interpretations of online communication in a graduate seminar. *Canadian Journal of Learning and Technology, 29*(2), 79-99.

Farrow, C. S. (1999, January). The electronic buffalo: A Web tale. *On Campus News* [University of Saskatchewan], p. 5.

Gutwin, C., & Greenberg, S. (1998). Design for individuals, design for groups: Tradeoffs between power and workspace awareness. *Proceedings of the ACM Conference on Computer Supported Cooperative Work* (pp. 207-216). New York: ACM Press.

Horn, S. (1997). *Cyberville: Clicks, culture, and the creation of an online town.* New York: Warner Books.

Kenny, R. F., Zhang Z., Schwier, R. A., & Campbell, K. (2005). A review of what instructional designers do: Questions answered and questions not asked. *Canadian Journal of Learning and Technology, 31*(1), 9-26.

Kessell, S. (1999). *Postgraduate courses on the WWW: Teaching the teachers and educating the professors.* Retrieved June 30, 2006, from http://technologysource.org/article/postgraduate_courses_on_the_www/

Kowch, E., & Schwier, R. A. (1997). Considerations in the construction of technology-based virtual learning communities. *Canadian Journal of Educational Communication, 26*(1), 1-12.

Kozma, R. (2000). Reflections on the state of educational technology research and development. *Educational Technology Research and Development, 48*(1), 5-15.

Kraut, R., Patterson, M., Lundmark, V., Kiesler, S., Mukophadhyay, T., & Scherlis, W. (1998). Internet paradox: A social technology that reduces social involvement and psychological well-being? *American Psychologist, 53*(9), 1017-1031.

McCalla, G. (2000). The fragmentation of culture, learning, teaching and technology: Implications for artificial intelligence in education research. *International Journal of Artificial Intelligence, 11*(2), 177-196.

Misanchuk, M., Anderson, T., Craner, J., Eddy, P., & Smith, C. L. (2000, October). *Strategies for creating and supporting a community of learners.* Paper presented at the Annual Convention of the Association for Educational Communications and Technology, Denver, Colorado.

Palloff, R. M., & Pratt, K. (1999). *Building learning communities in cyberspace: Effective strategies for the online classroom.* San Francisco: Jossey-Bass.

Schütt, P. (2003). The post-Nonaka knowledge management. *Journal of Universal Computer Science, 9*(6), 451-462.

Schwen, T. M., Kalman, H. K., Hara, N., & Kisling, E. L. (1998). Potential knowledge management contributions to human performance technology research and practice. *Educational Technology Research and Development, 46*(4), 73-89.

Schwier, R. A. (2001). Catalysts, emphases and elements of virtual learning communities: Implications for research and practice. *Quarterly Review of Distance Education, 2*(1), 5-18.

Schwier, R. A. (in press). Virtual learning communities. In G. Anglin (Ed.), *Instructional technology: Past, present, future* (3rd ed.). Englewood Cliffs, CO: Libraries Unlimited.

Schwier, R. A., & Balbar, S. (2002). The interplay of content and community in synchronous and asynchronous communication: virtual communication in a graduate seminar. *Canadian Journal of Learning and Technology, 28*(2), 21-30.

Schwier, R. A., & Daniel, B. K. (2007). Did we become a community? Multiple methods for identifying community and its constituent elements in formal online learning environments. In N. Lambropoulos & P. Zaphiris (Eds.), *User-evaluation and online communities* (pp. 29-53). Hershey, PA: Idea Group.

Schwier, R. A., & Dykes, M. E. (2007). The continuing struggle for community and content in blended technology courses in higher education. In M. Bullen & D. Janes (Eds.), *Making the transition to e-learning: Issues and strategies* (pp. 157-172). Hershey, PA: Idea Group.

Selznick, P. (1996). In search of community. In W. Vitek & W. Jackson (Eds.), *Rooted in the land* (pp. 195-203). New Haven, CT: Yale University Press.

Wenger, E. (1998). *Communities of practice: Learning, meaning, and identity.* Cambridge, UK: Cambridge University Press.

Wilson, B. G., Ludwig-Hardman, S., Thorman, C. L., & Dunlap, J. C. (2004). Bounded community: Designing and facilitating learning communities in formal courses. *International Review of Research in Open and Distance Learning, 5*(3). Retrieved June 30, 2006, from http://www.irrodl.org/index.php/irrodl/article/view/204/286.

CHAPTER 3

ONLINE LEARNING COMMUNITIES WITH ONLINE MENTORS

A Conceptual Framework

Shujen L. Chang

This chapter presents a model of online learning communities characterized by online mentors (OLCOM), a virtual online learning community, which is used to facilitate teaching and learning in online degree programs at a large southeastern state university. OLCOM was evaluated through student performance including course completion rates and grade point averages and student satisfaction with mentor performance. Findings indicate that students facilitated by the OLCOM team performed better than the cohort students in the same university. Student satisfaction with mentor performance was high.

INTRODUCTION

Online programs are growing dramatically in higher education in the United States. There were 2.3 million online students in the fall of 2004

Online Learning Communities
pp. 41–52
Copyright © 2007 by Information Age Publishing
All rights of reproduction in any form reserved.

(Allen & Seaman, 2005). The Department of Distance Learning (DDL) at a large southeastern state university established online degree programs in 1995 to enable students holding associate of arts degrees to pursue bachelor degrees. The DDL developed the online learning communities with online mentors (OLCOM) model to facilitate teaching and learning. The OLCOM team expands beyond students and faculty members to include online mentors, a mentor support team, and academic coordinators (Figure 3.1). Mentors, trained and supported by the mentor-support team, assist students and faculty members for effective online instruction. Academic coordinators facilitate students through proper online administrative procedures, unfamiliar to most students.

OLCOM was initially implemented in four undergraduate online degree programs: computer science, information studies, interdisciplinary social science, and nursing. There were 8 different courses offered totaling 26 sections, with 570 online students supported by 26 mentors. Each section had one online mentor and student-mentor ratio was about 20 to 1.

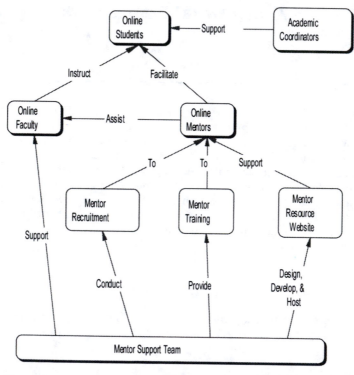

Figure 3.1.   Online learning community with online mentors (OLCOM).

Online degree programs at the university grew rapidly. By fall 2005, there were 3 undergraduate and 15 graduate online degree programs.

THE ONLINE LEARNING COMMUNITIES

The development of online learning communities (OLCs) is an expansion of face-to-face learning communities in traditional classrooms. OLCs are formed by online students and faculty members using course Web sites as platforms to achieve learning goals (Caverly & MacDonald, 2002). However, OLCs are distinguished from face-to-face learning communities in three ways. First, an OLC is a virtual learning environment in a course Web site where students and faculty interact synchronously or asynchronously through online learning activities. Second, the major means of communication in an OLC is telecommunication, rather than face-to-face communication. Online faculty and students post messages in discussion boards, participate in chat rooms, and exchange e-mails within course Web sites. Third, the identity of a learning community, or the sense of social connectedness, is critical for successful online learning (Charalambos, Michalinos, & Chamberlain, 2004).

Research indicates that building an online learning community requires course design that specifically supports the construction of an OLC. Encouraging interactions through communication, cooperation, and collaboration can help students build an OLC (Misanchuk & Anderson, 2001). Online instructional designs, such as learner structural-dependent and interaction-conducive strategies, can develop strong OLCs (Hill, 2001). OLCs are frequently used to support a wide range of learners. For examples, STAR-Online (Supporting Teachers with Anywhere/Anytime Resources) was designed and implemented for teacher professional development and continuing education (Charalambos et al., 2004). An OLC was constructed in a graduate-level course among diverse adult learners from the United States, Hong Kong, Japan, Argentina, and Venezuela (Sierra & Folger, 2003). The University of South Africa implemented online learning communities for greater accessibility to African communities (Heydenrych, Higgs, & van Niekerk, 2003). An OLC was built into an online course, which was delivered to two different educational cultures, one in Ireland and the other one in Denmark (Sorensen & Murchú, 2004).

ONLINE LEARNING COMMUNITIES WITH ONLINE MENTORS

Online learning communities with online mentors (OLCOM) are distinguished from other online learning communities by incorporating online mentors, the mentor-support team, and academic coordinators. Online mentors are included to encourage more interaction, facilitate effective communication, and support collaboration to enhance online learning, as suggested by previous studies (Charalambos et al., 2004; Misanchuk & Anderson, 2001). The mentor-support team trains online mentors so they can acquire necessary knowledge, skills, and attitudes for facilitating online learning and teaching. Academic coordinators are drawn from associated academic departments who assisted online students in the process of online admissions and registrations.

Online Students

Online students are students currently taking online courses in the undergraduate online degree programs. To be admitted, online students must meet the same admission criteria (e.g,. grade point average in high school, Scholastic Aptitude Test, etc.) as those of face-to-face undergraduate degree programs at the university. As in the face-to-face learning, online students are encouraged to contact faculty members for questions concerning course content. For technical problems and content clarification questions, online students can also ask online mentors to assist them. Online students can ask for help from academic coordinators concerning administrative procedures, such as online admissions and course enrollments.

Faculty Members

Faculty members were the professors who teach online courses in the undergraduate online degree programs. Online faculty members generally teach courses they designed and developed. Faculty members often play multiple roles—subject matter experts, online course managers, and computer technology consultants. Playing so many roles dramatically increases their teaching load and becomes a heavy burden to online faculty. The role of online course managers is significantly different from face-to-face classroom instructors, and the role of computer technology consultants is a new role for most faculty members. Both roles require advanced knowledge and skills regarding online course management and technical problem-solving. First-time online faculty members must spend extra time developing the new knowledge and skills, in addition to the time spent assisting students learn course content. To reduce this burden for online faculty, online mentors facilitate online learning by providing students with supplementary mentoring on course content and helping on technical problem-solving. The mentor-support team shares responsibility for online course management. Online faculty then have more time to focus on the activities related to learning goals, without being overwhelmed by online course management or solving technical problems.

Online Mentors

The majority of online mentors are faculty members from community colleges and university graduate students. Content expertise is required. Online mentors must possess either a master's degree related to the course or advanced knowledge of the course content. Computer literacy is preferred, and mentors are trained by the mentor-support team for online course management.

Online mentors played three roles supplementary to faculty members. They are subject-matter facilitators, learning-community builders, and technical supporters. As subject-matter facilitators, online mentors provide course-specific information to facilitate students to better understand course content. They monitor online discussion and provide additional feedback and resources to students who appear to be experiencing difficulties. Online mentors join online discussions to clarify and elaborate concepts, to draw attention to the focus of the discussion topics, to provide additional examples, to point out relationships among concepts, and to answer questions. As learning community builders, online mentors stimulate more interactions among students to build a strong sense of OLC community among online learners. Research indicates that online interactions are critical to effective online learning. Interactions between faculty members and students, and among students, motivate learners to engage more in learning activities and then facilitate sociocultural and sociocognitive development (Gilbert & Driscoll, 2002; Hill, 2001; Jin, 2002; Tu & Corry, 2002). Online mentors initiate interactions with students, including joining students' discussions, assisting group activities, guiding students toward their learning goals, providing just-in-time help, promoting collaboration to develop a team spirit, and contributing their own learning experiences. Interactions initiated by online mentors can build a social rapport and a sense of coherent learning communities that supports online learning (Brown, 2001; Gilbert & Driscoll, 2002). As online technical supporters, online mentors help students solve technical problems, making online learning possible. Students, with little or no online learning experiences, often encounter technical problems, such as accessing or navigating course Web sites, uploading or downloading course materials, posting messages onto online discussion boards, and so on. With assistance from online mentors, students are able to complete course work without being held back by technical problems.

The Mentor-Support Team

The mentor-support team includes a mentor coordinator and two or three assistants. This team recruits online mentors, conducts the mentor-training program, and hosts the mentor-resources Web site. To recruit mentors, the mentor-support team announces vacancies on the university Web site and to community college campuses through multiple media. The mentor coordinator visits community college campuses once or twice a year to meet with potential mentors and encourage them to apply for the positions. The mentor coordinator recommends the best candidates to faculty members, who make the final decisions. Selected online mentors are hired by the Department of Distance Learning and trained by the mentor-support team. The mentor-training program trains new online mentors to acquire the essential knowledge, skills, and attitudes for online mentoring. The mentor-training program is held every summer and can be held at other times as needed. The two phases of mentor-training program include face-to-face workshop and online training. Each phase takes approximately 16 hours.

Mentor-training Phase I is a 3-day workshop on the university campus. In this phase, online mentors learn the expectations of their roles and responsibilities, meet faculty members and other members in OLCOM, and get familiar with the online course management system. Representatives of each segment of OLCOM present the roles, responsibilities, and expectations for mentors from the perspective of students, faculty, and the university. Experienced online mentors are invited to meet with new online mentors in a casual setting and answer questions. Mentors also meet with faculty members to discuss any specific assistance the faculty members expect. At the end of Phase I, new mentors participate in an orientation on the online course management system that delivers online courses to become familiar with the learning environment in which they would be working. Mentor training Phase II is online training on the basic skills for operating the online course management system. New mentors are asked to complete training activities on two parallel training Webs ites. They experience two different roles: as a teaching assistant on one Web site and as a student on the other Web site. Training activities include how to login to the training Web sites, participate in online discussions, form small discussion groups, set up chat rooms, submit assignments, post grades, and so forth. Training in an authentic online learning environment provides new mentors the opportunity to learn, practice, and experience the results as both mentors and students. Mentors who successfully complete the mentor-training program receive mentor certificates awarded by the university.

A mentor-resources Web site is designed, developed, and hosted by the mentor-support team to provide a virtual space for professional development through comentoring partnerships or collaborative mentorship. The collaboration among mentors establishes a partnership support group, which forms a powerful force for professional development in mentoring (Mullen, 2000). The most significant feature of the mentor-resources Web site is the opportunity to obtain support from peer mentors through online discussions. Any mentors or the mentor coordinator can initiate a forum to discuss issues, exchange experiences, express opinions, send out early warnings of potential problems, and suggest solutions to problems. Most mentors comment that participating in the discussion on this Web site is extremely valuable for their professional development. The mentor-resources Web site, as the major communication tool between the mentor coordinator and mentors, keeps mentors updated about the news and recent events in the online learning community. The mentor coordinator frequently posts announcements on the mentor-resources Web site for all mentors regarding new mentoring resources, new mentors, recommendations for problem solving, explanations of mentoring models, conference calls, and new vacancies.

Academic Coordinators

Academic coordinators assist students with online administrative procedures. An academic coordinator from each associated academic department is assigned to assist students who are taking online courses in the undergraduate online degree programs. Academic coordinators team up with the office of admissions to help students to obtain admissions online, collaborate with the registrar's office to track online students' progress in course work, and cooperate with the graduation office to process graduation materials for the students who have met the graduation requirements. Like face-to-face students, all online students were admitted to the online degree programs each semester.

EVALUATION

The evaluation of OLCOM included student performance and student satisfaction with mentor performance. Student performance was evaluated by comparing students' course completion rates and grade point averages between undergraduate online degree programs and the cohort of all undergraduate degree programs (face-to-face and online) at the same university. Online students had higher course completion rate

Table 3.1.   Comparison of Course Completion Rates and GPAs in Online and Cohort Undergraduate Degree Programs

Undergraduate Degree Programs	Completion Rate	GPA	Number of Students in the First Year Completed the Course	Enrollment: Number of Students in the First Year
Online	87%	3.43	389	447
Cohort	82%	3.01	4,986	6,080

Data sources: Florida State University Fact Book (Kalb, 2002) and the Office for Distributed and Distance Learning (2002).

(87%) than the cohort students (82%) at the same university. Online students also had higher GPA (3.43) than the cohort students (3.01). Table 3.1 displays student completion rates and GPAs in online and cohort undergraduate degree programs.

The student satisfaction with mentor performance was assessed through an online survey and measured five aspects: response time, the quality of help, consistency of feedback, comfort level in the mentor student relationship, and whether or not students would recommend the mentor to other students. The questions capturing these five aspects of student satisfaction were: (1) My mentor's response time was reasonable. (2) My mentor's help in course content was valuable. (3) I received consistent feedback from my mentor and my instructor. (4) I would be comfortable having the same mentor in a future course. (5) I would recommend my mentor to other students who will be taking online courses. Students were asked to answer each question on a 5-point Likert scale: *strongly agree, agree, neutral, disagree,* and *strongly disagree.* This online survey was distributed at the end of the semester and encouraged students to voluntarily participate.

The five aspects of student satisfaction with mentor performance were based on online learning satisfaction reported in previous studies. Reasonable response time is the top attribute of the supportiveness to online learning and teaching (Maushak & Ellis, 2003; Northrup, 2002). Valuable online help, or sufficient online support, motivates and enhances learning achievement (Hill, 2001). Consistent feedback from faculty and mentors confirms right answers and corrects errors, which is essential to learning achievement and satisfaction (Kulhavy, 1977). A positive mentor-student relationship is a major factor promoting student satisfaction in online learning environments (Jung, Choi, Lim, & Leem, 2002). Comfortable relationship with the mentor motivates satisfied students to recommend their mentors to other students. Students who are satisfied with their learning experiences prefer having the same mentor in future courses (Maushak & Ellis, 2003).

Table 3.2.   Student Satisfaction With Mentor Performance

Question		Strongly Agree	Agree	Neutral	Disagree	Strongly Disagree	Positive Ratings*	Total
My mentor's response time was reasonable	n	469	288	80	63	44	757	944
	(%)	(50)	(31)	(8)	(7)	(5)	(80)	(100)
My mentor's help in course content was valuable	N	433	297	133	37	40	730	940
	(%)	(42)	(29)	(13)	(4)	(4)	(70)	(100)
I received consistent feedback from my mentor and instructor	N	451	289	129	46	30	740	945
	(%)	(44)	(28)	(12)	(4)	(3)	(71)	(100)
I would be comfortable having the same mentor in a future course	N	517	220	106	43	53	737	939
	(%)	(50)	(21)	(10)	(4)	(5)	(72)	(100)
I would recommend my mentor to other students who would be taking online courses	n	487	223	121	62	50	710	943
	(%)	(47)	(22)	(12)	(6)	(5)	(69)	(100)

Data source: Office for Distributed and Distance Learning (2002)
Note: *Positive ratings: sum of the strongly agree and agree ratings .

Findings indicate that students were satisfied with the performance of their mentor. Approximately three fourths of all students reported positive ratings of "strongly agree" and "agree." The range on positive answers was 80% to 69%. The survey return rate was 36% or 945 responses from 2,616 students. Table 3.2 displays the results of student satisfaction with mentor performance.

DISCUSSION

Findings endorsed the overall success of OLCOM; students supported by the OLCOM team scored higher completion rate and GPA than cohort students and reported high satisfaction with online mentor performance. The finding that online students achieved higher course completion rate and GPA than cohort students does not necessarily demonstrate that online learning had any significant advantages over traditional face-to-face learning, since this was not a controlled comparison. This finding strongly suggests that, with support from the OLCOM team, online students may perform as well as the students in face-to-face classrooms. The finding of online students' satisfaction with online mentor performance has several implications: (1) Online mentors might have effectively facilitated online students to build closely tied OLC for supporting online learning, (2) the mentor training program prepared online mentors very well for online mentoring, (3) the mentor-resources Web site supported online mentors in better assisting online learning.

With regard to learning effectiveness, online mentors appear to be more important for online learning than teaching assistants to face-to-face learning. Online learning has barriers, such as psychological disconnectedness and technical problems, which are unique to online learning environments (Wolcott, 1996). Online courses put great demands on faculty and students in dealing with these online learning barriers. With more online experience students have and technical assistance provided at the university level, online students may eventually need less help for technical-problem solving. However, the psychological disconnectedness will continue to be present in every virtual classroom. Building close-tie online learning communities will continue to be a critical factor to minimize psychological disconnectedness for successful online learning.

FUTURE TRENDS

With the widespread use of Internet in education, online education is growing at a tremendously large scale that was never imagined in the history of education. Learning is now distributed among diverse people and communities. In the era of globalization, online learning communities expand across geographic boundaries and embrace learners with various cultures. These global online learning communities may broaden learners' knowledge with multiple perspectives and develop learner networks at the global level. This is a unique feature that traditional education is not able to achieve easily. For future research, the online learning communities with online mentors (OLCOM) model presented here can serve as a basic framework from which online educators can explore various conceptual systems and instructional designs to build and sustain online learning communities for the growth of global online learning communities.

REFERENCES

Allen, I. E., & Seaman, J. (2005). *Entering the mainstream: The quality and extent of online education in the United States, 2003 and 2004.* The Sloan Consortium.

Retrieved   June   15,   2006,   from   http://www.sloan-c.org/resources/entering_mainstream.pdf.

Brown, R. (2001). The process of community-building in distance learning classes. *Journal of Asynchronous Learning Networks, 5*(2). http://www.sloan-c.org/publications/jaln/v5n2/v5n2_brown.asp

Caverly, D. C., & MacDonald, L. (2002). Techtalk: Online learning communities. *Journal of Developmental Education, 25*(3), 36-37.

Charalambos, V., Michalinos, Z., & Chamberlain, R. (2004). The design of online learning communities: Critical issues. *Educational Media International, 41*(2), 135-143.

Gilbert, N. J., & Driscoll, M. P. (2002). Collaborative knowledge building: A case study. *Educational Technology Research and Development, 50*(1), 59-79.

Heydenrych, J. F., Higgs, P., & van Niekerk, L. J. (2003). Implementing the online learning community in Africa: A UNISA case study. *African & Asian Studies, 2*(4), 421-474.

Hill, J. R. (2001). *Building community in web-based learning environments: Strategies and techniques.* Retrieved December 17, 2002, from http://ausweb.scu.edu.au/aw01/papers/refereed/hill/paper.html

Jin, Q. (2002). Design of a virtual community based interactive learning environment. *Information Sciences, 140*(1/2), 171-191.

Jung, I., Choi, S., Lim, C., & Leem, J., (2002). Effects of different types of interaction on learning achievement, satisfaction, and participation in Web-based instruction. *Innovations in Education and Teaching International, 39*(2), 153-162.

Kalb, J. (2002). *Undergraduate student dropouts during the first year of attendance Fall 1999 Cohort.* Retrieved October 10, 2002, from http://www.ir.fsu.edu/Factbooks/

Kulhavy, R. W. (1977). Feedback in written instruction. *Review of Educational Research, 47*(2), 211-232.

Maushak, N. J., & Ellis, K. A. (2003). Attitudes of graduate students toward mixed-medium distance education. *Quarterly Review of Distance Education, 4*(2), 129-41.

Misanchuk, M., & Anderson, T. (2001). *Building community in an online learning environment: Communication, cooperation, and collaboration.* Retrieved December 17, 2002, from http://www.mtsu.edu/~itconf/proceed01/19.html

Mullen, C. A. (2000). New directions for mentoring: Remaking the school-university culture. *Action in Teacher Education, 22*(1), 112-124.

National Center for Education Statistics. (1999, December 17). *Distance education at postsecondary education institutions: 1997-98* (NCES # 2000013). National Center for Education Statistics. Retrieved October 22, 2002, from http://nces.ed.gov/pubsearch/pubsinfo.asp?pubid=2000013

Northrup, P. T. (2002). Online learners' preferences for interaction. *Quarterly Review of Distance Education, 3*(2), 219-226.

Office for Distributed and Distance Learning. (2002). *Mentor performance report summary.* Office for Distributed and Distance Learning at Florida State University. Retrieved June 17, 2002, from http://online.fsu.edu/instructor/mentor/ongoing.html

Sierra, C., & Folger, T. (2003). Building a dynamic online learning community among adult learners. *Educational Media International, 40*(1/2), 49-62.

Sorensen, E. K. M., & Murchú, D. Ó. (2004). Designing online learning communities of practice: A democratic perspective. *Journal of Educational Media, 29*(3), 189-200.

Tu, C. -H., & Corry, M. (2002). eLearning communities. *Quarterly Review of Distance Education, 3*(2), 207-218.

Wolcott, L. L. (1996). Distant, but not distanced: A learner-centered approach to distance education. *TechTrends, 41*(5), 23-27.

CHAPTER 4

FOUNDATIONS AND PRACTICE FOR WEB-ENHANCED SCIENCE INQUIRY

Grounded Design Perspectives

Minchi C. Kim and Michael J. Hannafin

Corresponding to the calls from the National Research Council (1996) and the American Association for the Advancement of Science (1993), researchers and practitioners have implemented learner-centered, technology-rich environments that help students to investigate scientific phenomena through authentic inquiry. The proliferation of Web-based modules and tools underscores the need to re-examine the foundations on which such environments are grounded and the practice through which students and teachers utilize the modules and tools. With a focus on open-ended learning environments and grounded design perspectives, this chapter examines issues in science learning in Web-Enhanced Learning Environments (WELEs) and describes foundations and design principles to support scientific inquiry.

Online Learning Communities
pp. 53–72

INTRODUCTION

Researchers have explored numerous approaches for enhancing student-centered learning in science classes in alignment with the National Science Education Standards (National Research Council, 1996) and the benchmarks from Project 2061 (American Association for the Advancement of Science, 1993). Corresponding to these calls, computer-based tools have been widely investigated to improve student learning in science classrooms. Research has shown promising findings about the impact of computer-based modeling and simulation tools on student achievement in science learning. In a 3-year study for systemic reform with technology-enhanced curricula, Marx et al. (2004) reported a significant increase in student achievement based on test data from 8,000 students in Detroit public schools; moreover, they found a significant learning increase in low-achieving students when integrating research- and standards-based inquiry curriculum supported by professional development for teachers.

Such successes can be partly attributed to the affordances of technologies that enable students to do what they would not be able to accomplish otherwise. The World Wide Web allows learners to access and use an enormous repository of resources. Web-based tools enable students to manipulate and analyze scientific data as problems are engaged, strategies emerge, and understanding evolves. The ready incorporation of text, graphics, video, and audio allows students to build, evolve, and organize multiple representations of their knowledge. Online courses, modules, and self-study units have proliferated during the past decade, reflecting a wide range of beliefs about teaching and learning, system affordances, and learning strategies. To some extent, this is normal and predictable, given technology's adoption and diffusion history. However, while the number of online learning systems has grown exponentially, a corresponding technology of design has been disappointingly slow to emerge (Hannafin & Kim, 2003).

This has proven especially challenging in Web-based systems designed to support science learning. Several values are considered central to many in the science education communities, principal among them scientific inquiry. Simply providing online science courses without reflecting inquiry—or the corresponding values and beliefs of a different community for an online course in that discipline—may be perceived as *less than* nothing by the intended audience. Availability and access to *a* course or courses may no longer be sufficient; misaligned courses may be perceived as misrepresenting or as undermining widely held values considered fundamental to a discipline. Online courses for the sciences need to approximate the interactions with and engage students in the thinking among scientists. The purposes of this chapter are to discuss core issues in science learning in Web-Enhanced Learning Environments (WELEs) and to provide foundations and design principles to support Web-enhanced science inquiry.

FOUNDATIONS WEB-ENHANCED SCIENCE INQUIRY

Scientific Inquiry: An Emergent Framework for Teaching and Learning

The National Standards for Science Education (National Research Council, 1996) define scientific inquiry as "the diverse ways in which scientists study the natural world and propose explanations based on the evidence derived from their work" (p. 23). Proposed as a learning and teaching framework that guides students to learn science in a way that scientists investigate natural phenomena, scientific inquiry has proven somewhat elusive because it does not explicitly designate accompanying teaching and learning strategies. The National Research Council (1996) outlines the following core elements of scientific inquiry:

> Inquiry is a multifaceted activity that involves making observations; posing questions; examining books and other sources of information to see what is already known; planning investigations; reviewing what is already known in light of experimental evidence; using tools to gather, analyze, and interpret data; proposing answers, explanations, and predictions; and communicating the results. (p. 23)

However, to some, this description is not sufficiently clear to implement inquiry in everyday classrooms (Shiland, 2002). Fundamental differences exist between science inquiry and traditional science teaching methods, focusing on directed questioning and answering, and accompanying laboratory experiments guided by teachers. For educators accustomed to traditional didactic instruction, scientific inquiry requires a significant epistemological and pedagogical shift.

Table 4.1 presents key distinctions between traditional science instruction and scientific inquiry. Traditional science instruction, rooted in positivism, assumes that students acquire knowledge as they answer teacher-directed questions. Accordingly, pedagogical strategies involve providing explicit learning content and well-defined problem contexts. Students are taught what to know about science, but do not control their learning; rather, teachers take active roles in identifying to-be-learned content, organizing and sequencing instruction, and assessing competence in the identified knowledge and skills. Traditional approaches are often supported by externally-posed, criterion-referenced assessments (Hannafin & Hill, 2002).

Table 4.1. Comparison Between Instruction-Oriented Science Learning Environments and Student-Centered Science Learning Environments

	Instruction-Oriented Science Learning Environments	*Student-Centered Science Learning Environments*
Theoretical framework	Positivism	Constructivism
Nature of learning	Learners can understand knowledge by answering questions posed by teachers	Learners can construct their own knowledge by exploring and analyzing scientific phenomena
Views of inquiry	Inquiry as a teaching strategy	Inquiry as a teaching and learning framework
Focus	Directed learning	Open learning
Content	Well-defined	Ill-defined
Assessment	Criterion-referenced assessment	Context-driven evaluation
Student's roles	Answerer, knowledge-receiver	Inquirer, knowledge-builder
Teacher's roles	Questioner, knowledge source	Facilitator, knowledge coconstructor
Locus of control	External	Internal

In contrast, scientific inquiry, grounded in constructivism, posits that students construct their own knowledge via the process of exploring and interpreting scientific problems and observations, and communicating with peers, teachers, and scientists. Students learn how to think scientifically by engaging in inquiry in much the same ways as scientists do. As a learning environment, scientific inquiry is typically implemented in student-centered classes, posing ill-defined problems where students co-monitor their progress with teachers (Hannafin & Hill, 2002). While facilitating students' learning processes, teachers also clarify and modify the students' scientific understanding and reconstruct their knowledge accordingly.

According to Hannafin (1995), the strengths of traditional didactic instruction are in familiarity, efficiency, precision, accountability, manageability, and training. Teachers feel more familiar with conventional questioning-answering than with scientific inquiry because directed approaches are often efficient and precise ways to both teach and measure achievements of established, explicit curriculum objectives and learning outcomes. Teachers tend to use direct instruction when they are accountable for demonstrating specific student accomplishments. In addition, some believe that courses are more manageable and instructional materials are easier to develop using traditional didactic methods.

However, traditional methods also tend to engender outcomes that are inconsistent with the values of scientific inquiry, such as compliant cognition, oversimplification, functional fixedness, limited incubation, and context-bound knowledge. Scientific inquiry requires learners to engage in ill-structured problem solving (Shin, Jonassen, & McGee, 2003) that focuses on student-generated problems and scientific ways to investigate the problems and emphasizes depth of knowledge—values difficult to promote using directed question-answer strategies. Through scientific inquiry, students generate, test, and modify their hypotheses based on the weight of evidence; students rarely focus on complying their thinking with a teacher as they pursue problems and issues of their own making. Whereas teachers tend to oversimplify essential science concepts in didactic approaches, scientific inquiry requires that both learners and teachers become facile with core scientific knowledge and scientific processes by "doing science." Students, as scientists-in-the-making, conduct experiments and develop scientific ways of examining and interpreting the natural world. Fundamental, conceptual changes in understanding, not limited to a particular problem, emerge from the learning experience. Thus, students' scientific knowledge can be more readily transferred to other contexts. As new ideas, scientific procedures, and conclusions are incubated, students become more capable of reflecting on both their formal knowledge as well as their learning experiences.

There is no single theory that addresses all teaching-learning problems and issues or approaches upon which all designers agree. We argue that scientific inquiry is a crucial (and widely endorsed within the science and science education communities) pedagogical framework upon which standards-based, Web-based science learning environments should be rooted. The differences between traditional and scientific inquiry are not merely semantic in nature, but reflect fundamental differences in values, epistemology, and methodology that need to be addressed.

Science Learning With Technologies

Research has shown the great potential of technologies to enhance student learning (Marx et al., 2004). In this section, we examine three aspects of science learning that can be fostered with technologies: (a) technologies providing metacontext where students can be assisted in solving complex science problems, (b) technologies incorporating different representations, and (c) technologies enabling peers, teachers, and experts to collaborate through online communities.

First, technologies serve as a metacontext that frames complex science problems in order to help students monitor their inquiry processes and solve the problems. Typically, students face challenges linking prior and novel knowledge and decomposing ill-structured tasks. However, technology-enhanced science environments as a metacontext can propose a problem context in which students can identify personally meaningful problems, solve the problems, and receive metacognitive and procedural scaffolds (e.g., embedded cues and visualized learning paths). For instance, in Web-enhanced Inquiry Science Environments (WISE) (Linn, Clark, & Slotta, 2003), students encounter an engaging or challenging problem context, identify smaller problems to which they can provide answers, explore Web-based evidence, and present and justify their conclusions. In a selected project from the WISE library dealing with controversies around genetically modified foods, Seethaler and Linn (2004) found significant learning gains on the posttest from eighth-grade students using the Web-based project in six classrooms.

Second, technologies may assist students in connecting different science ideas by utilizing diverse representations embedded in simulations and modeling tools. For example, the Virtual Solar System (Barab, Hay, Barnett, & Keating, 2000) allows students to visualize abstract concepts in astronomy and to manipulate associated variables (e.g., size, distance, speed of planets) in order to see the virtual changes made by students' input. Keating, Barnett, and Barab (1999) reported significant gains in learning outcomes from the students participating in the Virtual Solar System course as compared to the typical introductory course for astronomy. In WorldWatcher (Edelson, Gordon, & Pea, 1999), students can visualize geographic information (e.g., world map), enter data values (e.g., temperature), and learn about global warming and energy balance. Wu, Krajcik, and Soloway (2001) reported a significant increase in 11th graders' comprehension of chemical representations after using eChem, a tool allowing students to construct molecular representations and interpret the corresponding symbolic representations.

Third, students have enormously increased opportunities to collaborate with peers, teachers, and scientists through online communities. Grounded in cognitive apprenticeship (Collins, Brown, & Newman, 1989) and situated learning (Lave & Wenger, 1991), Sandoval and Reiser (2004) proposed a framework of explanation-driven inquiry or designing authentic science inquiry. It emphasizes students' engagement in scientific reasoning and discussions, and such participation involves crucial inquiry activities such as generating "researchable" questions, designing "informative" investigations, and proposing "persuasive" arguments (p. 347)—the core value-oriented activities in the science discipline. ExplanationConstructor was designed to facilitate explanation-driven inquiry by helping students to articulate on causal relations of scientific variables and to develop scientific arguments. Using the text boxes and prompts embedded in ExplanationConstructor, a student can pose a question, a peer can respond to it, and they can then collaborate on formulating and revising a scientific explanation of the answer.

To foster students' science inquiry in Web-enhanced learning environments and to maximize the potential of different technologies, how should designers ground their design in the values of science inquiry? How can such values be embodied in Web-based learning environments? How can we design online activities and courses consistent with the values of scientific inquiry? We propose that open-ended learning environments provide a useful theoretical framework when grounded design principles guide the design and implementation of online scientific inquiry.

PRACTICE FOR WEB-ENHANCED SCIENCE INQUIRY ENVIRONMENTS

Open-Ended Learning Environments: A Design Framework

We propose open-ended learning environments (OELEs) as a framework to understand fundamental assumptions for learning and teaching with Web-enhanced environments for science inquiry. To distinguish the purposes and processes of traditional directed learning, Hannafin, Hall, Land, and Hill (1994) introduced OELEs as process-oriented, student-centered learning environments. The essential characteristic of OELEs is that it is the student "who determines what is to be learned and what steps are taken to promote learning" (p. 48). In inquiry science classes, students have primary ownership over finding driving questions, generating hypotheses to answer the questions, and investigating their own hypotheses with supporting evidence.

OELEs comprise four basic components: enabling contexts, resources, tools, and scaffolds. Technologies are frequently used as a tool to frame learning contexts and to provide resources, tools, and scaffolds customized to students' needs, interests, and relevant knowledge (Land & Hannafin, 2000). In this section, we analyze characteristics and examples of each component in the place of science teaching and learning.

Learning Contexts.   A learning context denotes either a physical or virtual place designed to foster meaningful learning. We highlight two key characteristics of learning contexts to promote science inquiry: (1) project-based, and (2) situated to students' daily experiences. First, project-based learning contexts supply the situation or problem area in which students can find a meaningful project to conduct an in-depth investigation. The learning context often guides students in recognizing or generating problems and framing learning needs. Externally-imposed contexts—often presented as explicit problem statements or questions—

clarify the expected learning outcome(s) and implicitly guide student strategies. Externally-induced contexts introduce a domain, but not the specific problems to be addressed.

The goal of project-based learning contexts is to help students practice inquiry activities in in-depth, authentic ways in contrast to the didactic teaching approach often leading to compliant cognition, oversimplification, and functional fixedness (Barab & Luehmann, 2003). To support students' meaningful participation, it is critical to provide a "tailored context" (Barab & Roth, 2006, p. 9) with challenging problems and scaffolds optimized for student needs. Typically, a scenario is encountered in which any number of problems or issues can be generated or studied. In generated contexts, specific problem contexts are not designed a priori. The learner establishes an enabling context based on needs and circumstances that are unique. As with induced contexts, students activate relevant knowledge, skill, and experience to guide their activities. Oftentimes, in project-based science classes it is essential for students to integrate knowledge from different subjects in order to construct an artifact.

Barak and Dori (2005) studied 215 undergraduate students in three chemistry classes to examine the effect of project-based, technology-supported learning activities on students' understanding of molecular models. They found that students who utilized a Computerized Molecular Modeling (CMM) tool incorporated into the project-based curriculum showed a significant increase from pre- to posttest, whereas students who did not use the tool did not.

Second, science learning contexts situated in students' daily experiences enhance transfer of science learning and increase student engagement in inquiry. In situated learning contexts when combined with project-based pedagogy, students find or choose a personally meaningful issue to investigate. Story-based problems that resemble everyday issues were found to be effective in increasing student engagement and learning in technology-assisted classes when carefully designed and incorporated with the curriculum (Cognition and Technology Group at Vanderbilt, 1997). Fortus, Krajcik, Dershimer, Marx, and Mamlok-Naaman (2005) reported that 9th- and 10th-grade students showed significant gains on transfer tasks when exploring and solving real-world science problems (i.e., "how do I design a structure for extreme environmental conditions?").

Resources.   Resources, which range from electronic databases and print textbooks to original source documents and humans, are source materials that support learning. In open-ended inquiry learning, resources provide an extraordinary reserve of source materials. The Web, for example, enables access to millions of source documents; however, their integrity and usefulness are difficult for individuals to ascertain (Hill & Hannafin, 2001). A resource's utility depends on its relevance to the enabling context *and* its accessibility. The more relevant and accessible, the greater its utility.

In science learning, resources typically have three goals: (1) to promote student investigation, (2) to support teacher facilitation, and (3) to enhance school and community collaboration from a distance. First, in order to promote student investigation, learning environments often involve electronic resources that students can access. Formats and functions of such resources for student inquiry vary: online daily newspapers for finding science issues relevant to the everyday world, government Web sites for looking up the data collected by scientists in the field, and Web search engines for perusing available information sources. Despite the diversity in formats and functions, all the resources are employed to promote students' inquiry activities, particularly in the process of evidence finding. Artemis was developed and tested to help students find and filter Web-based resources needed to answer their own driving questions. Hoffman, Wu, Krajcik, and Soloway (2003) studied how eight pairs of 6th-grade students utilized online evidence in a digital library. The library was specifically designed for middle- and high school students' inquiry with Artemis to help students develop content knowledge in earth and space science. This learning environment includes qualified online materials selected by librarians and sorted by topics and driving questions so that students can browse and find resources in systematic ways. After implementing the digital library and Artemis to four Web-based inquiry units for 9 months, Hoffman et al. (2003) reported that tools developed to assist student investigation of resources can increase student strategies in searching and linking evidence and boost students' conceptual understanding of subject matter.

Second, in order to support teacher facilitation in inquiry classes, learning environments provide a virtual place where novice and experienced teachers can share ideas and teaching exemplars for successful student inquiry. Inquiry Learning Forum is one example of online resources that allow in-service and pre-service teachers in science and mathematics to collaborate on developing and refining teaching practices for student-centered inquiry (Barab, MaKinster, Moore, & Cunningham, 2001).

Third, extending collaboration among teachers, shared online resources can enhance school and community collaboration as well. Research indicates that school and community culture is a critical factor when teachers implement technology-infused inquiry approaches in science classes. In particular, schools in urban settings face more challenges due to their lack of resources, support, and pedagogy (Songer, Lee, & Kam, 2002, p. 128). Moreover, it is more difficult for urban science teachers to motivate students whose interest and expectations are academically deficient and peer-focused (Seiler, Tobin, & Sokolic, 2001). Despite the long-overdue issue of urban science education, there is still a paucity of community-based resources and support for such diverse and often disadvantaged groups in urban settings. Learning environments for successful science inquiry necessitate more research-based development of community and school resources and practice-based teaching exemplars from diverse school settings.

Tools. Tools provide the means to engage and manipulate resources and ideas. Tools' functions vary according to the enabling contexts and the intentions of users; the same tool can support different functions. We classify technology-based tools for science into eight types based upon their purposes and roles: seeking, collecting, processing (visualizing), organizing, integrating, manipulating, generating, and communicating.

Seeking tools, such as keyword search, topical indices, and search engines, help learners to find and access information, scientific data, and needed resources corresponding to learners' hypotheses. **Collection tools** facilitate students' gathering of resources. For example, Web browsers typically save URL addresses visited and word processors allow users to capture and save documents, charts, pictures, and tables. **Processing tools** reduce the cognitive load required to process information by providing multi-representations and visualizations. The WorldWatcher, for example, renders complex data from a data library and displays weather maps that students can easily understand (Edelson et al., 1999). **Organization tools** assist learners in representing relationships among ideas, using graphical or semantic mapping to define relationships among ideas, concepts, or "nodes." Semantic networks and concept map are well-known cognitive tools supporting organization of ideas (Jonassen & Reeves, 1996).

Integration tools help learners to associate new information with existing knowledge. Prompts used in WISE (Web-based Inquiry Science Environment), such as what do you think, state your opinion, and defend your positions, facilitate reflecting on prior knowledge, elaborating new ideas, and deepening the associations between and among new and existing knowledge. **Manipulation tools** are used to test or explore beliefs and theories-in-action. For example, students can build a Virtual Solar System in order to test their hypotheses and verify conclusions (Keating, Barnett, Barab, & Hay, 2002). **Generating tools** help students to create artifacts of understanding such as presentations using both original and existing resources (Iiyoshi & Hannafin, 1996) or software for teaching peers about fractions (Harel & Papert, 1990). **Communication tools** (e.g., e-mail, listserv) support efforts to initiate or sustain exchanges among learners, teachers, and experts.

Scaffolding. Researchers (Metcalf, Krajcik, & Soloway, 2000; Hannafin & Oliver, 2001) have suggested that many students are not independently capable of utilizing the Web for higher-order tasks. Scaffolding—support through which learners can engage a task productively beyond their inde-pendent abilities—is often necessary to support and guide the student inquiry processes. Scaffolding has been characterized as a type of model-ing, coaching, articulation, reflection, and exploration (Collins et al., 1989). However, wide variations are evident in interpreting, adapting, and implementing scaffolding. Applebee and Langer (1983) proposed five essential features of scaffolding: intentionality, appropriateness, structure, collaboration, and internalization. Hogan and Pressley (1997) described process-oriented scaffolding elements: pre-engagement, shared goals, analysis of learners' understanding and needs, tailored assistance, goal maintenance, feedback, risk control, and independence.

In inquiry classes where students often lack relevant prior experiences, cognitive capacities, or intrinsic motivation, scaffolding is crucial. Kim (2006) classified scaffolding in technology-infused science classrooms into three types: technology-enhanced scaffolding, peer-enhanced scaffolding, and teacher-enhanced scaffolding.

First, technology-enhanced scaffolding is defined as various features embedded in tools with the goal of helping students overcome challenges in inquiry processes. According to Reiser (2004), computer-based tools scaffold students' inquiry activities by structuring and problematizing inquiry tasks. First, by structuring inquiry activities, science tools help stu-dents probe complicated inquiry tasks and center their cognitive atten-tion on key learning issues. Second, by problematizing inquiry tasks, science tools support students' capacities to deeply think about a prob-lem, to reflect on their reasoning processes, and to justify their solutions. For instance, Metcalf and his colleagues (2000) identified three examples of scaffolding that Model-It provides: supportive scaffolding that assists students in building their model by providing examples and explana-tions, reflective scaffolding that guide students in monitoring their model-building activities, and intrinsic scaffolding that helps students adjust the complexity of activities with the features for multiple represen-tations.

Second, peer-enhanced scaffolding has been researched extensively on the effects of peer interaction (Ge & Land, 2003) and peer discussion (Scardamalia & Bereiter, 1992) on solving higher-order problems in tech-nology-supported learning environments. Research indicates that dis-tance learners working in groups may perform significantly better than ones working alone in problem-solving tasks and show increased time on tasks (Uribe, Klein, & Sullivan, 2003). In science education, research also suggests that students might benefit from peer challenges or communica-tions by increasing their motivation and justification skills in inquiry tasks.

Third, research has shown the increasing importance of the teacher in science classes to be critical in the successful implementation of inquiry activities (Crawford, 2000). Specifically, teacher-enhanced scaffolding is crucial, considering that inquiry-oriented activities require students to take their own ownership of learning and that many students need guided assistance for generating science questions and structuring their inquiry tasks (Krajcik, Blumenfeld, Marx, Bass, Fredricks, & Soloway, 1998). However, more research is needed to examine peer-enhanced and teacher-enhanced scaffolding in technology-supported inquiry classes with a focus on their roles and collaborating patterns.

Scaffolding can be provided through various sources; furthermore, scaffolding complexity varies according to the locus of the problem(s) posed and the demands posed in the enabling context. During scientific inquiry, where the nature of use and learner needs cannot be definitively established in advance, scaffolding typically remains available continuously, although it is used less frequently as facility increases. Conceptual scaffolding guides learners regarding *what to consider* by identifying key conceptual knowledge related to a problem or creating structures that make conceptual organization readily apparent. Metacognitive scaffolding supports the underlying processes associated with individual learning management, such as *how to think* during learning, helping students to consider how or if to initiate, compare, and revise their representations. Procedural scaffolding emphasizes *how to utilize* the affordances of the learning environment, such as system features and functions, and otherwise aids the learner while navigating. Finally, strategic scaffolding focuses on *alternative ways* to analyze, plan, and act during open-ended inquiry by enabling students to identify and select needed information, evaluate resources, and integrate new and existing knowledge and experiences.

Grounded Learning Systems Design

Hannafin, Hannafin, Land, and Oliver (1997) defined grounded design as "the systematic implementation of processes and procedures that are rooted in established theory and research in human learning" (p. 102). As examined, OELEs provide a framework to understand key aspects of student-centered inquiry learning. In order to guide the design of OELEs, grounded design perspectives emphasize the alignment of learning theories and pedagogical strategies with practical considerations.

We identify five essential foundations in grounded design: psychological, pedagogical, technological, cultural, and pragmatic foundations (Hannafin & Land, 1997; Land & Hannafin, 2000). Each foundation co-

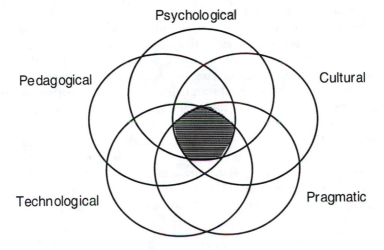

Source: Adapted from Hannafin and Land (1997).

Figure 4.1.   Fully integrated foundations in open-ended learning environments.

exists with every other foundation; the extent to which the foundations are congruent with one another determines the degree to which their influence is balanced across or dominated by one or more foundations. A conceptual illustration of a partially congruent relationship among foundations, where joint influence yields a balanced impact, is shown in Figure 4.1; congruence among foundations is represented by the shaded area.

Psychological foundations characterize how people think and learn based on validated theories and research. Reinforcement theory derived from behavioral psychology, information-processing theory from cognitive psychology, and situated cognition consistent with social constructivism are often cited as psychological foundations (Hannafin et al., 1997). Following from and consistent with psychological foundations, pedagogical foundations undergird the strategies used to facilitate teaching and learning. Direct instructional strategies flow naturally from both behavioral and cognitive psychology, while anchored instruction and scaffolded inquiry (Linn & Slotta, 2000) are consistent with the more constructivist approaches embodied in scientific inquiry.

Technological foundations refer to capacities and constraints of media in learning; that is, the potential and actual uses of a given learning environment's affordances. Technology tools can be used to support a number of different (but aligned) psychological and pedagogical foundations, but the uses will likely vary considerably. For example, simple tutorial and drill programs can be used as direct instruction grounded in behavioral psychology, but inquiry approaches are more likely to feature tools that assist in student-centered investigation. Cultural foundations emphasize the values of community where learning occurs. The beliefs of different communities vary substantially; back-to-basics advocates tend to stress knowledge and skill building through practice and repetition, while the scientific inquiry community values learning environments that enable the reconciliation of diverse perspectives and the developing and testing of formative theories and hypotheses. Finally, pragmatic foundations reflect "tradeoffs" between benefits and costs, the theoretical ideal and the practical, and the unique cultural mores of different communities. Pragmatic foundations define the resources and constraints, as well as the values, of both the community as a whole and individual parents, teachers, and students.

WISE: Web-Based Inquiry Science Environment

As an open-ended learning system, WISE provides reliable ways of building inquiry-oriented, open-ended learning environments, aligning psychological, pedagogical, technological, cultural, and practical foundations to its online scaffolding. WISE (Web-based Inquiry Science Environment, a funded project by National Science Foundation) promotes students' solving of interdisciplinary science problems and the debating of natural phenomena in scientific ways using the Science Controversy On-line (SCOPE) (Linn & Hsi, 2000). Extending initial work in Knowledge Integration Environments, WISE manifests four values: make science visible, make thinking visible, help students learn from one another, and foster lifelong learning (Linn & Slotta, 2000; Linn, Clark, & Slotta, 2003). (Figure 4.2, for examples, see http://wise.berkeley.edu).

According to the OELE framework, WISE initially utilizes externally-induced contexts associated with diverse scientific controversies and evidence. The contexts contain ill-defined problems with associated structured inquiry activities to guide students in using their prior knowledge and scientific data to solve problems. During the inquiry process, WISE encourages students to employ a variety of resources, including natural phenomena, results from experiments, pre-selected Web URLs potentially relevant to the problem under study, and everyday experiences. In addition, WISE helps students to integrate new scientific findings into existing knowledge using tools and scaffolding to manipulate and analyze scientific data with graphs and charts, as well as to communicate with peers, teachers, and scientists. WISE provides main organizing questions and prescribes student activities, but it also provides activities to connect

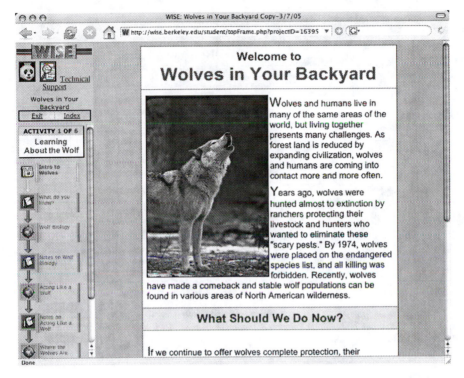

Figure 4.2.   WISE (http://wise.berkeley.edu).

new with existing knowledge and metacognitive scaffolding to monitor individual student learning processes.

According to grounded design principles, psychologically and pedagogically, WISE is grounded strongly in social constructivism, which stresses cognitive apprenticeship, scaffolded knowledge integration, and lifelong science as key pedagogies. Technologically, it utilizes a variety of interactive two-way features such as saving students' work using WISE note-taking tools (Figure 4.3), while supporting communication among teachers and students, and manipulating the data using, for example, charts. Culturally, WISE tools foster collaboration among members of the student learning community as well as support the teachers' community using tools such as Teacher's PET (Figure 4.4). Pragmatically, WISE features and options are the result of a wide range of input and expertise from teachers, technologists, scientists, and researchers to increase ownership and investment in its ideas and values, and it is readily adapted to different science classrooms.

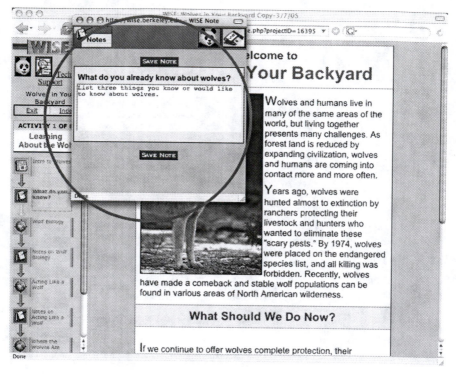

Figure 4.3.   WISE note.

CLOSING THOUGHTS

The design of online systems that support the values and methods associated with scientific inquiry requires that designers take several factors beyond "generic" design into consideration. The implications are tangible and meaningful to the science and science education communities; to support these communities, the implications must become tangible and meaningful to learning environment designers as well.

The question of how to promote scientific inquiry in Web-based learning environments is not limited to issues of generally effective online teaching and learning strategies, but to the specific values embraced by the science community and inextricably tied to corresponding pedagogical frameworks and design perspectives. In a sense, "good design" is situation-specific and contextually determined. Good learning systems design—appropriate, important, useful—is not absolute but a function of the practices and values shared by a given community. To the extent the design community recognizes this and enacts designs accordingly, we con-

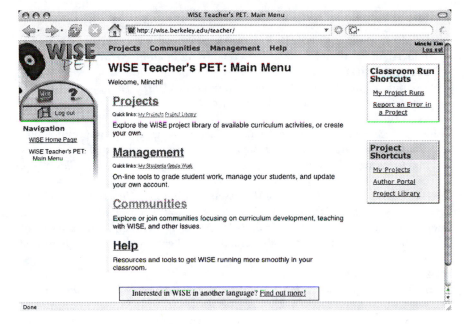

Figure 4.4. WISE Teacher's PET.

tribute meaningfully to a given community; to the extent we extol a unified "right way" in our designs, our effort will likely become increasingly marginalized and our field increasingly balkanized.

REFERENCES

American Association for the Advancement of Science. (1993). *Benchmarks for science literacy.* New York: Oxford University Press.

Applebee, A. N., & Langer, J. A. (1983). Instructional scaffolding: Reading and writing as natural language activities. *Language Arts, 60,* 168-175.

Barab, S. A., Hay, K. E., Barnett, M., & Keating, T. (2000). Virtual solar system project: Building understanding through model building. *Journal of Research in Science Teaching, 37*(7), 719-756.

Barab, S. A., & Luehmann, A. L. (2003). Building sustainable science curriculum: Acknowledging and accommodating local adaptation. *Science Education, 87*(4), 454-467.

Barab, S. A., MaKinster, J. G., Moore, J. A., & Cunningham, D. J. (2001). Designing and building an on-line community: The struggle to support sociability in the inquiry learning forum. *Educational Technology Research and Development, 49*(4), 71-96.

Barab, S. A., & Roth, W. -M. (2006). Curriculum-based ecosystems: Supporting knowing from an ecological perspective. *Educational Researcher, 35*(5), 3-13.

Barak, M., & Dori, Y. J. (2005). Enhancing undergraduate students' chemistry understanding through project-based learning in an IT environment. *Science Education, 89*(1), 117-139.

The Cognition and Technology Group at Vanderbilt. (1997). *The Jasper project: Lessons in curriculum instruction, assessment, and professional development.* Mahwah, NJ: Erlbaum.

Collins, A., Brown, J. S., & Newman, S. E. (1989). Cognitive apprenticeship: Teaching the crafts of reading, writing, and mathematics. In L. B. Resnick (Ed.), *Knowing, learning and instruction: Essays in honor of Robert Glaser* (pp. 347-361). Hillsdale, NJ: Erlbaum.

Crawford, B. A. (2000). Embracing the essence of inquiry: New roles for science teachers. *Journal of Research in Science Teaching, 37*(9), 916-937.

Edelson, D. C., Gordin, D. N., & Pea, R. D. (1999). Addressing the challenges of inquiry-based learning through technology and curriculum design. *Journal of the Learning Sciences, 8*(3-4), 391-450.

Fortus, D., Krajcik, J., Dershimer, R. C., Marx, R. W., & Mamlok-Naaman, R. (2005). Design-based science and real-world problem-solving. *International Journal of Science Education, 27*(7), 855-879.

Ge, X., & Land, S. M. (2003). Scaffolding students' problem-solving processes in an ill-structured task using question prompts and peer interactions. *Educational Technology Research and Development, 51*(1), 21-38.

Hannafin, M. J. (1995). Open-ended learning environments: Foundations, assumptions, and implications for automated design. In R. Tennyson (Ed.), *Perspectives on automating instructional design* (pp. 101-129). New York: Springer-Verlag.

Hannafin, M. J., Hall, C., Land, S., & Hill, J. (1994). Learning in open-ended environments: Assumptions, methods, and implications. *Educational Technology, 34*, 48-55.

Hannafin, M. J., Hannafin, K. M., Land, S. M., & Oliver, K. (1997). Grounded Practice and the Design of Constructivist Learning Environments. *Educational Technology Research and Development, 45*(3), 101-117.

Hannafin, M. J., & Hill, J. (2002). Epistemology and the design of learning environments. In R. Reiser & J. Dempsey (Eds.), *Trends and issues in instructional design and technology* (pp. 70-82). Upper Saddle River, NJ: Merrill/Prentice-Hall.

Hannafin, M. J., & Kim, M. C. (2003). In search of a future: A critical analysis of research on Web-based teaching and learning. *Instructional Science, 31*(4-5), 347-351.

Hannafin, M. J., & Land, S. M. (1997). The foundations and assumptions of technology-enhanced, student-centered learning environments. *Instructional Science, 25*, 167-202.

Harel, I., & Papert, S. (1990). Software design as a learning environment. *Interactive Learning Environments, 1*(1), 1-32.

Hill, J. R., & Hannafin, M. J. (2001). Teaching and learning in digital environments: The resurgence of resource-based learning. *Educational Technology Research and Development, 49*(3), 37-52.

Hoffman, J. L., Wu, H. K., Krajcik, J. S., & Soloway, E. (2003). The nature of middle school learners' science content understandings with the use of on-line resources. *Journal of Research in Science Teaching, 40*(3), 323-346.

Hogan, K., & Pressley, M. (Eds.). (1997). Scaffolding scientific competencies within classroom communities of inquiry. In *Scaffolding student learning: Instructional approaches and issues* (pp. 74-107). Cambridge, MA: Brookline Books.

Iiyoshi, T., & Hannafin, M. J. (1996, February). *Cognitive tools for learning from hypermedia: Empowering learners.* Paper presented at the Association for Educational Communications and Technology, Indianapolis, IN.

Jonassen, D. H., & Reeves, T. C. (1996). Learning with technology: Using computers as cognitive tools. In D. H. Jonassen (Ed.), *Handbook of research for educational communications and technology* (pp. 693-719). New York: Macmillan.

Keating, T., Barnett, M., Barab, S., & Hay, K. E. (2002). The virtual solar system project: Developing conceptual understanding of astronomical concepts through building three-dimensional computational models. *Journal of Science Education and Technology, 11*(3), 261-275.

Keating, T., Barnett, M., & Barab, S. A. (1999, April). *The virtual solar system project: Conceptual change through building three-dimensional virtual models.* Paper presented at the American Educational Research Association, Montreal, Canada.

Kim, M. C. (2006). *Scaffolding middle school students' problem-solving in Web-enhanced learning environments.* Unpublished doctoral dissertation, University of Georgia, Athens, GA.

Krajcik, J., Blumenfeld, P. C., Marx, R. W., Bass, K. M., Fredricks, J., & Soloway, E. (1998). Inquiry in project-based science classrooms: Initial attempts by middle school students. *Journal of the Learning Sciences, 7*(3-4), 313-350.

Land, S. M., & Hannafin, M. J. (2000). Student-centered learning environments. In D. H. Jonassen & S. M. Land (Eds.), *Theoretical foundations of learning environments* (pp. 1-23). Mahwah, NJ: Erlbaum.

Lave, J., & Wenger, E. (1991). *Situated learning: Legitimate peripheral participation.* Cambridge, UK: Cambridge University Press.

Linn, M. C., Clark, D., & Slotta, J. D. (2003). WISE design for knowledge integration. *Science Education, 87*(4), 517-538.

Linn, M. C., & Hsi, S. (2000). Computers, teachers and peers: Science learning partners. Mahwah, NJ: Erlbaum.

Linn, M. C., & Slotta, J. D. (2000). WISE science. *Educational Leadership, 58*(2), 29-32.

Marx, R. W., Blumenfeld, P. C., Krajcik, J. S., Fishman, B., Soloway, E., Geier, R., et al. (2004). Inquiry-based science in the middle grades: Assessment of learning in urban systemic reform. *Journal of Research in Science Teaching, 41*(10), 1063-1080.

Metcalf, S. J., Krajcik, J., & Soloway, E. (2000). Model-it: A design retrospective. In M. J. Jacobson & R. B. Kozma (Eds.), *Innovations in science and mathematics edu-*

cation: Advanced designs for technologies of learning (pp. 77-115). Mahwah, NJ: Erlbaum.

National Research Council. (1996). *National Science Education Standards: Observe, interact, change, learn.* Washington, DC: National Academy Press.

Oliver, K., & Hannafin, M. (2001). Developing and refining mental models in open-ended learning environments: A case study. *Educational Technology Research and Development, 49*(4), 5-32.

Reiser, B. J. (2004). Scaffolding complex learning: The mechanisms of structuring and problematizing student work. *Journal of the Learning Sciences, 13*(3), 273-304.

Sandoval, W. A., & Reiser, B. J. (2004). Explanation-driven inquiry: Integrating conceptual and epistemic scaffolds for scientific inquiry. *Science Education, 88*(3), 345-372.

Scardamalia, M., & Bereiter, C. (1992). Text-based and knowledge-based questioning by children. *Cognition and Instruction, 9*(3), 177-199.

Seethaler, S., & Linn, M. (2004). Genetically modified food in perspective: An inquiry-based curriculum to help middle school students make sense of tradeoffs. *International Journal of Science Education, 26*(14), 1765-1785.

Seiler, G., Tobin, K., & Sokolic, J. (2001). Design, technology, and science: Sites for learning, resistance, and social reproduction in urban schools. *Journal of Research in Science Teaching, 38*(7), 746-767.

Shiland, T. W. (2002). Reply to Pushkin. *Science Education, 86*(2), 167-170.

Shin, N., Jonassen, D. H., & McGee, S. (2003). Predictors of well-structured and ill-structured problem solving in an astronomy simulation. *Journal of Research in Science Teaching, 40*(1), 6-33.

Songer, N. B., Lee, H. S., & Kam, R. (2002). Technology-rich inquiry science in urban classrooms: What are the barriers to inquiry pedagogy? *Journal of Research in Science Teaching, 39*(2), 128-150.

Uribe, D., Klein, J. D., & Sullivan, H. (2003). The effect of computer-mediated collaborative learning on solving ill-defined problems. *Educational Technology Research and Development, 51*(1), 5-19.

Wu, H. K., Krajcik, J. S., & Soloway, E. (2001). Promoting understanding of chemical representations: Students' use of a visualization tool in the classroom. *Journal of Research in Science Teaching, 38*(7), 821-842.

PART II

DESIGN AND INSTRUCTION FOR ONLINE LEARNING COMMUNITIES

CHAPTER 5

DESIGNING EFFECTIVE ONLINE INSTRUCTION

Gary R. Morrison and Steven M. Ross

Distance education instruction presents a unique design problem when the instruction is presented in an asynchronous environment. The instruction must be well designed to account for the learner and content variables that can hinder or facilitate the development of understanding. In this chapter, we illustrate how to apply a traditional instructional design model to the design of distance instruction. Distance education courses can either start with a blank slate or can involve the repurposing of an existing course. We present two different approaches to front-end analysis to address these two starting points. Once the content is defined and analyzed, we present a series of heuristics to design appropriate instructional strategies that help the learner achieve the objectives.

INTRODUCTION

Designing instruction for distance education presents a unique environment for the instructional designer. During classroom instruction, whether K-12, higher education, or a training classroom; the teacher or instructor can make immediate adaptations to the instruction to correct misunderstandings and problems in the materials. Similarly, the instruc-

Online Learning Communities
pp. 75–85
Copyright © 2007 by Information Age Publishing
All rights of reproduction in any form reserved.

tor can read body language to identify when students are having difficulty during a lecture, and then make corrections or add additional examples to improve comprehension. In a distance education environment where the instructor and students are separated in time and place, the instructor may not receive feedback in terms of body language or real-time verbal feedback from students that allow him or her to make immediate adjustments to the instruction. While good instructional design is important in both classroom and distance delivery, the inability to obtain immediate verbal and nonverbal feedback implies a greater need for well-designed instruction.

The term distance education is interpreted in many different ways and can lead to a great deal of confusion unless it is defined by the authors (Garrison & Shale, 1987; Holmberg, 1989; Moore, 1977; Simonson, Smaldino, Albright, & Zvacek, 2000). We agree with Keegan's (1996) definition that requires the relatively permanent separation of the instructor and students in both time and location. Thus, our view of distance education is one that may involve a great deal of individualized instruction. That is, the designer works with the subject-matter expert/instructor to prepare a wide range of materials for use in a distance education course. Much of instructional load might be carried by text materials consisting of a textbook, previously published materials, or materials specifically developed for the course. Other forms of instruction might include streaming video or audio lectures. The environment described by Keegan's definition implies students have 24/7 access to the instruction, but seldom have 24/7 access to the instructor. This type of environment implies that the instructional materials should be designed and developed before the course starts, which also allows the design team to use time-on-task as an instructional adaptation for the learner (Block, 1971).

In the following pages, we will introduce two models that describe learning in a distance education environment and then we will describe how an instructional design model can be used to design distance education instruction. We will focus on how the Morrison, Ross, and Kemp (2007) model can be used to design effective instruction for distance instruction.

LEARNING IN A DISTANCE EDUCATION ENVIRONMENT

Delivery of distance instruction can be classified as either synchronous or asynchronous. For example, a two-way audio and video delivery system (compressed video) uses a synchronous delivery format while an e-learning course might exclusively use an asynchronous format. Courses can also use a combination of synchronous and asynchronous delivery. We should note that Keegan (1996) does not consider synchronous delivery

systems such as two-way audio and video as distance education, but classifies them as virtual courses. Our focus in the following discussion is on the
design of instruction for asynchronous delivery. Using this delivery mode
implies that the materials are designed prior to delivery.

This separation in time between the creation or design of materials
which Keegan (1996) labels as the instruction and the act of learning (i.e.,
delivery of the instruction) is different than the immediacy of the instruction in the classroom or synchronous delivery mode. In asynchronous
instruction, Keegan suggests that the instructional materials (e.g., the
teaching) are prepared months or maybe a year or more in advance of
their use for learning. According to Keegan, the learner must reintegrate
the acts of teaching and learning when the course is offered. For example,
a college instructor might work with a design team to develop a new introductory philosophy course. The planning and development work is all
done in the 2007-2008 academic year. The first offering of the course is in
the fall of 2008. Thus, the learner in September 2008 must read the
instructional materials developed in 2007, resulting in a separation of the
teaching and learning acts. This linkage of the instructional materials to
the learning is a critical component in the learning process. Our goal as
designers should be to keep this act of reintegration from being artificial.

One way to reintegrate the instruction and learning is with Holmberg's
(1989) guided didactic conversation. Holmberg suggests that designers
create materials that would initiate an internal conversation in the learner
to reintegrate the teaching learning act described by Keegan. We suggest
that this internal speech is similar to that proposed by Vygotsky (1962),
which the learner uses to plan and develop an understanding. Properly
designed instruction might facilitate this internal conversation if the
designer selects appropriate instructional strategies. While Holmberg
describes macro strategies like Keller's Personalized System of Instruction
(Morrison et al., 2007), we believe that micro strategies such as paraphrasing and elaboration (Ross & Morrison, in press) are more appropriate for the task.

In the following sections we will describe the front-end analysis tools
and instructional strategy design for a distance education course.
Depending on the nature of the course, the front-end analysis can be
approached with one of two methods.

FRONT-END ANALYSIS FOR A DISTANCE EDUCATION COURSE

The instructional design process begins with the identification of an
instructional problem that culminates in a listing of goals for the course
(Morrison et al., 2007). Designers can use a needs analysis and/or a goal

analysis to identify the problem and goals. This approach works well for designing a new course to address a problem. However, distance education courses sometimes involve the conversion of traditional courses to Web-based courses. If the decision has been made to convert an existing course, the use of a needs analysis and/or goal analysis might be redundant and a waste of resources if the course addresses a specific need.

Once the need for a course is identified through analysis or a need to convert a course to Web-based delivery, the designer can start the task analysis to define the content. Depending on the nature of the course, the task analysis might involve a procedural analysis, topic analysis, and/or a critical incident analysis. A procedural analysis is used to identify the sequential steps for completing a psychomotor or cognitive task. A topic analysis is used to identify the structure of information such as facts, concepts, and principles. A critical incident analysis is used to analyze interpersonal communication skills, such as conducting an interview. These three task analysis methods are used to identify the content needed to address the problem. Morrison and Anglin (2006) proposed a reverse-engineering approach when converting traditional course materials to Web-based delivery using the instructional disassembler. The process to break down or disassemble the information involved three steps. First, the existing materials are broken into the smallest units, much like a traditional task analysis. The main ideas in each sentence are identified and then reduced to key statements. The result may resemble an outline format (see Figure 5.1). Notice how the first sentence that defines points is broken down into five individual phrases or ideas. Second, content structures are identified using the expanded performance-content matrix (Morrison et al., 2007). This matrix is used to identify facts, concepts, principles, procedures, interpersonal skills, and attitudes that may be in the content. In Figure 5.1, "loan discount" is a concept. Third is the evaluation of the existing instructional design for teaching each of the identified structures. The evaluation consists of the needed content and instructional strategy. For example, the content required to teach a concept includes the concept name, definition, and best example (Tennyson & Cocchiarella, 1986). The concept of loan discount includes the name, definition, and example. After completing the disassembly of the content, the designer can determine if additional information is required and perform the needed task analysis. Similarly, the designer might determine that irrelevant information is included in the original instruction and should be deleted.

The result of this analysis step is a definition of the content needed to solve the instructional problem. Based on this analysis, the designer can specify the objectives for the course. Objectives can be written as behavioral or Mager-style objectives (see below) that are precise and identify an

Loan Discount ("raw" content): Also often called "points" or "discount points," a loan discount is a one-time charge imposed by the lender or broker to lower the rate at which the lender or broker would otherwise offer the loan to you. Each "point" is equal to one percent of the mortgage amount. For example, if a lender charges two points on a $80,000 loan this amounts to a charge of $1,600 (U.S. Department of Housing and Urban Development, 1997).

C   Loan Discount (disassembled content)

   1.   A one-time charge imposed by lender or broker
      a).   Lowers rate of the loan
   2.   Often called points or discount points
      a).   Each point is equal to 1% of the mortgage amount
   3.   Example
      a).   Lender charges two points on a $80,000 loan
         (1).   The charge is $1,600

Source: Morrison and Anglin (2006). Copyright 2006 by Information Age Publishing, Inc. Reprinted with permission.

Figure 5.1.   Disassembled content.

observable outcome (Mager, 1984). Or, the objectives can be written as a cognitive objective (Gronlund, 2004) that is best used for complex tasks that are not easily defined. With the specification of the objectives, the designer is ready to design the instructional strategies that will support the development of the knowledge and skills specified in the objectives. In the next section, we will describe a process we use in our model to design the instructional strategies.

DESIGNING INSTRUCTIONAL STRATEGIES
FOR DISTANCE EDUCATION

Keegan (1996) has suggested that we need to design instructional strategies that will help the learner reintegrate the teaching and learning process. Similarly, Holmberg (1989) suggests that designers engage learners in a guided didactic conversation as part of the instruction. The reintegration of the teaching and learning process can be achieved through strategies that actively engage learners in developing and modifying their schema that results in understanding. We are proposing that generative learning strategies (Wittrock, 1974, 1989) can engender a didactic conversation leading to the reintegration of the teaching and learning process.

Generative Strategies

Learning is an active process and involves the development of relationships between what the learner knows and new information presented in the instructional materials. A well-designed instructional strategy engages learners in a manner that motivates them to make the connections between the new information and prior knowledge. Wittrock (1974, 1989) describes this process as generative learning that promotes a deeper level of understanding and long-term retention. This active process of linking old information with new information may be the didactic conversation described by Holmberg.

There are four categories of generative strategies grouped by the function of the strategy (Jonassen, 1988). The first category, recall, is used when learning facts and lists for verbatim recall. Common strategies include rehearsal, repetition, and mnemonics (memory aids). The second category is integration strategies that are used to transform information into a more easily remembered format. Integration strategies include paraphrasing and generating examples or questions relevant to the material. Third is organizational strategies that help the learner understand how new ideas relate to existing ideas. Organizational strategies include outlining and categorizing information. An example of an organizational strategy is a table (West, Farmer, & Wolff, 1991) that the learner completes (see Table 5.1). In this example, the learner lists the types of hammers that a craftsman can use and then directs the learner to describe the intended application of the hammer. Fourth is elaboration strategies that motivate the learners to add their ideas to the new information. Elaboration strategies include generating mental images, diagrams, and sentence elaborations. The following paragraphs describe how these four groups of strategies are used to teach the different types of content.

Designing Instructional Strategies

The first step in designing an instructional strategy is to determine the type of content and level of performance specified in the objective. The expanded performance-content matrix (see Table 5.2) is used to deter-

Table 5.1.   Categorization Table

Types of Hammers	Application
Claw	
Ball Pein	
Club Hammer	
D	

Content	Performance	
	Recall	Application
Fact		
Concept		
Principle		
Procedure		
Interpersonal		
Attitude		

Source: Morrison, Ross, and Kemp (2007). Copyright 2007 by John Wiley & Sons, Inc. Reprinted with permission.

Figure 5.2.   Expanded Performance-Content Matrix

mine an appropriate instructional strategy (Morrison et al., 2007). The content specified in the objective is classified into one of the content categories. The behavior (i.e., performance) is classified as either recall or application. Recall is simply stating the content, while application can involve several activities in which the learner must apply the information such as identifying a new example of a concept or performing a procedure. Specific strategies are then selected for each cell of the matrix.

A Two-Part Instructional Strategy

We recommend designing a two-part instructional strategy. The first part is the initial presentation that provides the learner with content supporting the achievement of the objective. This presentation can take many forms including text and video demonstrations. A designer should try to identify presentations that present the learner with a concrete representation of the content. Information should be structured and presented in a way that facilitates comprehension. The second part of the presentation is a generative strategy that increases the depth of processing of the content. For example, if the objective is to learn the primary colors and their complements we might start by showing the primary colors (red, blue, and green) paired with their complements (cyan, yellow, and magenta) as our initial presentation. We could select a mnemonic ("Red Cars BY General Motors") as our generative strategy.

An appropriate strategy should be selected that facilitates recall, integration, organization, or elaboration of the instruction. Effective instructional strategies are the result of a well-designed initial presentation that presents the content in an easily understandable format and a generative strategy that motivates the learner to make connections between the new information and prior information.

Designing Instructional Strategies

The following paragraphs provide guidelines for designing strategies for each content type. A more detailed discussion of each strategy can be found in Morrison et al. (2007).

Strategies for facts. Facts are associations between two pieces of information, such as Columbus and 1492, which can only be recalled. The initial presentation for concrete facts (e.g., "Fire trucks are red") should involve a direct experience such as visit to a fire station. When designing instruction for abstract facts, the designer should try to provide a concrete representation through a picture, diagram, or animation. For example, to teach the fact that Indianapolis is the capital of Indiana, the initial presentation might be a map of Indiana with a star beside the name Indianapolis. Generative strategies for facts typically involve a rehearsal-practice strategy or mnemonics.

Strategies for concepts. Concepts are groups of similar objects like gloves, doors, racing bikes, and mammals. The initial presentation for a concept should include the label or name of the concept, the definition, and the one best example (Tennyson & Cocchiarella, 1986). If the performance level is application, then designers can select to use an integration, organization, or elaboration strategy. The traditional approach to concept learning is the use of an integration strategy requiring the learner to identify new examples and nonexamples.

Strategies for principles. Principles are stated relationships between concepts such as "Price increases when supply is less than demand." Initial presentations for principles follow one of two approaches (Markle, 1969). The first is rule-eg, where the principle is stated and then examples of the principle are given. For example, the text could state the rule showing the relationship between price and supply and then show a graph of the price of oil, oil production, and demand. The second is eg-rule where examples of the principle are presented to the learner and the learner derives the principle. Using an eg-rule approach, the instruction might first show several graphs of the price of consumer products such as oil and sugar and prompt the learner to state the relationship between price and supply based on the data in the graphs. An integrative generative strategy would ask the learner to paraphrase the rule, and an elaborative strategy would present the learner with a situation and ask for a prediction (i.e., application of the principle) of the results.

Strategies for procedures.   Procedures include both psychomotor tasks such as replacing a transmission, and cognitive tasks such as calculating the square footage of a home. The initial presentation for a procedure requires modeling the procedure. For psychomotor tasks, the modeling may require action using streaming video, or narrative with pictures may be adequate for less complex skills. The model for a cognitive task is a worked example (Sweller & Cooper, 1985). Worked examples are commonly found in math books and present the solution in a series of steps. The generative strategy for procedures involves two steps. The first is to have the learner paraphrase the procedure or elaborate on the specifics of each step. The second step is practicing the procedure through applications.

Strategies for interpersonal skills.   Interpersonal skills involve communication between two or more individuals. Examples of instruction for interpersonal skills include training individuals to answer a telephone, conduct a job interview, and deliver a traffic report on the radio. The instructional strategy of interpersonal skills is based on Bandura's (1977) social learning theory. First, the interaction is modeled for the learner through a videotape, role play, or case narrative. Second, the learner is prompted to develop a verbal model of the key steps and an imaginal model that includes an image of the interaction. Third, the learner is encouraged to mentally rehearse the interaction (covert practice). Fourth, the learner engages in overt practice such as a role play.

Strategies for attitudes.   Attitudes consist of a belief and an associated behavior, with the instructional strategy focusing on changing the associated behavior. The strategy is based on Bandura's social learning theory. The proper behavior is modeled, the learner develops a verbal and imaginal model, mentally rehearses the behavior, and finally engages in overt practice of the behavior.

SUMMARY

Asynchronous instruction presents a challenge to the designer to create effective instructional materials that a learner can use in relative isolation from an instructor or other learners. Using Keegan's suggestion that the learner must reintegrate the teaching and learning acts and Holmberg's suggestion of creating a guided didactic conversation, we have proposed the strategies recommended in the Morrison, Ross, and Kemp instructional design model for use in designing effective distance instruction. The instructional design model's approach to task analysis may need to be modified when converting a traditional course or materials for Web-based delivery. Morrison and Anglin's instructional disassembler provides an appropriate tool for reverse-engineering the content so the design can be evaluated and appropriate changes can then be made for a Web-based environment.

REFERENCES

Bandura, A. (1977). *Social learning theory.* Englewood Cliffs, NJ: Prentice-Hall.

Block, J. (1971). *Mastery learning: Theory and practice.* New York: Holt, Rinehart, & Winston.

Garrison, D. R., & Shale, D. G. (1987). Mapping the boundaries of distance education: Problems in defining the field. *American Journal of Distance Education, 1*(1), 4-13.

Gronlund, N. E. (2004). *Writing instructional objectives for teaching and assessment* (7th ed.). New York: Prentice Hall.

Holmberg, B. (1989). *Theory and practice of distance education.* New York: Routledge.

Jonassen, D. H. (1988). Integrating learning strategies into courseware to facilitate deeper process. In D. H. Jonassen (Ed.), *Instructional designs for microcomputer courseware* (pp. 151-181). Hillsdale, NJ: Erlbaum.

Keegan, D. (1996). *Foundations of distance education* (3rd ed.). London: Routledge.

Mager, R. F. (1984). *Preparing instructional objectives.* Belmont, CA: Pitman.

Markle, S. (1969). Good frames and bad: A grammar of frame writing. New York: Wiley.

Moore, M. (1977). *On a theory of independent study.* Hagen, Germany: Fernuniverisitat (ZIFF).

Morrison, G. R., & Anglin, G. J. (2006). An instructional design approach for effective shovelware: Modifying materials for distance education. *Quarterly Review of Distance Education, 7*(1), 63-74.

Morrison, G. R., Ross, S. M., & Kemp, J. E. (2007). *Designing effective instruction* (5th ed.). Hoboken, NJ: Wiley.

Ross, S. M., & Morrison, G. R. (in press). Research on instructional strategies in educational technology. In J. M. Spector, M. D. Merrill, J. J. G. v. Merriënboer, & M. P. Driscoll (Eds.), *Handbook of research on educational communications and technology* (3rd ed.). Mahwah, NJ: Erlbaum.

Simonson, M., Smaldino, S., Albright, M., & Zvacek, S. (2000). *Teaching and learning at a distance: Foundations of distance education.* Columbus, OH: Merrill.

Sweller, J., & Cooper, G. (1985). The use of worked examples as a substitute for problem solving in algebra. *Cognition and Instruction, 2*, 59-89.

Tennyson, R. D., & Cocchiarella, M. J. (1986). An empirically based instructional design theory for teaching concepts. *Review of Educational Research, 56*(1), 40-71.

U. S. Department of Housing and Urban Development. (1997). *Buying your home: Settlement costs and helpful information.* Retrieved October 24, 2001, from http://www.pueblo.gsa.gov/cic_text/housing/settlement/sfhrestc.html

Vygotsky, L. S. (1962). *Thought and language.* Cambridge, MA: The M.I.T. Press.

West, C. K., Farmer, J. A., & Wolff, P. M. (1991). *Instructional design: Implications from cognitive science.* Englewood Cliffs, NJ: Prentice Hall.

Wittrock, M. C. (1974). Learning as a generative process. *Educational Psychologist, 19*(2), 87-95.

Wittrock, M. C. (1989). Generative processes of comprehension. *Educational Psychologist, 24*, 345–376.

CHAPTER 6

THE USE OF DISCUSSION FORUMS IN LEARNING COMMUNITIES

Stephen Corich, Kinshuk, and L. M. Jeffrey

It is argued that distance learners face more obstacles to learning than their traditional classroom-based counterparts. Technology has the potential to address some of the obstacles that distance learners face, but only if the technology is utilized to its full potential. This chapter examines the use of discussion forums in social constructivist learning communities. It introduces two tools that have been designed to provide added functionality to the traditional discussion forum and explores how such tools can provide features that can assist with knowledge construction and collaboration in a virtual classroom.

INTRODUCTION

The expansion of distance education is transforming the higher education environment (Kriger, 2001). The number of tertiary institutes offering blended and fully online coursework is expanding rapidly and the number of Internet-based distance education courses is steadily increasing. Asynchronous tools, such as discussion forums, are being used to rep-

Online Learning Communities
pp. 87–108
Copyright © 2007 by Information Age Publishing
All rights of reproduction in any form reserved.

licate features available in traditional face-to-face education. When used to encourage knowledge building and social reinforcement, asynchronous communication tools provide opportunities for learning communities that are not available within the confines of the traditional classroom (Moller, 1998).

Asynchronous discussion forums are recognized as having the potential to support a learning environment in which learners actively interact and construct knowledge by sharing experiences and information (Jonassen, 1994). Educational researchers have reported positive outcomes using threaded discussions that encourage students to accept responsibility for building knowledge by reflecting on course materials and discussing content with fellow participants (Lamy & Goodfellow, 1999).

Learners who elect to study using distance education do so for convenience. Work commitments, location, health and personal circumstances are likely to persuade an individual to study online. Unlike campus-based students who regularly have opportunities to share problems and concerns with fellow students and faculty, the distance learner has to rely on asynchronous communication tools such as e-mail and discussion forums to interact with other course participants and faculty. To improve the communication process for students and staff in the distance learning environment, the Advanced Learning Technologies Research Centre (ALTRC) at Massey University in Palmerston North, New Zealand has undertaken a number of developments, several of which are aimed at enhancing the functionality of discussion forums.

This chapter describes two of the ALTRC projects. The aim of the first project was to design and build a tool that automatically evaluates the quality of student contribution to a discussion forum, providing feedback which could help improve the quality of contributions. The second project adds to the functionality of a discussion forum by providing a student-centered community of learning in which students can share and exchange study- and subject-related problems/solutions, join study groups, and receive expert advice.

BACKGROUND

Communities are said to share common goals, needs, and problems and can promote solutions by sharing collective knowledge (Rovai, 2002). Online communities are described by Rheingold (1994, p.57) as, "cultural aggregations that emerge when enough people bump into each other often enough in cyberspace." According to Whittaker, Isaacs and O'Day (1996), online communities have a number of core attributes:

- Shared goals, interests, needs or activities;
- Repeated, active participation, with intense interactions and strong emotional ties between participants;
- Access to shared resources with policies to determine access;
- Reciprocity of information, support and services between members; and,
- Shared context (social conventions, language, protocols).

Palloff and Pratt (1999) describe learning communities as places where people with mutual interests join together to examine a particular theme and learn by exchanging existing knowledge. Online learning communities exist where people sharing common goals, with appropriate access, can pose questions and respond with answers and suggested resources. Within an online learning community, knowledge and meaning are actively constructed, and the members of the community enhance the acquisition of knowledge and understanding, thereby satisfying learning needs (Rigou, 2004). Members of a learning community may be students, lecturers, tutors, researchers, practitioners, and domain experts.

Discussion forums are increasingly seen as one of the most powerful tools for creating online learning communities (Sergiovanni, 1999; Swan & Shea, 2005). Used appropriately, discussion forums can enable rapid dissemination of information and can encourage feedback and the refinement of ideas among participants (Hiltz & Turoff, 1978/1993). Discussion forums are being increasingly used to promote collaboration among a diverse variety of people from a wide range of settings and locations (Mayadas, 2001).

The pedagogy supporting the use of asynchronous communication tools within learning communities has its roots in constructivism and social constructivism (Knowles, Holton, & Swanson, 1998; Palloff & Pratt, 1999; Squire & Johnson, 2000). In a constructivist learning environment, control shifts from the instructor to the learner. One of the main principles of constructivism involves using open-ended questions that replicate realistic problem situations, enabling learners to develop skills in complex and unstructured problem-solving situations. Constructivism involves learning in a social context using group activities, collaboration, and teamwork. Participants in a constructivist setting have shared goals that are negotiated between instructors and learners and themselves and learners; in this situation, the instructor has the role of facilitator or coach.

Social constructivists suggest that the optimal learning environment is one in which there is a dynamic interaction between instructors and learners, and tasks provide an opportunity for learners to create their own understanding by communicating with others. McMahon (1997) claims that social constructivism emphasizes the importance of culture and context in understanding what is happening in society and constructing knowledge based on this understanding. Participants in a social constructivist environment collaborate by sharing experiences and information in a way that promotes critical thinking and knowledge construction.

COMMUNITY OF ENQUIRY

One of the most widely accepted models, which was specifically designed to guide the use of computer conferencing to support critical thinking in higher education, is the Garrison, Anderson, and Archer (2000) community of inquiry model. The model (see Figure 6.1) attempts to identify the elements that are crucial for a successful higher educational experience. In the model, the learning community undertakes deep and meaningful learning, the central goal of higher education, in a community of inquiry comprising of instructors and learners as the key participants in the educational process. The model assumes that, in this community, learning occurs through the interaction of three core components: cognitive presence, teaching presence, and social presence (Rourke, Anderson, Garrison, & Archer, 2001).

Cognitive presence is defined by Garrison et al. (2000) as "the extent to which participants of any particular configuration of a community of enquiry are able to construct meaning through sustained communication." Teaching presence includes facilitating the construction of learning, providing guidance relating to subject materials. Social presence is defined as the "ability of participants in a community of inquiry to project themselves socially and emotionally, as real people (i.e., their full personality), through the medium of communication being used" (Garrison et al. 2000).

The first of the two ALTRC projects described in this chapter relates primarily to the cognitive presence component of the community of enquiry model, while the second project has elements that relate to all three of the model's core components.

DISCUSSION FORUM CONTENT ANALYSIS

When investigating the use of asynchronous discussion forums, researchers have attempted to identify evidence of critical thinking, which, as Bloom, Englehart, Furst, Hill, and Krathwohi (1956) suggest, should be a prime objective of any form of education, including distance education.

In a discussion forum, critical thinking is evident when participants construct meaning while communicating with fellow participants. A number of models, most of them based loosely on Bloom's taxonomy, have attempted to measure the extent to which knowledge is constructed through the collaborative discourse among discussion forum participants. Bloom's taxonomy identifies six objectives: knowledge, comprehension, application, analysis, synthesis, and evaluation. A model using Bloom's taxonomy would classify each discussion message into one of the six objectives, and the distribution on all objectives would provide an indication of a learner's ability to formulate value judgments about theories and methods. The most commonly cited researchers involved in identifying evidence of critical thinking within discussion forums include Henri (1991), Gunawardena, Lowe, and Anderson (1997), Newman, Webb, and Cochrane (1995), Garrison, Anderson, and Archer (2000, 2001) and Hara, Bonk, & Angeli (2000).

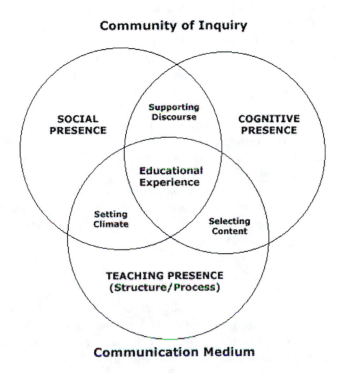

Source: Garrison, Anderson, and Archer (2000).

Figure 6.1.   Community of inquiry model.

The models used to measure critical thinking rely heavily on the use of quantitative content analysis (QCA) which is described as "a research technique for the objective, systematic, quantitative description of the manifest content of communication" (Berelson, 1952, p. 519). A researcher utilizing QCA breaks a discussion forum transcript into units, assigning the units to a number of recognizable categories and counting the number of units in each category. Researchers suggest that QCA is "difficult, frustrating, and time-consuming" (Rourke et al., 2001, p. 12), and agreement between coders coding the same transcripts varies considerably.

Two of the most popular content analysis approaches are those designed by Henri (1991) and modified by Hara et al. (2000), and one designed by Garrison et al. (2000). Several researchers have either duplicated or incorporated these models into their research. Corich, Kinshuk, and Hunt (2004) describe the application of these two methodologies to a first year undergraduate degree course.

QCA involves evaluating the transcripts of a discussion forum, which can usually be exported to a text file. McKlin, Harmon, Evans, and Jones (2002) suggests that even though transcripts can be converted to a machine-readable format, there is little evidence of using computers to assist with the task of text analysis using discussion forum transcripts. While there are a number of general software-based text analysis tools that could be used to assist with the task of identifying evidence of critical thinking, there is little evidence to suggest that that they have been utilized for that purpose. The software tools which include Wordnet, WordStat, NUD*IST/NVivo, HyperQual and General Inquirer are predominantly text processing systems that identify occurrences of strings within the text-based transcripts. The more powerful tools enable text to be classified into predetermined categories, producing results that can be transferred to statistical analysis packages for detailed analysis. The majority of these tools are generic and require users to create dictionaries that contain expressions associated with the each of the defined categories of adopted QCA model.

A review of extant literature would suggest that while there are numerous examples of researchers manually coding transcripts to identify evidence of critical thinking, there are few examples of using a computer to automate the analysis process. McKlin et al. (2002) and Chen and Wu (2004) provide two examples of automated systems that have been used to analyse the output from a discussion forum. McKlin et al. (2002) described using an automated tool that used neural network software to categorize messages from a discussion forum transcript. Chen and Wu (2004) used keyword contribution mining to measure the quality of a student's work.

McKlin et al. (2002) suggest that their automated tool could be used to gauge, guide, direct and manipulate the learning environment. Their analysis was based on the Garrison et al. (2000, 2001) community of enquiry model. The study reported high coefficient of reliability figures when compared to human coders, suggesting that the tool had the potential to code forum transcripts to identify cognitive presence. Despite efforts to contact the research team and a review of current literature, no evidence could be found of further work relating to the tool.

Chen and Wu (2004) describe how computers have been used to automatically grade assessments and how correlations of between 0.4 and 0.9 have been achieved when comparing human-assigned and computer-generated grades. They point out that the automated grading systems have been used to successfully grade the quality of single assessment items, and they suggest that such systems could be redesigned to cater for ongoing assessment items such as discussion forums. Chen and Wu (2004) describe a model that uses three measures: keyword contribution, message length, and message count, to produce a final score called a performance indicator. The results of the system were encouraging; however, they did point out that they did not expect the computer to entirely replace human instructors in evaluating student class performance.

AUTOMATIC CONTENT ANALYSIS TOOL (ACAT)

Encouraged by the findings of previous researchers using automated tools to grade assignments, and the reported successes of McKlin et al. (2002) and Chen and Wu (2004), a decision was made to develop a tool that could be used to automate the manual process of QCA coding. The initial system design described by Corich et al. (2004) included a transcript-importing module, a coding module, and an analysis module. The plan was to build a dictionary based on one of the commonly used QCA models and use it to categorise the postings from an undergraduate class discussion forum and then compare the results to those obtained by human coders using the same model. The results were encouraging, showing correlation levels between 70 and 80%. The tool was aimed at providing information to the teachers that would enable them to give advice to students on how they could improve the level of their discussion forum contribution.

Following on from the successes of the initial system, the scope was expanded to provide a number of additional features that should enhance the potential of the tool. The revised tool is a Web-based automated content analysis tool, referred to as ACAT. The ACAT system has six main components and it is designed to automate the process of transcript anal-

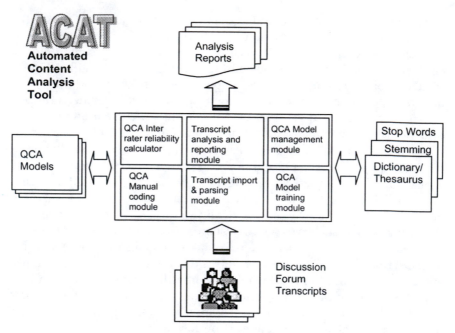

Figure 6.2. The concept model for the ACAT system.

ysis, providing information to students and teachers as they participate in discussion forum activities associated with an online learning community.

Figure 6.2 shows the concept model of the ACAT system. Users of the system can import transcripts, manually code transcripts, store the manually coded results, automatically code the transcripts, and then compare automatically the results of the manually coded transcripts with automatically coded transcripts.

The transcript import and parsing module allows any transcript saved as a standard text file to be imported into the system. The system breaks the transcript into individual units that are stored in a table ready for either automatic analysis or manual classification. While researchers have debated what should be used as a unit for classification, Campos (2004) suggests using the sentence as the human cognitive unit of analysis. The research conducted by Campos demonstrated that using the sentence as the basic unit for classification could produce encouraging results when manually coding transcripts. Following the promising results of the Campos study, the ACAT system was designed to use sentences as the basic coding unit. The ACAT system parses the imported text, breaking the transcript into sentences that are stored in a table.

Early versions of the ACAT system stored sentences taken directly from transcripts. In an attempt to improve the functionality of the system, algorithms were added to the transcript import and parsing module that enable the removal of stopwords and the reclassification of words into their word stems. Stopword removal involves the removal of frequently occurring words that do not carry meaning, which Ginsparg, Houle, Joachims and Sul (2004) suggest adds to the effectiveness and reliability of text analysis systems. Wordstemming is a process whereby suffixes are removed from words to get the common origins of words. Hull and Grefenstette (1996) suggest that wordstemming helps overcome some of the issues associated with incorrect spelling and it is also said to help when comparing texts to identify words with common meaning and form as being identical. Additional tables were added to the system so that the raw text, the stopword modified text, and the stemmed text versions of sentences could be saved for comparative analysis when automatically coding the system.

The QCA model management module enables users of the system to add a recognized QCA model to the system. It allows users to name the model and establish the number of categories that the model requires for analysis. Once the model has been created, the user can train the system using the QCA model training module.

The QCA training module allows users to create dictionaries for each of the QCA models that have been created using the model management module. The user enters an expression into the system and then places the expression in one of the categories associated with the QCA model being used. The same module also allows users to take a transcript that has been manually coded and add its units into the appropriate categories of a model dictionary.

The QCA manual coding module presents users of the system with the sentences that have been parsed by the import and parsing module and allows them to be categorized against the appropriate category of the chosen QCA model. The results are stored in a table so that they can be compared to automatically coded results to calculate the coefficient of coding reliability by the QCA interrater reliability calculator module.

The interrater reliability calculator automatically calculates the coefficient of reliability between two record sets. Normally the module would be used to compare a manually coded record set against an automatically coded record set. The module can be used, however, to compare two manually coded records sets if required. The coefficient of reliability represents a percentage agreement calculation which reflects the number of agreements between two systems as a proportion of the number of units represented. Two coefficients are in common use for QCA: Hosti's coefficient of reliability (Hosti, 1996) and Cohen's kappa statistsic (Rourke et al.

2001). There is some debate among researchers as to what constitutes an acceptable level of agreement. Riffe, Lacey, and Fico (1998) suggest that anything lower than 80% is unacceptable, while Garrison et al. (2000) report levels as low as 35%. The current version of the ACAT system calculates the coefficient of reliability using Hosti's coefficient.

The transcript analysis and reporting module is the heart of the ACAT system. This module produces reports for manually coded transcripts, listing for each category the number of units belonging to each category. The module also performs the automated analysis of the transcript units against a chosen model, producing a report similar to the manually coded report.

Chen and Wu (2004) report that while the idea of using computer software to grade student work has been around since the 1960s, there is little evidence of software being used to grade student work that accumulates over time. In recent times, models have been developed that grade varieties of student work, including computer programs (Jones, 2001), prose (Page, 1994) and essays (Foltz, Laham, & Landauer, 1999; Larkey, 1998). Rudner and Liang (2002) reported that there is promising literature in the information science field regarding the use of Bayes' Theorem as the underlying model behind text classification. Bayesian networks have become widely accepted and are being used in essay grading systems, help desk applications, medical diagnosis, data mining, intelligent learning systems, and risk assessment tools (Rudner & Liang, 2002). Bayesian Networks use probability theory to assign items to various categories. McCallum and Nigam (1998) provide an excellent overview of the use of Bayesian Networks. The apparent success of using Bayesian networks to classify text suggests that a similar process could be applied to classify transcripts. The analysis technique adopted within the ACAT development is based on a Bayesian-based essay scoring system described by Rudner and Liang (2002), who used a four-point scale to categorize the features of essays.

USING THE ACAT SYSTEM

The system has been trialed using the transcripts generated from an undergraduate first year data communications course that was offered in a blended delivery mode and which included an assessment that required students to participate in a discussion forum. The course consisted of 15 students; 3 females and 12 males, aged between 18 and 38 years and of varying academic abilities. Students were informed of the topic for discussion early in the course and instructions were given to students explaining what was expected from them. The instructions were given as guidance and to encourage higher-level critical thinking. All postings were monitored by an instructor who provided encouragement, feedback, and clarification when required. The discussion forum was made available to students for a 3-week period and, as a condition of the assessment, students were encouraged to post at least two times a week.

During the three weeks that the forum was available, a total of 104 posts were made, 30 of which were made by the instructor. Once the instructor postings were removed, the remaining 74 posts generated 484 sentences for coding. The 484 sentences were coded by two researchers using two coding schemes developed and tested by Garrison et al. (2001) and Hara et al. (2000). The results for the manual coding exercise were reported by Corich et al. (2004). When the results of the transcript analysis for the two researchers were evaluated to establish the level of agreement that existed, the Holsti coefficient of agreement was 87% for the Garrison et al. (2001) model and 81% using the Hara et al. (2000) model.

The QCA model with the higher coefficient of agreement was used for the ACAT system trial. The four category model developed by Garrison et al. (2001) was created using the ACAT model management tool. A dictionary based on experiences of the two researchers who undertook the manual coding exercise combined with the triggers identified within the Garrison et al. model was created using the ACAT model training module. The forum transcript was imported and parsed using the ACAT transcript import and parsing module and the results of the manual coding exercise were entered into the system using the manual coding module. The transcript analysis and reporting model was then used to analyse the individual coding units and reports for the manual coding and automatic coding processes were produced. A summary of resulting reports are shown in Table 6.1.

The manual coding exercise resulted in 20 sentences being uncategorized, while the automated process categorized all sentences. The automated system categorized sentences on the basis of highest probability of fit to a specific category, allocating sentences to categories only when the resulting probability was higher than the probability of a random occurrence in an individual category. When the system identified a sentence as having the same probability for more than one category, it automatically placed the sentence in the category that appears first in the model.

The number of sentences and the percentages were similar across all categories for the manual coding, the automatic coding of raw text, and the automatic coding of text with stopwords removed and stemmed text. The coefficient of reliability between the manual coding and the automatic coding of raw text was 0.64. The removal of stopwords slightly increased the reliability to 0.65 and the use of stemmed text increased the reliability to 0.71. While the results are not as high as those reported

**Table 6.1.   Number of Sentences in
Each of Garrison et al. (2001) Categories**

Category	Manual Coding	Automatic Coding (Raw Text)	Automatic Coding (Stopwords Removed)	Automatic Coding (Stemmed Text)
1. Triggering	73 (15%)	78 (16.1%)	80 (16.5%)	75 (15.5%)
2. Exploration	124 (25.6%)	128 (26.5%)	129 (26.7%)	119 (24.6%)
3. Integration	209 (43.2%)	218 (45%)	217 (44.8%)	225 (46.5%)
4. Solution	58 (12%)	60 (12.4%)	58 (12%)	65 (13.4%)
Not categorized	20 (4.1%)	0	0	0
Total number of units	484 (100%)	484 (100%)	484 (100%)	484 (100%)
Hosti coefficient of reliability		0.64	0.65	0.71

between manual coders (Garrison et al., 2001), they are similar to those of McKlin et al. (2002).

THE FUTURE OF THE ACAT SYSTEM

Rourke et al. (2001) suggest that the application of the QCA process to identify evidence of critical thinking within a discussion forum transcript is inherently subjective, inductive, and prone to errors. Fahy (2002) adds that coding is a difficult and time-consuming exercise. To help overcome the issue of coder subjectivity, multiple coders are used and results compared to ensure that agreement is reached for coding decisions. Automated systems, if they can be proven to be reliable, have the potential to eliminate the subjectivity issue and thus reduce the time and effort required for identifying the levels of cognitive activity.

The ACAT system described in this chapter is a work in progress. The system has only been used to code transcripts using the Garrison et al. (2001) model for small transcript samples. Provided time was invested in building dictionaries for alternate models, the system could be used to test any recognized cognitive QCA model. With multiple dictionaries, the system would be capable of automatically comparing the results of using different models.

The current ACAT system requires a text version of a discussion forum transcript to be imported before the analysis process can be conducted. The system does not recognize contributions from individuals, producing a single report for all the participants. The system could be modified to identify and report on individual participation so that it could provide feedback to individual participants. The system also could be redesigned so that it could be used as a plug-in to an existing learning management system, providing information to discussion forum participants as and when required. Such a system could aid students attempting to improve their level of participation.

The existing ACAT system performs its analysis using a Bayesian network probability theory. The system could be extended to include a number of different algorithms, such as Nearest Neighbor, Centroid-Based Document Classifier, Latent Semantic Indexing, Log-Entropy weighting, or Term Frequency & Inverse Document Frequency. If the system then allowed individual algorithms to be selected, from the effectiveness of each technique could be compared.

STUDENT CENTERED COMMUNITY OF LEARNING

The community of enquiry model (Garrison et al., 2000) identified social presence as one of the core components in an online learning community. Social presence is said to support cognitive objectives by sustaining and instigating activities that are engaging and rewarding. Such activities lead to increases in academic, social and institutional integration, resulting in an environment in which participants are more likely to see a course through to completion.

Angeli, Bonk, and Hara (1998) suggest that computer mediated communication (CMC) tools such as discussion forums have the ability to support highly affective interpersonal interactions. When analyzing the interactions of a course conducted entirely through CMC, they found that 27% of total message content was social in nature, leading to the development of community. Brookfield (1986), Slavin (1983), and Whitsed (2004) provide support for the concept that interaction among students is a key variable in learning communities.

Guanawardena et al. (1997), in discussing the process of knowledge construction within a group, suggests that a group goes through a five stage process of development. The five phases that are required for knowledge generation and understanding in groups are:

- sharing/comparing of information;
- the discovery and exploration of dissonance or inconsistency among ideas, concepts or statements;
- negotiation of meaning/coconstruction of knowledge;
- testing and modification of proposed synthesis or coconstruction; and
- agreement statement(s)/applications of newly constructed meaning.

For CMC to be used effectively in a learning community, it should provide support that enables the group to move through these five phases. With this concept in mind, the second of the two ALTRC projects was developed. The project known as eQuake (electronic QUestion and Answer Knowledge Environment) was funded by the Tertiary Education Commission under an e-Learning Collaborative Development Fund that was funded by the New Zealand Government to encourage initiatives within the e-learning community.

EQUAKE (ELECTRONIC QUESTION AND ANSWER KNOWLEDGE ENVIRONMENT)

The eQuake system is aimed at enhancing current Web-based discussion forums. The main goal of the system is to allow users to find and share information within a learning community. This is achieved by: identifying questions that have been previously answered; providing a mechanism to unite several educational institutes, creating the potential for a larger knowledge pool; automatically notifying teachers/moderators when there are several similar unanswered in the system questions in the system, so that an FAQ entry can then be created; and notifying participants that an answer to has been posted to a question in which they have expressed interest.

The system was developed as a collaborative exercise between Massey University, Auckland University of Technology, and the Eastern Institute of Technology. The eQuake system was developed with the aim of fostering cooperation between tertiary education institutions within New Zealand.

The eQuake system is a Web-based system incorporating intelligent software agents that allow students from New Zealand tertiary institutions to engage in a student-centred community of learning to share and exchange study- and subject-related problems/solutions, join study groups, and receive expert advice. The intelligent software agents built into the system have been designed to monitor student interaction and create profiles of students based on their interaction with other students. The system tags significant or repeated issues as well as queries from those students who rarely participate. It allows teachers to formulate responses in the form of frequently asked questions (FAQs) or respond individually to certain students. Once an FAQ item is added, intelligent software agents, based on students' profiles, identify those students who may benefit from that FAQ and advises those students accordingly. The next time that a student raises that particular issue, the intelligent software agents intercept the query and redirect the student to the FAQ. Students can then decide whether their query has been answered or if it should go to other students for further responses. A feedback loop, maintained by the intelligent software agents, enables revision of FAQs as and when required. Based on student profiles, the system is able to propose study groups among compatible students by taking into consideration the knowledge levels and learning styles of participants. The overview of the Agent-based Intelligent Help System is shown in Figure 6.3.

The eQuake system consists of several components/agents that work together to provide system functionality. Figure 6.4 shows how the various components/agents interact. The Query Display Component allows students to view, search, and retrieve queries available from the Query Store. The query display component was designed to interface directly into an existing learning management system (LMS). The current version of eQuake integrates directly into Moodle and Blackboard.

The Student Proxy Agent provides a two-directional interface to the students, allowing them to post queries, comments, or solutions, and rate the responses of other students to their queries. This agent also forwards

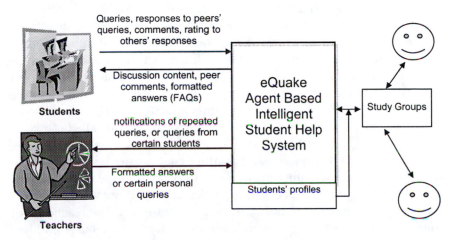

Figure 6.3.   Overview of the eQuake system.

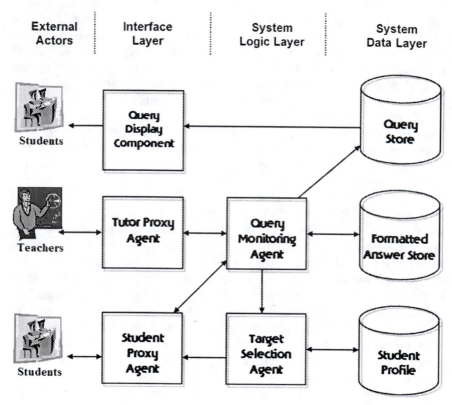

Figure 6.4.   Agents and components of the eQuake system.

to the teacher the formatted answer of a particular topic/query to designated students. It also identifies those students who either rarely participate or exhibit a lack of understanding of the already existing solutions.

The Query Monitoring Agent uses a filtering mechanism to monitor every query posted by a student. The Query Monitoring Agent also detects how many queries pertaining to a particular question/topic have been posted. If it identifies any frequently repeated queries on the same question/topic, then it flags the query and sends it with all the related postings to the teacher through the Tutor Proxy Agent. The system can be configured so that the queries and postings could either be sent to all the teachers (from participating institutions) who are involved with that subject area, or only to the teacher (of a particular institution) whose students had asked the majority of the questions on that topic. The teachers can then investigate, rearrange, rectify, and/or expound on the query and format the query and the answer to a generalized format.

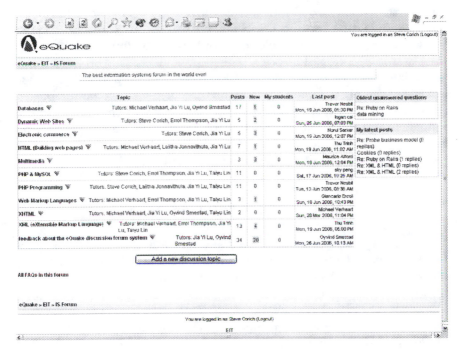

Figure 6.5.   The eQuake system.

The formatted answer (FAQ) is sent back to the Tutor Proxy Agent and further onto the Query Monitoring Agent. Here the original flag is removed and the answer is saved into the long-term Formatted Answer Store. During this process, the Query Monitoring Agent notifies the Target Selection Agent of the incoming formatted answer. The Target Selection Agent then looks up the participants who posted queries related to the issue and those who may benefit from the formatted answer and forwards the formatted answer to them. The opening screen of the eQuake system is shown in Figure 6.5.

The eQuake system is currently being tested by students from each of the three institutes involved in the project. Initial response to the system is very positive, with students and faculty expressing support for the concept. When testing has been completed, participants will be evaluated using a technology assessment methodology. The results of the evaluation will be reported to the project sponsors and will be discussed in academic publications in the future.

The initial evaluation of the eQuake system has identified a number of tangible benefits that are not always evident in traditional discussion forum systems. The benefits include: students have been able to help each other by suggesting posing questions and suggesting answers to questions; the system has been able to identify when a similar question has been posted and suggest answers, reducing the time taken for students to access information; accumulation of FAQs has created a knowledge base available to future students and faculty; the push technologies employed automatically inform students when a question has been addressed; the system automatically informs teachers when students do not participate; and the group work feature automatically identifies students who have similar interests and abilities, inviting them to join a group.

FUTURE OF THE EQUAKE SYSTEM

The initial eQuake system was hosted at a central location and collaboration between students at different institutes did not really occur. Distributing the system and encouraging students from a number of different institutes to participate in a shared environment will expand the learning community, giving participants a richer, wider perspective. The system also could be expanded to include secondary school participation; this would allow senior high school students to interact with junior tertiary students, giving the school students a glimpse of the tertiary environment, potentially helping to smooth the transition to higher-level study.

Enhancements planned for future versions of the system include providing the ability to add multimedia annotations, creating opportunities to enrich the question and answer processing. This should assist students with more visual learning styles, offering the opportunity for a more interactive experience.

The current eQuake system relies on students having access to e-mail and the eQuake discussion forum using personal computers or laptop devices. Since the ALTRC is involved in a number of projects involving the use of mobile devices, the eQuake system could be enhanced to provide access using mobile devices such a personal digital assistants and mobile telephones.

The eQuake system has been trialed in an information systems educational environment. The system has the potential to enhance any learning domain or commercial environment and should be tested on a wider community.

The eQuake query monitoring agent is one of the key components of the system. The current system conducts searches in the system knowledge base to find answers to student questions; perhaps this could be extended to include online knowledge bases like Wikipedia. Such an enhancement could produce a wider variety of answers, further reducing the need for teacher intervention.

CONCLUSION

This chapter has presented two different systems that have the potential to add to the functionality of existing discussion forums. Both systems are aimed at enhancing the experience of students and teachers as they participate in the learning community. Any system that enriches the online learning experience of students and provides tools that can assist in the knowledge building process is likely to improve student retention and satisfaction.

Tools such as ACAT and eQuake have been designed to assist with the constructivist approach to learning. When designing such tools, designers need to be mindful of the need to ensure that the tools are easy navigate and use, and that using them does not cause students to become frustrated or discouraged. Storey, Phillips, Maczewski, and Wang (2002) found that tools that were difficult to use can have a negative effect on learning, thus reducing the likelihood that a student will actively participate. Jonassen (1994) indicates that constructivist tools designed to enhance the learning community should support knowledge construction, collaboration between participants, and have a meaningful context. Lee (2006) suggests that the design process should be extended to ensure that the learning environment is also situated, social, and student-centered.

Distance learning can be a lonely and frustrating experience; students often feel they have nowhere to turn for advice and support. The retention rates in distance education courses are often lower than their equivalent face-to-face counterparts and students struggle to maintain enthusiasm for learning. Tools that improve the learning communities of distance learners and which encourage collaboration, knowledge construction, and sense of community, if well designed and thoroughly tested, can only improve the chances of success for the ever-increasing number of online students.

REFERENCES

Angeli. C., Bonk, C. J., & Hara, N. (2000). Content analysis of online discussion in an applied educational psychology. *Instructional Science, 28*(2), 115-152. CRLT (Center for Research on Learning and Technology) Technical Report

No. 2-98. Retrieved September 17, 2006, from http://crlt.indiana.edu/publications/journals/techreport.pdf

Berelson, B. (1952). *Content analysis in communication research*. Glencoe, IL: Free Press.

Bloom, B. S., Englehart, M. D., Furst, E. J., Hill, W. H., & Krathwohl, D. R. (1956). *Taxonomy of educational objectives: The classification of educational goals. Handbook 1: Cognitive domain*. New York: David McKay.

Brookfield, S. D. (1986). *Understanding and facilitating adult learning*. San Francisco: Jossey-Bass.

Campos, M. (2004, April). A constructivist method for the analysis of networked cognitive communication and the assessment of collaborative learning and knowledge building. *Journal of American Learning Networks, 8*(2), 1-29.

Chen, X., & Wu, F. (2004). Automated evaluation of students' performance by analyzing online messages. *Proceedings of IRMA*, New Orleans, LA.

Corich, S. P., Kinshuk, & Hunt, L. M., (2004). Assessing discussion forum participation: In search of quality. *International Journal of Instructional Technology and Distance Learning, 1*(12), 1-12.

Fahy, P. (2002). Use of linguistic qualifiers and intensifiers in a computer conference. *American Journal of Distance Education, 16*(1).

Foltz, P. W., Laham, D., & Landauer, T. K. (1999). The intelligent essay assessor: Applications to educational technology. *Interactive Multimedia Electronic Journal of Computer-Enhanced Learning, 1*(2).

Garrison, D. R., Anderson, T., & Archer, W. (2000). Critical thinking in a text-based environment. Computer conferencing in higher education. *Internet in Higher Education, 2*(2), 87-105.

Garrison, D. R., Anderson, T., & Archer, W. (2001). Critical thinking, cognitive presence, and computer conferencing in distance education. *The American Journal of Distance Education, 15*(1), 7-23.

Ginsparg, P., Houle, P., Joachims, T., & Sul, J. (2004). Mapping subsets of scholarly information. *Proceedings of National Academy of Sciences of the United States of America, 101*(1), 5236-5240.

Gunawardena, C., Lowe, C., & Anderson, T. (1997). Analysis of a global on-line debate and the development of an interaction analysis model for examining social construction of knowledge in computer conferencing. *Journal of Educational Computing Research, 17*(4), 395-429.

Hara, N., Bonk, C., & Angeli, C., (2000). Content analyses of on-line discussion in an applied educational psychology course. *Instructional Science, 28*(2), 115-152.

Henri, F. (1991). Computer conferencing and content analysis. In A. R. Kaye (Ed.), *Collaborative learning through computer conferencing: The Najaden papers* (pp. 116-136). Berlin, Germany: Springer-Verlag.

Hiltz, S. R., & Turoff, M. (1993). *Network nation: Human communication via computer* (rev. ed.). Boston: MIT Press. (Originally published 1978)

Hosti, O. (1996). Content analysis for social sciences and humanities. Don Mills, ON: Addison Wesley.

Hull, D. A., & Grefenstette, G. (1996) Stemming algorithms: A case study for detailed evaluation. *Journal of the American Society for Information Science, 47*(1), 70-84.

Jonassen, D. H. (1994). *Technology as cognitive tools: Learners as designers. IT Forum Paper #1.* Retrieved June 26, 2006, from http://it.coe.uga.edu/itforum/paper1/paper1.html

Jones, E. L. (2001). Grading student programs - a software testing approach. *The Journal of Computing in Small Colleges, 16*(2), 2001.

Knowles, M., Holton, E., & Swanson, R. (1998). *The adult learner: The definitive classic in adult education and human resource development* (5th ed.). Houston, TX: Gulf.

Kriger, T. J. (2001). A virtual revolution: Trends in the explosion of distance education. *USDLA Journal, 15*(11), 30-50.

Lamy, M. N., & Goodfellow, R. (1999). "Reflective conversation" in the virtual language classroom. *Language Learning & Technology, 2*(2), 43-61.

Larkey, L. S. (1998). Automatic essay grading using text categorization techniques. Proceedings of the 21st annual international ACM SIGIR conference on Research and development in information retrieval.

Lee, K. (2006). From engineer to architecture? Designing for a social constructivist environment. In E. Alkhalifa (Ed.), *Cognitively informed systems: Utilizing practical approaches to enrich information presentation and transfer* (pp. 185-209). London: Idea Group.

McCallum, A., & Nigam, K. (1998). *A comparison of event models for Naive Bayes text classification.* In AAAI-98 Workshop on Learning for Text Categorization. Available online http://citeseer.ist.psu.edu/mccallum98comparison.html

McKlin, T., Harmon, S., Evans, W., & Jones, M. (2002). Cognitive presence in web-based learning: A content analysis of student's online discussion. *IT Forum, 60.* Retrieved June 29 2006 from http://it.coe.uga.edu/itforum/paper60/paper60.htm.

Mayadas, F. (2001, June). Testimony to the Kerrey Commission on Web-based Education. *Journal of Asynchronous Learning Networks 5*(1), 134-138.

McMahon, M. (1997, December). *Social constructivism and the world wide web—A paradigm for learning.* Australian society for computers in learning in tertiary education. Perth, Australia.

Moller, L. (1998) Designing communities of learners for asynchronous distance education. *Educational Technology Research and Development. 46*(4), 115-112.

Newman, G., Webb, B., & Cochrane, C. (1995). A content analysis method to measure critical thinking in face-to-face computer supported group learning. *Interpersonal Computing and Technology, 3*(2), 56-77.

Page, E. B. (1994). New computer grading of student prose using modern concepts and software. *The Journal of Experimental Education 62*(2), 127-142.

Palloff, R. N., & Pratt, K. (1999). *Building learning communities in cyberspace.* San Francisco: Jossey-Bass.

Rheingold, H. (1994). A slice of life in my virtual community. In L. M. Harasim (Ed.), *Global networks computers and international communication* (pp. 57-80). Cambridge, MA: MIT Press.

Riffe, D., Lacey, S., & Fico, F. (1998). Analyzing media messages: Using quantitative content analysis in research. Mahwah, NJ: Erlbaum.

Rigou, M. (2004, February). On the development of adaptive web-based learning communities. *Proceedings of the IASTED International Conference Web-based Education*, Innsbruck, Austria.

Rourke, L., Anderson, T., Garrison, R., & Archer, W. (2001). Assessing social presence in asynchronous text-based computer conferencing. *Journal of Distance Education, 14*(2). Retrieved June 27, 2006 from http://cade.icaap.org/vol14.2/rourke_et_al.html.

Rovai, A. P. (2002). Sense of community, perceived cognitive learning and persistence in asynchronous learning networks. *Internet and Higher Education, 5*(4), 319-332.

Rudner, L. M., & Liang, T. (2002). *Automated essay scoring using Bayes' Theorem*. National Council on Measurement in Education. New Orleans, April.

Sergiovanni, T. (1999). The story of community. In J. Retallick, B. Cocklin, & K. Coombe (Eds.), *Learning communities in education: Issues, strategies and contexts* (pp. 9-25). London: Routledge.

Slavin, R. E. (1983). *Cooperative learning*. New York: Longman.

Squire, K., & Johnson, C. (2000). Supporting distributed communities of practice with interactive television. *Educational Technology Research and Development, 48*(1), 23-43.

Storey, M. A., Phillips, B., Maczewski, M., & Wang, M. (2002). Evaluating the usability of Web-based learning tools. *Educational Technology and Society, 5*(3), 91-100.

Swan, K., & Shea. P. (2005). Social presence and the development of virtual learning communities. In S. Hiltz & R. Goldman (Eds.), *Learning together online: Research on asynchronous learning networks* (pp. 239–260). Mahwah, NJ: Erlbaum.

Whittaker, S., Isaacs, E., & O'Day, V. (1996). Widening the Net: The theory and practice of physical and network communities. *SIGGroup Bulletin*, ACM Press.

Whitsed, N. (2004). Learning and teaching. *Health Information & Libraries Journal, 21*(1), 74-78.

CHAPTER 7

ENGAGING AND SUPPORTING PROBLEM SOLVING IN ONLINE LEARNING

David H. Jonassen

Based on the author's observations of numerous examples of online learning environments, more often than not, online learning functions and activities replicate face-to-face instruction. The pedagogies employed in online learning are similar if not identical to those typically employed in face-to-face instruction. Teachers or professors organize readings related to the topics being studied, tell the students their understandings about the topic, answer questions if any are raised, and then assess whether students remember what the textbook and the teacher told them. Most online learning begins with traditional assumptions and conceptions of learning and knowledge. The teach-and-test ontology and the reliance on traditional subject-matter ontologies ensure a lack of innovation in online learning. To the degree that online learning is perceived by educators as innovative, the author believes that online learning provides the opportunity, if not the obligation, to innovate. Online learning can and should escape the limitations of conventional, face-to-face instruction.

Online Learning Communities
pp. 109–127

INTRODUCTION

Why is innovation in online learning necessary? Because the conceptions of learning in formal educational contexts that online learning emulates and those in everyday and professional contexts (what some refer to as the real world) are diametrically opposed. In schools, universities, and corporate training contexts, learning is knowledge- (content-) based, highly organized and structured by rules and abstract formalisms. Learning is conceived of as "knowledge acquisition," which depends on how much "knowledge" was transmitted from online instruction to the learner. The knowledge that supposedly is acquired by learners is determined by an examination of the knowledge that did not leak out of the heads of the learners. This knowledge transmission paradigm assumes an absolutist epistemology where content is assumed to represent the truth (Jonassen, Marra, & Palmer, 2004).

In formal learning contexts, students or workers "learn about" the content they are studying. For example, in sociology classes, students learn about sociology. In biology classes, they learn about biology. However, they rarely, if ever, learn how to perform any of the functions of sociologists or biologists; that is, to think and act like sociologists or biologists. Again, learning in formal face-to-face or online learning contexts is diametrically opposed to how learning occurs in real world settings.

Learning in the real world, where people live and work, is omnipresent and essential to survival, let alone progress. In order to advance their culture (be it community or corporate) in any conceivable way, individuals and societies must learn. However, their learning cannot be described by any ontology of concepts and rules that supposedly describe the world in a hierarchical fashion. They learn as individuals and communities while learning to make sense of phenomena in order to solve problems. Their learning is activity-based, not content-based. Learning is situated in the problems they are solving, so the learning issues are emergent from those problems. Those issues cannot be predicted or prescribed in any curriculum. Learning and solving problems in the real world rely on knowledge distributed throughout a community of practice. The medium of learning is social negotiation of meaning, not content as determined by some agency, so knowledge emerges in the discourse of the community. Perhaps the most important difference is that in the real world, individuals and communities learn how to do things, not about the things. Most curricula describe the topics that teachers and professors teach about.

Here are the important questions: In corporate training and in higher education, the primary users of online learning, which world should we model in our instruction? Which skills need developing? Which conception of learning should drive our instruction? What should our students be learning?

My position is clear. Telling students about the world and quizzing their recall of what we told them is not only an insult to our learners (should not we expect more of them?), but that pedagogy retards their epistemological development, preventing them from developing knowledge-seeking skills needed to learn how to do something useful (Jonassen et al., in press). I believe that the only legitimate goal of professional education, either in universities or in corporate training, is problem solving. The rationale is simple. People in the real world (in everyday and professional contexts) are not expected to memorize information as presented. Rather, they are expected to solve problems and are rewarded for doing so. Therefore, we should focus instruction on how to solve problems. Content is the information, advice, and strategic knowledge needed to solve problems. Before describing how to do that, I need to articulate briefly what problem solving is.

What is Problem Solving?

Problem solving has two critical attributes. First, problem solving requires the mental representation of a situation in the world. That is, human problem solvers construct a mental representation of the problem, known as the problem space (Newell & Simon, 1972). Second, problem solving requires some active manipulation of the problem space. When we manipulate the problem space, we represent the components and dimensions of the problem, generate hypotheses about how to find the unknown, test those possible solutions, and draw conclusions. So, manipulation of the problem space, be it an internal mental representation or an external physical representation, necessarily engages conscious activity.

Having provided a generic definition, it is important to point out that problems are not the same and that different kinds of problems engage different problem-solving processes. Problems and problem solving vary in their structuredness, complexity, dynamicity, and domain specificity (abstractness).

Jonassen (1997) distinguished well-structured from ill-structured problems and recommended different design models for each. The most commonly encountered problems, especially in schools and universities, are well-structured problems. Typically found at the end of textbook chapters, these well-structured problems require the application of a finite number of concepts, rules, and principles being studied to a constrained problem situation. Well-structured problems typically present all elements of the problem; engage a limited number of rules and principles that are organized in a predictive and prescriptive arrangement; possess correct, convergent answers; and have a preferred, prescribed solution process. Ill-structured problems, on the other hand, are the kinds of problems that are encountered in everyday practice. Ill-structured problems have many alternative solutions; vaguely defined or unclear goals and constraints; multiple solution paths; and multiple criteria for evaluating solutions; so they are more difficult to solve.

Just as ill-structured problems are more difficult to solve than well-structured problems, complex problems are more difficult to solve than simple ones. Complexity of a problem is a function of the number of issues, functions, or variables involved in the problem; the number of interactions among those issues, functions, or variables; and the predictability of the behavior of those issues, functions, or variables.

Dynamicity is another dimension of complexity. In dynamic problems, the relationships among variables or factors change over time. "Why is this so?" Changes in one factor may cause variable changes in other factors. The more intricate these interactions, the more difficult is any solution.

A final dimension of problems and problem solving that is somewhat orthogonal to the other dimensions is domain specificity. In contemporary psychology, there is a common belief that problems within a domain rely on cognitive strategies that are specific to that domain (Mayer, 1992; Smith, 1991). Traditional conceptions of problem solving have been domain independent. That is, problem solving was conceived as a mental skill that could be generalized across domains. We now know that is not the case.

Jonassen (2000) described a typology of problems. This typology assumes that there are similarities in the cognitive processing engaged within these classes of problems. This range of problem types describes a continuum of problems from well-structured to ill-structured. Within each category of problems that are described, problems can vary with regard to abstractness, complexity, and dynamicity.

Logic Problems

Logic problems are abstract tests of logic that puzzle the learner. They are used in research studies to assess mental acuity, clarity, logical reasoning, and problem solving, despite their lack of authenticity. Examples of logic problems include Tower of Hanoi or cannibals and missionaries. Because this type of problem is used only for laboratory research on human reasoning, it will not be further analyzed or developed.

Algorithmic Problems

Most common in mathematics courses, algorithmic problems are those in which students are taught to solve algorithms using a rigid set of procedures. Algorithmic problems, according to McCloskey, Caramaza, and Basili (1985), require comprehension of the operations (e.g. associative and commutative properties and concepts of multiplication and division), execution procedures for calculating, and retrieval of arithmetic facts (e.g. times tables). The primary limitation of algorithmic approaches to problem solving is the over-reliance on procedural knowledge structures and the lack or absence of conceptual understanding of the objects of the algorithm and the procedures engaged. Examples of algorithms include factoring quadratic equations, calculating the derivative of an equation, or bisecting any given angle. Procedural problems also exist in the real world (e.g. starting a computer, checking out a book, or entering data in an accounting system.

Story Problems

In an attempt to situate algorithms in some kind of context, many textbook authors and teachers employ story problems. This usually takes the form of embedding the values needed to solve an algorithm into a brief narrative or scenario. Learners are required to access a problem schema and apply that schema to the current problem. If they access the correct schema, the solution procedure is usually embedded within that schema. However, numerous difficulties occur in extracting the values from the narrative and inserting them into the correct formula, and solving for the unknown quantity. Unfortunately, the story covers for the problems are too often uninteresting and irrelevant to students. So when they attempt to transfer story problem skills to other problems, they focus too closely on surface features or recall familiar solutions from previously solved problems (Woods et al., 1997). Story problems include elementary combine, cause/change, or compare problems in math (Joe has three marbles; Jane gave him three more; how many does he have?); calculating resistance given voltage and amperage; calculating reagents needed to form a specific precipitate in a chemical reaction; or calculating interest accrued on a savings account.

Rule-Using Problems

Many problems have correct solutions but have multiple solution paths or multiple rules governing the process. They tend to have a clear purpose or goal that is constrained but not restricted to a specific procedure or method. Rule-using problems can be as simple as expanding a recipe to accommodate more guests and as complex as completing tax return schedules or evaluating a loan application. Using an online search system to locate relevant information on the World Wide Web is an example of rule-using problems. The purpose is clear: find the most relevant information in the least amount of time. That requires selection of search terms, constructing effective search arguments, implementing the search strategy, and evaluating the utility and credibility of information found. Because there is little, if any, research on rule-using, knowledge about this kind of problem solving must derive from rule induction research.

Decision-Making Problems

Decision-making problems usually require making a decision from a limited number of alternative options. For instance, which marketing strategy will be most effective? Which health plan do we select? How am I going to pay this bill? What is the best way to get to the interstate during rush hour? Though these problems have a limited number of solutions, the number of factors to be considered in deciding among those solutions as well as the weights assigned to them can be very complex. More vexing, decisions often entail personal beliefs and biases. Decision problems usually require comparing and contrasting the advantages and disadvantages of alternate solutions.

Troubleshooting Problems

Troubleshooting is one of the most common forms of everyday problem solving. Maintaining automobiles, aircraft, or any complex system requires troubleshooting skills. Debugging a computer program requires troubleshooting. The primary purpose of troubleshooting is fault state diagnosis. That is, some part of a system is not functioning properly, resulting in a set of symptoms that have to be diagnosed and matched with the user's knowledge of various fault states. Troubleshooters use symptoms to generate and test hypotheses about different fault states. This kind of problem will be described more completely later.

Diagnosis-Solution Problems

Diagnosis-solution problems are similar to troubleshooting problems. Most diagnosis-solution problems require identifying a fault state, just like troubleshooting. However, in troubleshooting, the goal is to repair the fault and get the system back online as soon as possible, so the solution strategies are more restrictive. Diagnosis-solution problems usually begin with a fault state similar to troubleshooting (e.g. symptoms of a sick person). The physician examines the patient and considers patient history before making an initial diagnosis. In a spiral of data collection, hypothesis generation, and testing, the physician focuses on a specific etiology and differential diagnosis of the patient's problem. At that point, the physician must suggest a solution. Frequently, there are multiple solutions and solution paths, so the physician must justify a particular solution as well as consider the beliefs of the family and the requirements of the insurer, making diagnosis-solution problems more open system types. Additional examples of diagnosis-solution problems include any kind of psychotherapy or counseling, developing an individual plan of instruction for special education students, or diagnosing management problems in a corporation.

Strategic Performance

Strategic performance entails complex activity structures in a real-time environment, where the performers apply a number of tactical activities to meet a more complex and ill-structured strategy while maintaining situational awareness. In order to achieve the strategic objective, such as teaching in a classroom or quarterbacking a professional football offense, the performer applies a set of complex tactical activities that are designed to meet strategic objectives. Pursuing strategies through tactical activities requires applying a finite number of tactical activities that have been designed to accomplish the strategy. However, an expert tactical performer is able to improvise or construct new tactics on the spot to meet the strategy. For instance, devising a new strategy in a courtroom when unexpected evidence has been heard. Those adjustments are contextually constrained.

Systems Analysis Problems

Systems analysis problems are complex, multifaceted situations in which it is not clear what the problem is. These ill-structured problems are often solved in professional contexts. Systems analysis problems require the solver to articulate the nature of the problem and the different perspectives that impact the problem before suggesting solutions (Jonassen, 1997). They are more contextually bound than any kind of problem considered so far. That is, their solutions rely on an analysis of contextual factors. Solving business problems, including planning production, are common systems analysis problems. Deciding production levels, for instance, requires balancing human resources, technologies, inventory, and sales. Classical situated systems analysis problems also exist in international relations, such as "given low crop productivity in the Soviet Union, how would the solver go about improving crop productivity if he or she served as Director of the Ministry of Agriculture in the Soviet Union" (Voss & Post, 1988, p. 273). International relations problems involve decision-making and solution generation and testing in a political context. Justifying decisions is among the most important processes in solving case problems.

Design Problems

Among the most ill-structured problems are design problems. Whether designing instruction, an electronic circuit, a bicycle that flies, a marketing campaign for a new Internet company, or any other product or system, designing requires applying a great deal of domain knowledge with a lot of strategic knowledge resulting in an original design. What makes design problems so ill-structured is that there are seldom clear criteria for evaluating success. The client either likes or hates the result but cannot articulate why. Therefore, skills in argumentation and justification help designers to rationalize their designs. Although designers always hope for the best solution, the best solution is seldom ever known. Also, most design problems are complex, requiring the designer to balance many needs and constraints in the design and the clients. Despite the difficulties, design problems are among the most common in professional practice. Virtually every engineer, for example, is paid to design products, systems, or processes.

Dilemmas

Dilemmas are the most ill-structured kind of problem because there typically is no solution that will ever be acceptable to a significant portion of the people affected by the problem. The continuing problems in Palestine or the Balkans are dilemmas. Usually there are many valuable perspectives on the situation (military, political, social, ethical, etc.), though none is able to offer a generally acceptable solution to the crisis. The situation is so complex and unpredictable, that no best solution can ever be known. Dilemmas are often complex social situations with conflicting perspectives, and they are usually the most vexing of problems.

PROBLEM SOLVING IN ONLINE LEARNING

I have argued that online learning too often replicates face-to-face instruction and that face-to-face instruction teaches students about content but not how to solve problems. Further, I have argued that problem solving is the only legitimate kind of learning that universities and corporate training should engage because their learners will doubtlessly be required to solve problems in the everyday professional situations for which they are preparing. The obvious conclusion is that online learning for professional education should engage and support learners in solving problems. If you accept that conclusion, it raises another problem. That is that the pedagogical structures, functionality, and affordances of most online management and delivery systems, such as Blackboard, WebCT, E-College and most others, do not support the use of alternative forms of knowledge representation, authentic forms of assessment, or the use of distributed tools to scaffold different forms of reasoning (Marra & Jonassen, 2001). These functionalities are essential for supporting problem solving in online learning environments. For online learning environments to support problem solving, they must be re-engineered to provide the functionalities required for supporting learning to solve different kinds of problems. They must engage learners in solving problems and provide them the intellectual and social support systems that are required to solve the problems. First and foremost, this means that problems come first, and that content instruction, in whatever form it assumes, is provided in support of the problem solving activity. How will this be accomplished?

When designing problem-solving environments for online learning, we first need to analyze the kinds of problem solving that our learners need and then design and provide problem-based learning environments to help them learn how to solve those problems. In order to do that, we must develop cognitive models of each kind of problem solving using a variety of appropriate needs assessment and task analysis tools. Having analyzed problem types, we then must develop instructional design models for each kind of problem solving and map those models onto problem-based architectures for online learning. Finally, faculties and teachers must be reoriented and trained in how to use these problem-based architectures; that is, how to teach problem solving in a problem-based environment.

This work is ongoing. To date, I have developed preliminary cognitive models for each kind of problem solving. However, only two of these problem types have been articulated sufficiently to develop architectures. I will briefly review those models and how they can be used to develop online problem-solving architectures. Page restrictions preclude elaboration of these models.

Story Problems

In another paper, I have analyzed the most common type of problem, story problems. From simple combine, comparison, and cause/change problems in beginning mathematics (Riley, Green, & Heller, 1983) to complex story problems in engineering dynamics classes, story problems are the most commonly used and extensively researched kind of problems. Found at the back of thousands of textbook chapters, these problems require learners to identify key words in the story, select the appropriate algorithm and sequence for solving the problem, apply the algorithm, and hopefully check their responses (Sherrill, 1983). Solving story problems requires not only calculation accuracy but also the semantic comprehension of relevant textual information, the capacity to visualize the data, the capacity to recognize the deep structure of the problem, the capacity to correctly sequence their solution activities, and the capacity and willingness to evaluate the procedure that they used to solve the problem (Lucangelli, Tressoldi, & Cendron, 1998). Difficulties in story problem solving are more related to lack of structural knowledge of the problems than the ability to calculate. Text comprehension and working memory also play important roles in story problem solving.

Math and science story problems have traditionally been taught using the following procedure (Rich, 1960):

- Representation of unknowns by letters
- Translation of relationships about unknowns into equations.
- Solution of equations to find the value of three unknowns.
- Verification or check of values found to see if they satisfy to original problem.

More contemporary research has emphasized the importance of problem schemas in solving story problems. Problem schemas are the mental models that learners construct about different kinds of story problems. Successful problem schemas are comprised of a semantic model of the situation described in text, a model of the deep structure of the problem, and a model of the processing operations required to solve the problem (Riley & Greeno, 1988). Solving story problems has a significant conceptual component that drives the selection and application of the procedural process. Problem types vary by semantic structure (semantic relations) and identity of unknown quantity, both of which consistently affect problem difficulty, so identifying problem types is essential to transfer of problem solving. In order to solve story problems, learners must:

- Parse problem statement
- Search for appropriate problem schema
- Use schema to classify problem type
  - o Compare surface content to previously solved problems
  - o Compare semantic model to previously solved problems
- Generate problem space
  - o Identify problem components from surface content
  - o Map onto problem structure in semantic model
  - o Access processing operations
- Map values into formula
- Estimate type, units, and size of solution
- Solve the formula
- Reconcile with estimate (was result similar to estimate? If not, generate new problem space)
- Associate problem content with semantic model and file according to problem type

This relatively sequential model for solving story problems belies the conceptual nature of the process. Essentially, transferring the ability to solve any particular kind of story problem requires that learners construct a mental model of the problem type (a problem schema) that includes a situational model of the kinds of surface content and a semantic model of the structure of the problem. For example, simple mathematics motion problems typically use trains, cars, or airplanes traveling in one direction or another. In order to be able to solve motion problems, the learner's problem schema must include a structural model or semantic model of the relationships between the different entities in a problem. There are different kinds of motion problems, such as overtake (one vehicle starts and is followed later by a second that travels over the same route at a faster rate), opposite direction (two vehicles leaving same point traveling in opposite directions), round trip (vehicle travels from point A to B and returns), or closure (two vehicles start at different points traveling towards one another) (Mayer, Larkin, & Kadane, 1984). Each kind of motion problem has a different set of structural relations between the entities that calls on different processing operations. It is essential that learners construct problem schemas that indicate comprehension of the surface elements of the problem, the semantic relationships between the entities in the problem, and the mathematical relations implied by those semantic relations.

Given those cognitive requirements, instruction designed to support learning how to solve story problems should:

- Describe problem type and relate to graphic organizer highlighting problem type in taxonomy of problem types within domain
- Present conceptual model of problem space, including:
  o Surface content
  o Semantic model of problem
  o Processing operations
- Ask students to estimate solution type, units, and size
- Model problem solution through worked example using voice and animated agent (if online)
  o Classify problem type
  o Estimate outcome
  o Parse surface content
  o Map elements onto semantic model
  o Convert semantic model into formula
  o Solve for goal
  o Reconcile with estimate (units and size)
  o Model metacognitive strategies and reflection on solution
- Pose practice problems by selecting similar and then dissimilar surface content
- Ask students to practice mapping surface content onto semantic model
- Ask students to build formula (use spreadsheet to explicitly represent algorithmic process)
- Ask students to use spreadsheet to solve practice problems
- Provide feedback on problem solutions: relate to problem elements and problem type
- Review problem type and relate to problem taxonomy

The most obvious method for teaching story problem solutions is worked examples. However, prior to working through solution examples, instruction must present conceptual models of the kinds of problems being solved that are compared and contrasted with models of story problems that have already been learned and those that will be learned in the future. That is, instruction must show where the current problem type fits into the taxonomy of problem types in the domain being studied. Working through problems with similar surface content or situational features that have different structural relations can support discrimination between problem types. The worked examples must integrate the situational, semantic models and the structural relations with the processing operations.

Online instruction for story problems therefore must have at least the following components:

- A graphical organizer illustrating each kind of problem solved within the domain. This organizer should explicitly contrast the deep structural differences between the problems. Clicking on each problem type reveals a structural analysis of the problem type, along with examples mapped onto the problem space. Each problem space must consist of surface content mapped onto a semantic model of the problem and the processing operations required to solve it. For example, Figure 7.1 illustrates a structural model of a simple stoichiometry problem. This Stella model shows the effects of each part of the equation on each other.

- A worked example of a number of example problems that explicitly classifies problem type, estimates the outcome, parses the text of the problem distinguishing surface content from structural content, maps problem elements onto a semantic model, converts the semantic model into formula, solves for goal, reconciles the answer with estimate in terms of units and size, and models metacognitive strategies and reflection on solution.

- Practice problems for students.

- Student problem spaces for solving the practice items, including structural supports and coaching to classify the problem type, estimate the outcome, parse the text of the problem distinguishing surface content from structural content, map problem elements onto a semantic model, convert the semantic model into formula, solve for goal, reconcile the answer with estimate in terms of units and size.

- Feedback on problem solutions.

- Fading of problem space scaffolds.

This reasonably complete design model for online learning has not been tested. Only empirical research can validate its effectiveness.

Troubleshooting Problems

Troubleshooting is among the most commonly experienced kinds of problem solving in the professional world. From troubleshooting a faulty modem to multiplexed refrigeration systems in a modern supermarket, troubleshooting attempts to isolate fault states in some working system. Having found the fault, the part is replaced or repaired. Troubleshooting is often conceived of as a linear series of decisions that leads to a fault iso-

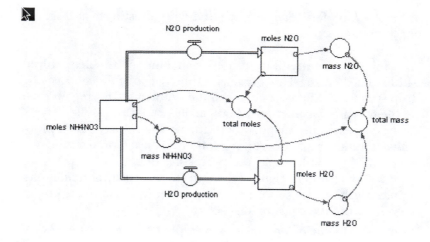

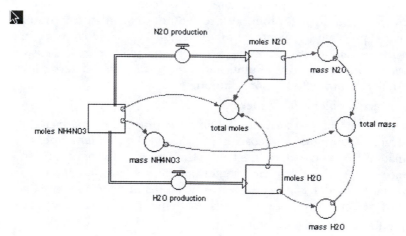

Figure 7.1.   Structural model of stoichiometry problem.

lation. That approach can work quite effectively in a performance support system for helping novices solve simple diagnosis problems; however, it is inadequate for training competent, professional troubleshooters. Effective troubleshooting requires system knowledge (conceptual knowledge of how the system works), procedural knowledge (how to perform problem solving procedures and test activities), and strategic knowledge (strategies such as search-and-replace, serial elimination, and space splitting) (Pokorny, Hall, Gallaway, & Dibble, 1996). These skills are integrated and organized by the troubleshooter's experiences. The troubleshooter's mental model consists of conceptual, functional, and declarative knowledge, including knowledge of system components and interactions, flow control, fault states (fault characteristics, symptoms, contextual information, and probabilities of occurrence), and fault testing procedures. The primary differences between expert and novice troubleshooters are the amount and organization of system knowledge (Johnson, 1988). Troubleshooting requires an integrated understanding of how the system being troubleshot works, which is best taught through functional flow diagrams (Johnson & Satchwell, 1993). In order to solve troubleshooting problems, learners must:

- Identify fault state and symptoms
- Construct problem space of system
  - o Describe goal state (how do you know when system is functioning properly?)
  - o Identify sub-system in which fault occurs (space splitting)
- Examine faulty sub-system(s)
- Complete diagnosis process
  - o Reminding from previous cases
  - o Rule out least likely hypotheses
  - o Generate initial hypothesis and assumptions
  - o Test hypotheses based on domain knowledge
  - o Interpret results of test
  - o Confirm or reject validity of hypotheses: If reject, generate new hypothesis
- Implement solution
- Test solution(s): is goal state achieved?
- Record results in fault database

In order to support learning how to troubleshoot, instruction should:

- Present system description with symptoms
- Present or help learner to construct a conceptual model of system
- Enable learner to identify fault state and symptoms
- Require learner to describe goal state (how he or she knows when system is functioning properly)
- Provide access to fault database, including fields:
  - o Fault
  - o Subsystem
  - o Symptoms

- o Failure mode
- o Strategies
- o Results
- o Effects
- • Require learner to examine faulty sub-system(s)
- • Test hypotheses in troubleshooter
  - o Action to be taken (test, remove/replace, eliminate, etc)
  - o Cost of action (time, materials, labor, downtime, etc.)
  - o Fault hypothesis
  - o Identify sub-system in which fault occurs on system model and provide feedback
  - o Result of action
  - o Interpret results of action
  - o Confirm or reject validity of hypotheses: If reject, take new action
- • Implement solution
- • Test solution(s): is goal state achieved?
- • Record results in fault database

The most effective way to learn to troubleshoot is by confronting trouble-shooting problems. Figure 7.2 illustrates the important components of a troubleshooting learning environment. In order to implement this environment in online learning, the following components are required:

- • Systems models illustrating the conceptual interconnectedness of systems components. The models must be interlinked with both the case library and the troubleshooter.
- • Case library or fault database consisting of as many troubleshooting instances as possible. Each case represents a story of a domain-specific troubleshooting instance. Case libraries, based on principles of case-based reasoning, represent the most powerful form of instructional support for ill-structured problems (Jonassen & Hernandez-Serrano, 2002).
- • Troubleshooter that allows the learner to troubleshoot new cases. For each action the learner takes, the troubleshooter requires the learner to estimate or look up the cost of action, state or select a fault hypothesis, identify sub-system in which fault occurs on system model and provide, receive feedback or the result of action, interpret results of action, and confirm or reject validity of hypotheses driving the action taken.

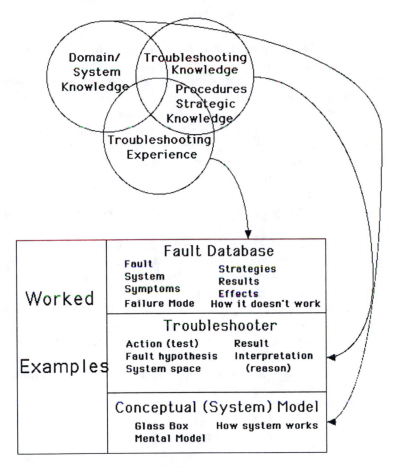

Figure 7.2.   Model of troubleshooting instruction.

- Each action taken by the troubleshooter shows up in the systems model.

The troubleshooter requires the learner to think and act like an experienced troubleshooter. The environment integrates the troubleshooting actions, knowledge types (conceptual, strategic, and procedural), and conceptual systems model with a database of faults that the learner and others have solved. Integrating knowledge, practice, and experience provides a powerful instructional model. As learners solve troubleshooting problems, the results of their practice cases can be added to the learner's case library of fault situations, so that the learner can learn from his or her own personal experience.

SUMMARY

In this chapter, I have argued that online learning in universities and corporate training should focus on problem solving. In order to support problem solving, problem and domain-specific problem architectures must be implemented in online delivery packages. I have described briefly examples of two such architectures, replete with the required instructional components. Because neither of these architectures has been built, no examples exist. Funding is being sought for that very purpose. The assumption is clear. We know that there are different kinds of problems, and we know what/how learners have to think in order to solve those problems. The next step will be to construct the different online architectures and disseminate them. That process will engage the greatest problem to date.

The most difficult problem in promoting problem solving in online learning will be to convince universities and businesses that learners should be learning to solve problems, that recalling and forgetting content is not sufficient for learning to solve problems, and that changes in the basic nature of their pedagogies are required. The dominant models of instruction in most universities and business are based on four centuries of practice. Changing pedagogies based on traditional, dualistic, and deterministic epistemological assumptions will require systemic changes within the institutions, which will represent an incredibly complex and multifaceted systems analysis problem.

REFERENCES

Johnson, S. D. (1988). Cognitive analysis of expert and novice troubleshooting performance. *Performance Improvement Quarterly, 1*(3), 38-54.

Johnson, S. D., & Satchwell, S. E. (1993). The effect of functional flow diagrams on apprentice aircraft mechanics' technical system understanding. *Performance Improvement Quarterly, 6*(4), 73-91.

Jonassen, D. H. (1997). Instructional design model for well-structured and ill-structured problem-solving learning outcomes. *Educational Technology Research and Development 45*(1), 65-95.

Jonassen, D. H. (2000). Designing constructivist learning environments. In C.M. Reigeluth (Ed.), *Instructional design theories and models: Their current state of the art* (2nd ed.). Mahwah, NJ: Erlbaum.

Jonassen, D. H., & Hernandez-Serrano, J. (2002). Case-based reasoning and instructional design: Using stories to support problem solving. *Educational Technology Research and Development, 50*(2), 65-77.

Jonassen, D. H., Marra, R. M., & Palmer, B. (2004). Epistemological development: An implicit entailment of constructivist learning environments. In N.

M. Seel & S. Dijkstra (Eds.), *Curriculum, plans, and processes in instructional design* (pp. 75-88). Mahwah, NJ: Erlbaum.

Lucangelli, D., Tressoldi, P. E., & Cendron, M. (1998). Cognitive and metacognitive abilities involved in the solution of mathematical word problems: Validation of a comprehensive model. *Contemporary Educational Psychology, 23*, 257-275.

Marra, R. M., & Jonassen, D. H. (2001). Limitations of online courses for supporting constructive learning. *Quarterly Review of Distance Education, 2*(4), 303-317.

Mayer, R. E. (1992). *Thinking, problem solving, cognition* (2nd ed.). New York: Freeman.

Mayer, R. E., Larkin, J. H., Kadane, J. B. (1984). A cognitive analysis of mathematical problem solving ability. In R. Sternberg (Ed.), *Advances in the psychology of human intelligence.* Hillsdale, NJ: Erlbaum.

McCloskey, M., Caramaza, A., & Basili, A. (1985). Cognitive mechanisms in number processing and calculation: Evidence from dyscalculia. *Brain and Cognition, 4*, 171-196.

Newell, A. & Simon, H. (1972). *Human problem solving.* Englewood Cliffs, NJ: Prentice Hall.

Pokorny, R. A., Hall, E. P., Gallaway, M. A., & Dibble, E. (1996). Analyzing components of work samples to evaluate performance. *Military Psychology, 8*(3), 161-177.

Rich, B. (1960). *Schaum's principles of and problems of elementary algebra.* New York: Schaum's.

Riley, M. S., Greeno, J. G., & Heller, J. I. (1983). Development of children's problem solving ability in arithmetic. In. H. P. Ginsburg (Ed.), *The development of mathematical thinking* (pp. 153-196). New York: Academic Press.

Riley, M. S., & Greeno, J. G. (1988). Developmental analysis of understanding language about quantities and solving problems. *Cognition and Instruction, 5*(1), 49-101.

Sherrill, J. M. (1983). Solving textbook mathematical problems. *Alberta Journal of Educational Research, 29*, 140-152.

Smith, M. U. (1991). A view from biology. In M. U. Smith (Ed.), *Toward a unified theory of problem solving* (pp. 1-19). Hillsdale, NJ: Erlbaum.

Voss, J. F., & Post, T. A. (1989). On the solving of ill-structured problems. In M. T. H. Chi, R. Glaser, & M. J. Farr (Eds.), *The nature of expertise.* Hillsdale, NJ: Erlbaum.

Woods, D. R., Hrymak, A. N., Marshall, R. R., Wood, P. E., Crowe, Hoffman, T. W., et al. (1997). Developing problem-solving skills: The McMaster problem solving program. *Journal of Engineering Education, 86*(2), 75-92.

CHAPTER 8

LAYING THE GROUNDWORK FOR THE DEVELOPMENT OF LEARNING COMMUNITIES WITHIN ONLINE COURSES

Jennifer V. Lock

Online learning environments are rapidly emerging across various sectors of society. In education, opportunities to access a wide range of courses and professional development services are now available on the Internet. Within these learning environments, a different kind of community is emerging— an online learning community. For educational leaders, developers, and practitioners, a serious question emerges: what must be done in the design of the online courses to promote the development of learning communities? On the theme of laying the groundwork for the development of online learning communities, we must first understand what is an online learning community and what are the characteristics and practices of such a community. How can active networks of people using technology develop and sustain a learning community? How do conceptual and theoretical frameworks guide the utilization of technology in creating and sustaining a learning community within an online learning environment? By developing a sound conceptual understanding of this phenomenon, educators designing such learning environments will be better prepared to explore various learning

Online Learning Communities
pp. 129–149
Copyright © 2007 by Information Age Publishing
All rights of reproduction in any form reserved.

community features and capabilities. The challenge is to integrate pedagogical and technological concerns through the design process to promote and foster the emergence of vibrant and stimulating learning communities.

INTRODUCTION

Conceptual Framework

A community is not an entity or a product. Rather, it is a process, which is fluid in nature. A community evolves through nurturing conditions. It "requires a highly interactive, loosely structured organization with tightly knit relations based on personal persuasion and interdependence" (Kowch & Schwier, 1997, p. 2). It is a supportive and empowering environment that accommodates and is responsive to the members' actions, interactions, and reactions. The relationships, the intimacy, the negotiations, and the engagement of participants all influence the evolution of a community. The growth and longevity of a community are directly related to the community meeting the needs of members. Conditions and characteristics associated with a viable community need to be fostered and nurtured if a learning community is to exist and evolve. It is through mediated communication within this online learning environment that a community comes to life.

Theoretical Orientation

Constructivist theory is the predominant philosophy in education and especially in online learning (Palloff & Pratt, 1999). Jonassen, Peck, and Wilson (1998) state that learning communities are "models of thinking about instruction, based on the dual platform of technology and constructivist theory" (p. 1). There is, however, a distinction between cognitive and social constructivist theory. The focus of cognitive constructivism is on "individual constructions of knowledge discovered in interaction with the environment" (Bonk & Cunningham, 1998, p. 32). From a Vygotskian social constructivist perspective, the sociocultural context influences the thinking and creation of meaning (Bonk & Cunningham, 1998). "Meaning making is a process of negotiation among the participants through dialogues or conversations" (Jonassen, Peck, & Wilson, 1999, p. 5). The opportunity to interact with other learners in sharing, constructing, and negotiating meaning leads to knowledge construction.

The theoretical orientation is critical when examining how a sense of community can be promoted in an online course. Within a constructivist philosophy, learning is based on constructing meaning from experience, and interpreting the world largely through the social environment. Learning involves both individual and social processes (Jonassen, 2000). "Active, constructive, intentional, authentic, and cooperative learning" (Jonassen et al., 1999, p. 7) are five attributes of meaningful learning. In this learning process, learners, groups of learners, working together and supporting each other, will use a variety of tools and information resources to achieve the learning goals (Wilson, 1996). Technology can be used as a tool in exploring, representing, and articulating knowledge. In addition, technology provides the medium for conversing and collaborating within this learning environment (Jonassen et al., 1999). A constructivist learning environment promoting community development fosters a social context in which all members, both students and teachers, are active participants in the learning process. Online learning communities are networks of social relationships in which engagement and interaction are critical factors within the constructivist learning environment.

CHARACTERISTICS OF ONLINE LEARNING COMMUNITIES

Cothrel and Williams (1999) defined community as "a group of people who are willing and able to help each other. In this sense, community is more than a way a group of people defines itself: it is a capability that can be developed and improved over time" (p. 60). Jonassen et al. (1999) defined it as "a social organization of people who share knowledge, values and goals" (p. 118). Rovai (2002) adds to this definition by noting key elements of community to be: "mutual interdependence among members, sense of belonging, connectedness, spirit, trust, interactivity, common expectations, shared values and goals, and overlapping histories among members." The social grouping of people in a community involves communication, relationships, activities, identities, memberships, and a shared history.

The concept of learning community has been defined by various scholars (e.g., Jonassen, et al., 1998; Kowch & Schwier, 1997; Mitchell & Sackney, 2000; Riel & Fulton, 2001). For example, Conrad (2005) has defined community in the online learning environment

as a general sense of connection, belonging, and comfort that develops over time among members of a group who share purpose or commitment to a common goal. The creation of community simulates for online learners the comforts of home, providing a safe climate, an atmosphere of trust and respect, an invitation for intellectual exchange, and a gathering place for like-minded individuals who are sharing a journey that includes similar activities, purposes and goals. (p. 2)

Those who form the membership of the community are drawn together for a common purpose, and, to some extent, a purpose that provides a boundary or exclusivity that assists in defining the community.

Virtual learning communities, as defined by Luppicini (2003), "are learning communities that are computer-mediated by interconnected computers. Communication characteristics of virtual learning communities include: asynchronous and synchronous communication, high interactivity, and multi-way communication" (p. 410). Online or virtual communities have been a part of the Internet since its beginning through the use of newsgroups, listservs, and virtual worlds (e.g., the WELL). However, Kearsley (2000) stated that the creation of online learning communities "is a new phenomenon in education" (p. 58).

Online learning communities involve a mutual knowledge-building process. "Members learn both by teaching others and by applying to their own situations the information, tools, know-how, and experiences provided by others in the virtual community" (Hunter, 2002, p. 96). The learning community, as described by Palloff and Pratt (1999) is "the vehicle through which learning occurs online. Members depend on each other to achieve the learning outcomes for the course.... Without the support and participation of a learning community, there is no online course" (p. 29).

To develop a deeper understanding of the complexity and multifaceted nature of this concept, we must examine some of the key elements. Schwier (2001, 2002) has articulated ten elements or characteristics of a virtual learning community. The following includes seven elements identified by Selznick (1996) and three additional elements that Schwier has identified: historicity, identity, mutuality, plurality, autonomy, participation, integration, an orientation to the future, technology, and learning (Misanchuck & Anderson, 2001; Schwier, 2001, 2002). Schwier asserts that all these characteristics may not appear in every community and that the degree of presence of each characteristic varies within and throughout the evolution of a community. Interactivity among these elements influences the evolution of a community.

Pedagogical Issues

Riel (1996) argued that building a community is not the same as building a physical space. Tools such as listservs, Web pages and conferencing forums do not define community. She claimed that it is the partnerships and interactions between and among the people who gather together that define community. Instructional designers and online educators who are developing courses with a view to promoting community need to have an understanding of the pedagogical issues and the factors that foster or hinder community development within an online learning environment. In the design of community, purposeful selection and use of digital technology with effective pedagogical and/or andragogical strategies needs to be addressed to create an environment in which people engage in learning experiences that foster the development of community (Lock, 2003).

Communication, collaboration, interaction, and participation are four cornerstones in a learning community framework. Nipper (1989) describes the third generation of distance learning as having a focus on both communication and learning as a social process. In this new generation, communication among learners is no longer marginal. This coincides with the development of the fifth generation of media, which includes digital networks that provide various types of interactivity between and among people and provide access to large quantities of multimedia information stored on digital networks (Bourdeau & Bates, 1997). This interactive communication technology has now advanced to a point where diverse interactions (one-to-one and one-to-many), synchronous (e.g., chat, desktop videoconferencing, and whiteboards) and asynchronous communication (e.g., e-mail, listservs, and bulletin boards), and multiple modes of communication are available to serve learners' needs and to facilitate the learning process and community.

Communication is pivotal in an online community. According to Schwier (2002), it "is the brick and mortar of virtual communities, and communities only exist as long as communication is available to participants" (p. 3). Without effective communication, it is not possible to generate interaction, engagement, or alignment. In other words, there can be no community (Schwier, 2001). Communication has to be open to all members. Frequent communication with members using various modes of communication needs to be part of the instructional plan (Bauman, 1997; Haythornthwaite, Kazmer, Robins, & Shoemaker, 2000). Individuals have the option and the ability to use such means as synchronous and asynchronous communication, private and public forums, and one-to-one and multiparty channels. Bauman (1997) recommended using a high level of public interaction to make all participants aware of the topic, to provide an electronic space for noncourse-related interactions, and for instructors to ask questions and to promote interaction among students. Hill (2001) noted that it is easy for people to lose contact with their online colleagues. She recommended that multiple means of communication be available to facilitate contact with others and to assist in maintaining a link to the larger community. Herrmann (1998) has found that language patterns become guideposts in community development. Civil language (e.g., being positive and friendly) and conflict resolution mechanisms are also important factors in creating and sustaining a community over time.

In their research using written contracts to foster community building within Web courses, Murphy, Mahoney, and Harvell (2000) identified four key communication factors that support an online community environment. First, there is a need for frequent and open communication between students and instructor, among students, and between groups. Second, the instructor's communication provides both information and feedback within the community. Third, the establishment of bonds and cohesion is based on group communication. Fourth, the use of well-written contracts assists in the creation of group cohesion. Contracts do provide a structure and framework within which students can work as a group. However, since communities function on the basis of commitment and not necessarily on contracts, it cannot be assumed that using contracts will lead to commitment, expanded communication, and community growth.

Collaboration is another factor that needs to be fostered in online courses to promote learning communities. Dennen (2000) defined collaborative learning as "a process that involves interaction amongst individuals in a learning situation" (p. 1). She described it as being grounded in a theory of learning that asserts that knowledge is constructed through social interaction. The collaborative learning process involves a learner-centred approach where "knowledge is viewed as a social construct, facilitated by peer interaction, evaluation and cooperation" (Benbunan-Fich & Hiltz, 2003, p. 299). McLellan (1997) summarized Schrage's (1990) position on collaboration by saying that the "goal in creating collaborative experiences is to create a shared experience rather than an experience that is shared" (p. 185). The experience needs to be participatory, not passive. Collaborative learning engages all participants (both students and instructors) in working together in the learning process.

Two other factors that contribute to community development within online courses are interaction and participation. Interaction is the dialogue that occurs "between the student and the instructor, other students or the content" (Kearsley, 2000, p. 80). Kearsley (2000) defined participation as "involvement and presences" (p. 80). Participation has both social and academic components that are integral parts of a community. Community members need to have opportunities to shape the style and degree of their participation. Guidelines and norms of participation need to be present, which can be established by the online educator and shaped by community members. In addition, the participant may perform multiple roles within an online course. For example, participants may interact at times as discussion moderators and at other times as discussion participants. According to Conrad (2002), "participation in online learning activities exist before community, that it contributes to community, that it is the vehicle for maintaining community, and that it eventually becomes the measure of the health of the community" (p. 16). Haythornthwaite et al. (2000) found that the interaction and the participation of community members need to be monitored and supported. Strategies need to be in place to launch dialogue and exchanges and to familiarize people with the environment that fosters a learning community.

Instructional context, more than instructional delivery, is a major pedagogical factor when designing online courses that promote community. Attention needs to be given to a relevant context that supports authentic learning. The use of real world problems, problem-based and case-based learning are instructional approaches that can be used. The use of collaborative learning environments helps to foster situated learning and to promote multiple perspectives among students and educators (Tam, 2000). These approaches help to cultivate an environment in which community members work together in a student-centered learning environment, sharing expertise, contributing to knowledge, and owning their own learning outcomes. In addition, they provide opportunities for leadership and for learners to take on various roles in support of their learning process (Palloff & Pratt, 1999). For this to occur online, learners need to have access to appropriate technologies that can be used in constructing and sharing knowledge. Kozma (2000) believed that creating learning environments will result in learners taking charge of designing the context of their learning using various tools and resources.

Jonassen et al. (1998) stressed that in learning communities the emphasis is on "the whole group, which should then collaborate and support each other towards their learning goals ... This model depends on both students and teacher taking responsibility for their learning and motivation" (p. 2). Garrison (2000) acknowledged the need for distance educators to understand that they are members of a community of learners, and not just external agents who are only involved in creating pre-packed learning materials. Rovai (2002) concurred by noting that if instructors believe their job is done after they design and put the course online, the result is that the "sense of community will whither unless the community is nurtured and support is provided in the form of heightened awareness of social presence." In the online environment, educators need to have an understanding of the learning community and need to play a dynamic role within the community to strengthen and support it as a community of learners.

An educator may take the lead role in an online course that promotes community development, but that lead needs to be shared among community members. For example, Enomoto and Tabata (2000) found that, as the course progressed, it transformed into a "student directed, peer learning experience." At the start of the course, students had limited exchanges with peers. However, as the assignments progressed, so did the number of interchanges among students. Their messages developed a more personal tone. Relationships developed among themselves, and they began to exchange messages on nonacademic subjects, shared frustrations and problems, and began to provide feedback and to introduce new materials to each other. This interaction and degree of engagement fostered greater social bonding and a more student-centered environment. Through their actions, members formed a community of "equals by supporting, complimenting, reinforcing and responding to each other" (Enomoto & Tabata, 2000). Although these findings are interesting, there is no discussion in this study of the design or instructional strategies used to promote engagement and social interaction. No information has been shared as to participants' familiarity with the technology. Nevertheless, their observations do indicate the capacity of an online course to evolve as a community.

Students need to be aware of the pedagogical framework of a learning community. Shapiro and Levine (1999) recommended that students need to be open and to be willing to reframe their roles as learners. A learning community does require students to be active learners, to use teamwork, to be interdependent (Riel & Fulton, 1998), and to understand that the community is the basis of authority. Wiesenberg and Hutton (1996) found that instructors need to encourage students in "becoming self-directed by creating a community of learners who depend on themselves and each other (as opposed to the teacher) for ideas, information and feedback" (p. 14). O'Sullivan and Miron (2000), in their research into building a learning community online in a computer science unit, recognized that students need to "make a paradigm shift in their learning strategies" (p. 7). Having students shift into a learner-centered, active learning environment that fosters a network of social relationships and promotes leadership and collaborative learning does require an induction into this new paradigm. Designers, developers, and online educators need to have support structures in place to foster this paradigm shift.

The development of pedagogical relationships and the collaborative nature of a learning community help to foster the learning process. Serious consideration of pedagogical issues from both instructional and student perspectives need to occur when planning an online course that is striving to promote a learning community. In addition, the pedagogical framework needs to guide access to and the use of technology in promoting a learning community.

Technological Issues

Communities need a gathering place or an online space. In the online environment, this place may be a listserv, chat room, bulletin board, Web site, or a combination. The gathering place has to be supportive of the purpose of the community and must meet the needs of users. Cothrel and Williams (1999) found that the lack of activity in a designated online place (e.g., asynchronous discussion forum) may not be reflective of a failed community. Rather, what is considered the community discussion space may need to be extended beyond what has been designated as the community place. Discussions going on outside the designated place may be contributing greater value to the community than those within the designated area. Therefore, consideration needs to be given to the various online places where people gather.

Jonassen et al. (1999) argued that technology plays a critical role in a constructivist learning environment, because it provides the means for "storing, organizing, and reformulating the ideas that are contributed by each community member" (p. 118). Technology assists in representing the synthesis of student and collective thinking within this community. Using these telecommunication tools and applications effectively in developing and sustaining learning communities within online courses is a challenge. However, scholarly literature in the areas of computer-mediated communication, online environments, and learning networks should be used to guide the selection and utilization of various technological tools and devices that may be appropriate within online courses.

One of the challenges in the creation of learning communities lies in creating a sound technological environment. Hill (2001) has found that technology needs to be flexible and people need to experience minimal technical "glitches" if community is to be fostered. In Kearsley's (2000) *Online Education*, a number of key questions arose in terms of hardware and software environments that impact the creation of online learning communities. He highlighted a few of the problems that may hinder the development of community. For example, participants who access the online environment using a lower bandwidth may not be able to successfully use compressed desktop videoconferencing or may become frustrated with the length of download times. The storing and archiving of threaded discussion messages may be an issue. Barriers such as connectivity may impact who can or cannot connect to the learning environment, as well as the quality and quantity of their interactions. Other issues, such as server connections and limitations or constraints within software, may hinder the depth and breadth of community development.

The technical design of the online environment has an impact on community development. Brown (1997) has studied the features of an effective online course focusing on the pedagogical rationale of the design. She has identified hypertext, active and collaborative learning, and learner-centeredness as three central design features that need to be considered in creating online courses that promote community. First, hypermedia and hypertext provide greater control for the user and provide diverse sources and pathways to explore. Second, designing a collaborative and active learning environment requires compatible technology to sustain purposeful learning. Third, learner-centeredness has an association with the interface design. The interface has to be responsive to the learner's needs. It needs to be intuitive to the user, must complement the learning goals, and put learning to the forefront. From a technical perspective, the interaction design of the online community needs to support intuitive and user-friendly orientation, navigation, usability, and functionality (Kristof & Satran, 1995).

Preece (2000) believed an environment that promotes community needs to address sociability (social interaction) and usability (focus on human computer interaction). Preece stated that good usability of software provides intuitive and easy completion of tasks. The interface also needs to be consistent. Items such as dialogue, navigation, feedback, and archiving features must all be factored into the design of technological environments suited to the target audience. The following dimensions of human diversity have an impact on online community design: physical, cognitive and perceptual, personality, cultural, experiences, gender, age, and capability (Shneiderman, 1998). Therefore, linking the needs of the target audience with user characteristics and preferences is critical when creating the interface design to support sociability.

Kowch and Schwier (1997) claimed that the technology needs to permit each of the following conditions to exist in a virtual learning community: negotiation, intimacy, commitment, and engagement. Selecting or designing digital media to meet such conditions is a serious challenge and has a bearing on developing online courses that foster community development.

The "use of the technology does not spontaneously cause communities to occur; communities of learners must be planned" (Moller, 1998, p. 120). The essence of community is related to the nature of human experiences and interactions mediated within the online environment. The creation and promotion of a community of learners involves an effort by all stakeholders and it takes time. In the design process, an instructional designer cannot create a community. Rather, one can plan and create conditions that foster and nurture the evolution of community. Given the establishment of relationships, intimacy, and trust through effective pedagogical strategies, technology can be used to create an environment in which people can engage in learning experiences that foster the development of community.

Community Building

Communities are complex. It is not simply a matter of applying a number of specific rules or guidelines. Rather, it "is an act of supporting the natural development of relationships" (Schwier, 2001, p. 1). Several factors need to be considered when creating learning environments that promote community. First, there needs to be an atmosphere within the online environment that is conducive to a learning community. The atmosphere of an online course needs to be "failure safe" (Hill, 2001, p. 9). Participants need a safe environment where they can express their feelings and thoughts, are able to freely work and communicate, and are able to learn from their mistakes without feeling intimidated. The development of community is based to a large degree on trust (McLellan, 1997, 1998; Poole, 2000). If members do not feel comfortable and safe or lack trust within a community, they might not actively contribute to the community (Haythornthwaite et al., 2000).

The encouragement of an "atmosphere of adventure" (Hill, 2001, p. 9) and the promotion of a togetherness environment are other factors to be nurtured within an online environment. Lowell and Persichitte (2000) found that developing a sense of connection within the course could assist in improving the quality of learner interactions within a virtual community. It is the nature, not the quantity, of interactions that leads to a sense of connection. To foster an environment of trust, friendship, and respect, communication barriers associated with the academic, social, and technological elements need to be eliminated. The "establishment of importance of community at the inception" (Hill, 2001, p. 10) must be made explicit to all members. This helps people to appreciate the benefits and the value of a community and to be aware of how they can take advantage of the various opportunities it provides. If this does not occur, it is more difficult to foster a learning community. For example, Brown (2001) found participants in her study who did not develop a sense of community. They did not perceive community to exist online and they did not place a high priority on devoting time to fostering relationships. If an educator and the designer want to foster a community philosophy, they need to make participants explicitly aware of it and to provide opportunities to engage in contributing to the evolution of a community and to fostering a sense of connection.

Selwyn (2000) demonstrated that participants need to foster community within the space they are using. It cannot be assumed that, if people have access to online forums and are of the same profession, a communal or a collaborative culture will emerge and prosper. In his study of teachers using electronic discussion groups over a period of 24 months, teachers used the forum for information and empathetic exchanges, but with no fostering of community. For example, a large portion of the online discussion originated with a small core group of participants. Why did the other participants not actively engage in the online forum? The discussions were stimulated by personal reasons. For this group, no community or group identity developed. Rather, only personal identities emerged.

Schwier (2001) described communities as being multifaceted. The social, personal, academic, and cultural dimensions cannot be overlooked in creating the online learning environment. In his learning community model for using asynchronous communication, Moller (1998) has identified two functions of a community: social reinforcement (meeting self-esteem needs) and information exchange (involves collaboration and constructing knowledge). He has put forth the idea that within the learning community there are three types of supports, which to some degree overlap with each other: academic, intellectual, and interpersonal. Providing support and activities in these three areas helps to foster the learning community.

The evolution of a community does take time and not all members within a course will have the same sense of community. As part of her theory, Brown (2001) has developed time triangles to represent the amount of time new and veteran online students spend in the following four areas: community building, course content, teaching method, and technology. She has found that veteran students spend a greater degree of time focused on community building because they are familiar with the technology and pedagogy used in online courses. In contrast, new students spend more time on becoming familiar with the technology, the content, and collaborative and learner-centred pedagogy. This time triangle concept is reflective of the experiences of most students in online courses and online programs. However, it may be inferred that a person works through each level of the time triangle in a linear fashion. But is that an accurate inference? Becoming familiar with specific technology, content, and pedagogy may occur simultaneously. In addition, course content and teaching methods have been identified as part of the triangle, but no explanation has been given as to what are the critical issues taking students' time. How can they be used to help support and foster community building?

Brown (2001) also identified three levels of community development. The first level is online acquaintance or the making of friends. At this level, participants find others who have similar backgrounds or ideas. Prior to this level, new participants need to become familiar with and confident with the technology and the learning environment. The second level is community conferment or acceptance. Brown noted that many participants referred to this as "being like a membership card for the community of learners" (p. 24). There is a sense of personal satisfaction and an affiliation with the larger community as a result of extensive interactions and discussions within the course. The final stage is camaraderie. At this level, participants have been involved in long-term interactions and have developed various affiliations with other participants. These individuals may have enrolled in other classes together, communicated outside of various courses and may use other technologies to interact. Brown's three levels help to promote an understanding of the process of community development. However, she does not examine the design of the course, specific pedagogical issues, or how specific technological factors influence the development process.

The process of developing a learning community in an online course is only one aspect of the capacity of a learning community. From Brown's (2001) research, when students associate at the camaraderie level they have developed long-term associations, trust relationships, respect for members of a community and identify as members of the community. This affiliation is associated with the online course but also with the larger learning community outside of the course. For example, McLellan (1997, 1998) found that the virtual community in a course dissolved at the end of the semester, but concurrently long-term relationships were established and were evident as part of a larger community. The essence of the community can extend beyond the online course. However, a degree of adaptability needs to exist for such a community to be resilient beyond the course. This leads to the question of what conditions help community members to foster this community association beyond the scope of the online course. How can educational organizations capitalize on the potential of long-term learning based on the existing community milieu?

CONCLUSION

A building contractor begins a construction project by carefully studying blueprints as a guide to laying the groundwork and building the foundation for the project. The careful installation of footings, the use of supports, and careful construction provide a solid foundation for what is to be constructed on this base. The same is true in laying the foundation for the creation of online learning communities. The foundation needs firm footings and structures in place to allow for future scaffolding and the building of a community.

Although there is as yet no accepted set of rules or blueprints for community building, there are concepts and theories (e.g., the seminal concepts of gemeinschaft and gesellschaft), studies, strategies, and examples that hold much promise and can be used to guide our thinking and practice in developing online courses that foster learning communities. Designing courses that support community development also calls for designing dynamic learning environments that foster a learning culture. It is dynamic action within social groups, which gather together, mediated by technology, taking on shared responsibility for their own learning, that nurtures community development. It involves members of the community sharing their expertise and, through multiple means of communication and collaborative effort, accomplish tasks and meet learning outcomes that are valued by the community (Bielaczyc & Collins, 1999). Synergistic relationships are vital components of a learning community.

One can extrapolate key factors from the literature and formulate a series of guidelines that educational stakeholders may use as they develop and nurture online learning communities. These guidelines fall into two distinct categories: the creating of online learning communities and the sustaining of online learning communities.

FIVE GUIDELINES FOR
CREATING AN ONLINE LEARNING COMMUNITY

Course developers and instructors must pay attention to a number of basic issues as they begin to plan and develop online courses that foster a strong sense of being a community of learners. First, there is a need for an awareness of community and of the sense and the value of a learning community. These individuals must ask themselves what factors they need to be aware of when designing and developing an online course and a learning environment that will foster a sense of community among course participants.

Second, design issues for online courses that support community need to be addressed. What can developers and instructors deliberately do in designing a learning environment that will provide opportunities for participants to develop and influence the growth of a community of learners? As they reflect on these questions, these individuals need to consider how they can create and implement mechanisms that will create an online culture based on the four cornerstones of communication, collaboration, interaction, and participation. For example, what role will communication have in online events? Is it practical for instructors and/or students to work together in small groups? How can various small groups and large groups interact within a course and at the same time interact with people outside of the online course structure? Consideration must be given to the technical design of the course and to the online communication applications used if the learning environment is to support interpersonal interaction and to foster the mediated sharing of human experience.

Third, mechanisms need to be in place that will facilitate the collaboration of community. Educational stakeholders, who support the development of learning communities, need to examine the mechanisms that are being used to sustain feelings of affiliation and connection within online courses, between online courses, and beyond particular course environments. It is one thing to strive to create a sense of community within an online course. But what mechanisms are in place to facilitate the sense of community connection beyond a particular course?

To achieve Brown's (2001) third level of community development, camaraderie, people must be aware of and have access to a variety of tools and applications that will accommodate and facilitate ongoing interaction and communication beyond the course environment. What technical factors and applications must educational stakeholders consider to accommodate the continuous evolution of a community of learners?

Fourth is the creation of community within the big picture. The starting point here is to understand what is a learning community within an online learning environment. If the notion of learning community is to be fostered within courses, it is critical for educators to look beyond the scope of courses and to understand how the concept of a learning community can be interwoven throughout the course, the curriculum, the institution, and globally within professional organizations and professional thinking. Kearsley (2000) suggests expanding community beyond the course environment by providing discussion forums that go beyond online courses, the creation and continuous updating of a directory of all participants, and the accommodation of functional user accounts for an indefinite period of time.

Within online course environments, educational organizations determine what will be learned. However, adapting learning modalities into noncourse environments puts greater control and autonomy in the hands of community members. As a result, leadership becomes a vital feature in fostering long-term learning relationships. Therefore, how can educational stakeholders work to develop and nurture a long-term learning philosophy within online learning communities?

Fifth and finally, ongoing research is required to provide direction and support for the development of learning communities. Designers and instructors of online courses are in a favourable situation, where they can take advantage of opportunities to conduct action research. Data gathered from online participants and online events can be used to feed into iterative design decisions for the purpose of enhancing the online learning community environment to best meet the needs of participants. Other research methodologies may also be used to extract empirical data that can be used to develop and sustain understanding of online learning communities.

SIX GUIDELINES FOR
SUSTAINING AN ONLINE LEARNING COMMUNITY

Although fostering and sustaining an online learning community can be addressed within particular online courses, consideration must also be given in how learning communities can be nurtured within educational institutions. As noted earlier, breaking down course walls with the purpose of expanding communication and facilitating greater interaction among learners is a continuing challenge in sustaining a learning community.

In Lock's (2003) multi-case study research, she examined how the concept of community was developed, realized, and sustained within virtual in-service teacher learning environments. From the study, she identified five elements required to sustain online communities: "commonality, commitment, communication, connection, and the capacity to grow" (p. 317). Further, she noted that there is an interconnecting relationship between the five elements. These elements can be used as guidelines for sustaining online learning communities.

First, commonality is the need for a common element that draws and keeps people together such as the articulation and acceptance of a shared vision, goals, and aspirations of the community. What is the purpose of the group and of the community and how does this purpose influence group and community members? Mitchell and Sackney (2001) claim that there needs to be "some sort of 'glue' that holds the members together." All factors creating the cohesiveness of the community must help to sustain it over time and through its evolution. Community members have an active role in shaping the vision, the understandings, and the goals of the community's development and must be continually responsive to the needs of the membership.

Second, there is a need for a level of personal commitment to the community. To sustain a learning community requires personal investment and commitment by all community members. What a person is willing to commit to in the community is based on personal motivation in belonging to and interacting within the community. The level of personal commitment varies with each person and within particular situations.

Third, communication needs to be "ongoing, mutual and responsive" (Lock, 2003, p. 318). Communication needs to be purposeful and relevant to the work of the community members. Consideration needs to be given to ways people can communicate online over time, private and public communication, and how communication can be archived so newcomers can glean an understanding of the evolution community.

Fourth, there is a need for a feeling of connection that reinforces the desire to continue to contribute to the community. The sense of meeting, participating, affiliating, trusting, and belonging are all attractors that may help in sustaining community. Embedded in the community is the need for communion, "the act of sharing in one another's traumas, joys, and eurekas" (Grubb & Hines, 2000, p. 375) if community is to survive the challenges of its evolution. Community membership will vary over time and this no doubt will have an impact on the cohesiveness of the community. Course designers and learning community members may need to explore ways in which, over time, they create opportunities for strengthening relationships and the sense of group affiliation.

Consideration needs to be given to the development and support of community leaders. Sustaining an online learning community requires the development of a philosophy of community that engages leaders, students, instructors, and administrators who value and support the idea of a learning community. These individuals must have a personal investment in nurturing and expanding the sense of community. It may well be these individuals who take a learning community to new levels of accomplishment and who expand the scope of the initial vision of the community. Those individuals, through their personal interactions and their sense of connectedness, may well act as role models for other members of the learning community. From a designer and developer perspective, then, how can the leadership role be supported and nurtured with the purpose of sustaining the development of a learning community?

Fifth, the capacity for the community to grow requires sufficient members interested and engaged in sustaining it. The community needs to have capability to evolve and expand to meet the needs of members. The technology used for the online gathering place needs to be flexible to accommodate growth and capable of functioning in support of life and longevity of the community within and beyond course environments.

A sixth guideline is the need to articulate and to apply necessary knowledge, skills, and attributes that facilitate the development and the evolution of a sense of community. Lawrence (1999) argued that online instructors have a critical role in developing and sustaining the online learning community. It is the instructors who must intentionally create a climate that fosters collaboration and interaction. For online instructors to be in a position to sustain a learning community, what knowledge, skills, and attributes do they need to possess in order to achieve this goal? What intentional actions do they need to take within the online environment to foster collaboration and to sustain a learning community? These questions need to be explored by all the online community participants.

Educational stakeholders who support an online learning community need to consider how institutional, organizational, and interpersonal factors can be utilized to meet these goals. Mitchell and Sackney (2001), in their learning community model, identify three capacities: personal, interpersonal, and organizational. It is in the building of organizational and interpersonal capacities that educational stakeholders must pay particular attention to expanding and sustaining a learning community over time.

Within an educational institution, decision makers must examine how they can utilize the knowledge, skills, and attributes of those who have developed a sense of community within and among online courses and who utilize this resource in transforming and sustaining the sense of community within a larger context. Consideration must also be given to the permeability of course walls in terms of accommodating interaction among and between community members (past and present) who may or may not be enrolled within specific courses. How flexible is the administrative structure in accommodating the fluid nature of the learning community over time?

In conclusion, it can be said that, as members of an online learning community, managers, designers, educators, and students must accept new responsibilities and new roles. The integration of such characteristics as "ownership, social interaction, group identity, individual identity, participation and knowledge construction" (Misanchuk & Anderson, 2001, p. 5) is needed in the evolution of strong online learning communities. Administrators, instructional designers, and online educators play key roles in planning and developing these structures and in fostering the relationships that help build communities. In a word, it is the informed initiative of members and the leadership of the community that influence and foster and sustain the vibrancy and resiliency of an online learning community.

REFERENCES

Bauman, M. (1997, April). *Online learning communities*. Paper presented at the Second Annual Teaching in the Community Colleges Online Conference TCC-L Conference. Retrieved July 14, 2006, from http://kolea.kcc.hawaii.edu/tcc/tcc_conf97/pres/bauman.html

Benbunan-Fich, R., & Hiltz, S.R. (2003). Mediators of the effectiveness of online courses. *IEEE Transactions On Professional Communication, 46*(4), 298-312.

Bielaczyc, K., & Collins, A. (1999). Learning communities in classrooms: Advancing knowledge for a lifetime. *NASSP Bulletin, 83*(604), 4-10.

Bonk, C. J., & Cunningham, D. J. (1998). Searching for learner-centered, constructivist, and sociocultural components of collaborative educational learning tools. In C. J. Bonk & K.S. King (Eds.), *Electronic collaborators: Learner-centered technologies for literacy, apprenticeship, and discourse* (pp. 25-20). Mahwah, NJ: Erlbaum.

Bourdeau, J., & Bates, A. (1997). Instructional design for distance learning. In S. Dijkstra, N. M. Seel, F. Schott, & R. D. Tennyson (Eds.), *Instructional design: International perspectives: Vol. 2. Solving Instructional Design Problems* (pp. 369-397). Mahwah, NJ: Erlbaum.

Brown, A. (1997). Designing for learning: What are the essential features of an effective online course? *Australian Journal of Educational Technology, 12*(2). Retrieved July 14, 2006, from http://www.ascilite.org.au/ajet/ajet13/brown.html

Brown, R. E. (2001). The process of community-building in distance learning classes. *Journal of Asynchronous Learning Networks, 5*(2), 18-35. Retrieved July 14, 2006, from http://www.aln.org/publications/jaln/v5n2/pdf/v5n2_brown.pdf

Conrad, D. (2002). Deep in the hearts of learners: Insights into the nature of online community. *Journal of Distance Education, 17*(1), 1-19.

Conrad, D. (2005). Building and maintaining community in cohort-based online learning. *Journal of Distance Education, 20*(1), 1-20.

Cothrel, J., & Williams, R. L. (1999). On-line communities: Helping them form and grow. *Journal of Knowledge Management, 3*(1), 54-60.

Dennen, V. P. (2000). Task structuring for on-line problem based learning: A case study. *Educational Technology and Society, 3*(3), 329-336. Retrieved July 14, 2006, from http://ifets.ieee.org/periodical/vol_3_2000/d08.pdf

Enomoto, E., & Tabata, L. (2000). *Creating virtual learning communities through distance learning technologies: A course examined.* Retrieved July 14, 2006, from http://kolea.kcc.hawaii.edu/tcc/tcon2k/paper/paper_enomotoe.html

Garrison, D. R. (2000). Theoretical challenges for distance education in the 21st century: A shift form structural to transactional issues. *International Review of Research in Open and Distance Learning, 1*(1). Retrieved July 14, 2006, from http://www.irrodl.org/index.php/irrodl/article/view/2/22

Grubb, A., & Hines, M. (2000). Tearing down barriers and building communities: Pedagogical strategies for the web-based environment. In R. A. Cole (Ed.) *Issues in Web-based pedagogy: A critical primer* (pp. 365-380). Westport, CT: Greenwood.

Haythornthwaite, C., Kazmer, M. M., Robins, J., & Shoemaker, S. (2000). Community development among distance learners: Temporal and technological dimensions. *Journal of Computer Mediated Communication, 6*(1). Retrieved July 14, 2006, from http://jcmc.indiana.edu/vol6/issue1/haythornthwaite.html

Herrmann, F. (1998). Building on-line communities of practice: An example and implications. *Educational Technology, 34*(1), 16-23.

Hill, J. R. (2001, April). *Building community in Web-based learning environments: Strategies and techniques.* Paper presented at the AusWeb01 Seventh Australian World Wide Web Conference, Lismore, Australia. Retrieved July 14, 2006, from http://ausweb.scu.edu.au/aw01/papers/refereed/hill/paper.html

Hunter, B. (2002). Learning in the virtual community depends upon changes in local communities. In K. A. Renninger & W. Shumar (Eds.). *Building virtual communities: Learning and change in cyberspace* (pp. 96-126). Cambridge, UK: Cambridge University Press.

Jonassen, D. H. (2000). *Computers as Mindtools for schools: Engaging critical thinking* (2nd. ed). Upper Saddle River, NJ: Prentice Hall.

Jonassen, D. H., Peck, K. L, & Wilson, B. G. (1999). *Learning with technology: A constructivist perspective.* Upper Saddle River, NJ: Prentice Hall.

Jonassen, D. H., Peck, K. L., & Wilson, B. G. (1998). *Creating technology-supported learning communities.* Retrieved July 14, 2006, from http://carbon.cudenver.edu/~bwilson/learncomm.html

Kearsley, G. (2000). *Online education: Learning and teaching in cyberspace.* Belmont, CA: Wadsworth.

Kowch, E., & Schwier, R. (1997). Considerations in the construction of technology-based virtual learning communities. *Canadian Journal of Education Communication, 26*(1), 1-12.

Kozma, R. (2000). Reflections on the state of educational technology research and development. *Educational Technology Research and Development, 48*(1), 5-15.

Kristof, R., & Satran, A. (1995). *Interactivity by design: Creating and communicating with new media*. Mountain View, CA: Adobe Press.

Lawrence, R. L. (1999). Cohorts in cyberspace: Creating community online. *Proceedings of the 19th Annual Alliance/ACE Conference*, Saratoga Springs, NY. Retrieved July 14, 2006, from http://www.nl.edu/academics/cas/ace/facultypapers/RandeeLawrence_Cohorts.cfm

Lock, J. V. (2003). *Building and sustaining virtual communities*. Unpublished doctoral dissertation, University of Calgary, Alberta, Canada.

Lowell, N. O., & Persichitte, K. A. (2000). A virtual ropes course: Creating online community. *ALN Magazine, 4*(1). Retrieved July 14, 2006, from http://www.sloan-c.org/publications/magazine/v4n1/lowell.asp

Luppicini, R. (2003). Categories of virtual learning communities for educational design. The *Quarterly Review of Distance Education, 4*(4), 409-416.

McLellan, H. (1997). Creating virtual communities via the Web. In B. H. Kahn (Ed.), *Web-based instruction* (pp. 185-190). Englewood Cliffs, NJ: Educational Technology Publications.

McLellan, H. (1998). The Internet as a virtual learning community. *Journal of Computing in Higher Education, 9*(2), 92-112.

Misanchuk, M., & Anderson, T. (2001). Building community in an online learning environment: communication, cooperation and collaboration. *Proceedings of the Annual Mid-South Instructional Technology Conference*. Retrieved July 14, 2006, from http://www.mtsu.edu/~itconf/proceed01/19.pdf

Mitchell, C., & Sackney, L. (2000). *Profound improvement: Building capacity for a learning community*. Lisse, Netherlands: Swets & Zeitlinger.

Mitchell, C., & Sackney, L. (2001). Building capacity for a learning community. *Canadian Journal of Education Administration, 19*. Retrieved July 14, 2006, from http://umanitoba.ca/publications/cjeap/articles/mitchellandsackney.html

Moller, L. (1998). Designing communities of learners for asynchronous distance education. *Educational Technology Research and Development, 46*(4), 115–122.

Murphy, K. L., Mahoney, S. E., & Harvell, T. H. (2000). Roles of contracts in enhancing community building in Web courses. *Educational Technology & Society, 3*(3), 409-421. Retrieved June 23, 2006, from http://www.ifets.info/journals/3_3/e03.pdf

Nipper, S. (1989). Third generation distance learning and computer conferencing. In R. Mason & A. Kaye (Eds.), *Mindweave: Communication, computers and distance education* (pp. 63-73). Oxford, England: Pergamon Press.

O'Sullivan, M., & Miron, D. (2000) Building a learning community online in a second year computer science unit. *UltiBASE Journal*. Retrieved June 23, 2006, from http://ultibase.rmit.edu.au/Articles/online/sullivan1.htm

Palloff, R. M., & Pratt, K. (1999). *Building learning communities in cyberspace: Effective strategies for the online classroom*. San Francisco: Jossey-Bass.

Poole, D. M. (2000). Student participation in a discussion-oriented online course: A case study. *Journal of Research on Computing in Education, 33*(2), 162-177.

Preece, J. (2000). *Online communities: Designing usability, support sociability.* Chichester, United Kingdom: Wiley.

Riel, M. (1996). *The Internet: A land to settle rather than an ocean to surf and a new "place" for school reform through community development.* Retrieved July 14, 2006, from http://www.globalschoolnet.org/GSH/teach/articles/netasplace.html

Riel, M., & Fulton, K. (1998, April). *Technology in the classroom: Tools for doing things differently or doing different things.* Paper presented at the Annual Meeting of the American Educational Research Association, San Diego, CA.

Riel, M., & Fulton, K. (2001). The role of technology in supporting learning communities. *Phi Delta Kappan, 82*(7), 518–523.

Rovai, A. P. (2002). Building sense of community at a distance. *International Review of Research in Open and Distance Learning, 3*(1). Retrieved July 14, 2006, from http://www.irrodl.org/index.php/irrodl/article/view/79/153

Schrage, M. (1990). *Shared minds: The new technologies of collaboration.* New York: Random House.

Schwier, R. A. (2001). Catalysts, emphases and elements of virtual learning communities: Implications for research and practice. *Quarterly Review of Distance Education, 2*(1), 5-18.

Schwier, R. A. (2002). *Shaping the metaphor of community in online learning environments.* Paper presented to the International Symposium on Educational Conferencing. Banff, Alberta, June 1, 2002. Retrieved July 14, 2006, from http://cde.athabascau.ca/ISEC2002/papers/schwier.pdf

Selwyn, N. (2000). Creating a "connected" community? Teachers' use of an electronic discussion group. *Teachers College Record, 102*(4), 750-778.

Selznick, P. (1996). In search of community. In W. Vitek & W. Jackson (Eds.), *Rooted in the land* (pp. 195-203). New Haven, CT: Yale University Press.

Shapiro, N. S., & Levine, J. H. (1999). *Creating learning communities: A practical guide to winning support, organizing for change, and implementing programs.* San Francisco: Jossey-Bass.

Shneiderman, B. (1998). *Designing the user interface: Strategies for effective human computer interaction* (3rd ed.). Reading, MA: Addison-Wesley.

Tam, M. (2000). Constructivism, instructional design, and technology: Implications for transforming distance learning. *Educational Technology & Society, 3*(2). Retrieved July 14, 2006, from http://ifets.ieee.org/periodical/vol_2_2000/tam.html

Weisenberg, F., & Hutton, S. (1996). Teaching a graduate program using computer-mediated conferencing software: Distance education futures. *Journal of Distance Education, 11*(1). Retrieved July 14, 2006, from http://cade.athabascau.ca/vol11.1/wiesenberg.html

Wilson, B. (1996). Introduction: What is a constructivist learning environment? In B. Wilson (Ed.), *Constructivist learning environments: Case studies in instructional design* (pp. 3-10). Englewood Cliffs, NJ: Educational Technology Publications.

PART III

RESEARCH ON ONLINE LEARNING COMMUNITIES

CHAPTER 9

CONNECTIONS IN WEB-BASED LEARNING ENVIRONMENTS

A Research-Based Model for Community Building

Janette R. Hill, Arjan Raven, and Seungyeon Han

The purpose of this chapter is to explore best practices for community building in Web-based learning environments (WBLEs). The study took place in two Web-based courses at 2 universities. An embedded case study design was used, and multiple sources of evidence (e.g., chat and bulletin board transcripts, interviews, and surveys) were gathered to inform the results. Overall, participants in both courses indicated some sense of community, albeit limited in scope. Learners also indicated a stronger connection with their team members than with the larger class group. While more research is needed, our study indicates that incorporating community building strategies during course design, and encouraging interactions between participants during the course, can contribute to the long-term viability and use of WBLEs in institutions of higher education.

Online Learning Communities
pp. 153–167

INTRODUCTION

The use of electronic technologies for the delivery of instruction has grown at an exponential rate over the last decade. Institutions of higher education, corporations, and K-12 environments continue to seek ways to use online tools to deliver instruction. Concurrently, the technological infrastructure has expanded in terms of its capabilities and power (Daniel, 1998; Dunderstadt, Atkins, & Van Houweling, 2002; Katz, 1999), increasing learner access to the technologies needed to acquire and share information with other participants. This convergence and growth in interest by educators and learners for learning via distance technologies has enabled an exponential increase in the quantity of distance education offerings across disciplines (e.g., art, history, information systems, education, science) and contexts (Saba, 2005).

While the increased interest in and need for distance education is an exciting development, several challenges associated with the successful implementation of instruction in Web-based learning environments (WBLEs) remain unresolved. Some of the challenges include: retention and high dropout rates, perceived isolation, and no significant difference in terms of learner performance (Hill, 2002; Howell, 2001). Retention has historically presented challenges for distance educators. According to Moore and Kearsley (2004), dropout rates have ranged from 30-50%. While this figure is inclusive of a variety of distance learning technologies (video, print, etc.), the low end of 30% is a considerable percentage to lose in a learning experience. WBLEs, with their high demands psychologically and technically, makes this challenge even more significant (Jun, 2005).

Several factors may contribute to retention challenges in distance education. Factors mentioned in the literature include: lack of prior experience with distance learning, external demands, self-management skills, and motivation (Glenn, 2003; Song, 2005). Another explanation for high dropout rates and dissatisfaction with distance-delivered courses may relate to a lack of a perception of community in courses that are not face-to-face. Learners may feel like they are isolated, creating an experience of lack of presence from others involved in the course (Howell, 2001).

Perception of a community may assist learners with feeling connected or belonging (Halaby, 2000; Joyce, Weil, & Calhoun, 1999). Research in online environments indicates that community building can occur in distance-delivered courses (Hill, 1999a; Palloff & Pratt, 2004), much like community building can occur in virtual teams in the business sector (Lave & Wenger, 1991; Raven, 1999). Given that a sense of a community has been demonstrated to contribute to group performance within a corporate context (Lave & Wenger, 1991), it may prove to be a benefit in a learning context. Discovering the best strategies and techniques for community building may lead to enhanced course outcomes (e.g., retention, satisfaction, learning outcomes) by participants in WBLEs.

Purpose

The purpose of this study was to explore the best practices for community building in WBLEs. In doing so, the study sought to examine specific strategies and techniques designed to facilitate the establishment of an online community. The study was guided by the following general research question: What are the best techniques/strategies to enable community building in WBLEs? This question was addressed through a number of sub-questions, two of which will be focused upon in this chapter: (1) What can we do as designers of, and instructors in, a WBLE to assist the learner in the effective building of community while learning in a Web-based environment? (2) What strategies can learners use to assist themselves (individually and with each other) in community building while engaged in learning in Web-based environments?

Significance of the Study

While considerable research has been conducted in the general area of distance learning, the data bank of empirical studies specific to Web-based environments for learning has only recently been growing (Goodyear, Banks, Hodgson, & McConnell, 2004). As the Web and Internet-based technologies (e.g., bulletin boards, e-mail, streaming video, instant messaging) continue to grow in popularity and use in higher education, we felt that institutions would benefit greatly from investigation of the best practices related to WBLEs; in our case, specifically examining best practices for community building.

Interest in building community is certainly not new, nor is it something isolated to study in the context of higher education. Lave and Wenger (1991) have spent considerable time examining the issues related to forming community in a business and industry setting. Joyce, Weil, and Calhoun (1999) called for the creation of communities of professional educators within a school setting. Halaby (2000) brings the notion of belonging into the classroom setting, emphasizing a need to help learners belong. More recently, Palloff and Pratt (2004) extended their work on community building within higher education settings, focusing on providing hints and tips for the online teacher.

Certainly, this work is useful and adds to our literature base. However, much of the work completed to date is primarily theoretical, and while based in experience, it is not primarily driven by empirical research. Further, the current work does not define specific models for how to enable community building in a Web-based environment—both from the teacher and student perspective. We need data-driven strategies and models, presenting techniques on both sides of the desk, so that others can test the robustness of the models in a variety of environments.

RESEARCH PLAN

Research Design

An embedded case study design was used for this study, involving the use of multiple cases or embedded units, within a larger context (Merriam, 1997). The unit of study in the case was the individual faculty member or student involved in the WBLE. Multiple sources of evidence (e.g., mid-term focus groups, end-of-term surveys, transcripts of online discussions (chat rooms and bulletin boards)) were used to triangulate the data, thus addressing possible concerns with internal validity (Yin, 2002). This approach has been used by one of the researchers in previous research (Hill, 1997b; Hill & Hannafin, 1997), and has proven successful when looking to describe rich contexts and for model development (Hill, 1999b).

Selection and Description of the Participants

Two groups of participants were engaged in this study. One consisted of an instructor and learners involved in the master's level course information technology infrastructures in a college of business at a university in a large metropolitan area. The other consisted of an instructor and learners involved in the master's level course instructional design in a college of education at a university in a rural area. The population included university instructors, instructional design experts, and working professionals returning to school from various sectors of business, industry (e.g., information technology management, technical support, Web development), and education (K-12 and higher education).

The courses were selected for two primary reasons. First, involvement in the courses was voluntary. Although for many learners the courses were required for completion of the degrees, they decided when and how to take the course. Most learners enter with a high level of interest and motivation. Second, learners begin the course with a variety of backgrounds, as well as differences in their technology experience. This variety is essential for examining strategies and techniques across potential learners. Two groups comprised the sample of this study: university faculty as subject matter experts to help inform the design, development, and implementation of the courses, and learners enrolled in the courses during summer term.

WBLE Development

A systematic approach for the design of instruction was used to guide the design and development of the courses Information Infrastructures and Instructional Design. The process was both in-depth and comprehensive, covering a 3-4 month period and involving a team of designers and subject-matter experts in both instances. Instructional design experts helped inform the design, development, and implementation of the courses while the subject matter experts informed the content used within the courses.

Various technologies were used in the development and implementation of both courses. These included: Dreamweaver for the development of Web pages, Active Server Pages with VisualBasicScript to enable high-end capabilities in the Web site, database technologies to support the overall site infrastructure, and Blackboard and WebCT for the integration of e-mail, bulletin board, and chat systems.

Measures and Instrumentation

A combination of positivistic and interpretivist techniques were used in gathering evidence for the study. Various instruments were used to facilitate data collection for the study: surveys, interviews, observations, and content analysis of discussion transcripts. Positivistic techniques were used to generate individual difference measures for each case. Interpretivist techniques were used to monitor the use of community-building strategies and techniques.

Settings and Procedures

Implementation of the courses took place over a 7-8 week period during a summer term. An initial face-to-face meeting was held for both courses, as was a mid-term face-to-face meeting for debrief of the experi-

ence to date. The classes met for asynchronous discussions in the chat
room. For chat room discussions, the classes were divided into two groups
of 10-15 learners to better facilitate asynchronous discussions. The chat
sessions for each group were held two times during the week and lasted,
on average, one hour. Follow-up bulletin board discussions were also held
each week to extend the conversations during chat sessions.

Data were collected in a variety of environments. Pilot testing with
learners in the spring and data gathering with learners in the summer
took place in the context in which the WBLE was used, including campus
computer labs and the learners' homes/places of employment (depending
on where they have access to the Web). A combination of questionnaires,
focus groups, and content analysis of transcripts from online discussions
were used to gather data from learners. The facilities and necessary
equipment for data gathering were fully established at each institution.

ANALYSIS

To the extent possible, the collection, organization, and initial analysis of
data occurred concurrently. Previous research indicates that this assists
with indicating gaps in data as they are gathered and allow for adaptations in the process (e.g., need for additional information) (Glaser &
Strauss, 1967; Hert, 1992; Hill & Hannafin, 1997). One "gap" that did
occur related to the number of participants. We did experience a small
reduction in participants in both courses, with the final number of participants being 21 in the information technology infrastructures course
(reduced from 23), and 22 participants in the instructional design course
(reduced from 24).

In-depth data analysis took place throughout the academic year following the offering of the courses. One level of in-depth analysis involved
reading through and coding the transcripts from the online chat and bulletin board discussions. As the researchers read the data, preestablished
codes were used to mark-up the data (Ericsson & Simon, 1993; Hill &
Hannafin, 1997). Additional codes were established as themes and patterns not readily applicable to the established categories emerged.

Another level of in-depth analysis involved chunking sections of the
data related to specific research questions according to preestablished
strategies and techniques for community building (Hill, 1999b). These
coding and analysis techniques have been documented in the literature
(Bogdan & Biklen, 2002; Krathwohl, 1998; Yin, 2002) and were used by
one of the researchers in previous studies (Hill, 1997b; Hill & Hannafin,
1997). Pattern matching was used to inform the generation of an overall
list of strategies and techniques—instructor and student—for community

building in WBLEs. The overall list was then analyzed for themes and patterns, enabling the creation of a theoretical model for community building in WBLEs.

Data Presentation. The content of each student's and instructor's postings in the chat room and on the bulletin boards was analyzed to determine the number and type of constructs. In total, over 400 pages of transcripts from the chat rooms and bulletin boards were analyzed and coded. Overall, 13 constructs in participants' postings were identified: active interaction, socially constructed meaning, expressions of support and encouragement, collaborative learning, sharing information/ resources, acknowledgement of others, chitchat, teacher initiative, student initiative, teacher response, student response, student evaluation, and teacher evaluation. To help inform the results, the data were first divided into two main categories: infrastructure strategies and interaction strategies. To refine our analysis, we further divided the codes in the interaction strategies category into two other categories: instructor strategies and student strategies. Codes and definitions for strategies included in these categories are displayed in Tables 9.1, 9.2, and 9.3.

The coding and analysis of the transcripts revealed patterns of behavior in the WBLEs. Other sources of data were then used as points of triangulation for the findings: focus group interview notes were reviewed, and

Table 9.1. Codes for Infrastructure Strategies

Codes	Constructs	Definitions Used in the Study
AI	Active interaction	Interactions involving both course content and personal communication; interactions that are purposeful, engaged, energetic.
SCM	Socially constructed meaning	Arguing with or questioning each other with the intent to achieve agreement on issues of meaning.
ESE	Expressions of support and encouragement	Validating other's ideas/sentiments by showing agreement or understanding.
CL	Collaborative learning	Sharing ideas and knowledge among and between learners. Comments directed primarily student to student rather than student to instructor.
SI	Sharing information/resources	Reference by learners to people, ideas, resources, etc.
ACK	Acknowledgement of others	Noting the presence of a person in the chat room or bulletin board space.
CC	Chit chat	Social interactions among participants that are not related to class.

Table 9.2.   Codes for Interaction Strategies—Instructor Strategies

Codes	Constructs	Definitions Used in the Study
TI	Teacher Initiative	Asking question(s) to lead and/or facilitate the discussion.
TR	Teacher Response	Responding to student contributions.
TE	Teacher Evaluation	Evaluation of student contributions.

Table 9.3.   Codes for Interaction Strategies—Student Strategies

Codes	Constructs	Definitions Used in the Study
SI	Student Initiative	Asking question to lead and/or facilitate the discussion.
SR	Student Response	Responding to the teacher or student contributions.
SE	Student Evaluation	Evaluation of student or teacher contributions.

end of term surveys were analyzed. Trends in these data were then compared to the trends and patterns established from the discussion transcripts. Overall, strategies and techniques were adjusted as needed based on the analysis of the additional data points.

FINDINGS

Analysis of the data was an intensive task, cognitively and logistically. Many hours were devoted to reviewing the data and refining the findings, individually and as a team. The results of our efforts are presented below and organized according to our research questions.

What can we do as designers of, and instructors in, a WBLE to assist the learner in the effective building of community while learning in a Web-based environment? Based on data gathered from the learners during implementation, as well as expert review of the course, the data indicated there are several things that designers and instructors can do during the design, development, and implementation stages to help with community building in WBLEs.

One strategy that proved very effective was ensuring that learners have sufficient opportunities to interact with each other as well as with the instructor. Our research indicates that learners want a variety of ways to interact with each other. In the end-of-term surveys, learners in the Information Infrastructures course and the instructional design course indicated that all of the communication technologies (e.g., chat, bulletin boards, e-mail, phone) were working well and were important for facilitating interactions. They also mentioned the importance of having face-to-face meetings. As one respondent put it: "I liked having the 2nd f2f because I think it helped connect with others and do real sharing of information, thoughts, and ideas."

Another strategy used in the instructional design course that proved effective was the use of CSM messages. CSM messages indicated to learners what they could be doing, what they should be doing, and what they must be doing. These messages were sent out by the instructor once or twice a week to remind learners of tasks for the week.

During the midterm evaluation, learners indicated that the CSM messages were important not only for keeping them on track, but also for letting them know that the instructor was there. When asked what they would keep in future classes, students noted: "The CSMs gave helpful information every week" and "CSM—great for organizing and planning."

Yet another strategy that proved effective for community building was the use of teams for completing course work. Because of the nature of the courses, team configurations differed. In the information infrastructures course, teams of two to four worked together; in the instructional design course, teams of two worked together (i.e., design buddies). During midterm focus groups in both courses, the learners indicated that the team members contributed very positively to their sense of belonging and a sense of connection with others in the course. This was also confirmed in the end-of-term surveys where learners reported that their teammates or "buddies" were the greatest contributor to their sense of belonging. The following two quotes illustrate this:

> It was difficult at first to experience any such "group" feeling with the online format. But interestingly enough, this grew exponentially as the course progressed, particularly with the project team.

> Having a design buddy and the interactions with instructor helped me feeling part of the class.

Additional comments related to successful strategies implemented in the course included:

> I found that talking to my design buddy helped a lot.

> I emailed by design buddy with questions.

> I have constantly asked questions to facilitator and to my buddy in order to be able to keep up with class work.

> Communication with Buddy, regular review of WebPages, questions to instructor when appropriate.

What strategies can learners use to assist themselves (individually and with each other) in community building while engaged in learning in Web-based environments? Analysis of surveys, as well as transcripts from various interactions in the courses, indicated that several strategies were used by learners to assist themselves with community building and learning in a Web-based environment. Learners were asked in the mid-term focus groups and end-of-term survey what they were doing to assist themselves with feeling connected in the WBLE. Several learners reported that a daily visit to the Web site to check for new messages on the bulletin boards was useful. While many learners indicated that this was frustrating ("takes too much time"), others stated that the frequent visits helped them with establishing a sense of belonging to the course. A large number of participants also mentioned that asking their buddy questions helped them a lot as a strategy:

> I looked at the website almost everyday. I also did a lot of research outside of the class site on the Internet for coding questions. I used my team members to bounce some questions off as well.

> I tried to stay in touch by going to the web site daily. I emailed my design buddy with questions and also I emailed [instructor] with specific questions. I read everything, probably too much. It was a lot of work to keep up with everything.

Two other closely related community-building strategies used by learners were providing encouragement and support to their peers. Evidence of this was seen throughout bulletin board postings and chat room interactions. Learners engaged in expressing encouragement and supporting each other on a regular basis throughout the term.

Several learners indicated that the experience was somewhat overwhelming. This comment related mainly to the number of messages learners had to read on bulletin boards, in chat sessions, and in e-mail. One strategy mentioned by several learners during mid-term focus groups and the end-of-term surveys was that of scanning; that is, reading for content, not for detail, in order to keep the information exchange manageable.

COMMUNITY BUILDING: A PROCESS-BASED MODEL

It would appear that various community-building strategies and techniques were used during the Information Infrastructures and the Instructional Design courses. To address the overall research question, "What are the best techniques/strategies to enhance community building in WBI?"

**Table 9.4.   Strategies and Techniques for
Community Building on Online Environments**

Infrastructure Strategies	Interaction Strategies
Access to multiple communication technologies.	Read for content not for detail.
Posting of announcements and "what's new" updates.	Encourage and support fellow learners in their efforts.
Personal Web pages for each learner.	Use CSM messages to indicate to learners what they Could be doing, what they Should be doing, and what they Must be doing in terms of the course.
Learners have sufficient opportunities to interact with each other as well as with the instructor.	Use of teams for completing work in the course.
	A daily visit to the Web site to check for new messages on the bulletin boards.

**Table 9.5.   Instructor and Learner Strategies for
Community Building in Online Environments**

Instructor Strategies	Learner Strategies
Provide multiple opportunities for interaction.	Visit the course Web site daily (or every other day at a minimum).
Send out management related messages (e.g., CSMs) on a regular basis.	Provide encouragement and support.
Establish teams so that learners work together to complete tasks.	Scan material posted on the Web site - do not read for detail.
Keep the Web site up-to-date and add in new information on a regular basis to keep things "fresh."	

the strategies and techniques have been divided into two main areas: infrastructure strategies and interaction strategies (see Table 9.4). We have also represented the strategies in terms of those most relevant to different participants, that is, instructor or learner (See Table 9.5).

The results of the study also enabled the creation of a theoretical model for community building and its potential relationship to the creation of a learning community (see Figure 9.1). While more empirical testing of the model is needed, it does exemplify a significant step toward identification of strategies and techniques that can enable community building in WBLEs.

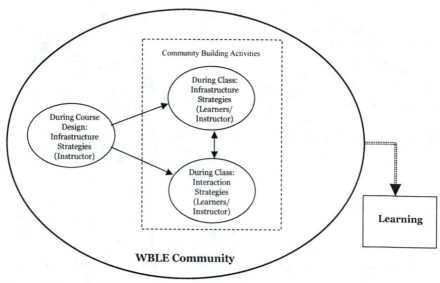

Figure 9.1.   Model for creating community in Web-based learning environments.

The model in Figure 9.1 illustrates how community building strategies may lead to community building activities that take place during a class. As discussed earlier, during course design, the instructor can implement a number of infrastructure strategies that provide a basic framework for community building (e.g., access to multiple communication technologies, posting of announcements and "what's new" updates, and personal Web pages for each learner that included a picture and biographical information). During the class, both instructor and learners can use interaction strategies (e.g., initiating, responding) for community building.

The two sets of strategies (infrastructure and interaction) can lead to enhanced communication during the class, creating opportunities for connections by and between learners and instructor. These connections, in turn, can lead to the emergence of a community that can support a learning outcome. Future research is needed to explore the extent to which the strategies and techniques enable learning to occur.

DISCUSSION AND SUGGESTED NEXT STEPS

This study investigated strategies and techniques for community building in WBLEs. Overall, participants in both courses indicated the use of some community building strategies, leading to some awareness of community, albeit limited in scope. Based on the data we gathered, the impact of the community building strategies seems to occur faster and more readily in teams or small groups. The learners indicated a stronger connection with their team members than with the larger class group. While further investigation needs to be completed to verify this finding, we do feel comfortable in proposing a preliminary implication: focus community-building strategies in small groups within the Web-based course, then look to extend those efforts to the larger class over the duration of the course.

Our recommendation of developing community across and between groups, and over time, mirrors research on learner engagement in online environments completed by Conrad and Donaldson (2001). In their model, Conrad and Donaldson recommend the implementation of strategies for engaged learning in phases, where phase one focuses on the individual and phase four (the last phase) focuses on the overall community. We believe that a similar approach would prove effective for building community in a Web-based environment—first focusing on the individual and, over the duration of the course, moving to teams and finally the overall community. Further research is needed to discover if moving from the individual to the team to the collective is an effective way to enable community building.

As we continue work in this area, we are also beginning to consider different questions and issues to explore. One issue we offer as an area for additional study is that of adjustments to a new teaching and learning environment. As compared to face-to-face classes, WBLEs place more demands on both instructor and learners in terms of amount of time worked, especially in regard to the number of student-instructor and student-student interactions (Briggs, 2005; Spector, 2005). As with regular face-to-face classes, it is better to wait with a summative evaluation of a Web-based course until it has been taught at least twice. The first time around is typically a learning experience for the instructor and the learner; better to use this as a vehicle to determine what works and what doesn't, and then make additional judgments the second—or third—time around.

We also recognize the need for assisting others in the implementation of community building strategies in their own WBLEs. Models and tools to assist with this effort would go a long way toward helping others interesting in building community in their own WBLE. We have proposed a preliminary model for community building in WBLEs. We also encourage others to explore this area and test the viability of the model.

CONCLUSION

By delivering engaging and meaningful instruction in WBLEs, universities can increase their visibility and viability in the twenty-first century educational arena. Further, results from this study can be used to guide and facilitate the design, development, and implementation of WBI to increase interaction and engagement. This, in turn, can lead to higher retention (our experience: 94%) and satisfaction (our experience: high) in online courses at institutions of higher education.

AUTHOR'S NOTE

The authors would like to recognize the work of Joan Davis and Michael Grant. Ms. Davis and the now Dr. Grant were PhD students in the Instructional Technology program at UGA during the study. Without their assistance with building and maintaining the course sites, as well as assistance with data collection, this research would not have been possible.

REFERENCES

Bogdan, R. C., & Biklen, S. K. (2002). *Qualitative research for education: An introduction to theory and methods* (4th ed.). Boston: Allyn & Bacon.

Briggs, S. (2005). Changing roles and competencies of academics. *Active Learning in Higher Education, 6*(3), 256-268.

Conrad, R. M., & Donaldson, J. A. (2004). *Engaging the online learner: Activities and resources for creative instruction.* San Francisco: Jossey-Bass.

Daniel, J. S. (1998). Mega-universities and knowledge media: Technology strategies for higher education. London: Kogan Page.

Dunderstadt, J. J., Atkins, D. E., & Van Houweling, D. (2002). *Higher education in the digital age: Technology issues and strategies for American colleges and universities.* New York: Praeger.

Ericsson, K. A., & Simon, H. (1993). *Protocol analysis: Verbal reports as data* (Rev. ed.). Cambridge, MA: MIT Press.

Glaser, B. G., & Strauss, A. L. (1967). *The discovery of grounded theory: Strategies for qualitative research.* Chicago: Aldine.

Glenn, J. M. L. (2003). E-learning e-volution: Your (digital) future awaits. *Business Education Forum, 57*(4), 8-15.

Goodyear, P., Banks, S., Hodgson, V, & McConnell, D. (2004). Research on networked learning: An overview. In P. Goodyear, S. Banks, V. Hodgson, & D. McConnell (Eds.), *Advances in research on networked learning* (pp. 1-10). Boston: Kluwer.

Halaby, M. (2000). *Belonging: Creating community in the classroom.* New York: Brookline.

Hert, C. A. (1992). Exploring a new model for understanding information retrieval interactions. In D. Shaw (Ed.), *Proceedings of the 55th ASIS Annual Meeting* (pp. 72-75). Pittsburgh, PA.

Hill, J. R. (1997b). The World-Wide Web as a tool for information retrieval: An exploratory study of users' strategies in an open-ended system. *School Library Media Quarterly, 25*(4), 229-236.

Hill, J. R. (1999a, April) *Learning about distance education at a distance: Rewards and challenges*. Paper presented at American Educational Research Association, Montreal, Canada.

Hill, J. R. (1999b). A conceptual framework for understanding information seeking in open-ended information systems. *Educational Technology Research and Design, 47*(1), 5-27.

Hill, J. R. (2002). Strategies and techniques for community-building in Web-based learning environments. *Journal of Computing in Higher Education, 14*(1), 67-86.

Hill, J. R., & Hannafin, M. J. (1997). Cognitive strategies in the use of a hypermedia information system. *Educational Technology Research & Development, 45*(4), 37-64.

Howell, D. (2001). Elements of effective e-learning: Three design methods to minimize side effects of online courses. *College Teaching, 49*(3), 87-90.

Katz, R. N. (1999). Dancing with the devil: Information technology and the new competition in higher education. San Francisco: Jossey-Bass.

Joyce, B. R., Weil, M., & Calhoun, E. (1999). *Models of teaching* (6th ed.). Boston: Allyn & Bacon.

Jun, J. (2005). Understanding e-dropout. *International Journal of E-Learning, 4*(2), 229-240.

Krathwohl, D. R. (1998). Methods of educational and social science research: An integrated approach (2nd ed.). New York: Longman.

Lave, J., & Wenger, E. (1991). *Situated learning: Legitimate peripheral participation*. Cambridge, UK: Cambridge University.

Merriam, S. B. (1997). Qualitative research and case study applications in education. San Francisco: Jossey Bass.

Moore, M. G., & Kearsley, G. (2004). *Distance education: A systems view* (2nd ed.). New York: Wadsworth.

Palloff, R. M., & Pratt, K. (2004). *Collaborating online: Learning together in community*. San Francisco: Jossey-Bass.

Raven, A. (1999). *Knowledge management for new product development meetings: The roles of information technology in shared knowledge creation*. Unpublished doctoral dissertation, University of Southern California.

Saba, F. (2005). Critical issues in distance education: A report from the United States. *Distance Education, 26*(2), 255-272.

Song, L. (2005). *Self-directed learning in online environments: Process, personal attributes, and context*. Unpublished doctoral dissertation, University of Georgia.

Spector, J. M. (2005). Time demands in online instruction. *Distance Education, 26*(1), 5-27.

Yin, R. K. (2002). *Case study research: Design and methods* (3rd ed.). Thousand Oaks, CA: Sage.

CHAPTER 10

IDENTIFYING FACTORS THAT EFFECT LEARNING COMMUNITY DEVELOPMENT AND PERFORMANCE IN ASYNCHRONOUS DISTANCE EDUCATION

Douglas Harvey, Leslie A. Moller, Jason Bond Huett, Veronica M. Godshalk, and Margaret Downs

Asynchronous distance education provides an opportunity for meaningful learning beyond the capacity of the traditional classroom if learning communities are created that encourage knowledge-building through information exchange and social reinforcement. This chapter describes the development of learning communities within the context of asynchronous distance education. To examine the argument that the community effects learning achievement, we studied 12 graduate students enrolled in a graduate-level asynchronous distance education class. The semester-long class, conducted using Internet-based conferencing software, worked on solving four different case studies. The students were arbitrarily assigned to 1 of 3, 4-person teams. The course was constructed as a regular class and not an

Online Learning Communities
pp. 169–187

"experiment." This plan, although sacrificing some research integrity, was felt to better capture the reality of this type of interpersonal interaction. All the student messages were saved for later analysis. The results of both the messages and case studies were compared, showing a significant pattern emerging, indicating the importance of community. The preliminary results indicate a relationship between learning achievement and strength of the community. While, due to a small sample, no statistical significance can be attached to these findings, the data do provide a foundation for a rich discussion. The empirical data are triangulated by qualitative analysis collected through interviews and student journals. The qualitative data support the empirical results and explain why the community may have had its impact by identifying factors that led to the communities' cohesion.

INTRODUCTION

Asynchronous distance education, as a learning tool, has evolved to a point where it is technologically feasible and socially acceptable. With concerns over its effectiveness largely resolved, asynchronous distance education (ADE) offers two potentially distinct advantages over face-to-face instruction: the ability to deliver instruction anytime and any place, thus increasing access for learners who could otherwise not be served and, second, for creating an environment that allows for knowledge-building based on collaborative and reflective learning (Barry & Runyan, 1995; Moller, 1998; Moore & Kearsley, 1996). However, for distance education to reach its potential for knowledge-building, existing pedagogy and the accompanying instructional strategies that include fostering community development must be expanded to exploit the capabilities presented by the technology. One key factor that can inhibit the potential effectiveness of asynchronous distance education is the strategic development of a learning community (Jonassen, Davidson, Collins, Campell, & Haag, 1995; Moller, 1998).

THE ROLE OF COMMUNITY

When the goal of asynchronous distance education is to attain knowledge-building levels, learners must have membership in a community dedicated to learning topic-specific information. According to Wilson and Ryder (1996), "groups become communities when they interact with each other and stay together long enough to form a set of habits and conventions and when they come to depend upon each other for the accomplishment of certain ends." This description is consistent with Shaffer and Anundsen (1993), who wrote that communities can be defined as a dynamic whole that emerges when a group of people share common practices, are interdependent, make decisions jointly, identify themselves with something larger than the sum of their individual relationships, and make long-term commitments to the general group's well-being.

The two basic functions of a learning community are to provide social reinforcement and intellectual exchange (Moller, 1998). A learning community, by providing social reinforcement, creates an opportunity to satisfy a human need for self-esteem, that encourages one of the internal conditions necessary for a learner to be ready and able to learn (Maslow, 1954). McIsaac and Gunawardena (1996) stated that social presence, the degree to which the person feels, or is seen by others as, "real" is a significant factor that affects satisfaction and achievement. Social reinforcement is a natural and positive outcome resulting from others in a community who contribute a sense of identity through shared values, norms, and preferences (Cathcart, Samovar, & Henman, 1996). According to Cathcart et al. (1996), cohesive groups "usually enjoy low turnover and higher participation because members desire continuation of the group and its commitment to goal accomplishment."

Intellectual exchange, a second function of a learning community, is concerned with collaboration and resulting knowledge-building. According to Jonassen (1998), computer-supported collaborative learning allows physically separated learners to create and share knowledge. Exchanging information allows alternate information and perspectives to be considered and learners to actively analyze or organize their own thoughts (O'Malley & Scanlon, 1990; Woodruff, 1996). Neilson (1997), in advocating collaborative learning through technology for organizational learning, states substantiated assumptions, including groups outperforming the best member in complex problem solving, sharing knowledge as a critical element in success, and leveraging knowledge in a rapidly changing environment as advantages of belonging to a community for information exchange.

Meaningful learning requires the learner to be actively engaged in cognitive manipulation of the instructional content or information. To a degree, learning occurs within the teacher or content expert-learner exchanges and dialogues. However, as Moore and Kearsley (1996) point out, "learner to learner interaction is desirable for pedagogical reasons" (p. 131). Intellectual exchange is described as invaluable for the application and evaluation of learning. Gay and Lentini (1995) confirm this assumption, noting that "learning is fundamentally built up through conversations between persons or groups; involving the creation and interpretation of communication." Furthermore, they argued, "conversations are the means by which people collaboratively construct beliefs and meanings as well as state their differences" (p. 2). It is evident that while their views and beliefs are individually held, these are, in fact, influenced and expanded by information received from other perspectives. Thus, individuals are more able to enlarge their own beliefs and more likely to take risks when supported by a community of other learners (Grabinger, 1996).

According to Scardamalia and Bereiter (1994), intellectual support communities are a "means for redefining classroom discourse to support knowledge building in ways extensible to out-of-school knowledge advancing enterprises." Scardamalia and Bereiter supported their argument by reporting that

> evaluations of CSILE (computer-supported intentional learning environments) students greatly surpass students in ordinary classrooms on measures of depth of learning and reflection, awareness of what they have learned or need to learn, and understanding of learning itself. Moreover, individual achievement, as conventionally measured, does not suffer. (p. 265)

Ahern, Peck and Laycock (1992) concluded, after their study of 80 undergraduate students, that asynchronous computer mediated communications improves the acquisition and application of knowledge without a teacher-centered orientation. Furthermore, their review of the research has shown "that this type of interaction is not merely noise in the instructional context, but essential to the cognitive development of the students" (p. 307).

In other words, a learning community contributes to effective learning by fostering cognitive development through communication, argumentation, and critical analysis. This occurs from increasing the range of ideas and capitalizing on the possibilities of brainstorming or collaborative idea generation. Furthermore, the community provides the necessary emotional support for growth or intellectual risk-taking behaviors. It is doubtful that learners would engage in substantive and rich conversations without the feelings of acceptance that a community provides. Learners also need support in terms of interpersonal encouragement and assistance to fully maximize their potential academic and intellectual development (Gunawardena, 1991; Moore & Kearsley, 1996). Those learners may see problems as overwhelming that may increase their anxiety, resulting in a lack of confidence. This will likely decrease their motivational level, expended effort, and the resulting learning achievement (Moller & Russell, 1994). Unlike learners in a face-to-face environment, the asynchronous distance learner may not have opportunities to observe other learners with similar problems or develop shared strategies that assist in solving those problems. Students who are unsuccessful at overcoming difficulties are more likely to discontinue their efforts to reach their educational goal (Kember, Lai, Murphy, Siaw, & Yuen, 1994; Kember & Murphy, 1992).

The purpose of this research effort was to explore the relationship between community and learning in asynchronous environments. Specifically, to first determine if a stronger learning community would lead to increased learning and productivity, as indicated by better solutions and higher grades in case studies and, second, to look for evidence or indications of what causes students to form a learning community via asynchronous technology.

METHODOLOGY

The study population consisted of graduate students enrolled in an asynchronous distance education class. The semester-long class, conducted using Internet-based conferencing software, worked on solving four different case studies. The 12 students were arbitrarily assigned to one of three four-person teams. Using a combination of quantitative and qualitative research methods, an analysis was conducted of the factors that affected community-building in the asynchronous course, and the possible relationships of these factors to learning outcomes. The factors considered included:

- Quantity of comments made by student teams is the sheer volume of messages exchanged between members of each team within their team conference.
- Amount of community-building types of comments made by student teams—the number of messages that were judged by a three-member panel to be practical, social, or interpersonal in nature.
- Degree of perceived responsibility and isolation of individual team members relative to their team.
- The methods by which each team appeared to form community—how connected each individual appeared to be to his or her teammates, how often they made community-building comments, and how quickly the team appeared to solidify their community identity.

Factors one and two above were studied quantitatively, while factors three and four were considered using the qualitative data gathered via end-of-course interviews and student journals. The following sections describe the methods utilized for the study and report the data collected. It should be noted that, as this was an exploratory study, the quantitative data were not analyzed using advanced statistical procedures. Rather, the data were used to determine specific trends and possible areas to be studied more closely using the qualitative data.

DESCRIPTIVE DATA

Total Comments

To determine if community affected achievement, we needed to determine if the groups differed in their community development process or intensity. The first step in examining community-building within the asynchronous course environment was to track the comments of each team. To manage this procedure for comparison to the case scores, comments were first grouped according to the case being considered. The learning outcomes were quantitatively measured on a team-by-team basis, using team-produced answers to four separate case studies. Three independent raters judged each team's answers to each of the four case studies. For each answer a score was assigned, ranging from 0 to 60 points, based upon a rubric that included 12 criteria each worth five points. The case scores were used as a measure of the team members' combined understanding of the course content (see Table 10.1).

The resulting data (see Figure 10.1) revealed that, in all but the third case, Team A produced the greatest number of comments of the three teams (Case 1 = 54 comments, Case 2 = 74 comments, Case 4 = 33 comments). In the third case, Team B produced the greatest number of comments (Case 3= 69 comments). However, in the first and second cases,

Table 10.1.   Rubric for Grading Case Answers

Please rate each answer, 1 (one) is poor, 5 (five) is strong.
1. Have the key issues, questions, and concerns in the case been clearly and coherently identified?
2. Have those issues been represented in a way that can be supported by the facts from the case and the research literature?
3. Does the solution take into consideration relevant constraints presented in the case?
4. Have the interests and perspectives of the different people involved in the case been considered?
5. Have various explanations and interpretations been considered?
6. Have various courses of action and their consequences been considered?
7. Does the solution recommend an alternative that is reasonable in light of the facts?
8. Does the solution recommend a workable alternative that is practical?
9. Has a coherent argument been made to support the recommended alternative?
10. Do proposed solutions fit with accepted instructional design practices?
11. Are proposed solutions specific and detailed?

Note: Adapted from 1998 Instructional Design Team Case Event, University of Virginia.

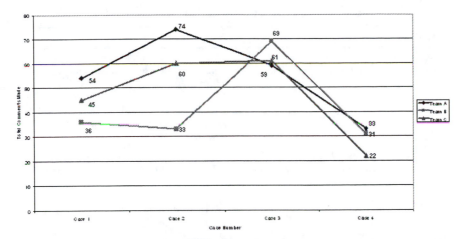

Figure 10.1.   Team comments across four cases.

Team B produced the fewest number of comments (Case 1 = 36 comments, Case 2 = 33 comments). Team C's comment totals were between the other two team's totals, except in the fourth case, in which they produced the fewest number of comments (Case 4 = 22 comments). It should be noted that less casework time was allotted, by the schedule, for the fourth case than the other cases, a likely explanation for the sharp decrease in comment totals for that case.

Community-Building Comments

Each comment made by students was judged by a team of three raters to determine if it was indicative of community-building activity. In order to determine which comments were related to building community, raters looked for criteria that would suggest whether an individual comment was meant to connect with other team members in one of three ways indicative of community-building: practical, social, and interpersonal (see Table 10.2).

Using this rating rubric, trends appeared in the data for the community-building comments (see Table 10.3) that were also in evidence for the total comments data. Team A had the highest number of community-building comments for Case 1 (42 comments), Case 2 (41 comments), and Case 4 (17 comments). Team B recorded the fewest community-building comments in Case 1 (22 comments) and Case 2 (14 comments), and Team C the fewest for Case 4 (10 comments).

Table 10.2.   Type of Comments and Examples

Type of Comment	Examples
Practical: designed to deal with issues of team coordination (time, responsibilities)	"I will post our team answer on Friday evening—please send me any changes before then."
	"I am out of town until next week—I will post my thoughts on Case 4 when I get back in town."
Social: fostering sense of group identity within assignment context (affirmation of ideas, valuing of opinions)	"That was a really interesting point—I had not thought of taking that perspective on the case."
	"We really did a great job of pulling our answer together!"
Interpersonal: provide personal glimpses of individual outside assignment contex (emotional, friendship)	"Sorry to hear about your problem at work—hope it improves soon."
	"I really enjoyed my vacation last week—it was nice to get away to the mountains for a change."

Table 10.3.   Total Community-Building Comments by Team and Case Number

Team	Case 1	Case 2	Case 3	Case 4
A	42	41	36	17
B	36	29	39	10
C	22	14	30	12

Discrepancies with the total comments data appear only in the third case. Team B, as opposed to Team A, recorded the lowest number of community-building comments for Case 3 (30 comments). Also, Team C recorded the highest number of community-building comments (39 comments) for the third case.

Case Scores

Case scores for the four cases (see Figure 10.2) revealed little difference in team scores for the first and third cases, with teams scoring within one or two points of each other. However, in the second and fourth cases,

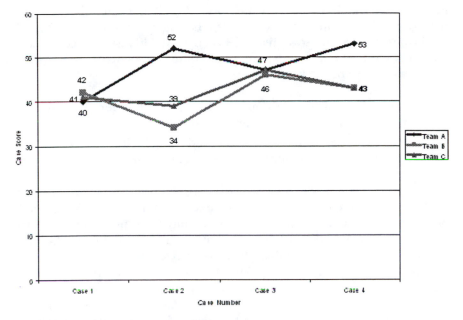

Figure 10.2   Case scores across four cases.

Team A scored 10 to 18 points higher than the other two teams (Case 2 = 52 points, Case 4 = 53 points).

SUMMARY OF QUANTITATIVE DATA

The general trend revealed that Team A, in all but the third case, made the most comments, as well as generating the highest number of community-building comments. Team A also scored consistently high on all four cases relative to the other two teams. Team A scored very closely to the other teams in the first and third cases, and much higher on the second and fourth cases.

Team B appeared to be the least-connected group, except in Case 3, as evidenced by recording a low number of comments. Closer inspection of the third case revealed that despite an increase in total comments, Team B had the fewest of community-building comments (30 out of 69 total comments) of the three groups for the case.

Team C exhibited an average amount of community-building in comparison to the other groups. In the first two cases, the quantity of comments fell between the extremes for total comments and community-building. For the third case, Team C showed the highest number of community-building comments, despite not having the highest number of total comments. For Case 4, Team C had both the lowest total comments and the lowest number of community-building comments. The following trends seemed to be in evidence:

- Teams B and C scored similarly on case answers for all four cases (within five points of the other team's score).
- Team A scored similar to Teams B and C on the first and third cases but scored much higher on the second and fourth cases.

Overall, Team A made the greatest number of comments (220), as well as the greatest number of community-building comments (136). Team A began making comments, including community-building comments, earlier (the first two cases) and at a higher rate (128 total comments, 83 community-building comments) than the other two teams.

Based on the trends apparent in the quantitative data, the qualitative data were analyzed to interpret whether the numbers of comments and case scores might be associated with other factors, such as individual responsibility, isolation, and social connection amongst team members. The following section reports the results of the qualitative methods used in the study. These results are the participants' reported perspectives of their experiences in this asynchronous course.

QUALITATIVE RESULTS

The teams each developed a community within their own team and among the other teams through asynchronous interactions. The teams revealed a sense of satisfaction and confidence with learning asynchronously, as they became more familiar with how to interact with each other and with what to expect from each other within the limitations of technology and asynchronous learning. Research on learning communities shows that people significantly connect through face-to-face and personal interactions, versus connecting on a personal expression-limiting level through technology-based communication.

Communication via messages was the link for developing a sense of community. The feelings of being part of a community varied between teams and changed over time. We believe, based on respondents' information, that feeling connected was caused by team members' senses of responsibility, and differences in sense of responsibility contributed to the difference in performance. Students also reported the need for more socializing and real-time communication, thus the missing link to community development in asynchronous learning. While socializing and real-time learning maybe the antithesis of asynchronous distance education, it does underscore the need to feel connected. The next sections report the findings of the major qualitative themes that revealed where community did and did not develop in the data. These themes include sense of responsibility, feeling connected, and learning.

Sense of Responsibility

One of the main themes that emerged from the interview and journal data is that teams felt a differing sense of responsibility to the other team members in doing their work. Team A seemed to feel the most responsibility to their team members. One student stated, "I feel a great responsibility to the team." A student in Team A relayed a sense of community responsibility in that they were aware that their actions affected everyone and wanted to have a positive outcome. "It's not just letting myself down, whereas let's say in class [traditional class], if I didn't read the assignment, I really see mostly that other people would participate, and it is my loss, versus this class [asynchronous class] I see it more like I'm letting my group down." Another participant related community responsibility to the smaller class size. "It [feeling responsible] might also be a function of the size of the group that in a class it's 26 people, and if I weren't to communicate, maybe somebody else would. Whereas in a group of 4, you are much more responsible."

A feeling of guilt also existed, for a Team A student, when there were challenges to active participation. This student had difficulties keeping up with the community because of work travel. "[I] feel guilty like I'm not keeping up my end of the work."

Team B members evidenced a less well-defined sense of responsibility within their community. One Team B member seemed confused about her responsibility: "The team work format is unclear, not sure of my responsibilities in this group." That statement was made at the beginning of the course and a sense of what was expected from each other was developed over time, as team members solved problems (cases) together. Over time, natural leaders emerged in Team B. A Team B student stated, "I am glad for the leadership roles that some students have taken." This may have been due to, or the cause of, the slow formation of community responsibility within Team B.

A member of Team C also expressed the sentiment that the team took some time to get to know each other and ultimately felt that everyone "carried their own weight" when she said, "This case was difficult for me because we were dealing with getting the program set up, feeling our way around one another as a team, and trying to decide how best to approach the case (our roles as team members), everyone carried their own weight." Another student stated "I feel a great responsibility to the group" and another student stated that she felt "more responsibility in this course than in traditional course." Another Team C member stated that she felt the learning opportunity was directly linked to the sense of responsibility shared by the team members: "if [I] expected to have more responsibility and had more time, [the] class would learn more."

We concluded that Team A more quickly developed a sense of responsibility, followed by Team C and, later, by Team B. This corresponds to the community-building comments and case score patterns. We believe that the posting of community-building comments encouraged the students in Team A to develop more intimate relationships, a contributing factor in developing a sense of responsibility. For example, a member of Team A noted this feeling of connection when she said, "I think I felt a little more connected with the group knowing a little more about what's going on with them." Most students noticed that there were fewer opportunities to feel connected in a distance education setting than in a traditional classroom setting, but that additional time helped them to feel connected to their team members. We suggest, based on the quantitative reporting of the types of comments, it is not time per se, but rather the increased degree of intimate communication that makes a difference.

A student in Team B noted that, over time, she "felt more connected at the end, not at all at the beginning, but it grew," while another stated that "getting to know each other helps." This is consistent with the increase of messages that resulted in a stronger community for Team B as time passed. Once again, it also could explain why Team B's case scores improved. One Team B student noted that "Our team members benefited, though not instantaneously, but through group dynamics of sharing information this way adds perspective that may not be available in one-on-one instruction."

The asynchronous communities developed more trust, as the result of the quantity and quality of feedback, and the community became stronger and more connected. We suggest that the quality of feedback is higher with stronger community. A Team A member stated that a "common problem builds community." Another Team A member said, "We have different ways of looking at a situation or question with regards to wanting more feedback to broaden their perspective." Conversely, a Team B member stated that "It would be good to have some type of feedback," indicating a lack of communication, possibly resulting from a lack of trust built within the community. A Team C member stated, "Team members feedback was good" and another member of Team C stated, "brainstorming and feedback were congenial." A Team C member stated, "learners developed a framework for feed back and solution/problem solving."

Once again, Teams A and C demonstrated behaviors associated with a community, while Team B lagged in this performance. This corresponds to Team B's lower case scores or team performance. Each of the teams stated that they would have liked more socializing, defined as: verbally talking to someone, talking in live-chat, classroom interactions, and face-to-face interactions. One Team B member reported that she would have liked to have been able to verbally talk to someone, and with a Team B member noted that "Email interactions seem less personal in chat." Another Team B member stated, "missed off-line communications." The team member reported, "I need to be in the social arena, but I would have arranged a telephone conversation because I think that is a viable alternative or a viable compliment." These Team B members were revealing their feeling and needed to have more personal interactions in their learning environment by verbally talking with their colearners. These types of comments were not expressed as strongly by Teams A or C.

Team members in all three groups mentioned classroom interactions and face-to-face interactions as a more desirable way to get to know their co-learners. For example, one Team A member said "Would like to see everyone discuss the class and socialize more." Another Team A member stated, "That [social interaction] is the only thing I miss about the classroom set-up." Two more students in Team A recalled that seeing others was important and missed in their asynchronous chat learning experience when they said: "Miss seeing her [fellow student] in class," and "Sometimes I think we would be able to connect better if we had face-to face talk."

Team B and Team C members also mentioned their desire to have more classroom interactions and face-to-face interactions. One Team B member stated, "There were two people in the class I knew, and I was really hoping that I could be on their team, because I think if you establish something … like if I am thinking 'I don't know how to respond to this', so you knew them and you could maybe deal with them, maybe, differently than with a stranger." A Team C student noted that "traditional class characteristics are taken for granted, you relate more in person." Another Team C student commented that the team would have liked to have gotten to know fellow students on a more informal basis:

> We thought it would be real neat idea to have the whole class get together for pizza or something at the end; the group seems to be talking to one another more than at the beginning of the class; would like to suggest more socializing—more socializing would help bring people closer together and be more interpersonal; develop bond with your team needs to happen more.

Another Team C student relayed that more chat time helped develop bonding between fellow team members: "In our chat a considerable amount of time was spent on interpersonal stuff. I liked learning more about my team members."

Learning

Learning occurred among the teams as their communities developed, working together to achieve the common goal of completing instructional design projects. Members of Team A reported that they learned through independent research, which happened in several different ways:

Learned through my own exploration and teams reference suggestions.

Being out there alone is a great help in that I am developing a way to learn to solve the cases by looking at the real issues and not making too many assumptions ... the cases are so realistic.

Posted ideas before chat so we could have time to review ahead of time.

Even though the research was accomplished independently, the team members collaborated on their ideas and shared their findings that were beneficial to their learning process and to contributing to a sense of community.

Members of Team B reported that they noticed having more time to think about the projects before posting their responses, whereas in the classroom setting, the time is limited and limits the ability to think through issues as thoroughly as in the asynchronous environment:

I put more time in, I would read the message, I would print it out, I would think it out, I would try and research it, respond to it, I would post it. Whereas face-to-face in class, you have those 3 hours, that's it.

Have ability to spend more time thinking about questions than in traditional classroom setting.

Members of Team C also noted that they liked having more time to think about their responses to the learning issues:

I like having time to reflect and react rather than just try to work as fast as you can off the top of your head in class. Finding solutions on your own is real-life experience.

Go onto the Internet to see if I can find an answer ... I am so excited I liked having time to think.

Can think about response, then post it. Able to research before responding go to the Internet to see other resources there.

Students on all three teams agreed that they were more satisfied with their contributions when having more time to think about their responses. The independent research activities among the teams revealed that a sense of satisfaction was achieved in the learning when they could spend more time thinking about their responses before posting their answers in chat. However, Team A and C students also noted the benefit in posting their research findings to share with other team members, as well as posting their responses early so that others could have a little time to think about it. Although shared learning was generally considered a positive experience across the teams, the types of social learning interactions that occur in the tradition classroom setting were missed.

Team A members reported that both shared experiences and independent research were valuable:

It's tough for me to say whether I learned more from our shared experience or from my own attempts to formulate a solution. I might feel more connected in a traditional class because others used to bring up a lot of stories of their work that were relevant to what we were learning in class.

I wonder if there may be a way for the teams to share our papers after they are completed. I would like to learn from them.

Team C members also reported that both shared experiences and independent research were valuable:

I learned from sharing.

Shared some of the stuff I found … posted it and decided they can read it or not.

Learned through my own exploration and teams reference suggestions.

I am very proud of our groups effort in coming up with solutions.

A Team C member stated, "This case gave me the encouragement to break away from the security of relying on the questions at the end of the case and rely more on my own judgment."

CONCLUSION

The purpose of this research effort was to explore the relationship between community and learning in asynchronous environments. Specifically, first, to determine if a stronger learning community would lead to increased learning and productivity, as indicated by better solutions and higher grades in case studies and, second, to look for evidence or indications of what caused students to form a learning community via asynchronous technology.

We believe that the descriptive data indicate that more peer interaction, as expressed by community comments, resulted in heightened learning, as evidenced by the case scores. This is consistent with Mason and Kaye (1990) who noted that "Growing out of this high level of interaction and the permanence of the discussion record is the possibility of a group creation, where people make leaps in understanding that are unlikely to happen in isolation" (p. 19). The importance of group interaction is supported by Grabinger's (1996) assertion that while our own views and beliefs are individually held, our views are, in fact, influenced and expanded by information we receive from other perspectives. Thus we are more able to enlarge our own beliefs and more likely to take risks when supported by a community of other learners. The descriptive describes a trend. This trend indicates the group that made the most community-building comments had higher scores on the case studies.

Further evidence can be found in the qualitative analysis of the learner journals and interviews. Once again, the team that usually performed the best expressed the strongest sense of responsibility to their fellow team members. According to Barab and Duffy (2000), "Most community members view themselves as part of something larger. It is this part of something larger that allows the various members to form a collective whole as they work towards the joint goals of the community and its members" (p. 38). Thus, we consider that "viewing yourself as part of something larger" was expressed in terms of an obligation or responsibility to meet the needs of the group.

In the years since this study was conducted and published (Moller, Harvey, Downs, and Godshalk, 2000), other researchers and writers in the distance education field have begun to use presence as a construct to explain findings similar to those in this study. Garrison, Anderson, and Archer (2000) define social presence as the social and emotional connection of a learner into a learning community. A study by Rourke, Anderson, Garrison, and Archer (2001) that attempted to test a measure of social presence suggests that comments similar to those scored as community-building in this study were indicative of social presence. This means that such comments were likely to include personal anecdotes, and suggest a level of personal connection to other group members.

Russo and Campbell (2004) examined social presence as mediated presence, with the media being asynchronous online communication, including threaded discussions such as those in this study. An interesting finding of the Russo and Campbell study was that students reported feeling most connected to the community during group projects. The students noted that both the conversational message styles (more informal than other parts of the course) and the inclusion of personal information made the interactions "more human."

Interestingly, Murphy (2004) has argued that development of social presence may be the initial step in forming collaborative online groups. Given the findings of this study, it would appear that argument may have some merit. Baskin, Barker, and Woods (2005) found that female students in an advanced business course that used an asynchronous online workgroup assignment reported valuing social interaction during their online discussions. These female students also appeared to develop stronger collaborative work skills as a result of their attention to developing social presence.

Such research and writings corroborate the findings of this study in that they also suggest that the social aspect of asynchronous communication is important to both the quality of the learning experience and the quality of the group work. In this asynchronous learning process, most students reported gaining a sense of confidence from the act of learning about the subject and themselves. Building their self-confidence through independent and collaborative research and being proud of their team's efforts and outcomes resulted in a sense of satisfaction among members of the learning communities. The desire for collaborative research was great when students wanted to get feedback, and this helped them feel connected to their team members. Even in the independent research activities, students reported wanting to share their research and benefit from others' research.

REFERENCES

Ahern, T., Peck, K., & Laycock, M. (1992). The effects of teacher discourse in computer-mediated discussion, *Journal of Educational Computing Research, 8*(3), 291-309.

Barab, S., & Duffy, T. (2000). From practice fields to communities of practice. In D. H. Jonassen & S. M. Land (Eds.), *Theoretical foundations of learning environments* (pp. 25-56). Mahwah, NJ: Erlbaum,

Barry, M., & Runyan, G. (1995). A review of distance-learning studies in the U.S. military. *American Journal of Distance Education, 9*(3), 37-47.

Baskin, C., Barker, M., & Woods, P. (2005). When group work leaves the classroom does group skills development also go out the window? *British Journal of Educational Technology, 36*(1).

Cathcart, R., Samovar, L., & Henman, L. (1996). *Small group communication: Theory and practice* (7th ed.) Madison, WI: Brown and Benchmark.

Garrison, D. R., Anderson, T., & Archer, W. (2000). Critical inquiry in a text-based environment: Computer conferencing in higher education. *Internet and Higher Education, 11*(2), 1-19.

Gay, G., & Lentini, M. (1995). *Communication resource use in a networked collaborative design environment.* New York: Interactive Multimedia Group.

Grabinger, R. S. (1996). Rich environments for active learning, In D. H. Jonassen (Ed.), *Handbook of research on educational communications and technology* (pp. 665-692). New York: Macmillan.

Gunawardena, C. (1991). Current trends in the use of communications technologies for delivering distance education. *International Journal of Instructional Media, 18*(3), 13-30.

Jonassen, D. H. (1999). Designing constructivist learning environments. In C.M. Reigeluth (Ed.), *Instructional design theories and models: Their current state of the art* (2nd ed., pp. 215-239). Mahwah, NJ: Erlbaum.

Jonassen, D., Davidson, M., Collins, M., Campbell, J., & Haag, B. B. (1995). Constructivism and computer-mediated communication in distance education. *American Journal of Distance Education, 9*(2), 7-26.

Kember, D., Lai, T., Murphy, D., Siaw, I., & Yuen, K. (1994). Student progress in distance education courses: A replication study. *Adult Education Quarterly, 45*(1), 286-301.

Kember, D., & Murphy, D. (1992). *Tutoring distance education and open learning courses.* Campbelltown, NSW, Australia: HERDSA.

Maslow, A. (1954). *Motivation and personality.* New York: Harper and Row.

Mason, R., & Kaye, T. (1990). Toward a new paradigm of distance education. In L. Harasim (Ed.), *On-line education: Perspectives on a new environment* (pp. 15-38). New York: Praeger.

McIsaac, M., & Gunawardena, C. (1996). Distance education. In D. H. Jonassen (Ed.), *Handbook of research on educational communications and technology* (pp. 403-437). New York: Macmillan.

Moller, L. (1998). Designing communities of learners for asynchronous distance education. *Educational Technology and Research Development, 46*(4), 115-122.

Moller, L., Harvey, D. M., Downs, M., & Godshalk, V. M. (2000). Identifying factors that effect learning community development and performance in asynchronous distance learning. *Quarterly Review of Distance Education, 1*(4), 293-305.

Moller, L., & Russell, J. (1994). An application of the ARCS model design process and confidence-building strategies. *Performance Improvement Quarterly, 7*(4), 54-69.

Moore, M., & Kearsley, G. (1996). *Distance education: A systems view.* Belmont, CA: Wadsworth.

Murphy, E. (2004). Recognising and promoting collaboration in an online asynchronous discussion. *British Journal of Educational Technology, 35*(4), 421-431.

Neilson, R. (1997). *Collaborative technologies and organizational learning.* Hershey, PA: Idea Group.

O'Malley, C., & Scanlon, E. (1990). Computer-supported collaborative learning: Problem solving and distance education. *Computer Education, 15*(1), 127-136.

Rourke, L., Anderson, T., Garrison, D. R., & Archer, W. (1999). Assessing social presence in asynchronous text-based computer conferencing. *Journal of Distance Education, 14*(2), 50-71.

Russo, T. C., & Campbell, S. W. (2004). Perceptions of mediated presence in an asynchronous online course: Interplay of communication behaviors and medium. *Distance Education, 25*(2), 215-232.

Scardamalia, M., & Bereiter, C. (1994). Computer support for knowledge-building communities. *The Journal of Learning Sciences, 3*(3), 265-283.

Shaffer, C. R., & Anundsen, K. (1993). *Creating community anywhere: Finding support and connection in a fragmented world.* New York: Putnam.

Wilson, B., & Ryder, M. (1996). Dynamic learning communities: An alternative to designed instruction. *Proceedings of Selected Research and Development National Convention of Association for Educational Research and Technology.* Indianapolis, IN.

Woodruff, E. (1996). The effects of computer mediated communications on collaborative discourse in knowledge-building communities. *Proceedings of Selected Research and Development National Convention of Association for Educational Research and Technology.* Indianapolis, IN.

CHAPTER 11

EXAMINING THE USE OF LEARNING COMMUNITIES TO INCREASE MOTIVATION

**Jason Bond Huett, Leslie A. Moller,
Douglas Harvey, and Mary E. Engstrom**

The purpose of this study was to determine if learning communities have an inherent motivational effect on learners and, if so, whether higher motivation impacts attitudinal change. As learning communities and groups become more established in distance educational settings, it is important to understand the impact these groups have on the motivation of the learners. This research project was conducted to determine if learning communities increase the effort level (motivation) expended by students in distance education. Based on this small sample study, groups do have a motivational impact on learners; however, in this case, that impact was not transferable to an attitudinal change.

INTRODUCTION

Distance education provides for ubiquitous and flexible learning opportunities, and many universities are turning toward this delivery system to address the needs of local and commuter students. In a U.S. Department

Online Learning Communities
pp. 189–203

of Education survey (1997-1998), 20% of the respondents—990 postsecondary institutions—reported that within 3 years they planned to join the 1,680 schools offering online distance education courses (National Center for Education Statistics, 2000). In a speech to the U.S. General Accounting Office (GAO), Cornelia M. Ashby (2002), director of education, workforce, and income security issues, stated that "Overall, about 1.5 million out of 19 million postsecondary students took at least one distance education course in the 1999-2000 school year" (p. 3). Ashby also noted that by 2002, more than 84% of four-year institutions were offering distance education courses. By most accounts, these numbers will continue to rise. For example, the University of Phoenix, the nation's largest private online college, is averaging more than 500 new students a month and has "pulled off the rarest of feats: Its stock has skyrocketed," hitting all-time highs, "despite the worst tech-stock bear market in history" (Symonds, 2003, p. 1).

In the corporate sector, the trend is even stronger with major e-learning initiatives now common in large Fortune 1000 companies. According to the annual training magazine survey, e-learning expenditures have grown to as much as 30% of the training budget in leading companies (Rosenberg, 2001).

With these dramatic increases, researchers are examining all aspects of the distant learning environment to determine what approaches, methods, and technologies are most appropriate and effective. One particular area that must be explored concerns what motivates and inspires the distance learner.

Motivation

Motivation is a critical component to learning (Keller, 1979a, 1987a, 1987b; Means, Jonassen, & Dwyer, 1997; Moller, 1993; Song & Keller, 2001), and there is considerable research regarding the importance of motivation in learning contexts. Researchers have attempted to define motivation on both ends of the spectrum, from external environmental conditioning, such as deprivation and reinforcement schedules (Skinner, 1953), to a humanistic, internal drive for self-actualization (Maslow, 1954; Rogers, 1951).

Both Bandura (1969) and Gagne (1985) argued that learning and motivation were a result not just of the environment (external) or the individual's free will (internal), but a combination of the two. According to Keller (1983), motivation provides the impetus to learn and to achieve one's ambitions and can be seen as "the choices people make as to what experiences or goals they will approach or avoid and the degree of effort they will exert in that respect" (p. 389). For this chapter, motivation is defined as the length and direction of effort expended by the learners in pursuit of achievement (Keller, 1979b; Moller & Russell, 1994).

Means et al. (1997) cite studies showing that motivation accounts for 16% to 38% of the variations in overall student achievement. Gabrielle (2003) feels that the literature supports three contentions about motivation and self-directed learning (SDL). Both motivation and SDL are influenced by external factors, are variable in that learners will be more motivated at some times and less motivated at others, and have an influence on performance.

Keller and Burkman (1993) acknowledge that much of what constitutes motivation is often seen as out of the hands of the instructional designer. However, they do not believe this to truly be the case. In fact, they feel that motivation is a systematic process that must be considered during all stages of design. Keller (1999) argues that there are stable elements of motivation that can be successfully manipulated and that "even some of the unstable elements are predictable" (p. 47). With careful forethought, Keller believes that instructors can design and manage the learning environment to create and to maintain learner motivation. Even if controlling an individual's internal motivational condition is not an option, "it is abundantly clear that the environment can have a strong impact on both the direction and intensity of a person's motivation" (p. 47).

Even though literature supporting the need for enhancing learner motivation can frequently be found, the study of motivation in distance education, Web-based environments, and other forms of distant CAI is lacking (Lee & Boling, 1996; Rezabek, 1994). This was clearly illustrated by Visser, Plomp, Amirault, and Kuiper (2002) in an in-depth study of the proceedings of the World Conferences of the International Council for Distance Education from 1988 to 1995. They found that only six of 801 studies addressed motivational concerns of online learners. They also noted a disturbing pattern in many of the handbooks published addressing distance education: very little if any attention was being paid to the motivational concerns of learners.

Motivation and Learning Communities

In terms of its role in learning achievement and motivation, the issue of learning communities has been at the forefront of distance education. Collaborative construction of knowledge through social negotiation often results in greater understanding (Jonassen, Mayes, & McAleese, 1993), and it is not much of a stretch to say that the current literature overwhelmingly supports the efficacy of collaborative learning (Sharp &

Huett, 2006). Whereas traditional distance learning models emphasize the independence of the learner (Downs & Moller, 1999; Moore, 1989) and the privatization of learning (Keegan, 1986), newer models emphasize collaboration. There is little doubt that collaboration can be a successful learning strategy. The idea of students working together in a teaching and learning experience to produce a product that is somehow more than the sum of its parts is not a new one. The theory behind successful collaborative learning is essentially the same whether one is in a face-to-face classroom or online. However, putting theory into practice for online learning is often difficult. Unlike face-to-face classes where social interaction is often taken as a given, online environments struggle to maintain a sense of social identity and engage learners in communal relationships that can lead to greater depth of learning (Sharp & Huett, 2006).

Online collaboration, in the form of peer work groups and learning communities, increases engagement in the learning process (Gay & Lentini, 1995; Moore & Kearsley, 1996). Kruger (2000) explains that distant students are capable of developing meaningful relationships with faculty and other students when they engage in learning communities "unbound by the barriers of time and place" (p. 59). Cifuentes and Murphy (2000) studied multicultural understanding and self-concept through distance learning communities and cited numerous benefits such as a sense of expanded worldview of students, increased multicultural awareness (when given the opportunity to interact with others from diverse cultures and backgrounds), increased student self-concept, and they concluded that distance education communities can "foster powerful relationships" (p. 81). Studies of written communications in distance education environments by Schallert and Reed (2004) support the contention that meaningfully creative and thoughtful learning experiences can be had within a community of online learners.

In a study of a Texas A&M online graduate class, Yakimovicz and Murphy (1995) found that a distance course which required students to work together improved learning outcomes and strengthened ties between students. Unlike local students with unfettered access to the campus and its personnel and resources, non-resident students must juggle a multitude of self-driven tasks in relative isolation. This is where online learning communities "may be the only viable path to greater student involvement" (Tinto, Goodsell-Love, & Russo, 1993, p. 21). Helping to form social bonds with peers, increasing academic motivation and participation, improving self-concept and self-awareness and, potentially, having a positive impact on achievement are some of the benefits of online collaborative learning. Not promoting collaboration in the online learning environment generally results in lower levels of participation but, when promoted, "collaborative work forms the basis for the student's ability to engage in a transformative learning process" (Palloff & Pratt, 1999, p. 127). Clearly, a deeper understanding of the role learning communities play and the potential for positive impact on student motivation is a significant research issue.

As learning communities and groups become more established in distance education settings, it is important to understand the impact these groups have on motivation of the learners. It is assumed that this configuration of learners has a positive effect and, thus, increases motivation or effort. The purpose of this study was to determine if learning communities have an inherent motivational effect upon learners and, if so, whether higher motivation impacts attitudinal change. This research project was conducted to determine if learning communities increase the effort level (motivation) expended by students in distance education.

FRAMEWORK AND RATIONALE

Regardless of how well content is presented, a learner must expend effort to be sufficiently engaged in the learning process so as to produce the desired outcomes (Keller, 1979a, 1987a, 1987b). Choosing to persist in a learning task is not a simple choice and is influenced by many variables (Driscoll, 2000). However, the literature on learning communities indicates there is a strong interpersonal commitment of the community members that should provide a supportive element to continuing motivation. The newer instructional models claim that significant and meaningful learning occurs as the result of learner-to-learner communication. This is more likely to occur when learners have access to a supportive community that encourages knowledge-building and social reinforcement (Foshay & Moller, in press; Moller, 1998). Thus, learner-to-learner dialogue is not only required for the intellectual exchange, but also necessary to create a proper emotional condition. This paves the way for the knowledge-sharing and growth. Then, learners are more able to enlarge their own beliefs and are more likely to take risks when supported by a community of other learners (Grabinger, 1996). According to Sharp and Huett (2006), "it seems reasonable to assume that improving learner-learner interaction [in distance education environments] helps to center the individual in a learning process that is as active and cognitively complex as possible" (p. 4).

Further insight into the motivation construct and support for the role of community can be found in Bandura's work on self-efficacy—which is better known as confidence. Confidence is the interplay between an individual's desire for success and his or her fear of failure. If the learner believes he or she can be successful at a given task (and that expending effort is a worthwhile choice), confidence increases and anxiety recedes. This desire to increase learner confidence and provide for instruction that helps learners feel in control and successful may be an even greater consideration in distance learning environments. Even with highly-motivated students, the learner isolation, an unfamiliar distance environment, the technology required in distance courses, the distance separating learner and instructor, and other mitigating factors have an effect on learner confidence (Huett, 2006). Studies have shown that technology brings with it new attitudes and anxiety levels that can have a direct effect on confidence (Yaghi & Ghaith, 2002). The instructor of the distance course must be especially concerned with increasing and maintaining learner confidence (Huett, 2006).

One way to help manage fear and anxiety in distance learners is with learning communities. Confidence, among other inputs, is influenced by vicarious experiences, such as seeing other learners achieve success. Confidence is also influenced by verbal persuasion or words of encouragement—particularly from one with whom there is an established prior relationship (Bandura, 1977; Driscoll, 2000). Simply put, a learning community provides external events that cause internal changes—a grounding principle of the instructional systems design discipline.

METHODOLOGY

In this study, there were 51 subjects. Subjects were graduate students at a Big Ten University. Twenty-two were in a naturally formed treatment group (Group A) and 29 were in a naturally formed control group (Group B). Of the original 51 participants, 6 were eliminated due to incomplete data.

In this quasi-experimental design, naturally formed means the subjects were traditionally in these study compositions and were not placed there for the purpose of the research. The treatment group was comprised of subjects working in learning communities. The control group was comprised of subjects working individually. Both groups took a pretest using an attitudinal measure for sexual harassment. Both the treatment and control groups completed a computer-based program on sexual harassment. A posttest attitudinal measure was administered as well as the Instructional Materials Motivational Survey (IMMS). The IMMS was developed by Keller (1993) and based on the ARCS model. The IMMS gauges the motivational effect of instructional materials. In relationship to the instructional material, it was designed to assess the four components of the ARCS model (attention, relevance, confidence, and satisfaction), as well as an overall motivation score. Prior scores obtained with this instrument (attention, relevance, confidence, satisfaction, and total ARCS score) have resulted in an overall Cronbach's alpha in excess of .80. For this study, the reliability estimate was .96.

The collected data were analyzed using an Independent Samples t-test to measure the differences between treatment and control groups for motivation and overall change of attitude. An independent samples t test is used when the researcher wants to compare the means of two independent groups on the dependent variable (Hinkle, Wiersma, & Jurs, 2003). Finally, a correlation was used to determine if the anticipated higher motivational scores were related to a change in attitude.

RESULTS

The research showed that there was no attitudinal change between the treatment (Group A) and the control group (Group B) with the means being almost equal from the pretest and posttest as well as between groups. Using an independent samples t test, we found that the pretest averages for Groups A and B were 2.75 and 2.82 respectively, with a significance of .310 at the .05 level. The posttest averages for Groups A and B were again 2.77 and 2.82 respectively, with a significance of .441 at the .05 level. In terms of motivation (see Table 11.1), there was statistical significance at the .05 level in motivation between Group A and Group B in every area except confidence.

DISCUSSION

It appears, based on this small sample study, that learning communities do have a motivational impact on learners; although, in this case, the impact was not transferable to an attitudinal change. This lack of attitude

Table 11.1.   IMMS Survey Scores

Motivation	Group	Mean Score	Sig. (.05 level)
Attention	A	3.71	.005
	B	3.27	
Relevance	A	3.75	.001
	B	3.08	
Confidence	A	4.00	.238
	B	3.8	
Satisfaction	A	3.14	.002
	B	2.34	
Overall Motivation	A	3.69	.001
	B	3.20	

change may be more related to the lack of potency of the instructional materials than to any effort, or lack thereof, on the part of the subjects.

Our findings are in contrast to a study done by Kelsey and D'Souza (2004), which found that student-student interaction was not a crucial component to online learning. However, the authors admit that in their particular study, "Student-student interactions were not formally provided in the majority of the courses" (p. 7). Qureshi, Morton, and Antosz (2002) found that distance education students were less motivated than their on-campus counterparts. However, one of the possible reasons they list for this finding is the lack of motivational value in distance education courses. This is an important point to highlight. Arguably, designers must intentionally foster learning communities if they are to have an impact on distance learner motivation. It stands to reason that unless learning communities are designed to be part of the structure of the class, one will likely not find increased motivation. Similar to our finding, Jung, Choi, Lim, and Leem (2002) did show positive changes in attitude, performance, participation, and satisfaction among online learners in placed social groups. What is practically significant about our finding is that intentionally designed learning communities will most likely increase the effort level (motivation) expended by students in distance education situations. If one builds the necessary support and makes community participation valuable, it seems likely that learners will take it upon themselves to be more engaged (motivated) to learn. If proven true, increased motivation through intentionally designed online learning communities may be a key to different findings than those of Qureshi, Morton, and Antosz.

Potential increases in motivation, as a byproduct of online learning communities, parallel research of face-to-face classes. Kerssen-Griep, Hess, and Trees (2003) cite numerous studies showing that social classroom environments can motivate learners. Such a sense of community may be part of the necessary support structure distance learners need (Kember, Lai, Murphy, Siaw & Yuen, 1994; Cathcart, Samovar, & Henman, 1996; Moller, 1998). According to Cathcart, Samovar, and Henman (1996), groups that are cohesive enjoy numerous benefits from higher participation and lower rates of turnover to increased bonding within the group and a greater commitment to group goals. Following the earlier definition of motivation being effort expended by the student, it seems plausible that this higher level of engagement comes from participating in a learning community.

Discussion tools (e.g., e-mail, discussion boards, and chat) are necessary communication mechanisms in online learning. In an exploration of studies concerning the use of computer mediated discussions (CMD), Schallert and Reed (2003) found many "affective and motivational responses associated with the social dynamics of online communication among students" (p. 6). Further, they found that students are often drawn to a deeper level of participation through discussion with other students. By the end of many discussions, some students showed progress from a naïve understanding of the subject matter to a much more sophisticated one. Thus, membership in a learning community can promote communication, social interaction, and deeper understanding. This, in turn, increases motivation, which strengthens the community. Arguably, this creates a positive cycle along the lines of a greater sense of community leads to greater motivation. This in turn leads to a greater sense of involvement and understanding, which increases participation within the community.

In this study, there was no statistically significant difference noted for confidence. While there are several possible explanations for this, the most likely is that confidence has proven itself difficult to measure accurately. With issues of maturity, anxiety, locus of control, and fear of failure (to name a few), confidence may not lend itself to accurate and consistent measurement. Perhaps there was a change in confidence, but the survey could not consistently detect the changes over the short term. Further research regarding confidence and its measurement is warranted.

FUTURE RESEARCH

Many researchers agree that facilitating the development of learning communities is a valuable strategy for helping students reach higher levels of learning. Moller (1998) finds learning communities provide three different types of support for distance learners: academic, intellectual, and interpersonal. Researchers, building on the works of individuals like Maslow (1954), work to remove the sense of isolation and to engender a sense of community and self-esteem that distance learners need to be successful. Such research is taking many forms. While not directly focused on community, researchers such as Song (1998, 2000) and Song and Keller (2001) are exploring ways to create motivationally adaptive computer-based courseware that can respond and adapt to the changing motivational needs of distance learners.

Focusing less on the course material and more on the communications aspect of distance education, researchers such as J. Visser (1990), Visser and Keller (1990), Visser (1998), Gabrielle (2003), and Huett (2006), are exploring ways to use electronic discussion tools and e-mail messages to improve learner interaction, motivation, and performance. This research is showing promise in helping to build a sense of community among distant learners and instructors.

However, at the opposite end of spectrum, some researchers are suggesting that creating a sense of community between learners in distance education courses may not be absolutely necessary. Philosophically, there is some debate about whether learner-learner interaction is really effective or even called for in distance education settings (Reisetter & Boris, 2004; Sharp & Huett, 2006). An examination of recent research on interaction in distance education presents interesting results. Two studies (Kelsey & D'Souza, 2004; Reisetter & Boris, 2004) concluded that learner-learner interaction was considered the least important type of interaction by students in distance education settings. In addition, a study by Sabry and Baldwin (2003) placed learner-learner interaction well behind learner-information in terms of student perception of interaction value. Some researchers argue that modern students engaged in distance education environments quite possibly neither need nor want interaction with other students (Reisetter & Boris, 2004; Sharp & Huett, 2006). According to Sharp and Huett (2006), one might trace this apprehension to engage in collaborative learning back to the current K-12 environment—which does little to promote collaborative interaction. Combine that lack of collaborative experience with the modern distance learner (who often tends to be adult, independent, with a high internal locus of control), and one has learners who "have significantly different goals and preferences when it comes to online learning that may not lend themselves well to learning communities" (Sharp & Huett, 2006, p. 5).

More research is needed before any definitive conclusion can be drawn about the value and appropriate use of learning communities in distance education settings. However, common sense and volumes of research still lead one to the tentative conclusion that increases in collaboration in distance learning environments should translate into numerous benefits in student learning, satisfaction, and motivation as well as increases in the overall quality of distance education initiatives.

CONCLUSION

While we believe that these results can be replicated with undergraduates, this study reflects only our experiences with graduate students. Success or failure in a study such as this can depend on unforeseen variables. While distance learning communities show great promise, Peters and Armstrong (1998) point to caveats concerning frustration among different types of learners, power transfers in which the students must assume greater responsibility for their education, and a redefining of teaching-learning relationships as hurdles that need to be cleared. Continued research on this topic is important. For example, in the document *Best Practices for Electronically Offered Degree and Certificate Programs* (The Higher Learning Commission, n.d.). developed by six regional accrediting bodies, one finds a call for "learning that is dynamic and interactive, regardless of the setting in which it occurs" (p. 3) and lists a distance education program's interactive component as vital to its success.

Palloff and Pratt (1999) write "it is the relationships and interactions among people through which knowledge is primarily generated. The [online] learning community takes on new proportions in this environment and consequently must be nurtured and developed so as to be an effective vehicle for education" (p. 15). We believe that, with proper design, the use of online learning communities will continue to enhance the learning experiences of all students. The resulting increase in motivation has potentially powerful benefits not only to the student but also to the group, the instructor, and the university. More importantly, such collaboration should lead to better classes and a greater sense of intrinsic, personal satisfaction for students and faculty. With this greater sense of satisfaction comes the hope that distance education might one day fulfill its potential and not wind up in the "academic pit that is filled with so many other panaceas for learning" (Jonassen et al., 1993, section 1.0).

REFERENCES

Ashby, C. (2002). *Growth in distance education programs and implications for federal education policy.* Testimony before the United States General Accounting Office. Retrieved October 28, 2003, from http://www.gao.gov/new.items/d021125t.pdf

Bandura, A. (1969). *Principles of behavior modification.* New York: Holt, Rinehart, & Winston.

Bandura, A. (1977). Self-efficacy: Towards a unifying theory of behavioral change, *Psychological Review, 84,* 195-215.

Cathcart, R., Samovar, L., & Henman, L. (1996). *Small group communication: Theory and practice* (7th. ed.) Madison: Brown and Benchmark.

Cifuentes, L., & Murphy, K. L. (2000). Promoting multicultural understanding and positive self-concept through a distance learning community: Cultural connections. *Educational Technology Research and Development, 48*(1), 69-83.

Downs, M., & Moller, L. (1999). Experiences of students, teachers, and administrators in a distance education course. *International Journal of Educational Tech-*

nology, 1(2). Retrieved October 1, 2004, from http://www.ao.uiuc.edu/ijet/v1n2/downs/index.html

Driscoll, M. (2000). *Psychology of learning for instruction.* Needham Height, MA: Allyn & Bacon.

Foshay, R., & Moller, L. (in press). Trends in the external environment as a context for critiquing the field of instructional design and technology. In G. Anglin (Ed.), *Critical issues in instructional technology.* Englewood, CO: Libraries Unlimited.

Gabrielle, D. (2003). *The effects of technology-mediated instructional strategies on motivation, performance, and self-directed learning.* Unpublished doctoral dissertation, Florida State University, Tallahassee.

Gagné, R.M. (1985). *The conditions of learning* (4th ed.). New York: Holt, Rinehart, & Winston.

Gay, G., & Lentini, M. (1995). *Communication resource use in a networked collaborative design environment.* Ithaca, NY: Interactive Multimedia Group.

Grabinger, R. S. (1996). Rich environments for active learning. In D. H. Jonassen (Ed.), *Handbook of research for educational communications and technology* (pp. 403-437). New York: Macmillan.

The Higher Learning Commission. (n.d.). *Best practices for electronically offered degree and certificate programs.* Retrieved October 1, 2004, from http://www .ncahigherlearningcommission.org/resources/electronic_degrees/

Hinkle, D. E., Wiersma, W., & Jurs, S. G. (2003). *Applied statistics for the behavioral sciences* (5th ed.). Boston: Houghton Mifflin.

Huett, J. (2006). *The effects of ARCS-based confidence strategies on learner confidence and performance in distance education.* Unpublished doctoral dissertation, University of North Texas, Denton.

Jonassen, D. H., Mayes, J. T., & McAleese, R. (1993). A manifesto to a constructivist approach to the use of technology in higher education. In T. M. Duffy, D. Jonassen, & J. Lowyck (Eds.), *Designing constructivist learning environments* (pp. 231-247). Heidelberg, Germany: Springer-Verlag.

Jung, I., Choi, S., Lim, C., & Leem, J. (2002). Effects of different types of interaction on learning achievement, satisfaction, and participation in web-based instruction. *Innovations in Education and Teaching International, 39*(2), 153-162.

Keegan, D. (1986). *The foundations of distance education.* London: Croom-Helm.

Keller, J. (1979a). Motivation and instructional design: A theoretical perspective. *Journal of Instructional Development, 2*(4), 26-34.

Keller, J. (1979b). Strategies for stimulating the motivation to learn. *Performance and Instruction, 26*(8), 1-7.

Keller, J. M. (1983). Motivational design of instruction. In C. M. Reigeluth (Ed.), *Instructional-design theories and models: An overview of their current status* (383-43). Hillsdale, NJ: Erlbaum.

Keller, J. M. (1987a). Strategies for stimulating the motivation to learn. *Performance & Instruction, 26*(8), 1-7.

Keller, J. M. (1987b). The systematic process of motivational design. *Performance & Instruction, 26*(9), 1-8.

Keller, J. M. (1993). *Manual for instructional materials motivational survey* (IMMS). Unpublished manuscript, Tallahassee, FL.

Keller, J. M. (1999). Using the ARCS motivational design process in computer-based instruction and distance education. *New Directions for Teaching and Learning, 78,* 39-47.

Keller, J.M., & Burkman, E. (1993). Motivation principles. In M. Fleming & W. H. Levie (Eds.) *Instructional message design: Principles from the behavioral and cognitive sciences* (2nd ed., pp. 3-53). Englewood Cliffs, NJ: Educational Technology.

Kelsey, K., & D'Souza, A. (2004). Student motivation for learning at a distance: Does interaction matter? *Online Journal of Distance Learning Administration,* 7(2). Retrieved October 1, 2004, from http://www.westga.edu/~distance/ojdla/summer72/kelsey72.html

Kember, D., Lai, T., Murphy, D., Siaw, I., & Yuen, K. (1994). Student progress in distance education courses: A replication study. *Adult Education Quarterly, 45*(1), 286-301.

Kerssen-Griep, J., Hess, J. A., & Trees, A. R. (2003). Sustaining the desire to learn: Dimensions of perceived instructional facework related to student involvement and motivation to learn. *Western Journal of Communication, 67,* 357-381.

Kruger, K. (2000). Using information technology to create communities of learners. *New Directions for Higher Education, 109,* 59-70.

Lee, S., & Boling, E. (1996). *Motivational screen design guidelines for effective computer-mediated instruction.* Paper presented at the Association for Educational Communications and Technology, Indianapolis, IN.

Maslow, A. (1954). *Motivation and personality.* New York: Harper.

Means, T., Jonassen, D., & Dwyer, F. (1997). Enhancing relevance: Embedded ARCS strategies vs. purpose. *Educational Technology Research and Development, 45,* 5-17.

Moller, L. (1993). *The effects of confidence building strategies on learner motivation and achievement.* Unpublished doctoral dissertation, Purdue University, West Lafayette.

Moller, L. (1998). Designing communities of learners for asynchronous distance education. *Educational Technology and Research Development, 46*(4), 115-122.

Moller, L., & Russell, J. (1994). An application of the ARCS model confidence building strategies. *Performance Improvement Quarterly,* 7(4), 54-69.

Moore, M. G. (1989). Three types of interaction. *The American Journal of Distance Education, 3*(2), 1-6.

Moore, M., & Kearsley, G. (1996). *Distance education: A systems view.* Belmont, CA: Wadsworth.

National Center for Education Statistics. (2000). *Distance education at post-secondary education institutions: 1997-98* [On-line]. Retrieved November 18, 2004, from http://nces.ed.gov

Palloff, R. M., & Pratt, K. (1999). Building learning communities in cyberspace: Effective strategies for the online classroom. San Francisco: Jossey-Bass.

Peters, J. M., & Armstrong, J. L. (1998). Collaborative learning: People laboring together to construct knowledge. *New Directions for Adult and Continuing Education, 79,* 75-85.

Qureshi, E., Morton, L. L., & Antosz, E. (2002). An interesting profile: University students who take distance education courses show weaker motivation than

202 J. B. HUETT, L. A. MOLLER, D. HARVEY, and M. E. ENGSTROM

on-campus students. *Online Journal of Distance Learning Administration, 5*(4). Retrieved October 1, 2004, from http://www.westga.edu/~distance/ojdla/winter54/Qureshi54.htm

Reisetter, M., & Boris, G. (2004). What works: Student perceptions of effective elements in online learning. *Quarterly Review of Distance Education, 5*(4), 277-291.

Rezabek, R. H. (1994). *Utilizing intrinsic motivation in the design of instruction* (Report No. IR 016 761). Nashville, TN: Association for Educational Communications and Technology. (ERIC Document Reproduction Service No. ED 373 751).

Rogers, C. (1951). *Client-centered therapy; its current practice, implications and theory.* Oxford, England: Houghton Mifflin.

Rosenberg, M. (2001). *E-learning: Strategies for delivering knowledge in the digital age.* New York: McGraw-Hill.

Sabry, K., & Baldwin, L. (2003). Web-based interaction and learning styles. *British Journal of Educational Technology, 34*(4), 443-454.

Schallert, D., & Reed, J. (2003). Intellectual, motivational, textual, and cultural considerations in teaching and learning with computer-mediated discussion. *Journal of Research on Technology in Education, 36*(2), 103-119.

Sharp, J., & Huett, J. (2006). Importance of learner-learner interaction in distance education. *Information Systems Education Journal, 4*(46), 1-10.

Skinner, B. F. (1953). *Science and human behavior.* New York: Free Press.

Song, S. H. (1998). *The effects of motivationally adaptive computer-assisted instruction developed through the ARCS model.* Unpublished doctoral dissertation, Florida State University, Tallahassee.

Song, S. H. (2000). Research issues of motivation in web-based instruction. *Quarterly Review of Distance Education, 1*(3), 225-229.

Song, S. H., & Keller, J. M. (2001). Effectiveness of motivationally adaptive computer-assisted instruction on the dynamic aspects of motivation. *Educational Technology Research & Development, 49*(2), 5-22.

Symonds, W. (2003). University of Phoenix Online: Swift rise. *Business Week Online,* June 23, 2003. Retrieved November 18, 2003, from http://www.businessweek.com/magazine/content/03_25/b3838628.htm

Tinto, V., Goodsell-Love, A., & Russo, P. (1993). Building community. *Liberal Education, 79*(4), 16-21.

Visser, J. (1990). *Enhancing learner motivation in an instructor-facilitated learning context.* Unpublished doctoral dissertation, Florida State University, Tallahassee.

Visser, L. (1998). *The development of motivational communication in distance education support.* The Hague, Netherlands: CIP- Gegevens Koninklijke Bibliotheek.

Visser, J., & Keller, J. M. (1990). The clinical use of motivational messages: An inquiry into the validity of the ARCS model of motivational design. *Instructional Science, 19*(6), 467-500.

Visser, L., Plomp, T., Arimault, R., & Kuiper, W. (2002). Motivating students at a distance: The case of an international audience. *Educational Technology Research & Development, 50*(2), 94-110.

Yaghi, H., & Ghaith, G. (2002). Correlates of computing confidence among teachers in an international setting. *Computers in the Schools, 19*(1-2), 81-94.

Yakimovicz, A., & Murphy K. (1995). Constructivism and collaboration on the internet: Case study of a graduate class. *Computers and Education, 24*(3), 203-209.

CHAPTER 12

LINKING COMMUNITY PARTNERS

Utilizing Videoconferencing in a Distributed Learning Environment

Pamela A. Havice, William L. Havice, Clint Isbell, and Larry Grimes

---

The purpose of the study presented in this chapter was to evaluate participants' reactions to the use of videoconferencing facilities to deliver educational/learning opportunities to communities and nonprofit organizations. Descriptive design principles were utilized to sample participants' formative reactions to the methods of a distributed learning environment. This study revealed that the participants' reactions were not negatively affected by the use of videoconferencing as a delivery method for staff development. Furthermore, there was limited evidence to support the idea that continued experience and use of videoconferencing technology by participants develops a more positive attitude towards the technology.

Online Learning Communities
pp. 205–216
Copyright © 2007 by Information Age Publishing
All rights of reproduction in any form reserved.

INTRODUCTION

In 1989, Wurman wrote in his book *Information Anxiety* that there is more information in one issue of the *Wall Street Journal* than was available in a lifetime of reading for a person in the seventeenth century (Wurman, 1989). When Wurman wrote this, the graphical interface that we use everyday to help us navigate the World Wide Web had not yet been introduced. Today we take the Internet for granted and are living and learning in an information society that continues to change at a dramatic rate. An example of this dramatic change is evidenced in the publishing industry, in which publishers are using multiplatforms to deliver information. These platforms include the traditional hard copy publication, as well as digital versions of the information ready for podcasts on portable media players (PMP), mobile devices and personal computers; video segments for cell phones (smartphones); and the Internet. With changes like these, the workplace has seen tremendous challenges and a need for continuously retraining workers to keep an up-to-date workforce.

In this digital age, emerging information technologies have made a dramatic impact on learning opportunities. Because of the influence of emerging information technologies like the Web, learners expect to access information at anytime and any place. Even "places" for learning have changed. With the globalization of learning, the boundaries among cultures and institutions of learning are blurred. As we delve into the twenty-first century, not unlike business and industry, educators all over the world are faced with the challenge of developing ways to manage, present, and best utilize information for themselves and their learners.

Distributed Learning Environment

Changes are taking place very rapidly with little time to develop or analyze trends and relationships in the use of emerging information technology for enhancing learning. Distributed learning has become a popular term used to describe the use of telecommunications to deliver synchronous and asynchronous instruction. In a world struggling to build learning communities within and between educational institutions nationally and worldwide, benefits of distributed learning environments are numerous. Distributed learning is giving opportunity to learners to access information in the traditional classroom, in traditional distance education, and to those participating in online courses. Additionally, within the technology-driven distributed learning environments, efficient, effective, and affective learning are made possible as the learner interacts with others and with the content (Hirschbuhl & Bishop, 1996, 2004; Havice & Havice, 2005).

"Distributed learning," as defined by Oblinger, Barone, and Hawkins (2001), "refers to technology-mediated instruction that serves students both on and off-campus, providing students with greater flexibility and eliminating time as a barrier to learning" (p. 1). Distributed learning environments integrate the interactive capabilities of networking, computing, and multimedia with learner-centered teaching approaches such as collaboration, discovery learning, and active learning. Distributed learning environments can include traditional course materials such as books, handouts, as well as delivered in part through electronic media, such as videoconferencing, videotape, audiographics, interactive television, CD-ROM, electronic mail, and Web-based instruction for the distant learner, the commuting learner, as well as the traditional on-campus learner (DeBourgh, 2003; Havice & Havice, 2005; Havice, Havice & Isbell, 2000).

According to Dede (1997; 2004), a distributed learning environment can be defined as one that facilitates the orchestration of educational activities among classrooms, workplaces, homes and community settings. "Emerging devices, tools, media and virtual environments offer opportunities for creating new types of learning communities" (Dede, 2004, p. 12). One or more of the instructional events that traditionally have occurred in the classroom are distributed to learners so they may occur while learners are separated by either time or space from one another and the course instructor.

Distance education is a part of the distributed learning model. The terms distance education, remote learning, and distance learning all refer to learning environments in which place and/or time separate the learner and instructor; thus the learner learns independent of face-to-face contact with the instructor and, often, other learners (Havice & Havice, 2005). The area of distance learning has especially gained advantage from the resources made available by the distributed learning environments and the various emerging technologies that support the learning process. Several of these technologies: networking advances, teleconferencing, wide band communication, two-way digital video, and Internet2 have created the infrastructure necessary to make the delivery of high quality interactive instruction a reality (Hirschbuhl & Bishop, 2004). The result of employing these technologies is the formation of highly interactive learning environments, which supports Cobb's (1997) redefinition of learning as "a highly interactive set of events shared between the learner and various human/non-human agents, tools, and media" (p. 24).

For this project, two-way videoconferencing was the medium of choice for delivering staff development workshops to three locations. The purpose of this study was to gain an understanding of participants' reactions to videoconferencing in a distributed learning environment.

Videoconferencing: Advantages and Challenges

Distance or mediated technology does not compromise good pedagogy, provided the technology enables interaction and two-way communication (DeBourgh, 2003). Two-way video/two-way-audio systems provide participants with simultaneous interactive image and voice communications, enabling individuals in different locations to communicate with each other as if they were in the same room. Users may be learners communicating with their teachers and other learners over a long distance (Minoli, 1996). Two-way video/audio allows the learner and instructor to interact face-to-face and is the closest match to traditional classroom instruction (Moore & Kearsley, 1996).

A videoconference allows two or more people at different locations to see and hear each other at the same time. It is an interactive instruction method by which a classroom is transmitted by an integrated system of video, audio, and/or computer signals to more than one location. This technology allows people to share information and ideas on a project via options such as document sharing or white-boarding (an electronic version of a blackboard). Depending on the electronic connection, as well as the hardware and software being used, the video frame rate allows videoconferencing to approach television quality (Barron, Orwig, Ivers, & Lilavois, 2002).

Similar to the traditional classroom situation, videoconferencing allows for two-way interaction among participants while those participants are at different locations. Videoconferencing allows the ability to reach more people with minimal travel time for both learners and instructors. Another positive attribute of videoconferencing is the interactive nature of this delivery format, whereby both participants and instructor receive immediate feedback. In the long term, videoconferencing can save money and resources (Havice & Knowles, 1995).

For several years, videoconferencing has been used as an effective means of communication in business and industry to provide conference calls, training, problem solving, sales demonstrations, and so forth, over a broad distance. However, issues with reliability, costs, compatibility, and ease of use have often discouraged expanded use of the technology. With recent technological advances, videoconferencing has become much more dependable and less cumbersome (Krell, 2001). However, the costs of videoconferencing equipment and communication services have widely deterred the expanded use of this technology in the small business, education, and nonprofit sectors. As time and travel costs of delivering training to distant locations in a timely manner becomes more valuable, the use of videoconferencing becomes more cost effective and attractive as a means of communication.

For years, large corporations have been able to afford the costs of videoconferencing through the use of satellite technology. Even at considerable costs, satellite communications provided large companies with the primary means to deliver cost effective and efficient training. As bandwidth has increased within the Internet and cable TV, small business and nonprofit organizations are now finding that accessibility to videoconferencing is an option to more traditional means of delivering content for training and development. Recent advances in technology have not only lowered costs of delivering videoconferencing, there has been a significant improvement in the quality of audio and video. The use of videoconferencing is becoming more widespread across the private sector, government, and education. As noted in the December 2001 issue of *Training*, there are a number of governmental agencies such as the U.S. Department of Labor and the Louisiana Department of Social Services and Welfare using videoconferencing in their programs and services. For example, the Louisiana Department of Social Services and Welfare uses videoconferencing to help its citizens learn basic computer, financial and resume-writing skills (Krell, 2001). The primary advantages of videoconferencing are the savings in travel costs that may be incurred while delivering information to geographically separated participants. However, as with any program, the impact on the training and success of the program must outweigh the costs of the delivery.

As efficient as videoconferencing can be, there are also challenges that arise when working with technology. There are numerous factors that must be taken into consideration for successful implementation of videoconferencing. Adaptation by both the learner and the instructor is an important aspect, as is the attitude of the learner toward the use of the technology. Quality of the audio and video and the environment also play a major role in the successful implementation of this technology. The key to accessibility is a dependable network that will lessen any frustration the user may encounter. This has never been truer than with the use of videoconferencing. Audio and video qualities are essential components and therefore have a major impact upon the success of the program. Acceptance of any new technology depends greatly upon the comfort level and level of frustration of the initial user. Audio and video interference may occur because of technical difficulties. Due to the nontraditional nature of videoconferencing, both the educator and the participants can become apprehensive and anxious. Thus, the educator may have a more difficult time maintaining the attention of the participants. Both the instructor and the participants may find the equipment intimidating and distracting (Havice & Knowles, 1995).

METHODOLOGY

The main purpose of this research project was to evaluate participants' reactions to videoconferencing in a distributed learning environment for educational/learning opportunities to communities and nonprofit organizations. The researchers worked with the South Carolina Center on Nonprofit and Grassroots Leadership, a center within Clemson University's Public Services Division that is managed on behalf of a group of charitable organizations in South Carolina. They developed and delivered a series of three staff development workshops (Workshops I, II, and III) through the South Carolina National Guard Bureau Distributive Training Technology Project (DTTP). Using the DTTP allowed for the use of two-way videoconferencing systems in distributing information across the state to three different locations (Sites A, B, and C).

The three workshops covered three distinctly different topics or themes. Furthermore, the workshop presenters originated from different workshop sites. For workshop I and III, the presenters originated from Site A. During workshop II, the presenters originated from Site C.

Descriptive design principles were utilized in this study to sample participants' formative reactions to the methods of a distributed learning environment. According to Gay (2000), descriptive research can be defined as a collection of data that serves to answer questions concerning the current status of the subject of study. Many descriptive studies are concerned with the measurement of attitudes, opinions, demographic information, conditions, and procedures. Questionnaire surveys, interviews, or observations are usually the means of collection for descriptive data. Gay (2000) also points out that the descriptive researcher has no control over what is, just as the historical researcher has no control over what was. The descriptive researcher can only measure what already exists. The descriptive method was appropriate for this study since the investigators were seeking to answer questions about participants' reactions to a distributed learning environment.

Distributed Learning Environment Groups

The participants in this study were selected from nonprofit literacy associations and councils, as well as directors of adult education programs in rural counties in South Carolina. Using a panel of education experts,

45 leaders in these fields were selected and sent letters announcing a stipend to assist in the costs of attending the series of three workshops. Leaders were selected from across the state and from as many counties as possible. The leaders ranged from having multiple years of experience in literacy education to being new to the job and field. Ultimately, 24 leaders were able to make the commitment that went with the conditions of the award and were distributed among the three sites for the workshop series. The majority of the 24 participants reported having never experienced a two-way videoconference prior to this project.

Participants were located at three sites for each workshop:

Workshop	Site A	Site B	Site C
Workshop #1	$N = 3$	$N = 4$	$N = 17$
Workshop #2	$N = 5$	$N = 6$	$N = 13$
Workshop #3	$N = 5$	$N = 7$	$N = 12$

This study was a sampling of participants' formative reactions to the distributed learning environment. The responses were collected three times over the course of the workshop series, resulting in 93 different comments. Different and changing random samples of participants were utilized with each collection of participant responses. Participants at all three sites were asked to complete statements about what they felt were the "best" and the "worst" things in the day's presentation.

RESULTS

To categorize the responses for the purpose of analysis, the investigator asked three independent judges, each an experienced educator, to view the responses to the reaction questionnaire collected from the control and experimental groups. The judges were asked to sort each response into one of the following categories: positive, negative, or neutral/unrelated. For the judges to rate a comment as "positive," they were to perceive the statement as favorable towards the workshop presentation. To rate the statement as "negative" the judges were to perceive the statement as unfavorable towards the workshop presentation. Responses that did not meet the criteria for being classified as positive or negative were perceived to be neutral or unrelated in regards to the workshop presentation. An inter-rater reliability coefficient of .97 (r) was computed among the three judges. Tables 12.1, 12.2, and 12.3 display the frequency distributions of the perceived categories of positive, negative, and neutral/unrelated com-

Table 12.1.   Responses to Participant Reaction Questionnaire by Site as Rated by Judges—Site A (21 comments)

Workshop	Positive Comments		Negative Comments		Neutral/Unrelated Comments	
	Frequency	%	Frequency	%	Frequency	%
First	6	60.0	4	40.0	0	00.0
Second	4	66.6	1	16.6	1	16.6
Third	4	80.0	0	00.0	1	20.0
Total	14	66.7	5	23.8	2	9.5

Table 12.2.   Responses to Participant Reaction Questionnaire by Site as Rated by Judges—Site B (26 comments)

Workshop	Positive Comments		Negative Comments		Neutral/Unrelated Comments	
	Frequency	%	Frequency	%	Frequency	%
First	5	41.7	6	50.0	1	8.3
Second	8	100.0	0	00.0	0	00.0
Third	6	100.0	0	00.0	0	00.0
Total	19	73.1	6	23.1	1	3.8

Table 12.3.   Responses to Participant Reaction Questionnaire by Site as Rated by Judges—Site C (46 comments)

Workshop	Positive Comments		Negative Comments		Neutral/Unrelated Comments	
	Frequency	%	Frequency	%	Frequency	%
First	8	53.3	5	33.3	2	13.3
Second	13	81.2	2	12.5	1	6.3
Third	11	73.3	4	26.7	0	0.0
Total	32	69.6	11	23.9	3	6.5

ments tabulated from the participant reaction questionnaires at the three sites.

Positive ratings by the judges were given a score of +1 for each comment, neutral/unrelated comments were set at zero, and negative comments were set at –1. The total number of ratings for each comment was computed, and then analysis of variance was completed to compare the

**Table 12.4.   Average Scores for
Each Workshop, Location, and the Interaction**

	A	B	C	Workshop Averages
I	0.20	−0.08	0.20	0.11
II	0.50	1.00	0.68	0.73
III	0.80	1.00	0.47	0.65
Site averages	0.43	0.50	0.47	0.46

average scores for the three workshops, the three sites, and the interaction. An interaction is the variation among the differences between means for different levels of one factor over different levels of the other factor. Table 12.4 gives the average scores for each workshop, site, and the interaction.

This study revealed no interaction between workshop and site. Therefore, differences among workshops were consistent for all sites. The three site scores were not different from each other and were all significantly positive ($p < .05$). The average score for workshop I was not different than neutral and was significantly lower ($p < .05$) than the average scores of either workshop II or III. Finally, the average scores for workshops II and III were positive ($p < .05$) and were not significantly different from each other.

DISCUSSION

This study revealed that participants' reactions were positive overall towards the use of videoconferencing technology as a way to gain staff development opportunities. In other words, participants' reactions were not negatively affected by the use of videoconferencing. Additionally, this study provided limited evidence to support the idea that continued experience and use of videoconferencing technology by participants develops a more positive attitude towards the technology.

One of the major outcomes identified in this study is there was not a significant difference in participants' reactions between sites regardless as to which site the presenter(s) was located. A study by Sorensen and Baylen (1999) found that the presence of the presenter at different sites appears to affect the class dynamics. They suggested that having the presenter rotate sites might equalize class participation across sites. Most importantly, they found that maintaining attention in the distance classroom appears to be a more difficult task than perhaps in the traditional class. The results of this study do little to support these conclusions. A factor for this difference is that each of the three workshops had different present- ers. If the same presenter had been used for all three workshops, the out- come in participants' reactions may have been different.

CONCLUSIONS

Advances in videoconferencing technology have greatly expanded oppor- tunities for the delivery of information in a much more effective and effi- cient means. There will be expanded opportunities for community outreach and cost-cutting opportunities for partnerships between the business community and the education community. Partnerships can bring experts from business and industry into the classroom. There will also be expanded opportunities for the use of videoconferencing for use of virtual therapy and training and development to build relationships between the educator/facilitator and the learner who are separated by dis- tance (Havice et al., 2000; Krell, 2001). Videoconferencing continues to show promise for distributed learning environments. Through this study we have learned some valuable lessons:

- Having "buy-in" from the presenter(s) is important;
- Regardless of delivery method, a presentation is only going to be as effective as the presenter;
- Presenters must be willing to adapt presentation strategies to enhance the videoconferencing environment;
- Technology support remains essential at all sites, especially if there are technical challenges;
- Collaboration and organization are key to the success of a multi-site videoconferenced workshop; and
- Using videoconferencing as a staff development tool was well received by the learners.

Therefore, to continue exploring the uses of videoconferencing tech- nology in developing distributed learning environments, it will be essen- tial that program designers and developers have a thorough understanding of all aspects of using the technology. Furthermore, having an understanding of the needs of the educator and users will be impor- tant. Adaptation of videoconferencing will depend greatly upon the qual- ity of the system, dependability of the system, the facilities, instructor training, and participant use and acceptance. Regardless of costs reductions, if videoconferencing does not gain acceptance from the end users by providing effective results for the intended use, then the application will not be worthwhile.

As learning environments continue to evolve, educators/facilitators will find themselves delivering instruction in the traditional format (face-to-face), while at the same time the presentation will be made synchronous to learners throughout the world transmitted via a Webcast, Podcast, or two-way videoconference. This same presentation will be recorded to storage/playback devices such as a server or devices like a CD-ROM, DVD, iPod™, smartphones, handhelds, or portable media players (PMP). This model allows for learners who cannot attend the original presentation because of time or physical constraints to be able to access the recorded presentation anywhere, anytime. Additionally, the recorded presentation would be available to all learners to assist in reinforcing important information by allowing the learner to play back the presentation as many times as needed.

In the distributed learning model, an educator or facilitator delivers content by communicating with learners through the use of a variety of delivery methods. The explosive growth of the Internet and emerging storage/playback devices has contributed to the increasing popularity of the distributed learning environment. Additionally, this all brings new issues and challenges not yet explored by researchers.

Kozma (1991) contended participants will learn a particular task regardless of the delivery system. He goes on to state that there is a growing understanding of the elements of learning with media, but questions remain in the cognitive effects of recently developed learning environments. Therefore, further research is necessary to better understand how media influences attitude and learning. This would include studying the effectiveness of distributed learning environments. Additional issues that need to be addressed in future research studies include cost effectiveness, the use of various instructional media for different types of subject matter, different types of participants, and different instructional methods.

REFERENCES

Barron, A. E., Orwig, G. W., Ivers, K., & Lilavois, N. (2002). *Technologies for education* (4th ed.). Greenwood Village, CO: Libraries Unlimited.

Cobb, T. (1997). Cognitive efficiency: Toward a revised theory of media. *Educational Technology Research and Development, 45*(4), 21-35.

DeBourgh, G. A. (2003). Predictors of student satisfaction in distance-delivered graduate nursing courses: What matters most? *Journal of Professional Nursing, 19*(3), 149-163.

Dede, C. (1997). Rethinking how to invest in technology. *Educational Leadership*, *55*(3), 12-16.

Dede, C. (2004). Enabling distributed learning communities via emerging technologies. *Technological Horizons in Education Journal*, *32*(2), 12-22.

Gay, L. R. (2000). *Educational research competencies for analysis and application* (5th ed.). New York: Macmillan.

Havice, W. L., & Havice, P. A., (Eds.). (2005). Distance and distributed learning environments: Perspectives and strategies. *54th Yearbook Council on Technology Teacher Education*. Peoria, IL: Glencoe/McGraw-Hill.

Havice, P. A., Havice, W. L., & Isbell, C. (2000). Rubrics and a strategy for integrating traditional instruction and distributed learning. In B. L. Mann (Ed.), *Web course management* (pp. 199-210). Toronto: Canadian Scholars' Press.

Havice, P. A., & Knowles, M. H. (1995). Two-way interactive video: Maximizing distance learning. *The Journal of Continuing Education in Nursing*, *26*(1), 28-30.

Hirschbuhl, J. J., & Bishop, D. (Eds.). (1996). *Computers in education*. Guilford, CT: Dushkin Publishing Group/Brown & Benchmark.

Hirschbuhl, J. J., & Bishop, D. (Eds.). (2004). Distributed learning. In J. J. Hirschbuhl & D. Bishop (Eds.), *Computers in education* (11th ed., pp. 188-212). Guilford, CT: McGraw-Hill/Dushkin.

Kozma, R. B. (1991). Learning with media. *Review of Educational Research*, *61*(2), 179-211.

Krell, E. (2001). Videoconferencing gets the call. *Training*, *38*(12), 36-42.

Minoli, D. (1996). *Distance learning technology and applications*. Norwood, MA: Artech House.

Moore, M. G., & Kearsley, G. (1996). *Distance education: A systems view*. Belmont, CA: Wadsworth.

Oblinger, D. G., Barone, C. A., & Hawkins, B. L. (2001). *Distributed education and its challenges*. Washington, DC: American Council on Education.

Sorensen, C., & Baylen, D. M. (1999, April). *Interaction in interactive television instruction: Perception versus reality*. Paper presented at the 1999 Conference of the American Educational Research Association, Montreal, Canada. (ERIC Document Reproduction Service No. ED 429 590)

Wurman, R. S. (1989). *Information anxiety*. New York: Bantam Books.

PART IV

INTERNATIONAL PERSPECTIVES ON ONLINE LEARNING COMMUNITIES

CHAPTER 13

EXPLORING ELEMENTS FOR CREATING AN ONLINE COMMUNITY OF LEARNERS WITHIN A DISTANCE EDUCATION COURSE AT THE UNIVERSITY OF SOUTHERN QUEENSLAND

**P. A. Danaher, Andrew Hickey,
Alice Brown, and Joan M. Conway**

Three crucial elements of creating and sustaining distance and online communities of learners are cognitive, social, and teacher presence. These elements are fundamental to ensuring that the educational contexts and environments framing a course of study are understood and engaged. This chapter interrogates a graduate preservice teacher education course at an Australian university in terms of its efficacy in facilitating and enacting these elements. The chapter identifies the centrality of presence, multiple and mutual responsibilities, the requirement for technologies to serve human needs, and the importance of explicating and interrogating contexts and environments as vital to sustainable communities of learners.

Online Learning Communities
pp. 219–240

INTRODUCTION

The notion of community underpins much of the recent and contemporary discourse framing social theory (Moriarty, Danaher, & Danaher, 2005). It seems that, as the certitudes of modernity have given way to the uncertainties of postmodernity, a focus on community holds some promise of establishing shared meaning-making and commonality of purpose, albeit within a carefully circumscribed context. This focus has certainly framed such concepts as imagined communities (Anderson, 1983), phantom communities (Durham, 1998), relational communities (Smith, 2005), and symbolic communities (Cohen, 1985).

Within education, community has been deployed as both a theory and a set of strategies to strengthen the bonds between learners and educators and among learners. This has been the case, for example, with the notions of communities of practice (Wenger, McDermott, & Snyder, 2002) and of cooperative communities (Johnson & Johnson, 1998). This approach is generally aligned with a socially constructivist conception of learning (Vygotsky, 1978), highlighting communication, dialogue, and interaction (Anderson, 2003) as crucial vehicles for the development of understanding.

This assumed and desired interplay between community and learning has particular resonance in the fields of distance and online education. Those commentators who privilege face-to-face contact as the educational "norm" insist that there is greater pressure on distance and online education to establish communities of learners to compensate for the inherent disadvantage arising from the absence of such contact (Kruger, 2000). By contrast, champions of distance and online education argue that asynchronous communication and multiple educational sites help to disrupt the educator-learner binary and create new opportunities for revisioning relationships, responsibilities, and roles across and within those sites (Edwards, 1995).

This chapter engages with this interplay between community and learning by exploring the dynamics and the tensions within one specific case of distance and online education: a graduate pre-service teacher education course at the University of Southern Queensland in Australia. The course, titled GDE3002 Contexts and Environments, was developed by a team of four, three of whom and a new academic staff member taught the course for the first time in Semester 1 (February to June) 2006 (and wrote this chapter). The authors deploy Anderson's (2004) useful distinction among cognitive, social, and teacher presence as a conceptual lens for reflecting on the processes and strategies underpinning the course's development and teaching and for interrogating the course's efficacy in generating and facilitating a community of learners. On the basis of that reflection and interrogation, four requirements for successful and sustainable communities of learners are distilled. The chapter is divided into four sections: a brief review of the current literature related to cognitive, social, and teacher presence; an account of the design and implementation of GDE3002 Contexts and Environments; an examination of the course's capacity for enacting cognitive, social, and teacher presence; and an elaboration of four implications for the success and sustainability of communities of learners as a contemporary trend in distance and online education.

LITERATURE REVIEW

It is easy to understand why cognitive, social, and teacher presence constitute an accessible and attractive conceptual framework for distance and online education researchers, particularly those concerned about establishing communities of learners. On the one hand, presence evokes the engagement and interaction assumed to lie at the center of the learner-educator relationship, whether face-to-face or mediated by space and/or time. Presence also betokens the empathy, encouragement, interest, and support and the emotional dimension of being human on which that relationship is presumed to be based. On the other hand, the cognitive, social, and teacher elements of such presence elicit the three commonly accepted modes of interaction in education: respectively student-content, student-student, and student-teacher (Anderson & Garrison, 1998). If distance and online programs and courses can facilitate genuine cognitive, social, and teacher presence and harness these modes of interaction, their pedagogical effectiveness would seem to be heightened, if not assured.

One caveat is appropriate here: the title of the chapter (Anderson, 2004) from which the framework deployed in this chapter is taken is "Teaching in an Online Learning Context." While the authors assert the utility of that framework in reflecting on and interrogating the course discussed here for its capacity to facilitate a community of learners, they acknowledge that that framework derives from the specific concerns and interests of the teaching staff in the course. It is hoped in subsequent research to glean and analyze the multiple perspectives of the students and other stakeholders in the course and the program to which it contributes.

That proviso having been noted, the authors turn to the model elaborated by Anderson (2004), based on earlier work by Garrison, Anderson, and Archer (2000), and represented in Figure 13.1. That representation

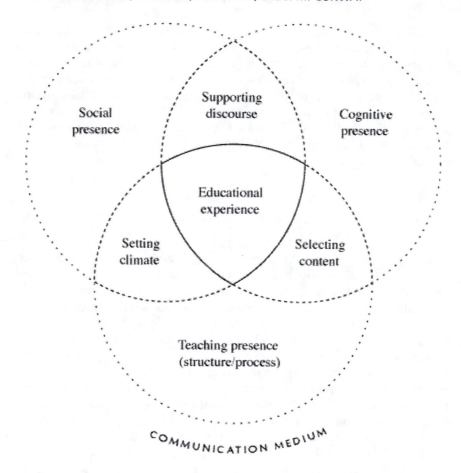

Source: Anderson (2004).

Figure 13.1.   Community of inquiry.

places central emphasis on the nature and quality of the educational experience, to which each of cognitive, social, and teaching presence makes a vital contribution, specifically by means of the simultaneous processes of selecting content, supporting discourse, and setting climate. Anderson (2004) contends that "deep and meaningful learning results when there are sufficient levels" (p. 274) of all three types of presence; they are therefore interdependent and iterative.

First, according to Anderson (2004), cognitive presence is crucial to ensuring "that serious learning can take place in an environment that supports the development and growth of critical thinking skills" (p. 274).

Furthermore, cognitive presence "is grounded in and defined by study of a particular content; thus, it works within the epistemological, cultural, and social expression of the content in an approach that supports the development of critical thinking skills" (p. 274). This form of presence accords directly with the student-content interaction mode noted by Anderson and Garrison (1998).

Second, Anderson (2004) states that social presence "relates to the establishment of a supportive environment such that students feel the necessary degree of comfort and safety to express their ideas in a collaborative context" (p. 274). It follows that the absence of social presence "leads to an inability to express disagreements, share viewpoints, explore differences, and accept support and confirmation from peers and teacher" (p. 274). This form of presence articulates particularly with the student-student interaction mode identified by Anderson and Garrison (1998).

Third, Anderson (2004) postulates that teaching presence "is critical" to "formal education" (p. 274). Drawing on the work of Anderson, Rourke, Archer, and Garrison (2001), he identifies "three critical roles that a teacher performs in the process of creating an effective teaching presence" (p. 274):

> The first of these roles is the design and organization of the learning experience that takes place both before the establishment of the learning community and during its operation. Second, teaching involves devising and implementing activities to encourage discourse between and among students, between the teacher and the student, and between individual students and groups of students and content resources.... Third, the teaching role goes beyond that of moderating the learning experiences when the teacher adds subject matter expertise through a variety of forms of direct instruction. (p. 274)

This form of presence links clearly with the student-teacher interaction mode posited by Anderson and Garrison (1998).

While the authors consider that the conceptual framework represented by Figure 13.1 is relevant and robust in relation to the course under review in this chapter, it is appropriate to acknowledge that other contemporary literature questions the centrality of the three types of presence. Some concern (Kehrwald, 2006) derives from the fact that the most commonly cited explanation of social presence occurred in the mid 1970s (Short, Williams, & Christie, 1976), and that it is likely to require some updating, particularly in view of the unprecedented technological developments since that time. Another source of critique has been the assertion that, rather than social presence helping to explain why particular media communicate the impression of the presences of others, "all media have an inherent degree of richness" (Hiltz, Coppola, Rotter, & Turoff, 2000), but also that "No medium is richest on all media characteristics, and the relationships between communication processes and media capabilities will vary between established and newly formed groups, and will change over time."

Although these concerns have some merit, the authors find more persuasive Luppicini's (2002) identification of what can be seen as an elaboration of social presence: the notions of sociopolitical and sociocultural presence. According to Luppicini, sociopolitical presence "concerns normative and pragmatic rules in sociopolitical structures" (p. 97). Distinguishing between, and studying, these rule types are important, because "there are political structures, contests, conflicts, environmental factors, and change at the base of any society" (p. 97). Similarly, sociocultural analysis "describes an inquiry into values, beliefs, and communication styles developed by a group of people in a particular human environment" (p. 97). In Luppicini's view, "Sociopolitical and sociocultural presence is gradually growing in recognition as an important aspect of computer-mediated learner communities" (p. 97). For the authors, this recognition attests to the understanding of the politicized contexts and environments in which distance and online education are enacted—an understanding that resonates with the concerns of the course as elaborated below.

Thus, Anderson's (2004) focus on cognitive, social, and teacher presence, leavened by current critiques of social presence, constitutes a timely and useful framework for the authors' interrogation of the capacity of GDE3002 Contexts and Environments to facilitate the development of a distance and online community of learners. That interrogation is preceded by an account of the design and implementation of the course in the first half of 2006.

DESIGNING AND IMPLEMENTING
GDE3002 CONTEXTS AND ENVIRONMENTS

The Graduate Diploma in Learning and Teaching was developed and accredited in 2005 by the Faculty of Education at the University of Southern Queensland in response to government changes to teacher education programs in Queensland. Until the mid 1990s, prospective teachers chose between a 4-year full-time undergraduate pathway and a 1-year full-time graduate entry pathway to qualify for registration, then from the mid 1990s to the mid 2000s the graduate entry pathway was doubled to 2 years full-time. A review of graduate entry programs recommended the reversion to 1 year full-time, partly to bring them into line with equivalent programs offered by universities in other Australian states.

In developing a new graduate entry program in response to this change, the Faculty of Education at the University of Southern Queensland decided to offer the program in two modes: on-campus (face-to-face); and online (using the WebCT course management system). Despite this distinction, all students in the program have a broad commonality of learning experiences; face-to-face students have access to intensive workshops throughout each course, but the central pedagogy is focused on online facilitation of engagement with written study materials to which all students have access (a point that highlights the cultural expectation at the university that all students, regardless of delivery mode, need to engage with contemporary technologies in their learning). This approach was intended to maximize development and teaching efficiencies in a situation in which the program had to be designed and implemented in a concentrated time period, and also to articulate with the demographics of the university's student population, nearly 80% of whom are external or distance students and 30% of whom are international students. The university has a well-established reputation for providing distance and online education, and the program developers sought to capitalize on that reputation in structuring and teaching the program.

The eight courses in the program are intentionally diverse, as befits a program seeking to certify contemporary registered teachers, yet they have some features in common:

- The courses support specialization in early years, primary, secondary, or further education and training;
- The courses are structured around a "problem-based" pedagogy;
- The courses are intended to prepare students for, and to be enriched by students' experiences during, periods of professional attachment in educational settings;
- The courses contribute to a compulsory initial residential workshop and/or optional supplementary workshops;
- Each course has its own Web site using WebCT, consisting of downloadable course materials (typically a course specification, a study guide, and additional readings), announcements, and asynchronous discussion lists, with the capacity for recorded lectures and/or Macromedia Breeze presentations to be added; and
- Each course has a series of face-to-face workshops for students able to visit Toowoomba, the university's principal campus.

Within that broader context, GDE3002 Contexts and Environments is one of four courses studied by full-time students in the first of the two semesters of the program (see also Danaher, in press). The course has the following rationale:

Socio-cultural and socio-political factors are powerful influences on the environments in which teachers conduct their work in schools and, in turn, on the environments that they establish for their work with students. In the broader context of globalisation, with its attendant homogenising forces, inclusive practice needs to recognise the differences that students and communities bring to the learning context. In order to design teaching and learning environments that are socially just and inclusive, teachers require an understanding of the socio-cultural realities of learners and the positioning of schools within particular cultural contexts and locations. (University of Southern Queensland, 2006, p. i)

Likewise, the course synopsis is as follows:

This course is designed to assist students to understand the range of social and political forces that interact to shape the nature of educational contexts and environments within schools, as well as the cultural identities of the individuals within schools. Understandings of these forces and trends are connected to exploration of whole-school and individual-teacher approaches to the establishment of inclusive learning environments. Awareness of how particular schools respond to particular features of their socio-cultural communities is explored through the lens of a social justice approach to meeting the needs of "at risk" groups. The course provides for a nominal 7.5 days of professional attachment to an identified school. During this period of attachment students will be immersed in the day-to-day operations of the school and in the work of a teacher, with a particular focus on the connections between that work and the issues covered in this course. (University of Southern Queensland, 2006, p. i)

The course has nine objectives, some specific to the course and others generic, whereby on completion of this course students will be able to:

- identify the key elements of inclusive learning environments;
- demonstrate knowledge of the socio-cultural, legislative, systemic and educational contexts that inform quality teaching for diversity;
- understand the application of ecological theory in a particular context;
- identify the implications and ramifications of actions taken at different levels of an education system;
- apply whole of school and community approaches to social justice in education;
- demonstrate knowledge, understanding and skill in the use of appropriate personal, professional and academic literacies;

- demonstrate knowledge, understanding and application of appropriate ICT uses for teaching and learning in a particular context;
- apply an understanding of contexts and environments in the professional attachment; and
- articulate an example of how the key concepts encountered in this course can be applied in an educational setting (University of Southern Queensland, 2006, p. ii).

The course content has been divided into four modules, each constituting one quarter of the study guide (Hickey, Collins-Gearing, Brown, & Danaher, 2006), one quarter of the facilitated online discussion, and one workshop for face-to-face students:

- Socio-cultural influences on individuals, schools and education,
- Whole-school and community approaches to inclusivity and social justice,
- Features of inclusive learning environments, and
- Educational reform and the role of the teacher (University of Southern Queensland, 2006, p. ii).

The course's summative assessment consists of three items: a proposal for problem-based presentation (10%), a problem-based presentation (40%), and a professional attachment (50%) (University of Southern Queensland, 2006, p. iv). Teaching team members assess students for the first two items; the remaining 50% is assessed by each student's professional attachment supervisor.

The course specification—and hence the rationale, synopsis, objectives, four content areas, and summative assessment items—had been written by the program coordinator as part of the program accreditation process; while he sought input and feedback from academic staff members, many of them had minimal involvement because they were not aware at that stage whether they would be developing and teaching specific courses. Three of the authors and another academic staff member wrote the four modules in the study guide over a period of three to four weeks at the beginning of 2006. The study guide and selected readings were loaded onto the course Web site prior to the commencement of the semester of the first teaching of the course, which at the time of writing this chapter is drawing to a close. Each of the four authors of the chapter facilitated the course's discussion list for the three weeks allocated to that person's module and presented one two-hour workshop at the Toowoomba campus for students who were able to attend; two of those workshops were recorded "live" and then uploaded onto the course site, while the facilitators of the other two workshops subsequently recorded Macromedia Breeze presentations with PowerPoint slides and an audio commentary that were loaded onto the site.

COGNITIVE, SOCIAL, AND TEACHER PRESENCE IN THE COURSE

The literature having been reviewed and the course having been outlined, the authors turn now to apply the three types of presence (Anderson, 2004) as a conceptual framework for evaluating the course's effectiveness in promoting a distance and online community of learners. This evaluation deploys a single case exploratory design within the case study method (Stake, 1995; Stark & Torrance, 2005; Yin, 1994), with the goal being an intensive examination of a contextualized phenomenon and the identification of possible implications beyond that phenomenon, rather than generalizability across contexts and phenomena.

Cognitive Presence

As was noted above, cognitive presence is designed to foster effective student-content interaction and to work "within the epistemological, cultural, and social expression of the content in an approach that supports the development of critical thinking skills" (Anderson, 2004, p. 274). This implies a capacity to help to bring the course content "to life" for students and to facilitate their making direct and substantial links between that content and their respective and shared lifeworlds and worldviews. In this respect, the focus was on using cognitive presence to develop shared pedagogical understanding in ways that were as dialogical as possible.

Each member of the course development team approached the task of writing her or his module for the study guide from the perspective of this goal—of making the text of the module as engaging and dialogical as possible. A number of textual strategies were used to further this goal, ranging from posing in-text questions to reflecting on multiple possible interpretations of particular readings to making explicit the author's specific standpoint with regard to the intentions of the module. This was particularly important with the first module, which provided the conceptual tools and vocabulary for students to develop their own positions in relation to complex contemporary educational issues.

Similarly, each member of the course teaching team used the three-week online facilitation of her or his module, and the two hour workshop for face-to-face students, to draw students' attention to aspects of the course content felt to be crucial to helping the students to meet the course objectives (and in the process to develop critical thinking skills) and to completing the summative assessment items. The emphasis was consistently on maximizing cognitive presence by explaining difficult or unfamiliar concepts of vocabulary, highlighting links and resonances across modules, identifying areas of debate and dissension within the content, and suggesting strategies for time-efficient approaches to engaging with complex and lengthy material.

Despite the development and teaching team members' best efforts, many students in the course's first cohort found the course content difficult and even inaccessible. Their initial degrees, on which their status as graduate entry teacher education students depended, varied widely, from arts and cultural studies to engineering and fine arts to law and media studies to nursing and science. Some students with backgrounds in arts, cultural studies, and sociology had an existing familiarity with many of the course concepts; others had no such familiarity and felt at a distinct disadvantage. Moreover, some students had completed those initial degrees one or two years before enrolling in this program, whereas others had last studied formally several years previously and some of them found the return to university study difficult. Furthermore, some students were resistant to the idea of developing their own philosophy and pedagogical approach, seeming to expect that teaching team members would tell them what that approach should be.

This situation of variability in students' capacity and/or willingness to engage with admittedly cognitively complex course content exercised the minds and challenged the respective pedagogical approaches of the teaching team members during and between team meetings (with varied views, for example, about the levels and types of cognitive scaffolding appropriate and possible to provide to students). Informal observation suggested that it was also a concern of teams teaching the three other courses in the first semester of the program. The team members will need to engage in careful and reflexive dialogue, informed by the students' final grades for the course and their completed course evaluation surveys, in order to see whether the presentation of the course content can be adapted in order to enhance the course's cognitive presence. At the same time, it is important for students and team members alike to recollect the course's intended contribution to certifying program graduates who are "industry ready" and capable of making the transition to effective classroom practitioners, so it is vital not to "water down" content in ways that render that contribution null and void.

Social Presence

Anderson's (2004) conception of social presence, which is focused particularly on student-student interaction, is that it "relates to the establishment of a supportive environment such that students feel the necessary degree of comfort and safety to express their ideas in a collaborative context" (p. 274), and that the absence of social presence "leads to an inability to express disagreements, share viewpoints, explore differences, and accept support and confirmation from peers and teacher" (p. 274).

The course online discussion list was the most prominent intended vehicle for the promotion of students' social presence. While it is not easy to identify the percentage of students who sent posts regularly compared with those who sent only one or two messages or who sent no posts at all, it is clear that several students were "lurkers" who read other students' posts and learned from them but for a variety of reasons declined to send messages themselves. Through e-mail messages and/or telephone calls to individual teaching team members, some students said that they felt overwhelmed by the course content and had a view that some other students had a far more decisive grasp on understanding that content than they had, rendering them disinclined to demonstrate what they perceived as their relative ignorance of the material.

At the same time, several students took advantage of the medium to send and respond to others' posts, and thereby to develop and display their social presence. These messages were of various types, including:

- Introducing themselves to other students and teaching team members;
- Asking questions of teaching team members, generally about content and/or summative assessment requirements;
- Responding to comments and/or questions posted by teaching team members;
- Responding to comments and/or questions posted by other students (for example, sending copies of readings that the posting students had been unable to download);
- Presenting alternative views to those posted by other students (for example, dissenting from a proposal for changing the dates of the optional midyear residential school, on the grounds that they had already made arrangements for attending on the previously advertised dates, and presenting an alternative experience of teaching in schools organized by specific Christian denominations);
- Striving to establish face-to-face study groups (for example, among students living in the same geographical area); and

- Striving to establish face-to-face social groups (for example, inviting students living in Toowoomba to meet for drinks at the university student club on Friday afternoons during the period of professional attachment).

A few observations are worthwhile making about the character and significance of these multiple enactments of students' social presence. The first and most striking for the teaching team members was the wide array of responsibilities that students continued to discharge at the same time as participating in full-time university study. These responsibilities ranged from paid employment (in some cases more than 30 hours per week), caring for family members, becoming married and giving birth during or at the end of the semester. While this trend conforms with McInnis's (2001) analysis that university study is not at the center of contemporary students' lives and has to compete with manifold other interests and pressures, teaching team members were concerned that some students had an unrealistic idea of the level of engagement needed to complete the course satisfactorily, and that this did not augur well for their understanding of what would be required of them as practicing educators.

The second and related observation is the apparently wide diversity of student attitudes and approaches to studying in the course (and presumably in the program as a whole). Some students had clearly read and reflected on the study guide and selected readings at considerable depth, and addressed numerous questions to teaching team members, both on the discussion list and via individual e-mail messages (in a few cases, seeming to fixate on relatively minor details of presentation). Others displayed a minimalist approach to study, sometimes allied with a high level of dependency on academic staff members that seemed to assume that it was the staff members' responsibility to provide the answers for the students to reproduce in their summative assessment items. One example of this was a few posts to the discussion list, along the lines that other universities that had student teachers at the same professional attachment site as these students expected far less of their students in terms of levels of commitment and engagement.

The third and perhaps corollary observation is the tension evident between students being willing to assist one another to find information and to suggest possible alternative ways of approaching their summative assessment items on the one hand and being covertly and overtly competitive with one another on the other. It was certainly the case that the summative assessment items were individualized and that no attempt was made to initiate online teamwork. At the same time, there was relatively little effort invested by students in building on other students' responses to questions in the online discussions.

Finally, in relation to social presence, as noted above, Luppicini (2002) provided a useful elaboration of this concept with his reference to sociopolitical presence, which focuses on the "political structures, contests, conflicts, environmental factors, and change at the base of any society" (p. 97), and to sociocultural presence, which "describes an inquiry into values, beliefs, and communication styles developed by a group of people in a particular human environment" (p. 97). Certainly GDE3002 Contexts and Environments is centrally concerned with these deeply embedded forces and structures that construct historical and contemporary meaning for multiple individuals and communities, particularly in relation to their impact on the possibilities and constraints of formal educational provision; this is exemplified in the first module in the course, "Socio-cultural influences on individuals, schools and education." Given that orientation, it was pleasing that students selected as their concept from that module such notions as agency, critical pedagogy, identity, and public pedagogies. Yet it is also fair to remark that students varied widely in the level of engagement with the sociopolitical and sociocultural dimensions of presence and in their demonstration of the degree of reflexivity required to assign to those dimensions the prominence that they warranted.

Teacher Presence

Anderson's (2004) major focus was on teaching presence and on the student-teacher interaction mode, which the authors have interpreted in terms of their capacity as teaching team members to facilitate the course's status as a community of learners. The authors follow Anderson's distinction among design and organization, facilitating discourse, and direct instruction as "three critical roles that a teacher performs in the process of creating an effective teaching presence" (p. 274).

Design and Organization

Anderson noted that "The first of these roles is the design and organization of the learning experience that takes place both before the establishment of the learning community and during its operation" (p. 274). As was outlined above, the development and teaching team members drew on their respective and shared experiential and theoretical knowledge in writing and/or facilitating their designated modules in the course. For example, the author and facilitator of the first module deployed his expertise in cultural studies and social theory to devise a conceptually rigorous yet empirically-grounded account of the interface between sociocultural ideas and education. The author of the second module, about whole-school and community approaches to inclusivity and social justice, interpreted that topic through the lens of her own indigeneity and her interest in Indigenous ways of knowing and understanding the world and education, while the facilitator of that module brought to the task her experience and research in school leadership and revitalization. The author and facilitator of the third module, which dealt with the features of inclusive learning environments, extrapolated from her working knowledge of, and teaching about, such environments in early childhood education and from the perspective of ecological theory. The author and facilitator of the fourth and final module, concerned with educational reform and the role of educators, framed the module in terms of his interest in the links between educators' work and identities and illustrated this framing by reference to teachers of occupational travelers such as circus and show communities, the subject matter of his research with other colleagues.

From this it was made clear to students that, rather than being neutral vehicles or passive ciphers for the delivery of content, the development and teaching team members were an integral part of the course's design and implementation. Moreover, individually and in combination they had significant and widely ranging experience as learners, educators, and researchers across a diversity of educational sectors and systems and across a number of different countries. In this way, the team members were modeling to students the kinds and levels of engagement and reflexivity that they expected the students to demonstrate throughout the course. Thus, the course design and organization both highlighted and depended on a strong level of teacher presence to set the parameters and lay the foundations of establishing a community of learners.

Facilitating Discourse

As the second element of teacher presence, Anderson (2004) noted that "teaching involves devising and implementing activities to encourage discourse between and among students, between the teacher and the student, and between individual students and groups of students and content resources" (p. 274). As with other types of presence, the online discussion list was the most appropriate medium for the facilitation of this discourse, enhanced by such strategies as a rapid rate in teaching team members responding to students' posts and individual e-mail messages and ensuring that such responses were phrased in ways that fostered ongoing dialogue rather than closed down conversation. Moreover, team members emphasized that they were also learners and asserted frequently the importance of listening to and understanding other people's opinions. Again as with other types of presence, the authors' analysis suggests a "mixed picture" about teacher presence being used to facilitate widely ranging and deeply reflexive discourse in the course.

On the one hand, it was clear that as the semester progressed the level of student commentary became more highly developed, with some students engaging with such issues as multiple and potentially conflicting understandings of social justice and the extent to which some teachers resisted what they perceived as the malign effects of specific educational reforms. This was particularly the case once students had commenced their periods of professional attachment: many of them seized the opportunity to use the theoretical concepts encountered in the course as lenses for reflecting on their practical experiences, and some of them also moved in the reverse direction, by subjecting the concepts to critique for relevance and utility on the basis of those practical experiences.

On the other hand, the great majority of student posts were submitted to the topics and categories which had been established by the teaching team members and which predictably focused on the four modules and the two summative assessment items that those team members were responsible for assessing. Students did have a capacity to create new discussion headings under "Default topic"; these ranged from "Reading 2.1 where is it?" and "Reading 2.1 found" to "assignment submitted to wrong course" to "Friday afternoon drinkies." Furthermore, the author and development and teaching team member who was also the course coordinator submitted 278 or nearly 28% of the 995 posts submitted at the time of writing this chapter. While many of those posts were intended to pose and respond to questions and thereby to facilitate discourse, the sheer volume of posts emanating from a single person who was also the course coordinator suggests the risk that much of the communication was monological rather than dialogical (Bakhtin, 1984).

Direct Instruction

Anderson (2004) identified direct instruction as the third element of teacher presence: "the teaching role goes beyond that of moderating the learning experiences when the teacher adds subject matter expertise through a variety of forms of direct instruction" (p. 274). Given the distributed and mediated character of the course design, direct instruction was not a prominent feature of GDE3002 Contexts and Environments; instead, the emphasis was on the course study guide, selected readings, and the course discussion list being used as vehicles to facilitate student engagement and understanding. The goal was to maximize links between the course content and the students' own settings, by posing questions such as "What is happening, and how does this relate to you and your setting?"

Direct instruction as an aspect of teacher presence was most clearly evident in the 2-hour face-to-face workshops conducted at the Toowoomba campus of the university, one workshop being facilitated by each of the four teaching team members. Yet even with those workshops the practice was generally to intersperse a relatively small amount of content from the respective module with suggested strategies for completing the summative assessment items. The provision of feedback to individual students about each completed assessment item was another opportunity for a form of direct instruction; a complication with that was that, owing to workload allocations, about 50 students' work was assessed by a contracted marker who was not a member of the course development or teaching teams and who was not paid to have direct contact with students apart from her marking of their work. Direct instruction was also facilitated by means of the Macromedia Breeze presentations, which dealt with summative assessment items and the importance of listening skills by means of focused input by two of the course teaching team members.

IMPLICATIONS FOR THE SUCCESS AND SUSTAINABILITY OF DISTANCE AND ONLINE COMMUNITIES OF LEARNERS

It is clear from the preceding analysis that the course development and teaching team members' efforts to establish cognitive, social, and teacher presence in GDE3002 Contexts and Environments have achieved varying degrees and levels of success. This is hardly surprising, given the complexity of and speed in developing and implementing a mixed mode course concerned with largely intangible yet pervasive and influential elements of educational provision.

From this analysis, the authors have distilled four key implications for what they envisage as the potential success and sustainability of distance and online communities of learners, which in turn they perceive as one of the key contemporary trends in distance and online education. These implications focus on the ongoing centrality of presence, the multiple and mutual responsibilities for establishing and maintaining communities of learners, the requirement for media and technologies to serve different kinds of human aspirations and needs, and the importance of explicating and interrogating the educational contexts and environments in which communities of learners are situated.

First, the analysis presented in this chapter has reinforced to the authors the ongoing centrality of cognitive, social, and teacher presence in any educational enterprise. Despite the concerns noted in the literature review about the continuing relevance of the concept of presence, the authors argue that these three types of presence have provided a relevant and robust conceptual framework for interrogating the course's efficacy in generating a coherent and productive community of learners. Furthermore, that framework will be indispensable in the enduring task of evaluating and refining the course so that it maximizes students' learning outcomes and the development of that community of learners. As Anderson (2004) noted at the end of his chapter about teacher presence:

> As yet, we are at early stages in the technological and pedagogical development of online learning. But the fundamental characteristics of teaching and learning and the three critical components of teacher presence...will continue to be critical components of teaching effectiveness in both online learning and classroom instruction. (p. 291)

Second, the preceding analysis reinforces the interdependence of students, course development and teaching team members, and other stakeholders if learning is to be maximized and if a community of learners is to be generated and sustained. The responsibilities of individuals and groups within such a community need to be both multiple and mutual. In a sense, this point has been exemplified by the development and teaching team members who, despite not having worked together previously, have quickly found common ground as well as areas of individual contribution, derived from their separate and collective abilities and interests. This kind of interdependent and iterative working relationship is very difficult to render scaleable, particularly across space and time, yet it is crucial to do so as one of the pillars underpinning a genuine community of learners. Here the five principles of cooperative communities (Johnson & Johnson, 1998)—positive interdependence, individual accountability, promotion of one another's success, interpersonal and small group skills, and group processing—would seem to be particularly helpful in providing some possible navigational tools for ways to proceed.

Third, the analysis in the chapter calls attention to the relativities of the relationship between media and technologies on the one hand and human beings on the other. Communities of learners work most effectively when media and technologies serve the aspirations and needs of human beings, rather than vice versa. The best utilization of media and technologies in educational settings occurs when those media and technologies are seamless and invisible parts of the educational process, not when they act as frustrating or even ominous gatekeepers (as, for example, when some students were unable to work out how to submit their summative assessment items electronically via the course studydesk). Hodas's (1993) notion of "technology refusal" is a timely reminder that what some technology developers regard as benign and innocent media of instruction can be seen by other people as malign instruments of control, to be resisted at all costs. The technological framework for distance and online community of learners must facilitate shared meaning-making and understanding, not replicate existing sociocultural inequities and/or create new ones.

Fourth, the subject matter of the course under review highlights the importance of explicating and interrogating the educational contexts and environments in which particular communities of learners are situated. Some aspects of those contexts and environments are clear and visible; many other aspects are intangible and invisible, rendering that explication and interrogation even more necessary and significant. To that end, with appropriate alterations to broaden its scope and reach, the course's rationale might serve as a useful starting point for discussions of how to make the educational contexts and environments of communities of learners part of the process of establishing and sustaining those communities:

> Sociocultural and sociopolitical factors are powerful influences on the environments in which teachers conduct their work in schools and, in turn, on the environments that they establish for their work with students. In the broader context of globalization, with its attendant homogenising forces, inclusive practice needs to recognise the differences that students and communities bring to the learning context. In order to design teaching and learning environments that are socially just and inclusive, teachers require an understanding of the socio-cultural realities of learners and the positioning of schools within particular cultural contexts and locations. (University of Southern Queensland, 2006, p. i)

CONCLUSION

This chapter has presented a case study of the development and implementation of a single graduate preservice teacher education course at the University of Southern Queensland in Australia. That case study used cognitive, social, and teacher presence (Anderson, 2004), leavened by sociopolitical and sociocultural presence (Luppicini, 2002), as a conceptual framework for evaluating the course's efficacy in generating a community of learners. The evaluation demonstrated that, while the course development and teaching teams have achieved some positive outcomes in terms of such a community, ongoing work is required to consolidate and sustain that community.

The chapter began by pondering the continuing focus on communities. The analysis presented in the chapter helps to explain why community persists in exercising the minds and engaging the spirits of learners, educators, and other educational stakeholders, regardless of educational sector, system, and mode. Certainly the course development and teaching team members, and many of the students, have felt that the elements of a community of learners help in the complex task of communicating some-times cognitively difficult content and of assisting students to engage with that content and of making links between it and their professional attachments. Assumptions about the co-construction of knowledge and that learning is cooperative rather than individualized or competitive under-pin the aspiration to make the course the framework and vehicle for fostering lifelong and lifewide learning partnerships, pathways, and pedagogies (Orr, Nouwens, Macpherson, Harreveld, & Danaher, 2006).

Yet the four implications distilled from that analysis highlight that achieving this aspiration is neither automatic nor easy. The authors contend that the centrality of presence, multiple and mutual responsibilities, the requirement for technologies to serve human needs, and the importance of explicating and interrogating contexts and environments are necessary but by no means sufficient conditions for the attainment of successful and sustainable communities of learners. The importance of continuing educational work—learning, teaching, policymaking, and research—to ensure that attainment is undeniable; the authors hope that this chapter and the book to which it contributes will augment the effectiveness, energy, and equity of that work.

ACKNOWLEDGMENTS

The authors are grateful to Rocci Luppicini for the invitation to participate in this project; they acknowledge Brooke Collins-Gearing's contribution to developing, Catherine H. Arden's role as initial respondent to, and Rebecca Statton's assistance in marking, the course reported here; and they express their thanks to the students enrolled in the course's initial cohort and to their colleagues in the program in which the course is located, particularly Rick Churchill for his original conceptualization of the course and the program. John Brown provided timely technical support at a crucial juncture in publication.

REFERENCES

Anderson, B. (1983). *Imagined communities: Reflections on the origin and spread of nationalism*. London: Verso.

Anderson, T. (2003, October). Getting the mix right again: An updated and theoretical rationale for interaction. *International Review of Research in Open and Distance Learning, 4*(2). Retrieved April 5, 2006, from http://www.irrodl.org/index.php/irrodl/article/view/149/230

Anderson, T. (2004). Teaching in an online learning context. In T. Anderson & F. Elloumi (Eds.), *Theory and practice of online learning* (pp. 273-294). Athabasca, Alberta, Canada: Athabasca University.

Anderson, T., & Garrison, D. R. (1998). Learning in a networked world: New roles and responsibilities. In C. Gibson (Ed.), *Distance learners in higher education* (pp. 97-112). Madison, WI: Atwood.

Anderson, T., Rourke, L., Archer, W., & Garrison, R. (2001). Assessing teaching presence in computer conferencing transcripts. *Journal of Asynchronous Learning Networks, 5*(2). Retrieved June 25, 2006, from http://www.aln.org/publications/jaln/v5n2/v5n2_anderson.asp

Bakhtin, M. M. (1984). *Problems of Doestoevsky's poetics* (C. Emerson, Ed. and Trans.). Minneapolis, MN: University of Minnesota Press.

Cohen, A. P. (1985). *The symbolic construction of community.* Chichester and London, UK: Ellis Horword and Tavistock.

Danaher, P. A. (in press). The social control–social capital debate about distance and online teacher education: Critical reflections on two courses at the University of Southern Queensland, Australia. *Journal of Open Learning and Teacher Education.*

Durham, S. (1998). *Phantom communities: The simulacrum and the limits of postmodernism.* Palo Alto, CA: Stanford University Press.

Edwards, R. (1995). Different discourses, discourses of difference: Globalisation, distance education and open learning. *Distance Education, 16*(2), 241-255.

Garrison, D. R., Anderson, T., & Archer, W. (2000). Critical thinking in text-based environment: Computer conferencing in higher education. *The Internet and Higher Education, 2*(2), 87-105.

Hickey, A., Collins-Gearing, B., Brown, A., & Danaher, P. A. (2006). *GDE3002 Contexts and environments: Study guide* (Semester 1 2006). Toowoomba, Queensland: Faculty of Education, University of Southern Queensland.

Hiltz, S. R., Coppola, N., Rotter, N., & Turoff, M. (2000, September). Measuring the importance of collaborative learning for the effectiveness of ALN: A multi-measure, multi-method approach. *Journal of Asynchronous Learning Networks, 4*(2). Retrieved June 25, 2006, from http://www.sloan-c.org/publications/jaln/v4n2/v4n2_hiltz.asp

Hodas, S. (1993, September 14). Technology refusal and the organizational culture of schools. *Education Policy Analysis Archives, 1*(10). Retrieved April 10, 2005, from http://epaa.asu.edu/epaa/v1n10.html

Johnson, D. W., & Johnson, R. T. (1998). The three Cs of effective schools: Cooperative community, constructive conflict, civic values. *Connections: Journal of the Australian Association for Co-operative Education, 5*(1), 4-10.

Kehrwald, B. A. (2006, June). *Inhabiting online spaces: Reconsidering social presence in contemporary online learning environments.* Paper presented at the 4th international lifelong learning conference, Yeppoon, Central Queensland, Australia.

Kruger, K. (2000). Using information technology to create communities of learners. In B. Jacoby (Ed.), *Involving commuter students in learning* (New directions for higher education) (pp. 59-70). San Francisco: Jossey-Bass.

Luppicini, R. J. (2002). Toward a conversation system modeling research methodology for studying computer-mediated learning communities. *Journal of Distance Education, 17(2)*, 87-101.

McInnis, C. (2001, August). *Signs of disengagement? The changing undergraduate experience in Australian universities.* Inaugural professorial lecture presented in the Centre for the Study of Higher Education, Faculty of Education, University of Melbourne, Australia.

Moriarty, B. J., Danaher, P. A., & Danaher, G. R. (2005). Pedagogies and learning in cooperative and symbolic communities of practice: Implications for and from the education of Australian show people. *International Journal of Pedagogies and Learning, 1(2)*, 47-56.

Orr, D., Nouwens, F., Macpherson, C., Harreveld, R. E., & Danaher, P. A. (Eds.) (2006). *Lifelong learning: Partners, pathways, and pedagogies: Keynote and refereed papers from the 4th international lifelong learning conference* (pp. i-x, 1-370). Rockhampton, Queensland, Australia: Lifelong Learning Conference Committee, Central Queensland University Press.

Short, J., Williams, E., & Christie, B. (1976). *The social psychology of telecommunications.* London: Wiley.

Smith, M. K. (2005). Community. In *The encyclopedia of informal education.* Retrieved June 10, 2005, from http://www.infed.org/community/community.htm

Stake, R. (1995). *The art of case study research.* Thousand Oaks, CA: Sage.

Stark, S., & Torrance, H. (2005). Case study. In B. Somekh & C. Lewin (Eds.), *Research methods in the social sciences* (pp. 33-40). London: Sage.

University of Southern Queensland. (2006). *GDE3002 Contexts and environments: Course specification.* Toowoomba, Queensland, Australia: Author.

Vygotsky, L. S. (1978). *Mind in society: The development of higher psychological processes.* Cambridge, MA: Harvard University Press.

Wenger, E., McDermott, R., & Snyder, W. (2002). *Cultivating communities of practice: A guide to managing knowledge.* Boston: Harvard Business School Press.

Yin, R. (1994). *Case study research: Design and methods* (2nd ed.). Thousand Oaks, CA: Sage.

CHAPTER 14

BUILDING LEARNING COMMUNITIES AROUND NEW PARTNERSHIP FOR AFRICA'S DEVELOPMENT E-SCHOOLS INITIATIVE

Peter E. Kinyanjui

This chapter gives an African perspective on open and distance education and accompanying technologies as driven by the New Partnership for Africa's Development (NEPAD). One of its flagship projects is the NEPAD e-Schools Initiative, aimed at building information and communication technology (ICT) skills in the African population. The attributes of a NEPAD e-School are viewed in light of the great potential that such a school will have as a community resource, and the effects it will have within the school community and beyond. The creation and enhancement of learning communities is one of the strategies for bringing about better quality of life and wellbeing for all. The author concludes that the NEPAD e-Schools Initiative has all the ingredients of success and should be strengthened, supported, and expanded throughout the continent in order to create and sustain learning communities.

Online Learning Communities
pp. 241–255
Copyright © 2007 by Information Age Publishing

INTRODUCTION

The New Partnership for Africa's Development (NEPAD) has been widely accepted as the framework for Africa's development. A brainchild of the African Union (AU), NEPAD draws its legitimacy from the transformation of the Organisation of African Unity (OAU), and informed by the new thinking reflected in the Constitutive Act of the AU. The transformation of the OAU to AU and the birth of NEPAD mark the beginning of a new era for Africa. For the continent to take advantage of the new opportunities created by NEPAD and the AU and for it to undergo the renewal process, it will need to harness the energy, creativity, talent, and enthusiasm of all its people—including women, who constitute over 52% of its population, and the youth (those under 25 years) who constitute over 60% of the population.

THE NEW PARTNERSHIP FOR AFRICA'S DEVELOPMENT (NEPAD)

NEPAD, a program of the African Union, is a vision and strategic framework for Africa's renewal. Its primary objectives include poverty eradication, placing African countries on a path of sustainable growth and development, acceleration of women empowerment, stopping the marginalization of Africa in the globalization process, and enhancing Africa's full and beneficial integration into the global economy. To achieve these objectives, NEPAD is guided by the principles of:

- Good governance as a basic requirement for peace,
- Security and sustainable political and socioeconomic development,
- African ownership and leadership, as well as broad and deep participation by all sectors of society,
- Anchoring the development of Africa on its resources and resourcefulness of its people,
- Partnership between and among African peoples,
- Acceleration of regional and continental integration,
- Building the competitiveness of African countries and the continent,
- Forging a new international partnership that changes the unequal relationship between Africa and the developed world,
- Ensuring that all partnerships with NEPAD are linked to the Millennium Development Goals and other agreed development goals and targets.

THE NEPAD E-AFRICA COMMISSION (THE COMMISSION)

The Commission was established in 2001 and was formally adopted by the NEPAD Steering Committee as its Task Team for Information and Communication Technology (ICT) in September 2002. The NEPAD Heads of States and Government Implementation Committee (HSGIC) endorsed the action of the Steering Committee in November 2002. The Commission is located in Pretoria, South Africa. As of April 2006, it had a staff complement of 15. The head of the Commission secretariat is the executive deputy chairperson, while the governing body is the executive committee. The executive committee comprises of top government officials with ICT responsibilities in the five NEPAD initiating countries: Algeria, Egypt, Nigeria, Senegal, and South Africa. The executive committee reports to the NEPAD Steering Committee, which in turn reports to the HSGIC.

The Commission's mandate is to manage the structured development of the ICT sector on the African continent in the context of NEPAD. It is also required to develop broad strategies and a comprehensive action plan for ICT infrastructure and its use for ICT applications and services. The NEPAD ICT program is divided into 10 focus areas:

- E-policies, e-strategies and global ICT governance,
- ICT infrastructure and development,
- Human development (e-schools and e-health skills),
- Business development and entrepreneurship,
- Special programs (LDC's, youth, and women),
- Local content,
- Internet and software development,
- E-applications (e-government, e-commerce, e-tourism),
- Research and development, space applications, and
- Public e-awareness.

In March 2003, in Abuja, the Commission presented a list of six ICT projects to the Sixth meeting of the HSGIC. The Committee endorsed these projects as high-priority NEPAD ICT projects and requested the Commission to press ahead with their implementation as a matter of urgency. The six priority projects are:

- NEPAD e-Schools Initiative,
- The low-cost satellite access project for NEPAD e-schools,
- East African submarine cable project (EASSy),

- NEPAD broadband access fibre-optic project for landlocked African countries,
- NEPAD capacity-building project for e-learning in Africa (based on the Africa Virtual University),
- The e-policies and e-strategies project.

The Commission is currently implementing the NEPAD e-Schools Initiative, the EASSy project, the ICT broadband network for East and Southern Africa, and will shortly embark on the ICT broadband network for Central, West, and North Africa. These projects broadly fall into two categories: those that relate to the need to establish an adequate broadband ICT infrastructure on the African continent, and those that relate to imparting ICT skills in the African population. The basic idea is that infrastructure and skills are key prerequisites to bridging the digital and knowledge divide in Africa. This chapter deals only with the NEPAD e-Schools Initiative.

NEPAD E-SCHOOLS INITIATIVE

More than 60% of Africa's population is made up of people below the age of 25 years. These young people are likely to be the most affected by the digital and knowledge divide. They also form the basis on which the future economic activity of Africa will be built.

The United Nations Millennium Development Goal (MDG) number 2 aims to ensure that, by 2015, children everywhere, boys and girls alike, will be able to complete a full course of primary schooling and that boys and girls will have equal access to all levels of education. This goes further than improving enrollment numbers, but improving the quality of education. The first phase of the World Summit on Information Society (WSIS), held in Geneva in 2003, agreed to harness the potential of ICT to promote the development goals of the Millennium Declaration.

In its report titled "Achieving the Millennium Development Goals in Africa," the African Development Bank recognized that African states must invest adequate resources in human development if they are to achieve the MDGs (African Development Bank, 2002). In response to these challenges, the Commission is implementing the NEPAD e-Schools Initiative, whose aim is to impart ICT skills to young Africans. Approximately 600,000 schools on the continent will be converted into NEPAD e-Schools over a 10-year period. The objectives of the Initiative are:

- To provide ICT skills and knowledge to learners that will enable them to function in the emerging information society and knowledge economy,

- To provide teachers with skills to enable them to use ICT as tools to enhance teaching and learning,
- To provide school managers with ICT skills so as to facilitate the efficient management and administration in the schools,
- To make every learner health literate.

A NEPAD e-School is one which will:

- Produce young Africans with skills to participate in the knowledge economy,
- Have appropriate ICT equipment and infrastructure,
- Be connected to the Internet,
- Have teachers trained to impart ICT skills to students according to agreed curricula and content,
- Have teachers trained to integrate ICT for teaching and learning,
- Have access to, and contribute to, availability of locally appropriate teaching and learning materials
- Have ICT tools to enhance the administration and management of the school,
- Be equipped with a "health point."

The implementation approach is based on continental coordination and national implementation. Senior officials nominated by the participating governments of the first phase countries have agreed on a concept framework for the NEPAD e-Schools and on an implementation structure for the execution of the initiative. This coordinating body is tasked to approve strategies, frameworks, and work-plans necessary for the continental coordination. The Commission, working with participating governments and other key stakeholders, will coordinate the development of standards, implementation, and monitoring and evaluation whilst national teams will manage the day-to-day activities within their own countries. The main components of this Initiative include the NEPAD e-Schools demonstration project (Demo), the business plan, content development and teacher training, the National Implementing Agencies, and the NEPAD e-Schools satellite network.

NEPAD E-SCHOOLS DEMONSTRATION PROJECT

The Demonstration Project (Demo) is a critical initial step in the implementation of the NEPAD e-Schools Initiative. It is intended to provide a learning mechanism, based on real-life experiences of implementing ICT in schools across the African continent, that will serve to inform the roll-out of the broader NEPAD e-Schools Initiative. It provides a platform to investigate and report on the typical scenarios, circumstances and requirements for implementation, challenges in large-scale implementation, effectiveness of partnerships and partnership models, and benefits of the envisaged satellite-based connectivity network.

The Demo is being undertaken in all countries that make up phase one of the Initiative, being the first 20 countries that have acceded to the African Peer Review Mechanism (APRM, 2006).[1] The participating countries in the Demo are: Algeria, Angola, Benin, Burkina Faso, Cameroon, Congo, Egypt, Ethiopia, Gabon, Ghana, Kenya, Lesotho, Mali, Mauritius, Mozambique, Nigeria, Rwanda, Senegal, South Africa, and Uganda. Six demonstration schools, at secondary level or equivalent, have been established and monitored in each of the participating countries. It is expected that the Demo will directly impact approximately 150,000 African learners and teachers.

The official launch of the Demo project in each participating country is presided over by the respective head of state and government. This is meant to create awareness among all stakeholders, facilitate the buy-in process, as well as publicize the partnership. Five lead consortia from the private sector are each responsible for providing, deploying, and operating end-to-end technology solutions for about 20 schools at their own cost. The five consortia are led by Advanced Micro Devices, Cisco Systems, Hewlett-Packard, Microsoft, and Oracle. The five consortia have assembled between them over 40 other companies to provide end-to-end technology solutions for the schools, with at least two consortia in each country for comparison purposes. Tripartite memoranda of understanding have been drawn up between the participating governments, the lead consortia, and the NEPAD e-Africa Commission outlining the specific roles and responsibilities of each party in the partnership.

A comprehensive monitoring and evaluation plan (M&E Plan) has been put into place from the outset. The M&E exercise is conducted by the Commonwealth of Learning in partnership with the InfoDev of the World Bank at the request of the NEPAD e-Africa Commission. The purpose of the monitoring and evaluation process during the demonstration project phase is twofold. It provides the project managers and decision-makers responsible for implementing the project with information and feedback as the project proceeds in order for them to make any necessary adjustments. Further, it analyses and synthesizes the lessons learned during the demonstration project and makes recommendations for the comprehensive rollout of the e-Schools Initiative in a summary report at the end of the demonstration period.

The M&E Plan will report on the extent to which the Demo will have met the overall objectives of NEPAD e-Schools, the suitability of the solutions, and the effectiveness of the partnership model. The first interim report was produced by the Commonwealth of Learning (COL) in February 2006, the second report in June 2006, and the final report will be out in December 2006. Running parallel with the Demonstration Project are six other strands that are also interconnected with each other and leading to the rollout of the NEPAD e-Schools Initiative. The six strands are: Business Plan, National Implementing Agencies (NIA), NEPAD e-Schools Satellite Network, Teacher Training, Content Development, and Development of Standards and Overall Coordination.

The Business Plan

The Commission, with funding from the South African Government, has engaged a consultant to develop the business plan for the NEPAD e-Schools Initiative. The business plan will bring together, all the critical elements, inputs, and processes that will form the basis for the execution of the roll-out. The plan is expected to provide the information necessary to substantiate funding requirements and the associated plan of action. It will include, among other things: assessing present environment for implementing an e-schools program in each participating country, identifying existing similar projects at regional or country level, identifying education and training requirements for students, teachers, managers and administrators of schools, funding requirements of the rollout phase, potential sources of funding, Strategic partnership issues, sustainability mechanisms, benefits and risks, quality assurance mechanisms, and the implementation plan.

It would also guide and inform the developmental phases of the project, starting at the school level, through the country, and at the continental level. The preparation of the plan will involve close consultation with experts nominated by the participating governments, the regional economic communities (RECs), and various stakeholders that will include public, private, and civil society organizations. The final business plan document will be finalized by November 2006.

The National Implementing Agencies (NIA)

The NEPAD e-Schools will be coordinated continentally through the Coordinating Body, but will be implemented nationally through the National Implementing Agencies (NIA) to be set up in each of the participating countries. These agencies will consist of various government departments, private sector organizations, development agencies, as well as civil society organizations within the country. The Commission will support the Agencies to manage the roll-out in their respective countries. The implementation of the NEPAD e-Schools Initiative at the country level will depend, to a large extent, on the quality, composition and capacity of each National Implementing Agency to carry out the tasks agreed upon.

The specific roles of the national implementing agency can be grouped into four categories as follows:

- *Operational.* These include supervising the installation, operation and maintenance of ICT hardware and software in the schools, working with experts and other stakeholders to provide educational portals to facilitate the flow of educational materials between appropriate sources and the schools, supervising and facilitating the timetable and other targets established for the NEPAD e-Schools in the country and making recommendations to the Commission concerning schools that are fit to qualify as "NEPAD e-Schools."

- *Coordination.* The NIA will coordinate with ministries and departments of education about the modalities for the ICT training of teachers and school administrators and their deployment to the schools, work with the appropriate certifying authorities to set ICT skills proficiency standards for graduating students, and establish sound working relationships with all other authorities and stakeholders within the country. On the issues of health, NIA will coordinate with ministries of health regarding the installation and operation of "health point" facilities.

- *Fund Raising.* A major task of the NIA will be to raise funds from the various sources, create and sustain effective partnerships with the private sector and civil society organizations, and to create and sustain public support and enthusiasm for the NEPAD e-Schools Initiative in the country.

- *Management.* The NIA will establish sound financial and managerial operations and manage and operate its affairs in an ethical and professional manner and in accordance with standards and norms established for the NEPAD e-Schools Initiative across the continent.

It is worth emphasizing here that whatever structure the governments decide upon, it would be helpful if the chosen entity is provided with sufficient leeway as well as human and financial resources to be able to fulfill the agreed functions. Provision should also be made for the NIA to invite experts to assist in the performance of its functions. Appropriate capacity-building measures should also be provided to make the NIA effective and sustainable. Although the agency may be located or attached to one of the government ministries or departments, the leadership and composition of this agency should be drawn from a wide representation of the main stakeholders to include other relevant government departments, the private sector, the civil society organizations, and individuals. It should also be gender sensitive in its composition. The quality rather than the size of this agency should be the prime consideration in constituting such a body.

The NIA will ideally comprise representatives from the ministries of education, health, finance, ICT, and communications, the private sector, the civil society organizations, and development partners. The NEPAD e-Africa Commission will be represented as a way of ensuring adherence to the standards and norms expected of the NEPAD e-Schools. The NIA will plan the implementation, mobilize resources, and execute the roll-out of the NEPAD e-Schools in a particular country. While the participating governments will be expected to establish and fund their own NIA, there will be need for material, human, and financial assistance and support in order to expedite the work of these agencies, particularly at their nascent stages. The Commission will seek resources to nurture and support these agencies that will, in turn, expedite the implementation of the NEPAD e-Schools in their respective countries.

Nepad E-Schools Satellite Network

Given the relatively poor state of connectivity on the African continent, a satellite network is being established to provide communications to all NEPAD e-Schools. One of the major functions of the NEPAD e-Africa Commission is to establish an Africa-wide satellite network that will connect the schools to the Internet as well as to points within each country from which educational content will be fed to the schools on a continuous basis. The Commission will procure satellite capacity in bulk and make it available for the connection of schools to the Internet. By establishing a common network and common operations for the continent, it should be possible to optimize use of scarce technical skills as well as leverage the benefits of a large network and common standards to reduce the cost of equipment, technology, and airtime. The Commission will develop common standards to ensure sound and effective operations of NEPAD e-Schools in a wide range of areas including technical, operational, educational, financial, and managerial. The Commission has appointed a consultant who will definehand preliminarily designing the NEPAD e-Schools satellite network. The final report is expected at the end of August 2006 and will also serve as an input into the Business Plan.

Teacher Training

Teacher training is a key component in the NEPAD e-Schools Initiative. The International Telecommunications Union (ITU) has funded a consultant to develop the teacher training framework. Once approved by the participating countries, this framework will form the basis upon which the countries will implement their national programs for teacher training and professional development to achieve the objectives of the NEPAD e-Schools, and to ensure the effective use of ICT for improved teaching and learning and effective administration and management of the schools. The framework is focused on the development of the 21st Century Skills as identified in the Partnership for 21st Century Skills (UNESCO, 2003). However, in a multinational program such as NEPAD's, the input from participating countries must influence the scope of this framework to reflect the broad needs of each country. Ultimately, the framework will need to be broad, flexible, and relevant to allow for customized interpretation of its content within each country's education and training system.

Content Development

In addition to developing the teacher training framework, the Commission will facilitate the development of an online content strategy. The objective here is to ensure that the content accessible via the e-Schools infrastructure is, wherever possible, in local languages and accommodates the cultures of its users. The strategy will outline the content gaps, ownership, audiences, priorities, and projects on the African continent. Furthermore, the strategy will outline the role to be played by the Commission in facilitating the partnerships in the development and dissemination of content through appropriate education portals to ensure that Africans are not just consumers of content developed elsewhere, but also originators and creators of their own content.

Development of Standards and Overall Coordination

As part of its role in continental coordination, the Commission will develop norms and standards to ensure sound and effective operations of NEPAD e-Schools in a wide range of areas, including technical, operational, pedagogical, financial, and managerial. The Commission will seek to bring to bear international best practice in all operations of the Initiative. Further, the Commission will strive to develop and nurture capacity at the national and regional levels for effective implementation of the projects and programs.

TOWARDS CREATING LEARNING COMMUNITIES

The NEPAD Secretariat has created an Office of Gender and Civil Society Organizations as a response to recommendations made by different stakeholders and experts. The creation of this office reinforces the commitment by NEPAD to gender issues as well as a desire to actively involve civil society organizations in the implementation of the various programs and projects. This will ensure that NEPAD initiatives and projects are all-inclusive and aligned with the needs and aspirations of the special groups. The NEPAD e-Schools Initiative, for example, will call for support from the local communities to provide the necessary security and maintenance of the facilities. In turn, the local communities will benefit from the information available through the Internet. The "health point" at every NEPAD e-School, for example, will disseminate appropriate information related to health matters such as epidemics, nutrition, and personal hygiene.

By combining the synergies of the NEPAD e-Schools with those of community-based organizations, it should be possible to demonstrate that a viable platform can be created for rural communities, including women and youth, to interact among themselves in local languages, exchange news, knowledge, and information at the local level, and use this knowledge to empower themselves at personal and community level, to fight poverty, ignorance, and disease, and to create wealth. The learning communities will thus evolve from this mutual learning environment.

UNESCO published a *Global Directory of Community Multimedia Centres* (CMC) around the world (UNESCO, 2005). In this directory, at least 28 centers from eight African countries were identified and described in some detail on how they were able to combine both traditional knowledge and media with the huge potential of information sourcing and sharing provided by the Internet and other new information and communication technologies.

What now remains to be done is to build on the NEPAD e-Schools and scale up their numbers and outreach in the rollout through broad-based ownership and management by the National Implementing Agencies described earlier. Each country will therefore need to prepare a strategy for scaling up the investments in these technologies and for their effective management and sustainability. This process will be accelerated by bringing in lessons and experiences garnered from other similar initiatives such as those from Schoolnet Africa and the Community Multimedia Centres.

THE ROLE OF GOVERNMENTS

All participating governments have a pivotal role to play in ensuring that the mission of the NEPAD e-Africa Commission is accomplished as planned. African governments are the key stakeholders in these initiatives and must ensure that all their citizens are both participants and beneficiaries of ICT programs and activities. Specific actions that every participating government should take include the following:

- Advocacy of ICT and ensuring that it is high on the national agenda, both at the national and sectoral levels;
- Establishing appropriate legal and regulatory frameworks that encourage more open competition in the telecommunication and other ICT industries and thus make the related goods and services more affordable;
- Encouraging the application of open, nondiscriminatory, and affordable access to the terrestrial, satellite, and submarine cable networks across the borders;
- Agreeing and supporting the principle of public-private partnerships to these networks;
- Formulating objectives and strategies for ICT in education and training within the national development context;
- Promoting and encouraging universal access to ICT for disadvantaged groups and geographical areas;
- Promoting the use of ICT in diverse fields of education and training, including the promotion of open learning and distance education;
- Establishing opportunities for, and facilitating, education and training using ICT capacities;
- Championing ICT use through promoting e-Government services at the national and local levels;
- Facilitating linkages between government and businesses and creating opportunities for civil society groups to identify opportunities for, and contribute to, the development of an information society;
- Encouraging private enterprise through the establishment of an enabling environment at the national and local levels;
- Attracting foreign direct investment into the development of ICT-related capacities, including the development of infrastructure and the reduction of connectivity and access costs;

- Encouraging domestic investment in the ICT industry and in ICT applications by small and medium businesses through appropriate incentive schemes and fair competition.

PROSPECTS FOR E-GOVERNMENT

The entry-point to e-Government is the e-Parliament. This is the level at which the parliamentarians will be introduced to ICT and how it contributes to national development. This way, the lawmakers themselves will get to appreciate and therefore support policies and programs of ICT in their respective countries. It is expected that the next big project for the NEPAD e-Africa Commission will be e-Parliament that will, inter alia, connect all the 55 African Parliament and train the parliamentarians in requisite ICT knowledge and skills. This way, the parliamentarians will understand the values that technology can bring by uplifting citizens and accelerating development and, therefore, support and secure the correct levels of investment for these initiatives. From there, technology will undoubtedly have an easier route into enabling the concept of e-government to gain ground and flourish in Africa. To this end, plans are at an advanced stage to launch e-policies and e-strategies project as one of the six priority projects of the Commission.

NEW PARTNERSHIP MODEL

NEPAD is founded on the bedrock of partnership. It represents a unique commitment by Africans to drive decisively the social, economic, and political transformation of the continent in partnership with the international community. Through the NEPAD framework, there is a new way of doing business in Africa. In a speech delivered in India in March 2006, UN Secretary-General Kofi Annan said "There are many positive ways for the business to make a difference in the lives of the poor … not through philanthropy but through initiatives that, over time, will help build new markets."

The partnership model that NEPAD has adopted is working well and yielding results. The NEPAD e-Schools Initiative is a good example, in which 20 African governments have joined hands with over 40 private sector companies and about a dozen development agencies and civil society organizations on a common project that will affect over half of the African population in the first phase. There is no doubt that, in terms of size and scope, the NEPAD e-Schools Initiative is the largest of its kind that has ever been tried anywhere in the world. It has already demonstrated some ingredients of success from the monitoring and evaluation process that was built in from the start and is continuing in step with the development of the Business Plan.

Africa will re-invent new ways of using and sharing technology. The case in point is the mobile technology. Africa today is one of the fastest growing markets for cellular phones, and the impact on people's lives is palpable—as families are able to stay in touch, farmers can find out the best markets for their produce, and fishermen are warned of storms at sea. At the same time, peer learning on how to use the new technologies is rampant at the marketplaces, community centres, and cyber-cafes. With technology and infrastructure becoming readily accessible and easily affordable, the NEPAD e-Schools should ideally become community resources and focal points for growth and development, and thus support learning communities. These community resources will need to be well serviced and supported through repairs and maintenance as and when required. Technical and managerial support will need to be created and sustained at the local level. Armed with the knowledge and skills, the new generation of young Africans will increasingly become job creators rather than job seekers.

In order to achieve the lofty goals of the initiatives to build ICT infrastructure and human skills, the NEPAD e-Africa Commission will require adequate human, financial, technological, and material resources. Significant human capacity is required to successfully implement and sustain the projects already started, and to expand them substantially in order to benefit from economies of scale. The provision and management of ICT infrastructure, tools, and skills will require that all partners in this venture work together to complement governments' efforts. The Commission recognizes the importance of partnerships in mobilizing skills and resources, including those from the African Diaspora, and these will be pursued with all organizations and individuals that have a stake in Africa's future.

AUTHOR'S NOTE

The author is responsible for the choice and the presentation of the facts contained in this chapter. The views and opinions expressed here are not necessarily those of NEPAD and do not commit the Organization.

NOTE

1.   APRM, a NEPAD initiative, is a voluntary process acceded to by African countries with a view to enhancing progress in key governance and socio-economic development areas.

REFERENCES

African Development Bank. (2002). *Achieving the millennium development goals.* Tunis.

African peer review mechanism. (2006). Retrieved September 1, 2006, from www.nepad.org

UNESCO. (2003). *Final Report: The Workshop on the Development of Guidelines on Teacher Training in ICT Integration and Standards for Competency in ICT.* Asia and Pacific Regional Bureau for Education.

UNESCO. (2005).*Community multimedia centres around the world: A global directory.* Paris: Author.

CHAPTER 15

INTERNATIONAL PERSPECTIVES ON DISTANCE EDUCATION AND LEARNING COMMUNITIES WITHIN ANGLOPHONE COMMONWEALTH COUNTRIES

Badri N. Koul

This chapter brings together various experiences from the Anglophone Commonwealth currently comprising 54 countries spread east to west from Tonga to Belize and north to south from the United Kingdom to South Africa.

INTRODUCTION

The expression "distance education" (DE), from among the many in use then, was accepted formally at the 1982 ICCE/ICDE Conference[1] held in

Online Learning Communities
pp. 257–276
Copyright © 2007 by Information Age Publishing

Vancouver to mean the kind of educational transaction best exemplified by the pioneering model put forth and implemented by the British Open University (UKOU) beginning in 1969, in which the course content was/is provided in self-instructional printed modules supplemented by limited audio and video (TV) materials and supported by well-organized student support services including some tutorials and counseling in person. The term implied spatial as well as temporal distance between the learner and the teacher/institution as the main feature of this new modality. In this paper, however, "distance education" is used as a cover expression to include its various manifestations along the path of its evolution—correspondence education, distance education, open distance education, tele-conferencing, online education, virtual education, and transmodal and/or blended education. Second, only briefly touching on the achievements and the potential of DE, which are neither in question nor lacking in extensive exposition, this paper focuses on its weaknesses as they obtain in the developing countries of the commonwealth and suggests possible solutions to overcome them. Third, within the broad international perspectives on DE and learning communities, this paper brings together various experiences from the Anglophone Commonwealth currently comprising 54 countries spread east to west from Tonga to Belize and north to south from the United Kingdom to South Africa.

BACKGROUND

Though correspondence education has been available in many parts of the world for over a century now, it was the establishment of the British Open University in 1969 that pioneered the thought and practice of open distance education in the Commonwealth. The impact of this experiment was startling, as soon after dedicated open universities were established throughout the Commonwealth one after the other, as if the chocked higher education system was waiting for just this vent to burst forth. The immediate purpose of the UKOU was to provide a second chance to take up university education to those who had missed the first one for whatever reasons (the aftermath of the War being one of them), while the open universities in the rest of the Commonwealth, especially in the newly-established independent developing countries, came to serve three distinct purposes: meeting the diverse demands of vast numbers aspiring for higher education and thereby compensating for the lack of higher education institutions otherwise required to meet that demand, providing affordable education with convenience even to working adults, and leap-frogging to fill up the educational gap (between the developing and the developed countries) that has been becoming more and more obvious and painful with every passing year. Argued opposition from various quarters notwithstanding, the mad rush for the new promising band-wagon was unprecedented, as the pioneers shouldered it robustly with systemic research and prolific supportive writings, and the politicians favoured it for its promise of being cost-effective/efficient. Then came the applications of information and communication technologies (ICTs) to build its potential for universal coverage eliminating the traditional barriers like geographical and political borders, restricted access, and limitations of inequity.

Thirty-six years on the tide, DE is poised to become the main mode of education any time now. This claim is not unfounded. In a short span of less than four decades, the Anglophone Commonwealth has experienced a meteoric drive across five generations of DE—marking a departure from the first generation DE (i.e. correspondence courses), the second generation DE (self-instructional print materials together with learner support services, now labeled "traditional distance education") was pioneered in 1969, as said above; in the following decade, increased use of audio, video, and teleconferencing at the institutional level brought the third generation DE to the scene, which took no time to be overshadowed in the mid-1990s by the advent of the fourth generation DE in the form of online courses and, by the turn of the last century, work on learning objects and instruction management systems laid the foundations of the fifth generation of DE, promising to overwhelm the institution of education like nothing before (Taylor, 2001).

There was just one open university in Africa in 1988, when India had four. Today, Africa has four and India 13, and the Government of India would like to see 40% of all higher education students studying through the distance mode by 2010. Overall, there were 10 open universities in the Anglophone Commonwealth in 1988; today this count stands at 23. Nearly 3 million learners took advantage of the open distance education system in the Anglophone Commonwealth in 2003, and today this number is said to have crossed the 10 million mark (Kanwar & Koul, 2006). This growth is not surprising, as some of the developing Commonwealth countries are faced with pressures from the youth (over 54% of the population in India) (Paul, 2005) and over 50% in Zambia (Direct Relief, 2006) are less than 25 years in age in addition to those from adults seeking avenues for upward mobility and updating of skills demanded by the fast-changing work market. Further, in view of the contribution of higher education in the economic growth and wellbeing of advanced countries, the developing countries with less than 10% Age Participation Rates (APRs) in higher education (around 7-8% in South Asia and 4% in Sub-Saharan Africa) are aiming at 40-50% APRs in search of parity with advanced countries (World Bank, 2002). If this objective is to be achieved in a reasonably short time, DE modalities have to be used increasingly in the developing world as has been done in the advanced world—today 81% of the face-to-face institutions in North America offer one or the other kind of blended learning option to a variety of students (Geith, n.d.).

Being a cost-efficient/effective means of educating and training, DE has attracted the attention of politicians and policy makers all over the Commonwealth. Second, the unprecedented developments in ICTs and their applications in educational transactions ranging from simple online courses through transmodal education to mobile learning are enabling diversification in flexible learning options, making it possible for institutions to reach learners at all levels, in all climes, for diverse disciplines and newly developing professions. Third, the inexorable march toward globalization is forcing people—young, adult and old alike—to seek relearning and retraining, to be multiskilled and mobile to improve their quality of life and to equip themselves for living in diverse cultures and thus become true world citizens. This scenario portends colossal pressure on the age-old institution of education, which to survive and maintain its symbiotic relation with human society, must change and also contribute to that change. As a result, traditional face-to-face education systems are accommodating distance modalities and, overall, DE is emerging not only as an all-powerful educational modality, but also as an effective means of universal development. This trend is evidenced by:

- mergers (we have now only one open university in Canada, while the other two have merged with traditional universities),
- grafting distance education units onto traditional institutions, as exemplified by the more than 100 such units in Indian universities,
- establishing new open universities, some of which deliver courses exclusively online,
- forging consortia of diverse (culturally as well as in terms of their specializations) institutions to achieve a common goal,
- cooperative efforts in building learning objects and learner/learning management systems, and
- nonformal DE applications for developmental purposes—combating AIDS, popularizing environmental education, providing health education, and so forth.

So far, so good! There are issues, however, that beset the progress of DE universally, particularly so in the Anglophone Commonwealth. Of these the major ones are, socioacademic credibility of DE, location/country specific systemic research, training for and among the DE personnel, awareness/understanding of intellectual property and copyright issues, adequate levels of technology required to utilize DE to its full potential, and quality of DE products, processes, and outcomes. The following sections will focus on these issues and also point to solutions that are being contemplated, proposed, and put to practice.

THE ISSUE OF SOCIOACADEMIC CREDIBILITY

In the developing part of the Commonwealth, a major hurdle in the promotion, acceptance, and sustenance of DE as an effective alternative system of education/training is its poor socio-academic credibility vis-à-vis the traditional face-to-face education that has a history of over 900 years to back it. This issue presents a glaring contrast between the developed and the developing countries. The former have since overcome hang-ups regarding the potential of DE modalities and embarked on its extensive and innovative applications, while the latter, in a state of hesitation, find it difficult to own the system wholeheartedly at the societal level and invest in it what it deserves in terms of funds, time, and commitment.

The case of the University of Southern Queensland, Australia, is that the mode of education has ceased to be a measure of the standards of education being imparted (Smith, 2006). They practice three modes—the conventional face-to-face mode, the traditional distance mode (i.e., the second generation DE), and the ICT enhanced online mode—each complementing the other and all are available simultaneously, leaving the choice to the learners. Besides, their firm belief in the multimodal operation, which they have built, motivates them to provide such content, learner activities, and support services as help them in offering their courses across their borders. On the other hand, we are told that "(t)he major challenges to quality assurance in online programs in Africa will continue to include...negative perceptions about distance education" (Dzvimbo & Kariuki, 2006) and that "the expansion of (open distance learning) ODL has also generated a different set of responses, particularly from the government and segments of the general public who ... see the unregulated growth of ODL as a threat to the quality of higher education and even to access and equity" (Umar, 2006).

But why is this growth (in Africa and in many developing countries) unregulated? It is usually because the policymakers and the implementing bodies are not sufficiently convinced of the utility and the potential of the DE modalities and a free-for-all attitude prevails. It is not unusual for some institutions to use their DE units as milk cows, as the funds generated through DE operations are ploughed into face-to-face operations at the cost of quality in their DE dispensation. In the same vein, academics, especially in dual-mode institutions in developing countries (India is a case in point), resist the development and integration of DE courses/programs with the on-campus ones. This is partly because they do not like the idea of undermining the face-to-face delivery (which constitutes education as tradition would have it) by integrating it with DE operations which, from their viewpoint, do not make education. Clearly, it is partly the conventional mindset of the educationists and academics, and partly some of the known poor local DE operations in many developing countries that militate against the immensely desirable promotion of DE, rendering it suspect as an alternative or complementary mode of education/training.

THE ISSUE OF SCANT COUNTRY-SPECIFIC SYSTEMIC RESEARCH

The UKOU started with an uncharted idea that was materialized through meticulous implementation, which together with its products, processes, and consequences was and is researched on continually and the conclusions drawn and insights gained were and are being used to improve and extend the system of education/training born of that idea—DE. They had no research findings to build their DE system on, nor any training to do what they embarked on, but they had in ample measure what pioneers need most—a firm conviction in what they were/are doing and the will to do it well. As the idea caught on and was adopted here, there, and everywhere, in some cases because of euphoria and in others under the compulsion of circumstances, it was essentially alien and remains so in many cases even today. As a result, many countries have not been able to assimilate it into their educational environment and ethos, which have their moorings in the traditional face-to-face system of education and training. If an alien idea and the related operations have to find a local habitation in a host country, she has to research on both within the specific local context, understand and appreciate them, and then adjust their odds and ends to suit her needs.

Apart from the advanced countries, few developing countries in the Commonwealth can boast of quality native and original research on their DE operations, the learning habits and strategies of their students, the very precise educational needs of their society, their DE-related financial and technology requirements, and the like. If there is any, the findings thereof are not used to enhance their DE enterprise. Neither the research for library shelves nor the one borrowed or adopted from other countries can address native issues—psychological, societal, and practical. For DE to benefit the developing countries in the Commonwealth to its full potential, they have not only to place systemic research in their DE operations prominently on their agenda, but also use its findings to address their country-specific issues. As Wenger (2003) remarks, the Research and Innovation Facility (RIF) of the African Virtual University

> is intended to assist in the deconstruction of such academic hierarchies that currently exist in the African academy ... (and it) will be pivotal in building a reflexive, transformative and emancipating educational discourse for the development of authentic, original, and indigenous African communities of practice and local virtual and physical infrastructures for learning and teaching that benefit the entire network as far as quality assurance is concerned. (Wenger, p. 237)

THE ISSUE OF TRAINING FOR AND AMONG THE DE PERSONNEL

Most of the personnel appointed at DE institutions throughout the Commonwealth, including those at the UKOU, be they academics, administrators, professionals, or technical hands, are from conventional systems. They enter this new system along with their respective mindsets, assumptions, and purposes—some for just a change, some for upward mobility, some as they have nothing else to do, but very few for what the system is or what it entails and promises. This statement holds for most of the staff in DE institutions even today, though formal training for DE personnel has been available for sometime now. Obviously, if a newly-established DE institution is to function purposefully and must take off immediately, training of the staff is a major and decisive prerequisite. In the 1970s and 1980s, this requirement was met (though only partially, as large numbers of DE personnel worked without any training coming their way) through workshops, attachments, and professional visits. Before the impact of the formal training programs (for traditional DE operations) that emerged during the mid-1980s was discernible, advances in and applications of the contemporary ICTs, which brought online education, e-learning, virtual institutions, and learning objects in their wake, extended the gap between the training available for ICT-enhanced DE operations at that time and the skills and know-how required of the personnel concerned. Once again, the system had to fall back on workshops, attachments, and the like. DE institutions throughout the developing Commonwealth have suffered immensely on account of these rapid developments.

As pointed to above, in many DE institutions, the prevailing financial management, administrative setup and so the attitude towards the introduction and applications of technology, the existing faculty and the support staff all are geared to working in and for the traditional on-campus course delivery. In dual-mode institutions making serious inputs (policy-wise, financial, and academic) in DE operations is seen as an "add-on" to routine responsibilities. An efficient and complete, even if gradual, switch over to a new/different system necessitates fundamental and a wide range of changes in the core constituents and activities of the institution. Unless there are timely and sound pre-service and in-service training programs (to cover both the traditional and the ICT-enhanced DE) built into the institutional strategies and operations and supported by incentives for the personnel to benefit from them, DE operations will remain slipshod and wanting throughout the developing Commonwealth.

THE INTELLECTUAL PROPERTY AND COPYRIGHT ISSUES

Dismissal of an academic at a DE institution on account of plagiarism may be a rare happening, but it is not unheard of in the developing Commonwealth. Overall, the people concerned, both the academics and the administrators, do not have accurate and dependable information regarding intellectual property and copyright laws they need to follow in dealing with course materials, printed as well as electronic (audio and video). Many of the concerned may not be able to tell whether their countries are signatories to the Berne Convention, the Universal Copyright Convention, or both, or which convention governs transactions of video materials in their country, and so on. Online materials and those on the Web have made the going more difficult as, for example, people confuse what is for public access with what is in the public domain and the like. These issues are of significance in DE operations that primarily pertain to the creation, manipulation, adoption, adaptation, sale, purchase, storing, construction, deconstruction, and repurposing of intellectual assets/property. Awareness regarding these issues, the relevant conventions and laws, and what entails their violation has to be an obligatory component of any training or awareness program meant for DE personnel.

ADEQUATE LEVELS OF TECHNOLOGY
VIS-À-VIS DISTANCE EDUCATION

Other than a few advanced countries of the Commonwealth, most developing countries suffer from a shortage of contemporary technology required for effective and efficient DE operations. To illustrate the point, cited below are data collected by the author in the Anglophone Caribbean (Koul, 2005) (see Table 15.1).

The level of connectivity and the cost of dial-up links in relation to population and GDP per capita as shown below point to the nature of the divide—the regional (Caribbean) connectivity is just 3.5% in comparison

Table 15.1. Connectivity Levels and Costs: The Country/Regional Profile

	Country	Area (Sq Km)	Population* in (000)	Connectivity			Dial-Up Costs in US$	
				Internet Connections in (000)	% Connections	GDP** per Capita US$	Dial-up Monthly Costs US$	% of GDP/Capita per Month
1	Antigua & Barbuda	442	67.4			7,900	40 +	6.1
2	Barbados	431	276.6	30.0	10.8	11,200	44 u	4.7
3	Belize	2,960	262.9	6.0	2.3	3,000	201	8.0
4	British Virgin Islands	151	21.2	3.0	14.2	10,000	59 u	7.1
5	Cayman Islands	264	36.2	—	—	24,500	60 l/+	2.9
6	Dominica	450	70.1	4.0	5.7	3,300	33 u	12.0
7	Grenada	345	89.2	4.0	4.5	3,500	48 u	16.4
8	Guyana	214,970	698.2	3.0	0.4	2,500	34 u	16.3
9	Jamaica	11,424	2,680.0	75.0	2.8	3,300	40 u/+	14.6
10	Montserrat	103	8.4	0.6	7.1	8,330	52	7.5
11	St. Kitts & Nevis	269	38.7	4.0	10.3	6,000	30 u	6.0
12	St. Lucia	616	160.1	5.0	3.1	4,100	52 u/+	15.2
13	St. Vincent & the Grenadines	388	116.3	3.0	2.6	2,400	52 u/+	26.0
14	Suriname	163,820	436.4	—	—	3,500	17 u/+	5.8
15	Trinidad & Tobago	5,128	1,163.7	60.0	5.2	8,000	50 u	7.5
	Overall		5,585.4	197.6 →	3.5	6,769	42 →	7.5
16	USA		280 m	44		31,500	20 u	0.76

*Data Derived from U.S. Census Bureau International Data Base (2000).

**Derived from Almanac—World and News: World Stats and Facts (mid-2002 estimates)

Note: (a) Blank cells indicate nonavailability of the relevant data. (b) In the last but one column, l stands for limited time, u for unlimited time and + for additional costs, such as cost for telephone calls, cost for the additional time beyond the scheduled limit, etc. c) "Overall" denotes totals in the Connectivity Column and means in the Costs Column, while → points to the direction of computation.

with the U.S. figures of 44%, which is more than 12 times the Caribbean level (Eadie, 2000). Considering the costs, the average regional rate at 7.5% of the GDP per capita per month is nearly 10 times costlier than 0.76% the rate available in United States. Though a part of the Anglophone Commonwealth, the Anglophone Caribbean belongs to the North American context geographically. Accordingly, connectivity costs beyond 1% (or so) of the GDP per capita per month in the Caribbean should be considered expensive. Obviously, in view of both the levels of connectivity and the costs thereof, the Caribbean lacks the very basic prerequisites for technology-enhanced DE operations. This situation is further aggravated by low levels of computer literacy and the poor availability of e-professionals in the region.

It is, therefore, not surprising that of the six native universities, namely the University of the West Indies, the University of Guyana, the Anton de Kom Universiteit van Suriname,[2] the Northern Caribbean University in Jamaica, the University of Technology in Jamaica and the University of Belize, only two—the University of Technology and the University of the West Indies—have any significant DE operations to write about. In fact, the former is the only university in the Caribbean which is adequately equipped for delivering technology-enhanced education. In terms of infrastructure, training of the staff, enabling university legislation, and the positive attitude of the management and the staff, it has a firm base for its potential as a DE provider, but until recently it had just three courses online and those too for campus-based students only. The University of the West Indies is a regional institution. As the oldest and a major provider of higher education in the Caribbean, it provides traditional distance education through its Distance Education Centre (UWIDEC), which caters to distance learners from 16 Anglophone Caribbean countries. Apart from this operation, the university has two full programs available online and efforts are on to provide more and more programs/courses through the traditional print-based technology as well as electronically. The overall situation is that applications of contemporary ICTs in educational dispensation in the Caribbean need more time to be extensive and visible.

The above details relate to physical objects and activities that have been improving progressively, and therefore must be better today. But they do give us an idea of what the developing countries are faced with when it comes to applications of contemporary technology in educational dispensation. The situation of the other developing countries in the Commonwealth is, more or less, the same as it is in the Caribbean, but the fact is that no two countries display the same levels of technology in terms of its availability, capacity to maintain it, and the human resources to run it. As a result, no single formula or strategy can be evolved to pull up these countries along any reformative ladder. It is a challenging situation, as developmental efforts have to be country-specific and to be successful they need local details with higher levels of specificity.

There is, however, a silver lining—the cost of connectivity and the related hardware is falling very fast and the institutions engaged in second generation DE (which is doubtlessly quite a robust and effective mode) can move on to the fourth generation modalities gradually by installing an instructional server initially and then enhance it by adding another for media materials, while the students would need low-band connectivity (ordinary cyber-cafes could serve the purpose) initially and later relatively advanced equipment and better bandwidth. Moving to the fifth generation DE applications would require higher levels of expertise in ICT applications, more advanced equipment, and dependable connectivity at the learner end. To make a beginning here, entering collaborative projects for the promotion of the fifth generation operations may be the best way out, as it will provide the needed expertise and confidence to take up the task of reengineering at a convenient time.

THE ISSUE OF QUALITY IN DE PRODUCTS AND PROCESSES

All said and done, the paramount issue in DE operations is that of quality and quality assurance (QA)—does the system provide quality education/training and has it arrangements in place to secure it? The details given under Background point to the current and the prospective exponential expansion of DE operations. Such expansion, especially in the developing world, in the face of disproportionately limited infrastructure, technology, and human resources available to support it, has disturbing negative implications for the quality of education/training delivered through the distance modality. Apart from this core problem of expansion against scant resources, there are some other reasons that make the issue of quality assurance challenging. For example, expanding democratization, value of education as a human right, and globalization of trade and service sector put a premium on the expanding range of offerings, the increasing flexibility in delivery systems, and the extending institutional reach to the needy. While negotiating the immense demand thus created in a climate of scant funds, institutions can survive and grow only if they strive for and offer quality education.

Secondly, to evolve and run a socially responsive educational system now (remember, universities in the Commonwealth have been elitist institutions), institutions have to review and reengineer their educational philosophy and content, modalities of its dispensation, student support services, and financial management in terms of the social utility of the education they provide.

Thirdly, with the advent of cross-border and transmodal education beginning to be offered by ever-multiplying provider institutions, the traditional institutions in developing countries are increasingly exposed to risks they had never thought of—in competition with quality education/training dispensed from abroad, they will either inadvertently promote even the sub-standard content doled out by foreign provider institutions or face extinction slowly but certainly. On the other hand, to remain in the swim, they need to improve the quality of their operations, services, and products significantly—and the sooner the better.

Fourthly, with the emerging connectivist educational paradigm, the traditional and well-known features of teaching-learning transactions are being challenged and changed by both the new learners and the digital natives (Prensky, 2005). Rather than fitting into the straightjacket of stereotyped syllabi, they emphasize and look for what they want to study, where and how while taking the onus of learning onto themselves and using ICTs to suit their individual learning habits and strategies. This trend portends elimination of educational enterprises that lack quality in their products and operations.

Different countries and institutions perceive the above trends differently and scan them at differing levels of specificity. Consequently, quality issues are addressed differently and with differing levels of intensity in different countries. Of late, taking cues from the approaches followed by the corporate sector, educational institutions have adapted quality improvement strategies not only for the face-to-face educational transactions, but also for the DE operations. Among the country-specific operations, for example, we may mention those of the United Kingdom, Australia, and India.

The United Kingdom established its Quality Assurance Agency for Higher Education (QAAHE) in 1997 (QAAHE, 2003). It prescribes a code listing principles of good practice with respect to 10 concerns that include collaborative activities; provision for differently able learners; learner assessment; postgraduate research activity; learners' complaints/appeals related to academic matters, approval, monitoring and review of programs; information, counseling, and career guidance, and so forth; and also the guidelines for practicing these principles. All the higher education institutions, including DE institutions, must submit self-assessment reports indicating the degree of their adherence to prescribed principles. These reports are reviewed by QAAHE and statements/facts ascertained through audit visits to the institutions concerned. Assessment is then recorded using the terms "broad confidence," "limited confidence," or "no confidence," in the quality of institutional performance. In the

United Kingdom, state funding is linked to institutional performance. As a result, assessment done by QAAHE safeguards educational standards/ quality in the country and also assures continuous improvements in the quality of educational content as well as dispensation.

The Australian University's Quality Agency) was established in 2000 (AUQA, 2005). As in the United Kingdom, this national body promotes quality in all types of higher education including distance education. Unlike QAAHE, it does not prescribe any code of principles/practices. Instead, each Australian institution of higher education must have its own quality assurance mechanism in place. AUQA audits institutional quality assurance mechanisms on request, and their assessment leads to the identification of "commendable practices" as well as the "areas for improvement." Funding from the federal, the territorial, and/or the state governments is linked to how the institutions respond to the audit report and what follow-up action is taken with regard to the identified areas for improvement.

In comparison with the United Kingdom and Australia, the size of operations in India is colossal—13 open universities, over 100 dual-mode institutions, nearly 360 universities, and around 14,000 colleges imparting higher education. In addition to the National Assessment and Accreditation Council (NAAC), which assesses and accredits higher education operations, the Distance Education Council (DEC) was established in mid-1980s to support and assure standards/quality in DE institutions/ operations. It does not seem to have satisfied the policymakers, as efforts are currently on to modify this arrangement. Given the size of the operation in India, that country may require a mechanism like the Council on Higher Education Accreditation (CHEA) in the United States, which functions as a federal accreditation agency mandated to accredit other accreditation agencies within the country.

With the emergence of cross-border education in the Commonwealth, regional and international accreditation bodies too have come up. The Asia-Pacific Quality Network (APQN) was established in Hong Kong in 2003 (Stella, 2005). Its mandate is to promote cooperation among the quality assurance agencies of the region and also to help them in reaching their full potential. It helps in establishing QA agencies in the countries where they do not exist, provides relevant training to the staff where they exist, trains trainers engaged in staff development within the regional QA agencies, and also provides consultancy services to the existing QA agencies to reengineer their operations for better services.

Generally, all the above formal QA mechanisms combine internal and external assessment as a standard practice, which for its objectivity in assessment is rated highly in terms of social credibility. Additionally, it makes cross-institution as well as cross-country comparisons of educational standards easy, facilitates decision-making for funding agencies and, above all, improves the quality of DE uniformly over the regions. These advantages notwithstanding, such mechanisms are not a norm throughout the Commonwealth, as they are expensive and time-consuming. There is an argument that, instead of working for costly and tiring mechanisms of QA, it may be of a long-term advantage and value to work for creating and then sustaining a culture of quality in DE operations.

Most of the developing countries in the Commonwealth are engaged in overhauling centuries of educational deprivation and at the same time they must improve their abysmal levels of participation in higher education. They cannot afford elaborate QA mechanisms and yet they must address the issue. In so doing, in such countries quality assurance measures seemingly override the concerns of accreditation. Here are a few examples.

Created by a responsive government committed to reengineer the country's educational content and dispensation, the Botswana College of Distance and Open Learning, facing scarcity of funds, took recourse to decentralized inclusive democratic management as it had no models to go by except its own will to provide the best to the fellow countrymen (Tau & Thutoetsile, 2006). Progressively, it carved appreciation for and faith in DE among the academic and administrator fraternities, offered quality study materials and support services, and has established itself as an exemplar of quality education for the rest of the country. The resource-starved Kyambogo University, Uganda, offers a teacher training program through DE modalities (Binns & Otto, 2006). There is no question of internal and external assessments here. They rate the quality of their dispensation in terms of the care the institution provides to its students. Their tutors/counselors walk miles and miles in sun and shower to meet their students on the roadside, under a tree, and so on. For them, quality lies in the attitude and ethos. In operational terms, they assure the quality of their offerings in the quality of their materials supported by learner support that is intimate, non-commercial, and highly satisfying for learners living in remote and abject situations. Yet another case is that of a nonformal program meant to train the elected members (many of them illiterate) of local self-government in the basics of self-governance in Madhya Pradesh in India. Offered by the Indira Gandhi National Open University, the strengths of the program were the meticulous planning it was based on, the identification and utilization of structural components most suited to the program content, the learner-friendly media-mix, and the language of the common man on the one hand and, on the other, the training provided to course writers, tutors, counselors, and other support staff to ensure efficient implementation (Aslam, 2006). The program claimed a Commonwealth of Learning award.

Obviously, quality assurance in DE products and operations has differing purposes and meanings in different situations. There is a long way to go before any universally uniform mechanisms for QA become acceptable and applicable. In the mean time, however, focused attention to the following three groups of factors should help in promoting quality in any DE enterprise whatever its level of operations (Koul, 2006).

The core factors are course materials including instructional design, the teaching-learning transaction, and learner support services. Their quality constitutes the foundation of quality assurance, whatever the context or generation of DE. Further, to ensure learner-friendliness in the operations, these factors require direction and support from country-specific systemic research as a prerequisite, making such research an allied core factor.

The systemic factors refer to the formal mechanisms for quality assurance. They include the State that must introduce relevant legislation and demand strict compliance from institutions; the institutional leadership for imaginative, responsive, and pro-active stewardship; the institutional commitment reflected in the policies and procedures, practices of adherence to the relevant state legislation, staff recruitment and development, delegation of powers, monitoring systems, incentive plans, developmental strategies, and attitude towards students on the one hand and towards institutional inertia, inefficiency, and indifference on the other; the innovative management that is capable of flexibility through participatory management (especially in dual-mode institutions), of pragmatism in the selection and application of technologies, of vision for perceiving possibilities and introducing innovations, and of professional integrity for eliminating all that is sick or does not work; the long- and short-term plans that are born of extensive and inclusive deliberation, provide space for modifications against risk factors, and are implemented meticulously; and, finally, the quality-assurance mechanisms as integral constituents of institutional structure as well as processes in the form of (an) administrative unit(s) for work audit, staff development, institutional capacity building, assessment of institutional products, processes, and outcomes and for helping the management in implementing correctives and reforms.

The resource factors, especially in view of the fourth- and fifth-generation DE enterprises, have become more significant than ever. They include technology, technical and academic expertise, learning resources, and physical infrastructure. Special mention needs to be made of technology and human resources. Of what is available and in operation in the Anglophone Commonwealth, the second generation DE (self-instructional study materials in print supported by audio-video supplements and tutorials/counseling) is quite robust and enjoys universal applicability. But it is going to be assimilated by the fifth-generation DE, which is a technology-intensive enterprise. The needed technology, however, is not available uniformly across the countries, nor the professional workforce to run and maintain it either. This constraint will have to be resolved through collaborations and developmental aid to be sought from the international community—the African Virtual University is a case in point. Second, the academic community, including the policy makers and administrators, need to feel the changing winds, examine their traditional roles, and accept multiple responsibilities, some of them real strangers, dictated by the changing modalities of education, come forward to get trained and retrained as new technologies enhance educational dispensation, equip themselves to meet diverse learner needs, and be prepared for didactic transactions at any time of the day, anywhere, using any technology.

CLOSING REMARKS

With the UKOU pioneering the second generation DE and the Anglophone Commonwealth having the same educational system as that of the UK, DE should have enjoyed greater integrity in, exercised greater impact on, and done more towards development in a large number of developing countries in the Commonwealth. As outlined in Background, DE has contributed significantly in improving the content and reach of education in and so to the overall development of these countries. But this development has, by and large, remained circumscribed by the limitations of the second generation DE model. By my reckoning, the main hurdle for DE in the developing Commonwealth lies in the lack of peoples' appreciation for and comprehension of the historical status as well as the evolutionary role of distance education (Koul, 1999). Unless that status is recognized unambiguously and the inevitability of that role appreciated fully and universally by the developing society as a whole, the developing countries will remain half-hearted regarding DE applications.

All along the course of human history, education has indeed been the single most significant agent of change. What we have achieved thus far is attributable to education, and what we have not to lack of it. DE is a mere mode of education and not education in itself. If education remains what it intrinsically is, a mode of it should not attract hurdles or become an issue in itself! To elaborate on this assertion, however briefly, we must trace the evolution of education as a social institution as well as an agent of change while touching upon the inevitability of corresponding changes in its modes from time to time.

The earliest forms and content of education must have been drawn entirely from the environment, which the primitives lived in. Generation after generation, their environment dictated what tools they learnt to

make, whether they learnt to fish, gather fruit, or hunt and how they pro-
tected themselves from rivals. Observation must have been the main
mode.

Advancing into tribes living within well-defined precincts, our ances-
tors must have shrunk the locale of education to sites of actual action, and
its content to some kind of primitive agriculture and, of course, the way of
life that the tribe practiced. Need for the division of labour must have initiated different types of education for different work-groups, though
loosely at this stage. Here examples and hands-on would have served as
modes.

With our forefathers grouping into ideology-driven larger sects, the site
of education shifts to places like monasteries. The educator had to be spe-
cially prepared for the task, as the content included sectarian ideology
and values. Crafts must have flourish at the workplaces under masters
training willing apprentices. The word of mouth and practice would have
been the modes. Extending intellectual horizons supported by explorations of diverse societies bring in liberal arts and the locale of learning
shifts to schools, colleges, and other similar institutions attracting more
and more young people than ever before. The word of mouth, together
with research, reading, and writing must have been the major modes. As
our attention shifted from human societies to the material world we live
in, we turned to matter and other than human life forms and the related
phenomena. This gave us new and more promising content, and the
locale of education shifted again—this time to laboratories. Natural sciences brought in profound changes in our outlook and ways of life. Simulation and experimentation must have been added to the already
available modes. Soon the practical utility of sciences dawned on us and
the concomitant development of technology entered the content of education along with a shift in the locale of learning—institutes of technology
and industries were born. Application and utilization got added to
enhance the then-existing repertoire of educational modalities. It is only
now that the significance of democratic values, importance of ecological
balance, and the inevitability of globalization that condition our collective
lives have started making sense to us. The content, locale, and modes of
education have to change. DE as a mode of didactic transaction is a conse-
quence of this change, and not a gimmick, as some would have it.

Overall, over the ages humans have become more and more humane
and the quality of life has improved with every passing age. Clearly, development and education are linked by a symbiotic bond. From the stage of
being environment-driven through its crafts orientation and socio-scien-
tific explorations and applications and now as a means of economic and
social growth, education has come a long way, but it has only just begun to
address the allied issues of the survival of the human race and the planet

it inhabits. It has responded to human needs age after age, has accommodated changes in its own salient features, and in turn brought about and successfully managed changes in human affairs. It is in place, therefore, to consider DE as the latest stage of socioeducational evolution outlined above. It is no more a mere mode to fill the distance between the teacher and the taught, but a flexible response to the times that brings the desired kind of education to learners' doorsteps. Looked at from this viewpoint, it broaches no scepticism.

Lest the future generations find us wanting, it is time that all the concerned—policymakers, academics, administrators, professionals, support staff, parents, employers, and certainly the international community work hard and collaboratively to promote, sustain, and develop DE. It is the mode now and for the future, the mode that helps in changing the content that needs to be changed and in bringing in the new content and the related transactions that need to reach learners wherever they are.

NOTES

1. The International Council for Correspondence Education (ICCE) was renamed the International Council for Distance Education (ICDE) at the same Conference held at Vancouver in 1982. Now, it is called the International Council for Open and Distance Education, but the latter acronym holds.

2. Suriname was the only non-Anglophone country involved in the survey referred to here.

REFERENCES

Aslam, M. (2006). Application of ODL methodologies in non-formal settings and quality Assurance: A case study from the Indira Gandhi National Open University, India. In B. N. Koul & A. Kanwar (Eds.), *Perspectives on distance education: Towards a culture of quality* (pp. 45-58). Vancouver, British Columbia, Canada: The Commonwealth of Learning.

Australian Universities' Quality Agency. (2005). *AUQA audit manual (version 2.1)*. Melbourne, Australia: Author.

Binns, F., & Otto, A. (2006). Quality assurance in open distance education—Towards a culture of quality: A case Study from the Kyambogo University, Uganda. In B. N. Koul & A. Kanwar (Eds.), *Perspectives on distance education: Towards a culture of quality* (pp. 31-44). Vancouver, British Columbia, Canada: The Commonwealth of Learning.

Dzvimbo, K. P., & Kariuki, C. W. (2006). Quality assurance in the African Virtual University: A Case Study. In B. N. Koul & A. Kanwar (Eds.), *Perspectives on dis-*

tance education: Towards a culture of quality (pp. 59-72). Vancouver, British Columbia, Canada: The Commonwealth of Learning.

Eadie, A. (2000, November 12). The consumer: Ready or not for e-tail. *The Globe and Mail*.

Geith, C. (n. d.). *North American Perspective: Business models and practices for online learning in the US*. Retrieved from http://www.unisa.edu.au/ odlaaconference/PPDF2s/132%20odlaa%20-%20geith.pdf

Kanwar, A., & Koul, B. N. (2006). Quality assurance and accreditation of distance learning in the Commonwealth of Nations. In Y. C. López et al. (Eds.), *Higher education in the world 2007* (pp. 152-158). Barcelona, Spain: GUNI/ Universitat Politècnica DE Catalunya.

Koul, B. N. (1999). DE as an agent of change and development. *Journal of Education & Development in the Caribbean, 3*(2).

Koul, B. N. (2005). *Higher distance/virtual education in the Anglophone Caribbean*. Caracas, Venezuela: International Institute for Higher Education in Latin America and the Caribbean (IESALC-UNESCO).

Koul, B. N. (2006). Towards a culture of quality in open distance learning: Present possibilities. In B. N. Koul & A. Kanwar (Eds.), *Perspectives on distance education: Towards a culture of quality* (pp. 177-187). Vancouver, British Columbia, Canada: The Commonwealth of Learning.

Paul, V. (2005). *India going global: India's rapidly growing influence in international markets*. Retrieved from http://www.asiasociety.org/speeches/sf_paul05.html

Prensky, M. (2005, November). *The future is now: Strategies for reaching today's students*. Presentation at the WCET Conference, San Francisco, CA.

Quality Assurance Agency for Higher Education. (2003). *A brief guide to quality assurance in UK higher education*. Gloucester, UK: QAAHE.

Direct Relief. (2006). Retrieved from http://www.directrelief.org/sections/ information_center/countries/zambia.html

Smith, A. (2006). Using integrated systems and processes to achieve quality: A case study of the University of Southern Queensland. In B. N. Koul & A. Kanwar (Eds.), *Perspectives on distance education: Towards a Culture of Quality* (pp. 165-176). Vancouver, British Columbia, Canada: The Commonwealth of Learning.

Stella, A. (2005). *Cooperation in quality assurance: Developments in Asia and the Pacific*. Retrieved from http://www.wes.org/ewenr/o0oct/practical.htm

Taylor, J. (2001, June). 5th generation distance education. *DETYA's Higher Education Series*, Report No. 40.

Tau, D. R., & Thutoetsile, T. (2006). Quality assurance in distance education: Towards a culture of quality in Botswana College of Distance and Open Learning. In B. N. Koul & A. Kanwar (Eds.), *Perspectives on distance education: Towards a culture of quality* (pp. 19-30). Vancouver, British Columbia, Canada: The Commonwealth of Learning.

Umar, A. (2006). Quality assurance procedures in teacher education: The case of the National Teachers' Institute, Kaduna, Nigeria. In B. N. Koul & A. Kanwar (Eds.), *Perspectives on distance education: Towards a culture of quality* (pp. 73-84). Vancouver, British Columbia, Canada: The Commonwealth of Learning.

Wenger. E. (2003). *Communities of practice: Learning meaning and identity.* Cambridge, United Kingdom: Cambridge University Press.
World Bank. (2002). *Constructing knowledge societies: New challenges for tertiary education.* Washington, DC: Author.

CHAPTER 16

ORCHESTRATING ETHICS FOR DISTANCE EDUCATION AND ONLINE LEARNING

Ugur Demiray

One of the most significant features of distance education and online learning compared to traditional education is opening the doors of global education to the student at his or her desktop. What is critical to the success of this mode of education is to have ethical principles and practices in place. Ethical codes, mainly introduced by traditional education to distance education, form a very significant base for the future of distance education and online learning. The author of this chapter discusses how the issues of ethics affect online university teaching and learning in Turkey. Suggestions are given on how ethical values can be incorporated into practices and why there remain strong and urgent demands for codes of ethics in distance education and online learning.

INTRODUCTION

Distance education has become one of the most effective, economical, and productive ways of delivering instruction by corporations, institutions, colleges and universities when properly and timely used. Histori-

Online Learning Communities
pp. 277–285
Copyright © 2007 by Information Age Publishing
277

cally, distance education has continuously evolved as technology has improved. From the early 1800s to the present day, educators have utilized this method of instruction to reach those unable to interact face-to-face due to various circumstances.

During the mid 1990s, the introduction of new technologies helped online program delivery become popular worldwide. This is indicated by the amount of higher education institutions that offer courses and/or full degree programs via distance learning methods. According to the National Center for Education Statistics (1999), the number of degree-granting higher education institutions offering distance education courses increased from 33% in 1995 to 44% in 1997-1998. More specifically, the use of computer-based technologies has increased from 22% in 1995 to 60% in 1997-98, and more than 80% in 2000s. The growing dimension and rate of increase in the delivery of distance education should be carefully examined under contemporary circumstances. Today, open and distance learning (ODL) represents an alternative to the conventional system. Distance education theorists, such as Holmberg, Wedemeyer, and Moore have identified the centrality of the learner in ODL. The emergence and developments in ODL methodologies have brought certain theoretical and pragmatic approaches to the field, including the emergence of virtual classrooms and the reliance on online communication through e-mail, discussion forums, list-serves, electronic chat, bulletin board systems, WebCT and other Web-based communication.

Virtual learning environments are seen as a space for teacher and learner activities, within which learning is seen as an active process taking place in a multi-informational, co-operational networked environment. Virtual learning environments are associated with learning flexibility and learner mobility through the use of modern information and communication technologies. Virtual learning environments are becoming popular because of advancements in connectivity and image compression technology, along with their compatibility with constructivist pedagogy. For constructivists, knowledge has to be constructed through the learner's active participation. Learning means interacting with the learning environment, experimenting with skills development, and dealing with complex knowledge. The ability to simulate real-life situations is a unique feature that constructivist oriented virtual learning environments can provide. For example, it is quite easy in a virtual learning environment to simulate traffic congestion that causes car accidents. This kind of simulation is very useful for a traffic controller to use when learning about the consequences of mishandling the situation and ways to avoid disaster. Winn's recent study showed that "artificial environments can help students to reify abstractions, can scaffold students to solve complex problems, and can immerse students into dynamic phenomena. When artificial environments apply to distance learning, the empowerment effect in learning can be explosive" (Winn, 2002).

BRIEF HISTORY OF DISTANCE EDUCATION IN TURKEY

When distance education history and significant applications were examined in Turkey, it was found that the conceptualization of distance education was first discussed during a meeting on the problems of education in 1927, although the applications started in 1982. The concept of distance education was thought to be beneficial in increasing the literacy rate of the citizens (Alkan, 1987, p. 91). At this time, other countries had initiated correspondence courses. Part of the problem with correspondence courses was that people often could not learn how to read and write without a teacher. As a result, the idea of distance education was not considered until 1956. Thus, the period 1927-1955 is described as a "period when the distance education merely remained an idea" (Kaya & Odabas, 1996, p. 31).

In 1956, this first distance education application was initiated at Ankara University in the Faculty of Law (Research Institute of Bank and Trade Law). In this application, the personnel in the banks were taught through correspondence. In 1961, The Center for Education through Letters was established as a suborganization of the National Ministry of Education and preparation courses were given to people who wished to complete their secondary education without attending courses. These attempts were extended in 1966. These applications were followed by the establishment of High Teacher School (Kaya, 1996, p. 13).

Teaching by mail (correspondence education) was applied in the 1974 to 1975 academic year. Applications were administered under the Ministry of Education Strategy without universities' support, but these open education practices were not successful. In 1975 and 1978, the establishment of an open university was proposed; however, it was not accepted.

In the 1970s, the Eskisehir Academy of Economics and Commercial Sciences (EAECS) was formed. This institution took the name Anadolu University in 1982 after a reorganization of Turkish universities in 1981 through the higher education law (Article 2547). During reorganization, Turkish universities were given the opportunity to offer distance education from the Turkish Higher Education Council Law. At this time, it was decided that Anadolu University Open Education Faculty would start offering distance education courses (Demiray, 1990). Thus, in 1982, Anadolu University created the Open Education Faculty (Acikogretim Fakultesi), the first university faculty of distance education in Turkey.

In the 1982-1983 academic year, Anadolu University's Open Education Faculty (OEF) enrolled 29,445 students in business administration and economics departments. In the beginning, the OEF instructed its students through printed materials, TV courses, and academic counseling (face-to-face). Later on, OEF added radio programs, video education centers, newspaper, computer centers, CD-ROMs, and various "e" applications such as e-books, e-exams, e-essays, e-TV, e-academic counseling, etc. (Demiray, Candemir, Inceelli, & Unal, 2004).

In the last decade, Anadolu University and other Turkish universities have opened online certificate and degree programs. For example, Middle East Technical University (METU) has several online certificate programs on information technology, English language training, and computer skills. METU and Bilgi University have been providing an online degree program called e-MBA for almost 2 years. Videoconferencing capabilities were introduced at Bilkent University in 1996 and Istanbul University in 2000. Firat University also provides distance education via Firat TV programs. There are also initiatives being undertaken at Sakarya University.

However, most of these efforts are still at the preliminary stages of development or are limited to just a few online courses and certificates. Home pages on the Internet have become a part of daily life at most Turkish universities, but there have been few studies on the use of the Internet for education (Usun, 2006), especially in the context of virtual learning environments where social and ethical concerns often arise. Moreover, when Turkish distance education literature is reviewed, few scholars and institutions have studied theoretical and ethical aspects of distance education/learning systems and their applications. This author believes that such studies are needed. The next section focuses on cheating and plagiarism.

ONLINE CHEATING AND PLAGIARISM

Despite the growing popularity of virtual learning environments, learners face a plethora of new challenges, such as dehumanization, role conflict, privacy debates, and other sociopsychological issues. Ethical issues are becoming a serious problem for many universities. For instance, obtaining unauthorized access to someone's electronic mails, presenting oneself as another within electronic chats, and creating nuisances by flashing abusive language during the communication are serious concerns. Protecting the privacy of messages is very difficult in online communications. Although encryption technologies have developed, institutions are using most of them insufficiently. In particular, online cheating and plagiarism has emerged as an important concern within traditional and distance education. Online cheating and plagiarism is one of the most common ethical issues faced by learners and instructors in teaching and learning processes. Copying assignments from other people's work or taking material from Internet is seen as the easy way out for the students.

According to Hinman (2000), there are four possible approaches to minimizing (online) cheating and plagiarism. First, there is the virtues approach, which seeks to develop a student attitude that does not contain cheating. The most serious disadvantage with the first approach is the instructor's inability to ascertain who is actually taking an online assessment. Second is the prevention approach, which seeks to eliminate or reduce students' chances of cheating and to reduce the pressure of cheating among students. The second strategy for minimizing academic dishonesty in online student assessments is to acknowledge the disadvantages, and find ways to overcome them. A second strategy for minimizing academic dishonesty in online student assessment is to take the necessary time to design effective online assessments. This is a disadvantage because of the possibility of students' collaborating with each other in taking an assessment. There is an important disadvantage with the online assessment that is an instructor's inability to control a student's unauthorized use of resources in completing an assessment. The simplest way to combat this difficulty is to make all assignments open-book.

In this manner, Olt (2002) discusses ethics and student assessment, as applicable to the growing field of distance education. In particular, she stresses the strategies for minimizing academic dishonesty in online student assessment. Among the strategies discussed are acknowledging the disadvantages of online assessment and overcoming them, designing an effective, cheat-proof online assessment, keeping online courses current, and providing students with an academic dishonesty policy.

A third one is concerned with the possibility of students collaborating with each other in taking assessments. The third strategy to reduce academic dishonesty is to rotate the curriculum by assigning original assignments and readings, or even considering alternative, project-based assessments that require creativity. Obviously, the less frequently instructors modify assignments and assessments, the easier it becomes for students to share graded papers from previous semesters.

Finally, there is a police approach that mainly seeks to catch and punish those who cheat. The fourth and final strategy to minimize academic dishonesty is to provide students with an academic integrity/dishonesty policy. According to McMurtry (2001), instructors should take the necessary time to discuss their academic policy with students. Unfortunately, a recent study reveals that few instructors take up the topic of academic integrity/dishonesty with their students (McMurtry, 2001).

Fass (1990) discussed how contemporary students have been raised in an era of decline of public morality involving scandal and corruption by public servants, major corporations, and private citizens. These events must surely affect students' attitudes about ethical behavior. Informal polls show that as many as three quarters of students on campuses today admit to some sort of academic fraud (Fass, 1990). This is an increased concern of faculty teaching at a distance whether the student who is doing the work is indeed the student enrolled. It is also important to understand the motives that lead to cheating, such as pressure for grades, the testing environment, lack of understanding of academic regulations, personality characteristics, and lack of moral reasoning. Furthermore, Fass (1990) commented in his study that many colleges, universities, and companies do not adequately spell out information on cheating in their handbooks and catalogs. Students coming from high schools do not understand the issues of collegiate ethics and academic honesty.

Recently, cheating and plagiarism have been receiving a good deal of attention in education circles. The rise of virtual paper mills has tuned educators in to the fact that students, when given the chance, will often resort to dishonest measures in order to get high marks in a course. Many professors have reacted very strongly to the rise of cheating. Some have strengthened their policies on the matter, others have added new paragraphs to their syllabi addressing the issue directly, and still others have been spending hours online trying to find any paper they believe to be from a source other than the student (Belle, 2006).

ANADOLU UNIVERSITY COUNCIL OF ETHICS CENTER (AUCEC)

In spite of number of universal ethics codes, some institutions and especially science institutions regulate their "Institutional Scientific Ethical Codes" or "Rules of Scientific Ethical Codes." The Anadolu University Council of Ethics Center (AUCEC) was formed in order to prepare the *Ethical Codes Guide of Anadolu University* in 2002. The guide concerns mainly ethical issues for researching and publishing in science and in educational applications process. These rules are focused on the following topics:

- Ethical rules and factors dealt with researching and publishing in science;
- Ethical rules for participants for human and animals;
- Ethical rules and factors for research results;
- Scientific negligence;
- Scientific deviation;
- Ethical rules and factors for publishing and presenting process;

- Complete plagiarism;
- Scientific piracy;
- Plagiarism;
- Self-plagiarism;
- Ethical rules and factors for editing and referring process;
- Ethical rules and factors for author names;
- Ethical rules and factors for editors;
- Ethical rules and factors for referees;
- Ethical rules and factors for reviewers;
- Ethical rules and factors for membership of jury;
- Ethical rules and factors for advisors and member of advising committee;
- Ethical rules and factors for academics and students exam process;
- Ethical rules and factors for academics exam process; and
- Ethical rules and factors for students exam process (Ethics Codes Guide of Anadolu University, 2002).

In addition to the specific strategies identified for each of the stated goals, Anadolu University is seeking funding to institutionalize the CEC initiative to establish an interdisciplinary ethics center. The center will have as its fundamental aim to enhance the overall ethical culture within the University community and beyond. Ethics centers based at other universities are used as models to design a center that will provide leadership for a wide variety of ethics initiatives including the following:

- Provide leadership for ethical campus and off campus education system programming.
- Promote the teaching of ethics, including professional development for both traditional and distance education department staff.
- Support research into both normative ethical theory and applied ethics in both traditional and distance education, including interdisciplinary research.
- Arrange for campus visits by nationally renowned scholars in ethics.
- Sponsor conferences and symposia focusing on ethical issues within and across disciplines.

CONCLUSION

The incredible growth of ODL and virtual learning environments have led to ethical dilemmas. More and more, faculties are being asked to teach at a distance, often with little to no training. Consequently, ethical practices can take a back seat in the rush to be prepared each semester. Suggestions for avoiding such dilemmas include:

- ODL faculty and administrators need to become ethical leaders in the field.
- ODL educators must interact with others honestly, fairly, respectfully, and consistently, along with developing policy that is ethical in practice.
- ODL educators must interact with general administrators and ICT sector administrators honestly, fairly, respectfully, and consistently, along with developing policy that is ethical in practice.
- ODL educators need to consider ethical practices in course design, development, and in interaction with learners.
- ODL educators need to make sure that learners (especially if dealing with high school or mature learners) understand what is ethical behavior as a learner.
- ODL administrators need to consider ethical practices in managing programs and developing policies and procedures.

To conclude, this chapter discussed the necessity of ethics for both teachers and students as well as administrators and instructors who design teaching materials in the field of distance education. In particular, this paper discussed strategies for minimizing plagiarism and cheating in ODL assessment. Among the strategies discussed are: acknowledging the disadvantages of online assessment and overcoming them; designing an effective, cheat-proof online assessment; keeping online courses current; and providing students with an academic dishonesty policy. The author of this chapter tried to consider how the issues of ethics affect online teaching and learning. Suggestions were provided on how values can be maintained and why there is a strong and urgent need for a code of ethics developed by various online universities. But, the question still remains as to whether the majority of distance educators and administrators today are following ethical practices.

REFERENCES

Alkan, C. (1987). Açikogretim: Uzaktan Egitim Sistemlerinin Karsilastirmali Olarak Incelenmesi [An open learning: Comperative investigaton of the distance education systems]. *Ankara Universitesi Egitim Bilimleri Fakültesi Yayinlari, 157*, 91.

Belle, V. G. (2006). *How cheating helps drive better instruction*, Retrieved April 2, 2006. Available from http://www.plagiarized.com/vanb.html

Demiray, U. (1990). *Undergraduates of the Open Education Faculty* (Publishing Number: 452/205). Eskisehir, Turkey: Anadolu University Publications.

Demiray, U., Candemir, O., Inceelli, A., & Unal, F. (2004). *A review of the litrature on the open education faculty in Turkey (1982-2002). A revised and expanded fourth edition*. Retrieved April 2, 2006, from http://www.tojet.net Sakarya University, Turkey.

Ethics Codes Guide of Anadolu University. (2002). Anadolu University Council of Ethics Center-AUCEC, Anadolu University Publications, Eskisehir Turkey.

Fass, R. A. (1990). Cheating and plagiarism. In W. W. May (Ed.), *Ethics and higher education* (pp. 171-173). New York: Macmillan

Hinman, L. M. (2000). *Academic integrity and the World Wide Web*. Retrieved April 2, 2006, from http://ethics.acusd.edu/presentations/cai2000/index_files/frame.htm

Kaya, Z. (1996). *Uzaktan Egitimde Ders Kitaplar (Açkögretim Lisesi Ornegi)* [Printed course books in distance education (A case of open high school)]. Ankara, Turkey. Gazi Üniversitesi Endüstriyel Sanatlar Egitim Fakültesi,

Kaya, Z., & Odabasi, F. (1996). *Türkiye'de Uzaktan Egitimin Gelisimi* [Developments of Distance Education in Turkey]. *Egitim Fakultesi Dergisi [Journal of Education Faculty]*, *6*(1), 23.

McMurtry, K. (2001). E-cheating: Combating a 21st century challenge. *THE Journal Online*. Retrieved November 6, 2006, from http://thejournal.com/magazine/vault/A3724.cfm

National Center for Education Statistics. (1999). *Teacher quality: A report on the preparation and qualifications of public school teachers*. (NCES 1999–080). Washington, DC: U.S. Department of Education.

Olt, M. R. (2002). Ethics and distance education: Strategies for minimizing academic dishonesty in online assessment. *Online Journal of Distance Learning Administration*, *5*(3). Retrieved October 7, 2006, from http://www.westga.edu/~distance/ojdla/fall53/olt53.html

Usun, S. (2006). *The role of the socio-cultural context in designing appropriate support services and enhancing interaction in Turkish distance education*. Department of Educational Sciences Canakkale Onsekiz Mart University, Canakkale, Turkey. Unpublished paper for *Turkish Online Journal of Distance Education*.

Winn, W. (2002, May). *What can students learn in artificial environments that they cannot learn in class?* Paper presented at the 20th anniversary celebrations, Open Education Faculty (AOF) First International Symposium, Anadolu University, Eskisehir, Turkey. Retrieved August 2, 2006, from http://aof20.anadolu.edu.tr/program.htm

PART V

TRENDS IN ONLINE LEARNING COMMUNITIES

CHAPTER 17

ONLINE SELF-ORGANIZING SOCIAL SYSTEMS

Four Years Later

David Wiley

It 2002, Brewer and Wiley first attempted to analyze interesting informal online learning interactions through the lens of biological self-organization (Wiley & Edwards, 2002). The approach proved quite fruitful. However, both the Internet and the field of instructional technology have changed significantly in the intervening years, and a fresh application of the analytical approach seems justified.

ONLINE SELF-ORGANIZING SOCIAL SYSTEMS (OSOSS), 2002

In the original paper, we posited that "the OSOSS structure allows large numbers of individuals to self-organize in a highly decentralized manner in order to solve problems and accomplish other goals" (Wiley & Brewer, 2002, p. 33). We thought that blogs would be "a fertile primordial soup from which online self-organizing social systems can emerge." Slashdot was the best and only model of a very large-scale community capable of

Online Learning Communities
pp. 289–298

sustaining the number of interactions necessary for supporting the emergence of anything like intelligent behavior, though we obviously expected
to see others emerge. We claimed that the ways an OSOSS overcomes
issues of teacher bandwidth while simultaneously increasing the level of
social interaction in online learning was the primary benefit of the model.
We also saw the OSOSS as providing an alternative framework for thinking about cataloging, finding, using, and evaluating educational
resources:

- Indexing and Discovery: Learning objects are not cataloged with
  metadata and submitted to a central curator repository. Community members know of existing resources and local resource collections. Individual resources are discovered through "community
  queries" in which community members respond with pointers to
  resources they know about personally. When a sufficient portion of
  the community responds in this manner, the learner locates satisfying resources.
- Combination: Learning objects are not automatically populated
  into one of many instructional templates. Without the direction of
  any single grand architect, peers contribute relevant resources and
  descriptions of how they might be employed within the context of
  the initiator's problem. Much like a colony of ants, peers autono-
  mously build on one another's work and create a satisfying resource
  structure without centralized direction (Bonabeau, Dorigo, & Theraluaz, 1999).
- Use: Learners do not sit through a temporal sequencing of
  resources and assessments linked to decontextualized instructional
  objectives. They employ resources provided by peers as media-
  tional means in the solution of a self-selected problem or accomplishment of another self-selected goal.
- Evaluation: Learning objects are not critiqued out of an instructional context with a summative quality rating of 1-5. Learners evaluate the relevance and suitability of resources within a specific
  learning context. (Williams, 2001, contains an excellent description
  of the impasse created by attempting to apply current context-
  dependent evaluation methodologies to extremely decontextualized educational resources.)

We likened the OSOSS model to an amalgamation of several instructional approaches, including collaborative problem solving, case-based
scenarios, legitimate peripheral participation, and cognitive apprentice-

ship. Finally, we listed what might be seen as some of the weaknesses of the OSOSS model:

- A standard curriculum may be difficult to impose on individuals in an OSOSS.
- Assessment of individuals may be difficult to carry out in an OSOSS.
- Required feedback may not be immediate in an OSOSS.
- Establishing identity and trust relationships within an OSOSS may take longer than in higher bandwidth channels.

Looking back, we took several positions that would be simple empirical questions years later. How did we do in our predictions? What has changed since then?

ONLINE SELF-ORGANIZING SOCIAL SYSTEMS, 2006

Updating the Definition

I believe our working description of an OSOSS is still fairly accurate, though I would alter it now to remove some of the repetitive redundancy it contains, since self-organization implies decentralization. If I had to write a new definition today (which, oddly enough, I do), I would say an online self-organizing social system exists when:

- a large number of people engage in a large number of direct or indirect interactions via the network,
- these interactions help individuals accomplish things they have reason to value,
- no central authority provides extrinsic incentives for participation in the system,
- no central authority regulates or controls the interactions.

The key components of the definition are a large number of people, a large number of interactions, participating individuals deriving value, and the decentralization of system management functions.

As Predicted, More OSOSS's Have Emerged

In the four years since the publication of the first OSOSS paper, MySpace (http://myspace.com/) and Digg (http://digg.com/) have both emerged as leaders in the OSOSS space. According to Alexa's Top 500 ranking of Web sites, MySpace is currently the sixth most popular Web site in the world (Alexa, 2006a) and Digg is currently the 49th most popular Web site in the world (Alexa, 2006b). So, both sites definitely qualify with regard to part 1 of the definition of an OSOSS.

Like Slashdot, these are both sites where users share information and build relationships with others. In the case of Digg, users help one another find technology news and related items. In the case of MySpace, users help one another find information about movies, music, dating possibilities, and classifieds-style information. In these ways the two sites meet part 2 of the definition.

As a moderately relevant aside, one may ask, "is an environment that helps people keep up on current events, movies, and music really a learning environment?" I would answer a resounding yes. You need only stand once by the copy machine while others discuss the most recent episode of Lost (which you didn't see), to remember the feeling of sitting down for the test you forgot was scheduled for today. Whether the content around which the learning interactions in an OSOSS happens to be valuable or not is not for me to decide on your behalf. It may as well be quantum physics, auto body welding, or fantasy sports. As instructional technologists, we are perfectly justified in studying the mechanisms and interaction structures that support learning in this wide variety of domains.

In the cases of both MySpace and Digg, an extrinsic incentive to use the sites obviously exists. If you fit a certain socioeconomic profile (age range, etc.), there is a rather strong social expectation that you will be a user of MySpace. Likewise, if you work in certain computer-related fields, there is a rather strong social expectation that you will be a user of Digg. But while peer pressure is a very real motivator, it is not one that is provided by a central authority. In fact, peer pressure is the epitome of a broadly distributed incentive system. It is probably the case that peer pressure is like gravity, in that the further you are from another person (where distance is measured by hops in your social network) the weaker their influence on you becomes, but this does not mean that the cumulative influence of an entire society of peers is insignificant. MySpace and Digg both meet part 3 of the definition.

Finally, MySpace and Digg are wonderful examples of user-run sites. Users find, contribute, and bookmark the technology news, music, videos, etc. Both sites are really structured shells into which users pour content and a set of tools by which users send signals to one another indicating their preferences for individual bits of content. Both sites meet part 4 of the definition.

There has been buzz recently that MySpace may begin exercising a stronger, more centralized control of what happens on the site (in response to concerns about users' privacy and safety). If this actually comes about, it places the site's phenomenal scale and success at risk to the extent that it violates the OSOSS way of doing things.

Blogs and RSS Move the Net Forward

While our predictions regarding the emergence of additional OSOSSes were partially accurate, we failed to be sufficiently radical in our projections of where the Net and OSOSSes would go. We should first discuss where the Net has gone. Blogs have soared in popularity since the first article, and with blogs came the popularity of RSS. These two have conspired to partially break one of the pillars of the OSOSS framework in the first paper: that collections of content indexed with metadata and collected in repositories will never happen.

Of course, they never happened the way people "hoped" they would. But there is now actually a huge amount of content catalogued with metadata and indexed in repositories. But instead of using the heavier metadata specifications like those from IMS or the IEEE, blog-based content is indexed with RSS or Atom. And bloggers submit their RSS feeds to sites like Technorati that regularly and automatically harvest everything new on tens of millions of blogs (as of July 2006, Technorati covers 49.8 million blogs (Technorati, 2006)), providing users the opportunity to search through all this distributed content from one location.

The magic of RSS is, of course, that bloggers never hear the word metadata or knowingly creates metadata. They just writes their posts, and the metadata is created automatically. RSS has proven so easy to use that an entire class of very popular applications called aggregators has sprung up, allowing people to maintain their own dynamically updated, personalized, local repositories.

Suddenly there were hundreds of millions of blogs out there, overflowing with content, all of it indexed with RSS, and much of it harvested by sites like Technorati. People still asked members of their communities for help finding resources, but the ability to search through indexed collections of content did manage to come about, after all.

Then Comes Web 2.0

The "Web 2.0" meme captures much of where the net has come in the time since the "dot-bomb" of the early 2000s when Erin and I originally wrote about OSOSSes. Tim O'Reilly (2005) attempts to define the Web 2.0 construct by comparison to what came before (Table 17.1).

Table 17.1.   O'Reilly's Web 2.0 Definition By comparison

Web 1.0		Web 2.0
DoubleClick	→	Google AdSense
Ofoto	→	Flickr
Akamai	→	BitTorrent
mp3.com	→	Napster
Britannica Online	→	Wikipedia
personal Web sites	→	blogging
evite	→	upcoming.org and EVDB
domain name speculation	→	search engine optimization
page views	→	cost per click
screen scraping	→	web services
publishing	→	participation
content management systems	→	Wikis
directories (taxonomy)	→	tagging ("folksonomy")
stickiness	→	syndication

Drawing out O'Reilly's comparison, we might make a similar chart comparing where the world has been and where it is now (Table 17.2).

Table 17.2 causes little heartburn until one realizes that formal education, and higher education in particular, seems trapped in the "From" column of Table 17.2. In testimony to the Secretary of Education's Commission on the Future of Higher Education, I expanded on the increasing disconnect between school and everything else:

A typical experience in a higher education classroom might be characterized as follows:

Students are inside a classroom (*tethered* to a place), using textbooks and handouts (*printed* materials), they must pay tuition and register to attend (the experience is *closed*), talking during class or working with others outside of class is generally discouraged (each student is *isolated* though surrounded by peers), each student receives exactly the same instruction as each of her classmates (the information presented is *generic*), and students are students and do not participate in the teaching process (they are *consumers*).

Compare the classroom learning experience with the same student's learning experiences outside the classroom:

From her dorm room / the student center / a coffee shop / the bus a student connects to the Internet using her laptop (she is *mobile*), uses Google to

**Table 17.2.   Differences in the
World of the 1990s and the World of the 2000s**

From	To	Examples
Analog/Print	Digital	Voice over IP (VOIP), e-books, digital newspapers (*New York Times*, *Washington Post*)
Closed	Open	Open source software, Public Library of Science journals, open access to weather and astronomical data
Tethered	Mobile	Batteries in laptops, cell phones, wireless Internet access
Isolated	Connected	Email, instant messaging, hypertext, web services; massive interconnection of people, content, and systems
Generic	Personal	Customized interiors for cars; skins and ring tones for cell phones; hard drives, RAM, and video components in computers
Consuming	Participating	Creating blogs, podcasts, and video podcasts

find a relevant webpage (a *digital* resource which is *open* for her to access). While carrying out her search, she chats with one friend on the phone and another using instant messaging to see if they can assist in her search (she is *connected* to other people), she follows links from one website to another exploring related information (the content is *connected* to other content), she quickly finds exactly the information she needs, ignoring irrelevant material (she gets what is important to her *personally*), and she shares her find with her friends by phone and IM (she *participates* in the teaching process) (Wiley, 2006).

One might say, "You're ignoring online classes! They show what the future of education is about." I certainly hope this statement isn't true. Yes, online classes were innovative in 1995. Now, in 2006, they're again woefully behind the times. Online classes are digital and mobile (i.e., you can do them online in your pajamas), but they fail to meet the core criteria that define the modern Web: open, connected, personal, and participatory. Students still have to register and receive a password to get into a course (online courses are closed), collaborating on assignments is even more zealously discouraged online than off (leaving students isolated), every student reads the same textbook-converted-to-Web pages as every other (the content is not personalized for individual students), and students neither create educational content for each other nor engage directly in teaching each other (they are consumers). We might arrange these principles as connected, open, personal, and participatory to get the mnemonic "COPP." Perhaps if professors and instructional designers (many of whom don't use the new Web) could remember these principles, they could begin to incorporate them into their instructional designs.

The New OSOSS and the New Stigmergy

One of the interesting characteristics of self-organizing systems is the way information is shared between system agents. One of these mechanisms is known as "stigmergy":

> Pierre-Paul Grasse first coined the term stigmergy in the 1950s in conjunction with his research on termites. Grasse showed that a particular configuration of a termite's environment (as in the case of building and maintaining a nest) triggered a response in a termite to modify its environment, with the resulting modification in turn stimulating the response of the original or a second worker to further transform its environment. Thus the regulation and coordination of the building and maintaining of a nest was dependent upon stimulation provided by the nest, as opposed to an inherent knowledge of nest building on the individual termite's part. *A highly complex nest simply self-organises due to the collective input of large numbers of individual termites performing extraordinarily simple actions in response to their local environment.* Since Grasse's research, stigmergy has been applied to the self-organisation of ants, artificial life, swarm intelligence and more recently, the Internet itself (Elliot, 2006, emphasis added).

Elliot and others look at the collaboration occurring within wiki environments and see stigmergy in action. The argument makes sense if you view stigmergy as collective action mediated by the environment—individuals start articles, those articles persist in the environment, other agents encounter the article, and make addition or corrections in response to the encounter.

I believe those who see wiki-based collaborative authoring as an example of stigmergy miss some important parts of the stigmergy equation. Wiki-based authoring, while it certainly is an aggregation of several small inputs from independent agents, is mediated by *language* far more than by the *environment*. To me, stigmergy is collective action mediated solely by operations on the environment, and does *not* involve any communication mechanism as powerful as language. In stigmergetic interaction, the environment is the communication medium. A higher fidelity example of stigmergy on the Internet would be delicious.

Delicious (http://del.icio.us/) is first and foremost a bookmark management tool—a Web site where users can keep their bookmarks. Storing your bookmarks online instead of directly in your browser allows you to access your bookmarks whether at work, at home, or at a friend's place, and that's a good thing. Delicious also lets its users organize bookmarks by adding (and later sorting by) keywords or "tags," making it easy to find everything you've bookmarked about "linux," "recipes," or "cricket."

Over and above being a bookmark management tool, Delicious is a *social* bookmarking site. This means that users can all see each other's bookmarks. They can also filter all the bookmarks in the site by keyword (e.g., see every bookmark that has been tagged "recipes" regardless of who bookmarked it). The front page of the site, as well as the Recent and Popular pages, show the sites that have recently been bookmarked (by anyone) and indicate how many total users have bookmarked them. While the primary benefit of using a social bookmarking system is being able to access your bookmarks no matter where you are, a very powerful second- ary benefit is the way the social aspect of the site helps users finding new, interesting sites.

To me, the bookmarking behavior of Delicious users seems much more akin to the woodchip stacking behavior of termites than correcting gram- matical errors in an encyclopedia article does. When an individual book- marks a site in Delicious, the Recent page is modified to include a link to that site and the total number of users who have linked to it. If another user quickly bookmarks the site, the Recent page is updated again with the new larger number of people who have bookmarked the site.

Internet users who frequent the Recent page or its derivatives (like http://opencontent.org/oishii/) see that certain sites appear on the page and have numbers next to them. Some users respond to this modification in the environment (the presence of sites and corresponding link num- bers on the Recent page) by bookmarking these sites themselves, further modifying the environment as experienced by the next user (the modifi- cation comes in the incrementing of the number of users who have linked to the site).

The careful reader will argue that these Delicious-based interactions are still language-based. This is true. But the role of language seems much less important in mediating the behavior of Delicious users (the behavior being adding a bookmark) than in mediating the behavior of wikipedia users (the behavior being editing language or creating addi- tional linguistic expressions). This self-organizing mechanism for helping people find interesting content gets better the more people there are par- ticipating in the system, unlike most systems that strain and eventually grind to a halt when large numbers of people all try to participate at once. Some doctoral students and I are currently working to better understand and model the pattern of these environmentally-mediated interactions.

CONCLUSION

The idea of the online self-organizing social system has proven to be quite robust by Internet-time. Brewer and I never imagined that OSOSSes would become the dominant form of Internet site, but this seems to be exactly what is happening. Understanding these groups and the structure of their interactions was an interesting curiosity for instructional technologists 4 years ago. These groups and the structure of their interactions have now moved to the front and center of the instructional technology research agenda. Any instructional technologists who wishes to have more current tools in their bag than the Web-based courses of 1995 must become fluent in the language of the OSOSS—including RSS, self-organization, aggregation, and social software. To the extent that instructional technologists are incapable or unwilling to become fluent in this language, our field will languish in the "From" column of Table 17.1, while the world moves on. Let's not be left behind.

REFERENCES

Alexa. (2006a). Related info for MySpace.com. http://www.alexa.com/data/details/traffic_details?q=&url=myspace.com/

Alexa. (2006b). Related info for Digg.com. http://www.alexa.com/data/details/traffic_details?q=&url=digg.com/

Bonabeau, E., Dorigo, M., & Theraluaz, G. (1999). *Swarm intelligence: From natural to artificial systems*. New York: Oxford University Press.

Elliot, M. (2006). Stigmergic collaboration: The evolution of group work. *M/C Journal, 9*(2). Retrieved from http://journal.media-culture.org.au/0605/03-elliott.php

O'Reilly, T. (2005). *What is Web 2.0. Design patterns and business models for the next generation of software*. Retrieved from http://www.oreillynet.com/lpt/a/6228

Technorati. (2006). *About Technorati*. Retrieved from http://technorati.com/about/

Wiley, D., & Edwards, E. K. (2002). Online self-organizing social systems: The decentralized future of online learning. *Quarterly Review of Distance Education, 3*(1), 33-46.

Williams, D. D. (2001). Evaluation of learning objects and instruction using learning objects. In D. A. Wiley (Ed.), *The instructional use of learning objects: Online version*. Retrieved June 1, 2007, from http://reusability.org/read/chapters/williams.doc

CHAPTER 18

EXPLORING QUALITATIVE METHODOLOGIES IN ONLINE LEARNING ENVIRONMENTS

Mary Beth Bianco and Alison A. Carr-Chellman

Qualitative inquiry is rich in personal interaction between participant and researcher. The researcher is an instrument (Creswell, 1998) and the participant an active sharer in the process. This discussion seeks to consider the issues related to conducting qualitative inquiries in online settings and the implications for using electronic means in interview and observation. Consideration should be given to the ramifications of online interview techniques and, particularly, observation experiences. Personal interviews may not be "face to face" in online environments, but may be only available via other synchronous forms such as telephone or online discussion. The implications for electronic discussion formats for collecting data will also be discussed but, more importantly, the implications for distinguishing between interview, observation, and document/artifact analysis when conducting research via electronic data collection. The tactical issues discussed here are those that relate to the interview and observational legs and also include artifact and document analysis of triangulation in conjunction with possible avenues for clarifying the lines between these 3 methods of data collection. Various strategies for testing online qualitative inquires will be considered and discussed related to their potential value in the inquiry process. This

Online Learning Communities
pp. 299–317
Copyright © 2007 by Information Age Publishing
All rights of reproduction in any form reserved.

inquiry examines the tactical implications for data collection and their impact on the qualitative process in online situations or by electronic means.

INTRODUCTION

There are a growing number of research studies being conducted on distance education—in particular, online learning environments (Donaldson & Tomson, 1999; French, 1999; Gunawardena, Lowe, & Anderson, 1998; Hengni, 1998; Hiltz, 1998; Jannasch-Pennell, DiGangi, Yu, Andrews, & Babb, 1999; Levin & Ben-Jacob, 1998; McFerrin, 1999; McIssac, Blocher, Mahes, & Vrasidas, 1999; Moon, 1998; Schlough & Bhuripanyo, 1998; Thompson & Nay, 1999; Truman-Davis & Hartman, 1998; Yong, 1998). Online delivery is becoming more and more prevalent as an integral part of today's college curriculum. Instructors and university professors are providing more Web support and universities are soliciting students to participate in online coursework in the "anytime, anywhere" model of instructional delivery (Dunn, 2000; Gladieux & Swail, 1999). Increasingly, "blended" courses that originate as face-to-face classes with regular meeting times integrate a certain amount of online requirement, resources, or student collaboration.

As a result of the increased interest in research of online learning environments, there has been a subsequent increase in the interest and use of qualitative methods to gain a deeper understanding of online learning environments. In particular, there have been a large number of studies that have examined, qualitatively, student perceptions of online learning experiences (e.g., McIsaac, Blocher, Mahes, & Vrasidas, 2000; McNeil, Robin, & Miller, 2000). However, there has not yet been adequate exploration of the use of qualitative methods of online learning environment investigations in terms of differentiation among strategies for data collection via qualitative online inquiry. Specifically, we seek to discuss qualitative methods literature in which the electronic "field" and electronic means of data collection are generally omitted and what may become blurred lines of distinction among the most common qualitative research strategies—interview, document analysis, and observation.

In an effort to understand students' perceptions of their learning in this emerging environment, much research is being conducted in connection to online learning. Among the current topics of interest are studies that compare online to traditional delivery of the same course material; effectiveness of learning; student perceptions; fostering collaboration; peer relationships and various course delivery models (e.g., Bianco, 2002; Diaz & Cartnal, 2000; Ryan, 2000). This chapter is an attempt to discuss some of the potential implications of doing qualitative research with online populations as well as future trends in this growing qualitative methodology.

Understanding Culture

An attempt has been made to understand the culture of online learning using qualitative methodology (specifically ethnography) as a natural choice with regard to research design. Ethnographic methods seek to understand a culture by describing the routines and daily activities of a particular culture (Fetterman, 1998). In utilizing ethnographic methodologies in online learning environments, we can attempt to understand the culture of these learning environments by observing as well as interacting with the participants.

Hine's (2000) publication, *Virtual Ethnography*, encapsulates the tenets of ethnography via the electronic milieu. For example, if the participants in a computer-mediated communication environment think of themselves as part of a group, it creates for them a social connection to the group which in turn is thought of as a cultural identity (p. 16). The field site then becomes the group interaction experience of the participants and they interact and communicate with one another, as in an online class setting, a listserve, an interactive blog or an interactive document sharing experience, such as Mediasite or Elluminate where access points are shared and multiple computers can interact via real time across geographic boundaries. Several issues with this type of interaction arise, but one of the most prevalent is that of identity (Hine, 2000; Mann & Stewart, 2000). It is difficult to assess the identity of a person in a virtual environment where identity is basically held to the honor system.

The tenets of phenomenology (Creswell, 1998; Moustakas, 1994) also lead us to deeper understandings of the experiences of the participants and the interpretation that informs our understandings. Phenomenological research assumptions carry with them the importance of the voices of the participants, their descriptions of their experiences, and their reflections on their lived experiences (Creswell, 1998; Moustakas, 1994). In considering online learning environments, these experiences are critical when attempts are made to gain deeper understandings of the lived experience of learners.

Online Learning—Attitudes and Perceptions

In light of the growing interest in these new learning environments, online learning has both its advocates (Dede, 1997) and its detractors (Noble, 1998). These new technologies in instructional delivery carry both support for, and definite opinions against, online learning environments and their potential effect(s) on learning. If learning is at the heart of our choice regarding instructional delivery options, researchers and educators are obligated to fully understand student experiences in many types of learning situations. Student perceptions and experiences should be priorities in instructional design processes and should be considered prior to media selection decisions. It is difficult not to design for the delivery method or media du jour, however popular, convenient, or well-funded online learning options may be—their impact on learners' experiences as understood through qualitative inquiry should be carefully considered by all practicing instructional designers. Noble's (2000) outcry against online learning and technology is largely aimed at the politics of technology. He argues that the technology itself is value-laden and the demand for online education is non-existent, simply created by university administrators (Young, 2000) primarily for profit motives.

Noble suggests that the motivations for online learning are nothing more than greed on the part of university administrators and should be resisted by faculty in the same ways that Luddites resisted the new technologies that they believed would put their own children out of future work. Others (Bowers, 1999; Woody, 1999) also argue that while the Internet is an excellent dispenser of information, education is not merely the acquisition of information. By making learning primarily about the acquisition of information, there is the potential to commodify higher education—learning becomes a product for sale rather than the experience of learning and growth (Carr-Chellman & Carr-Chellman, 2001). Like Noble, many are concerned with the financial emphasis placed on online learning environments with a lack of focus on "learning" (Noble, 1998; Woody, 1999).

Many supporters of online education (Dede, 1997; Dunn, 2000) envision a future in which students will come to universities only for the social aspects of higher education, such as sports or other non-academic activities. In a report prepared by the college board, predictions about the future of online learning environments included the demise of the university, as we know it, within 30 years (Dunn, 2000; Gladieux & Swail, 1999). Gladieux and Swail go on to cite examples of complete degree programs offered by "traditional" universities online and refer to them as leaders in the electronic market. While considerations need to be made about the access to these new technologies and the target populations who benefit from technological advancement, other issues should be considered as well. The need exists for a qualitative examination of online instruction. Collaboration, social interaction, and relationship building activities that exist in face-to-face instruction have been addressed somewhat in the design literature (Jonassen, Davidson, Collins, Campbell, & Bannan-Haag, 1995).

The Match Between Qualitative Inquiry and Online Learning

Qualitative methodologies are social at the core (Creswell, 1998; Denzin & Lincoln, 1998a). There has always been an understanding that part of the qualitative inquiry experience is "being in the field" (Wolcott, 1995). Doing fieldwork, in which the inquirer works in a natural setting to collect stories by observing, examining documents, and interviewing indigenous populations, has always been a cornerstone of the qualitative research experience (Lincoln & Guba, 1985). What is the implication of doing qualitative research in online settings? Where is the field located? Can it be electronic? If so, does it exist only within wires or flowing through the air? What does it mean to have a "virtual" field or to do "virtual" fieldwork where the field itself is no longer bound a physical space or by geography?

Collecting data at a distance begs the question: can qualitative research occur in the exploration of online learning? Well, actually, this has already been answered: it most certainly can happen. The question is the extent to which we need to redefine some of our terms in doing so... and if so, how will that experience be defined? Will qualitative research lose a certain social quality when we translate these methods from naturalistic inquiry (Lincoln & Guba, 1985) into "e-inquiry"? Will the researchers enjoy the experience of doing qualitative research in an e-field as much as they enjoy being in a physical field? Will there be some important essence of the stories that are lost by doing qualitative research electronically? Or is the fidelity actually boosted by doing the inquiry in the same sort of culture that the students are experiencing for their own learning? Is there any way to do qualitative research among online populations in a face-to-face mode, and what is gained or lost in this choice? And what of the qualitative tactics themselves? Will the traditionally separate tactics of interview, observation, and document analysis become blurred in online settings? If an interview is conducted in a chat mode, is it a document to be analyzed, or an interview? Clearly, we cannot answer all of these questions in any complete way here; we raise them as serious considerations for those engaged in qualitative research among online populations as well as for those who supervise students who wish to pursue qualitative inquiry projects in online education.

QUALITATIVE RESEARCH EPISTEMOLOGICAL VIEWPOINTS

Qualitative research is conducted in an effort to understand the experiences and attitudes of people in contextually and typically geographically bound settings. It is understood to be descriptive, rather than prescriptive; not seeking truth of objectivity (Creswell, 1998). Purposes of qualitative research include inquiry in natural rather than contrived settings and understanding the ontological viewpoints of the participants. Perspective, perception, and experience are epistemological notions that are sought in the interpretation and understanding of specific contexts or situations. Because we wish to understand the perceptions and lived experiences of learners in online environments, there is a viable match between qualitative inquiry and online learning environments. However, online qualitative inquiry methodology has not been clearly delineated or explicated, nor is it definitively prescribed in the qualitative inquiry literature.

As previously mentioned, the book entitled *Virtual Ethnography*, by Hine (2000), is one of the few sources that discusses qualitative inquiry in online settings from a methodological standpoint. A second, *Internet Communication and Qualitative Research* by Mann and Stewart (2000), also focuses on communication and research executed in an online milieu. While Hine's inquiry context is not online learning environments, she does discuss in detail the implications of using aspects of the Internet as a cultural setting in qualitative research and questions whether or not our definition of culture and society have or will become altered due to the increased use of the Internet and other forms of computer-mediated communication.

Mann and Stewart (2000) specifically refer to the benefits of being able to investigate "hard to reach populations," working with sensitive issues that may be a deterrent to soliciting participants, and the ability to collect a mass of information. Other benefits include cost savings in terms of access, time savings in terms of travel to get to populations, and the convenience that is brought by online access to people. Oddly, many of these benefits are those enjoyed by online learning students themselves and cited by learners and administrators as justifications for the enterprise overall (Bianco, 2000). This can certainly be criticized and we would be naïve not to recognize that the benefits of time and money in a labor-intensive project, be it teaching or inquiry, will also have significant, though perhaps less measurable, costs.

Epistemological philosophies inherent in naturalistic inquiry methods such as phenomenology and ethnography differ from more positivistic qualitative methods, such as grounded theory. In exploring student experiences through qualitative inquiry, we seek to understand them in a way that is more natural, rather than building theories or juxtapositions about these experiences. We are using qualitative inquiry because it appears to be an epistemological match with our goals for understanding online learning environments prior to truly exploring the impacts of this application on the field of qualitative inquiry and the underlying epistemological foundations on which that discipline is built. However, great caution must be exercised when determining and qualifying methodology and its purpose. The discussion that follows is an overview of the three most common qualitative data collection tactics (interviewing, observations, and document analysis) and their relevance to the understanding of online learning environments. We explore some of the implications of using qualitative tactics and base these implications on our own experiences conducting qualitative studies in online environments.

QUALITATIVE DATA COLLECTION TACTICS

Interviews

Interviews and observations are used as key tactics for recording people's experiences, perceptions, and attitudes in qualitative inquiry (Creswell, 1998). Interviews range in type and length and are used for different purposes, but are present in virtually all qualitative traditions. Interviewees are often selected utilizing purposeful sampling processes and are contacted or recruited in many different ways. Telephone interviews have been used for many decades and are conducted when access to participants in a face-to-face environment is hindered in some way (Bruce, 1979; de Leeuw 1992). Telephone interviews carry the advantage that the participant can be interviewed at a remote location, saving travel time and money, but the researcher loses the opportunity to observe nonverbal communicative actions that can substantively alter findings. Focus group interviews are used in situations where the interaction among participants is determined to be beneficial for the inquiry (Fontana & Frey, 1994). Ideal interview situations are personal, face-to-face contexts where the interviewer and the interviewee have the opportunity to interact in an open atmosphere and establish rapport (Fontana & Frey, 1994). Typically, qualitative interviews are recorded either by audio or video and are transcribed for the analysis of data. There are a number of ways of approaching interviews, from highly structured to open-ended interview protocols.

Computer-mediated interviewing (CMI) techniques add quite another dimension. Media utilized to conduct CMIs include synchronous chat, e-mail, and discussion forums. As with telephone interviews, in CMI, face-to-face contact is lost. Voice tone and inflection, hesitation or eagerness, and other audible indications that lead to deeper understandings that are not possible through CMI, are also lost. While not without benefit, interviews conducted via chat may arouse questions regarding the conveyance of meaning, since both voice and body language are absent. On the other hand, little is left unquestioned in terms of specific data because it is necessary to ask for continual clarification from the participant throughout

**Table 18.1.   Similarities and Differences Among
Three Different Interview Techniques**

Face-to-Face	Telephone	Computer-Mediated
Visibility of facial expressions	Absence of facial expressions and body language	Absence of facial expressions and body language
Personal qualities of establishing rapport with the participant	Voice tone assistance in establishing rapport	Absence of personal contact to aid in establishing relationship with participant(s).
Communication is more natural to most people in conversation form	Conversational tones are possible	Conversational tones are absent and limited to inference based on text.
Travel time required	Travel time saved	Travel time saved
Transcription costs incurred	Transcription costs incurred	Transcription costs saved
Travel costs incurred	Telephone costs may be incurred depending on type of long distance utilized	Typically no or low cost via internet hookup
Opportunities for on-site experiences are preserved	Opportunities for on-site experiences lost	Opportunities for on-site experiences lost
Ability to interview a limited number of respondents	Ability to interview more respondents	Ability to interview many respondents including those abroad, disabled, elderly, housebound

the CMI (Mann & Stewart, 2000). Table 18.1 presents a comparison of interviewing techniques, as they are relevant to this discussion.

It is possible to see from Table 18.1 a comparison of the advantages and disadvantages of the three possible media for conducting qualitative interviews. Obviously, the primary advantage of using the telephone or the CMI options are resource related, (e.g., time and money to travel to remote sites). However, there is no clear indication of precisely how much is lost in terms of the deep understanding of the stories being told by the respondents by losing their affective, interpersonal, voice and body reactions to questions. It is not clear how much data may be lost by the very different type of rapport that is established online or by telephone. It is almost impossible to quantify or qualify this loss (if it exists) because qualitative data are so individualized that there is no easy comparison study that can be conducted to establish what is truly lost and/or gained in these three environments. In fact, such a study would be rather ironic, as it would require an experimental approach to understanding a qualitative problem and would fall out of alignment, epistemologically, with the goals of qualitative research. Instead, we believe understanding these tradeoffs is more enlightened by reflective practice; by an understanding of the art rather than the science of qualitative inquiry.

We are concerned that these methodological decisions are likely to be made too often because of cost considerations. Rather than seeking additional resources to allow the researcher to be in the natural setting, the breadth of respondents will be valued and the choices will be made to use cheaper methods than traveling to geographically dispersed sites. It is the same principle we use in the assignation of media in instruction. We ought not use a medium merely because it is available, new, convenient, cheap, popular—or even well-funded, but rather because it is what is called for in the instructional design based on the needs assessment, strategy selection, goals, and objectives for the learning. The cost and convenience issues are only part of the picture (Romizsowski, 1981). In this same way, we should select telephone or CMI options for collecting qualitative data because they are supported by the research question. Tactical choices should not be made for financial reasons alone, any more than they should be made for convenience reasons alone—thus, the negative perception of samples of convenience studies. Instead we should allow our research question to drive our interview technique choices among face-to-face, telephone, and CMI as responsive choices to the research question.

Future trends in online interviewing may include the use of interactive media, thereby allowing a more authentic interview experience among participants. A brief analysis of the potential of this technological advancement includes "face-to-face" interaction in which voice, tone, and body language are visible with the benefit of breaking through the geographical barrier that previously precluded some populations from participation. Interactive media, such as the use of a Webcam allow for observations more closely aligned to traditional methods of observations in which the observer can access the field in an unobtrusive manner while having access to the culture.

As a qualitative research tool, a Webcam can unblur the lines between observation and document analysis while assisting with obstacles of time, geography, access to hard-to-reach cultures and allow for a more true observational technique. Skype, a Voice over Internet Protocol (VoIP), for example, allows for free Internet calling to anyone, anywhere, provided the other person has downloaded the product. This product has calling and chat capability, allows for as many as 100 users in a group chat, and has great implications for cost-savings with regard to travel, time and expanding the population of participants.

Observations

Qualitative observations (Adler & Adler, 1994) elicit some of the same issues as interviews, but the concerns here are even more pronounced. How is it possible to "observe" an online class? We know what it means to observe a face-to-face classroom, and we know how to design an observation instrument to assist us in focusing on the proper interactions, experiences, cultures, and environmental cues when in a physical "field." However, we don't know what any of this means in the online environment. Do we observe individuals at their machines in their home space? Do we observe the class as it interacts online? Is the electronic space the actual classroom—is it a virtual "field"? What sorts of things are we looking for and what type of instrument will help us to focus on those things? Participant observations where the researcher is part of the culture in which the observation is being conducted, as is the case with ethnographic studies, leave the role of the researcher even more undefined in online environments. It is important to consider the practical as well as the theoretical and philosophical aspects of participant observations in online class settings.

In our experiences, this is perhaps one of the most difficult things to handle in online learning environment inquiry. Because we do have certain "scripts" (mental or physical) that guide our interview protocols, the interview procedures are still somewhat familiar to us in electronic media. Although the social nature of the interview is significantly altered, the pragmatics of how to go about it are still relatively similar—that is, to set out a series of questions (structured, unstructured, semi-structured) and begin conversing with respondents. But how do we go about really observing the online learning environment? Is it even possible? Here is an even more evident exposure of the social nature of qualitative inquiry (Wolcott, 1995). Here we have a real conundrum. What sort of observational techniques should we use; can we rely on the old checklists for observations that we had used traditionally? Do we have to shift foci in the same ways that we do in traditional settings? Unfortunately, our experience raised more questions than answers in this regard. We attempted to "observe" online settings by reading through the ongoing synchronous exchanges, such as chats and asynchronous discussion forum communications. To the end, our experience was limited in this regard, and thus we are less than comfortable offering specific recommendations or guidance. Nevertheless, we feel that there is a certain amount of merit in suggesting that good data can be found in e-inquiry through a number of different sources. We feel that observing individual students in their home space will offer a significantly deeper understanding of the experience and setting that the learner is engaging in online courses. We also feel that observations of the online setting itself, via discussion boards, chats, listserv, e-mail, and other course activity spaces are rich sources of understanding. Observation may need to be somewhat recast in our minds. How we go about observing the online classroom should, naturally, respond to our research question and should yield the most important and significant data possible. The same warning regarding costs can be made in this instance as well. While it may be tempting to feel that the entire understanding of the online course culture can be captured as an extant document after each class session, this may not yield the best possible data for answering the research question. It is extremely inexpensive in travel monies and particularly in terms of time. But it must be asked, does an extant documentation of a class session that the observer obtains after-the-fact qualify as an observation or is it more appropriately considered a document for analysis?

Advanced technologies, including the use of Webcams, as previously discussed, also have the potential of advancing observations in an unobtrusive manner, maybe even less obtrusively than a physical observation. The placement of a Webcam, which automatically digitizes the scenes for analysis, has the potential to provide an even truer picture of the culture or scene being observed.

Online focus groups can also be enhanced using newer, more advanced technologies in online or computer-mediated data collection. Chat rooms and new technologies such as a product called Elluminate Live! allow for online collaboration in which more than one participant at a time has the capability of interacting in real time and often with video and other collaboration activities. Technological advances are also beginning to allow greater numbers of participants to connect via Webcam, allowing for a more seamless interaction. In qualitative research, participants in geographically different locations but with commonalities inherent to the research study can more easily participate in a study. A broader, more in-depth perspective on a culture or community can be investigated and has financial implications as well.

Document Analysis

Document analysis (Hodder, 1994) is perhaps the least difficult qualitative data issue to be resolved. Since there are fewer abstractions that are important (e.g., voice tone, culture of a classroom, etc.) in document analysis, the issues are less complicated. Clearly, online course materials, as with face-to-face course materials, are prime candidates for document analysis in such studies. And, quite often, the online setting is rife with course materials because of the nature of online interactions and the necessity for specificity and clarity due to the lack of verbal resources. In the same way, student materials are also documents, but in the online environment, there are typically many more "print" resources than there may be in the face-to-face environment. What is to be considered a document? Is the chat that the students conduct on regular Monday meeting times, for example, to be considered documentary, observation, or interview data? Documents typically included in qualitative research for data analysis appear in the form of written text. Written text assumes a purpose depending on the author and the intended use of the document. Creswell (1998) distinguishes between texts written as records of information (i.e., public documents, reports, and contracts) and others such as diaries or journals, written for personal use. Journals, logs, and diaries are sometimes requested by the researcher as a way for participants to keep track of and reflect on their activities in a particular situation or context. Blogs, short for Web log can be interactive or personal. Blogs are online journals or diaries in which issues are commented on by multiple participants as in a shared blog, or journals or diaries are posted for others to view but generally considered private, one person's thoughts. As a primarily textual document, blogs, because of their purpose, should be considered as most appropriate as document analysis. In terms of research, the benefits of considering this type of document deal with the elimination of transcription and the easy import into a qualitative data analysis software.

In online learning environments, information is presented in the form of written text in several aspects including (but not limited to) synchronous chat, discussion forums, project submissions, e-mail communications, and written reports or summaries. As these class activities are utilized in ways that intend to mirror activities typically integral to face-to-face learning environments, they would not be considered as document analysis, but rather as observation or interview data. In what ways does this change the nature of data collected? In the case of document analysis, wherever this cautious distinction is drawn and assuming that there is care to maintain authenticity in the documents themselves, it is likely that there will be the least impact. This is primarily because there is inherently less "socialness" to the procedures within most document analyses, even within the qualitative tradition. It is more anthropological in nature, uncovering the cultures and understandings of authors as a result of careful dissection of documented artifacts. The main conundrum likely to emerge in document analysis, therefore, will be the distinction between observation/interview data and document analysis—that is, the clarification of what counts as a document and what does not. There may also be the problem of being overwhelmed by the sheer volume of documents available in the online setting and determining what is really relevant to the inquiry.

DISCUSSION

With the growing interest in online education and the vast difference in teaching and learning between online and face-to-face learning environments, it is becoming more and more necessary to gain a better understanding of the experiences students face in new distance education endeavors of many institutions of higher education. While there is limited research available in this area, we believe qualitative methods in seeking this information are not only appropriate, but also necessary in developing a greater understanding of student experiences.

However, the employ of qualitative methods founded on assumptions of the social nature of inquiry can only be used with great caution. It is essential that as we continue to examine online learning environments in qualitative ways that we carefully reflect on the experience of doing online interviews, online observations, and electronic document analysis and try to capture how we see these experiences as differing from previous experiences in qualitative research. The blur among the methodological strategies is most pronounced when attempting to differentiate the predominantly textual nature of data collection online. For example, what distinguishes an observation from a document analysis? There are various ways to conduct and online observation. The observer can be a participant observer, engaging in conversation with a group of participants collaboratively making meaning of the dialogue (Crichton & Kinash, 2003; Sade-Beck, 2004). Likewise, in an online environment, the interactions of participants are currently predominately displayed in text format. The differentiation and distinction of the researcher's intent must be clearly articulated. The "lurking" observer who observes the text-based interaction in a real-time chat or an asynchronous discussion without actually participating has only text from which to extract data. All the physical, nonverbal cues are absent as are the emotion, tone, and feeling from the participant's expression of ideas (Sade-Beck, 2004). Questions regarding the purpose of the interaction or data collection should be carefully considered. The purpose of the tool, such as with the blog, changes based on the participants and the purpose for which it is being used. A blog used as a diary, one person's thoughts, should be considered a document. Conversely, an interactive blog in which many participants are interacting, may be considered an electronic observation.

We call, here for more research that involves careful inquirer-reflection on the processes of collecting qualitative data in electronic environments.

Attempts to intentionally vary techniques and reflect on those data and processes is an essential next step to a deeper understanding of the ways in which e-inquiry relates to the traditional forms of qualitative inquiry.

In our experience in qualitative inquiry in online learning environments, we found it essential that we not only define our contexts but also the methods we choose to employ. It is very difficult, for example, to define an online observation. In defining online observation, it is important to consider the purpose of an observation. If the purpose of the observation is to examine class interactions, then it may be appropriate to "lurk" in a synchronous chat in which students are "meeting"—assuming you can mitigate any ethical considerations. It may also be appropriate to define observation as the "reading of the discussion forum," as this type of discussion is typically asynchronous interaction designed to take the place of class or group meetings. Therefore, qualitative inquiry in online environments may call for a re-definition of these basic tactical practices. Class discussion as defined by an online learning environment is often asynchronous in nature and, while the instructor may or may not participate, monitoring of such discussion for purposes of monitoring student interactions probably then becomes a form of observation. Observational techniques have the purpose of watching how people interact with each other and making inferences as to the nature of those interactions through field notes or journals (Adler & Adler, 1994; Creswell, 1998). In arguing that an asynchronous discussion is meant for the purpose of student interaction, a logical conclusion may be drawn based on not only the purpose of the interaction, but the purpose of the observation of those interactions.

Our experiences with interviews using computer-mediated communications (CMC) were limited to e-mail and synchronous chat formats. E-mail interviews presented difficulties with communication in the general flow and rapport. In face-to-face qualitative interviews, where questions can be open-ended and the discussion left to the discretion of the interviewer, the lack of immediate interaction between interviewer and interviewee when using CMC felt disjointed and the flow was severely disrupted. We believe that the quality of the interviews suffered. Not only were the qualities of tone and voice inflection lost in the e-mail interviews conducted, it was also very cumbersome when clarifications were sought. Meaning appeared to be lost in the time span between question posing and question answering. Interviews conducted via synchronous chat interaction more closely resembled that of a personal face-to-face interview but still lacked voice inflection and any non-verbal data. Typing skills of both the interviewer and the interviewee become a factor as well. While at first a chat interview appeared to be more closely reminiscent of a face-to-face personal interview, it was hard to determine if a pause was an indication of a typing deficit or a long thoughtful break. In our limited experience, chat interview responses also appeared to be less descriptive and shorter than telephone or face-to-face interviews. Even if the participant was comfortable in the environment and a self-described "good typist," this impression that the data was "flatter" persevered. While it may be more convenient and cost-effective, it seems we should understand synchronous and asynchronous chats and discussion board to be a more limited form of interview data.

FUTURE TRENDS

With the recent advances in technology that allow for higher broadband and streaming media or video capabilities, computer-mediated interviews should become more easily managed. The limitations to chat interviews and the loss of face-to-face communications may be eliminated as the technology becomes more advanced and accessible to various groups. Microphones and cameras have the capability of breaking through the barriers of strictly text-based observations, interviews, and document analysis. The obstacles that must be very clearly delineated and described in terms of process, purpose, and method will more closely mirror the more traditional methods of qualitative inquiry as the technology becomes more advanced. And one thing technology always seems to be good at is advancing. There have been several recent additions to the technology used for data collection online that were woven into discussion related to tactics previously explored. Newer, more advanced, technologies have the potential to more closely simulate immersion through observation and face-to-face—albeit computer-mediated—communication for interview and focus group purposes.

Transcription tools and voice recognition, coupled with blogging, Webcams, interactive collaborative software, and other more common tools, such as chat rooms and discussion forums, have great potential in qualitative inquiries. These electronic tactics for collection data and analysis transcription, voice recorders alongside transcribing software and voice recognition software, are making it increasingly compelling to consider using traditional interviews with audio recordings that are getting cheaper, easier to store and to destroy, and far easier to transcribe than ever before. This may help to ameliorate some of the inappropriate use of already transcribed data via chats and discussion boards or e-mail interviewing.

New technologies have the potential to move qualitative data collection forward while in some ways preserving the epistemological integrity of conducting qualitative inquiry. As tools, online interactive collaboration experiences that allow for real-time, face-to-face interactions maintain the tenets inherent in delving into the culture under study. Bearing in mind that it is essential that all good qualitative research have certain hallmarks of quality, and in one final note, we wish to emphasize the importance of disclosing one's researcher identity. Even more so than in many other areas, the online revolution has recently turned into an online opinion war with many folks lining up on both sides, pro (Dede, 1997) and con (Noble, 1998). It is, therefore, essential that we are clear with all readers on our own feelings and biases with regard to new innovations and their impact on the enterprise of qualitative research. We have seen far too many recent reports of qualitative findings regarding online learning communities, relationships, interactions, and the like. Without the "road map" of a clearly disclosed researcher identity, it is difficult to really know how to read some of these reports within the epistemological framework of qualitative inquiry.

Finally, it may seem that the sorts of distinctions we are drawing here and the cautions we are issuing are really semantic differences. However, they are crucial to a deep understanding of the differences between online learning inquiry and the more traditional face-to-face experience of qualitative inquiry. These distinctions must be carefully considered and, perhaps most importantly, they must be clearly and honestly discussed within the qualitative research write-up. Honesty and disclosure of precise tactics, techniques, and strategies is imperative in all rigorous qualitative inquiry (as is disclosure of researcher identities and biases). However, in this case, we can no longer rely on the traditional meanings of "observation," "interview," and "document analysis" that makes purpose a fundamental and critical disclosure. We must explicate their meanings within the qualitative report so that all readers will understand the ways in which data were handled and analyzed. These differences are not merely semantic; they speak to the fundamental differentiation between online and traditional inquiry—the social nature of "the field."

REFERENCES

Adler, P. A., & Adler, P. (1994). Observational techniques. In N. K. Denzin & Y. S. Lincoln (Eds.), *Handbook of qualitative research* (pp. 377-392). Thousand Oaks, CA: Sage.

Bianco, M. B., (2002). The nature of peer relationships in an online learning context: A qualitative exploration. *Dissertation Abstracts International, 63*(7), 2513. (PUB No. 3051624)

Bowers, C. A. (1998). The paradox of technology: What's gained and lost? *Thought and Action, 14*(1), 49-57.

Bruce, F. J. (1979). Advantages and disadvantages of different survey techniques. *New Directions for Institutional Advancement, 6*, 11-19.

Carr-Chellman, A. A., & Carr-Chellman, D. J. (2001). *Mr. Jones' E-Z Elixir: Marketing higher education on the Web*. Unpublishd manuscript.

Crichton, S., & Kinash, S. (2003). Virtual ethnography: Interactive interviewing online as method. *Canadian Journal of Learning and Technology, 29*(2). Retrieved June 6, 2006, from http://www.cjlt.ca/content/vol29.2/cjlt29-2_art-5.html

Creswell, J. W. (1998). *Qualitative inquiry and research design: Choosing among the five traditions*. Thousand Oaks CA: Sage.

Dede, C. (1997). Distributed learning: How new technologies promise a richer educational experience. *Connection: New England's Journal of Higher Education and Economic Development, 12*(2), 12-16.

De Leeuw, E. (1992). *Data quality in mail, Telephone and face-to-face surveys*. Amsterdam: T. T. Publikaties, Plantage Daklaan 40, 1018CN

Denzin, N. K., & Lincoln, Y. S. (1998a). *Collecting and interpreting qualitative materials*. Thousand Oaks, CA: Sage.

Denzin, N. K., & Lincoln, Y. S. (1998b). *Strategies of qualitative inquiry*. Thousand Oaks, CA: Sage.

Diaz, D. P., & Cartnal, R. B. (2000). Students' learning styles in two classes. *College Teaching, 47*(4), 130-136.

Donaldson, J. L., & Thomson, J. S. (1999). Interpersonal communication strengthens web-based instruction. *Journal of Applied Communications, 83*(3), 22-32.

Dunn, S. L., (2000). The virtualizing of education. *The Futurist, 34*(2) 4-38.

Fetterman, D. M. (1998). *Ethnography: Step by step*. Thousand Oaks, CA: Sage.

Fontana, A., & Frey, J. H. (1994). Interviewing: The art of science. In N. K. Denzin & Y. S. Lincoln (Eds.), *Handbook of qualitative research* (pp. 361-376). Thousand Oaks, CA: Sage.

French, D. (1999, February). *A qualitative and quantitative evaluation: Innovative use of internet based collaboration*. In SITE 99: Society for Information Technology & Teacher Education International Conference, San Antonio, TX.

Gladieux, L. E., & Swail, W. S., (1999). The virtual university & educational opportunity: Issues of equity and access for the next generation. *College Board Publications* (ERIC Document Reproduction Service No. ED428637).

Gunawardena, C. N., Lowe, C. A., & Anderson, T. (1998). Transcript analysis of computer-mediated conferences as a tool for testing constructivist and social-constructivist learning theories. In *Distance Learning '98. Proceedings of the Annual Conference on Distance Teaching and Learning*. Madison, WI. (ERIC Document Reproduction Service No. ED422854)

Hegngi, Y. N. (1998, April). *Changing roles, changing technologies: The design, development, implementation and evaluation of a media technology and diversity on-line course*. Paper presented at the annual meeting of the American Educational Research Association, San Diego, CA.

Hiltz, S. R., (1998). Collaborative learning in asynchronous learning networks: Building learning communities. In *WebNet '98 World conference of the WWW,*

Internet, and Intranet Proceedings, Orlando, FL. (ERIC Document Reproduction Service No. ED427705)

Hine, C. (2000). *Virtual ethnography.* Thousand Oaks, CA: Sage.

Hodder, I. (1994). The interpretation of documents and material culture. In N. K. Denzin & Y. S. Lincoln (Eds.). *Handbook of qualitative research* (pp. 393-402). Thousand Oaks, CA: Sage.

Jannasch-Pennell, A., DiGangi, S. A., Yu, A., Andrews, S., & Babb, J. S. (1999). Impact of instructional grouping on navigation and student learning in a web-based learning environment. In *proceedings of selected research and development papers presented at the National Convention of the Association for Educational Communications and Technology*, Houston, TX. (ERIC Document Reproduction Service No. ED436156)

Jonassen, D., Davidson, M., Collins, M., Campbell, J., & Bannan-Haag, B. (1995). Constructivism and computer-mediated communication in distance education. *The American Journal of Distance Education, 9*(2), 7-36.

Levin, D. S., & Ben-Jacob, M. G. (1998). Collaborative learning: A critical success factor in distance education. *Distance Learning '98. Proceedings of the Annual Conference on Distance Teaching and Learning*, Madison, WI. (ERIC Document Reproduction Service No. ED422843)

Lincoln, Y., & Guba, E. (1985). *Naturalistic inquiry.* Thousand Oaks CA: Sage.

Mann, C., & Stewart, F. (2000). *Internet communication and qualitative research: A handbook for researching online.* Thousand Oaks, CA: Sage.

McFerrin, K. M. (1999). Incidental learning in a higher education asynchronous online distance education course. *SITE 99: Society for Information Technology & Teacher Education International Conference*, San Antonio, TX.

McIsaac, M. S., Blocher, J. M., Mahes, V., & Vrasidas, C. (1999). Student and teacher perceptions of interaction in online computer-mediated communication. *Educational Media International, 36*(2), 121-31.

McNeil, S., Robin, B., & Miller, R. (2000). Facilitating interaction, communication, and collaboration in online courses. *Computers and the Geosciences, 26*(6), 699-708.

Moon, B., (1998, April). *Towards a generation of open learning programmes in teacher education: Lessons for us all.* Paper presented at the annual meeting of the American Educational Research Association, San Diego, CA.

Moustakas, C. (1994). *Phenomenological research methods.* Thousand Oaks, CA: Sage.

Murray, B. (1999). Technology invigorates teaching, but is the pizzazz worth the price? *APA Monitor Online, 30*(4). http://www.apa.org/monitor/apr99/.

Noble, D., (1998). *Digital diploma mills: The automation of higher education.* Retrieved January 15, 2001, from http://www.firstmonday.dk/issues/issue3_1/noble/

Romiszowski, A. J. (1981). *Designing instructional systems.* London: Kogan Page.

Ryan, R. C. (2000, January). Student assessment comparison of lecture and online construction equipment and methods classes. *T.H.E. Journal.* Retrieved January 15, 2001, from http://www.thejournal.com/magazine/vault/A2596.cfm

Sade-Beck, L. (2004). Internet ethnography: Online and offline. *International Journal of Qualitative Methods, 3*(2). Retrieved June 6, 2006, from http://www.uaalbera.ca/~iiqm/backissues/3_2pdf/sadebeck.pdf

Schlough, S., & Bhuripanyo, S. (1998, March). *The development and evaluation of the Internet delivery of the course "Task Analysis."* Paper presented at SITE 98: Society for Information Technology & Teacher Education International Conference, Washington, DC.

Seidman, I. (2006). *Interviewing as qualitative research: A guide for researchers in education and the social sciences.* New York: Teacher's College Press.

Thompson, J. C., Jr., & Nay, F. W. (1999, October). *Distance interaction through the World Wide Web in graduate teacher education: A follow-up analysis of student perceptions.* Paper presented at the Annual Meeting of the Mid-Western Educational Research Association, Chicago, IL.

Truman-Davis, B., & Hartman, J. (1998, November). On-line with the future: Web-based program development at the University of Central Florida, Designing a University for the 21st Century. 4 *WebNet 98 World Conference of the WWW, Internet, and Intranet, Proceedings*, Orlando, FL.

Wolcott, H. (1995). *The art of fieldwork.* Lanham, MD: AltaMira Press

Woody, T. (1999). *Academics rebel against an online future.* Retrieved January 20, 2001, from http://www.suite.101.com/discussion/.ctm/higher_education/6062 #message_1

Yong, Y., (1998). Learners' perceptions on learning through the Web. *Journal of Instruction Delivery Systems, 12*(1), 23-26.

Young, J. R. (2000). David Noble's battle to defend the "sacred space" of the classroom. *The Chronicle of Higher Education, 46*(30), A47-49.

CHAPTER 19

REVISITING CATEGORIES OF VIRTUAL LEARNING COMMUNITIES FOR EDUCATIONAL DESIGN

Rocci Luppicini

Developing rich learning environments using computer-mediated communication and strategies to connect individuals in various ways is a major challenge within educational technology. Creating virtual learning communities is recognized as a potential means of building commonalities and connections essential to education and society. Knowledge of instructional design does not provide the necessary understanding of learning environments and human interaction required to allow learning communities to form (Luppicini, 2003; Schwier, 2001). First, this chapter presents a topology of virtual learning communities within formal and informal learning environments to advance knowledge of educational design. Second, it explores elements of virtual learning communities pertaining to educational design and suggests parameters for designing different types of virtual learning communities. Finally, future trends in virtual team classification and virtual community sustainability are discussed as supporting tools for guiding the design of virtual learning communities.

Online Learning Communities
pp. 319–332
Copyright © 2007 by Information Age Publishing

INTRODUCTION

The notion of "learning communities" generates widespread interest in a variety of contexts. Organizations apply the term "learning communities" to describe an approach to team building and improving connectedness within organizations (Senge, 1990). In higher education curriculum literature, this term "learning communities" is employed to describe common cohorts of students enrolled in courses clustered around interdisciplinary themes (Weber, 2000). Within this framework, learning communities are considered to be curricular structures that link different disciplines around a common theme or question and promote shared inquiry among faculty and students (Gabelnick, MacGregor, Matthews, & Smith, 1990). In the situated cognition literature, this same term describes a specific orientation to learning and instruction in educational contexts based on cognitive apprenticeships, anchored instruction, communities of practice, and collaborative learning approaches (Brown, Collins, & Duguid, 1989; Cognition and Technology Group at Vanderbilt, 1990; Lave & Wenger, 1991). The term is also employed in the broader sense to describe the phenomenon of groups (communities) of individuals learning together with an emphasis placed on the social nature of cognition and meaning (Imel, 2001).

Virtual learning communities are learning communities that are computer-mediated by interconnected computers. Communication characteristics of virtual learning communities include: asynchronous and synchronous communication, high interactivity, and multiway communication. Virtual learning communities are known under variety of labels including, "virtual communities," "chat rooms," "social networks," "online forums," "virtual academies," "academic networks," "computer conferences," and "collaboratories."

VIRTUAL LEARNING COMMUNITY TYPES

The nature of virtual learning community focus depends largely on community purpose. Virtual learning communities are created for a variety of purposes, including educational advancement, faculty revitalization, socialization, team building, etc. This discussion is framed around virtual learning community types and underlying structures found in formal and informal learning environments. Fundamental functions of virtual learning community types are described along with distinguishing features (see Table 19.1).

Table 19.1.   Categories of Virtual Learning Communities

Category	Description	Distinguishing Features
Virtual learning communities of knowledge building	Allows members to focus on topics of interest and construct communal data bases of information.	Shared common interest and personal responsibility of contributing to community knowledge-building
Virtual learning communities of inquiry	Goal-based orientation among participants that requires active involvement from community members.	Shared purpose and active solution seeking
Virtual learning communities of practice	Based on learning lived practices of the community.	Active participation and reflection.
Virtual learning communities of culture	Based on shared history, common sense of ideology, or ritualistic traditions.	Strong group identification and sense of tradition
Virtual learning communities of socialization	Based on connecting individuals with common interests or a common background for social exchange.	Emphasis on social interaction and entertainment.
Virtual learning communities of counseling and development	Provides support services to individuals and nurturing individual growth	Empathetic relationship building and concern for human well being

Virtual Learning Communities of Knowledge Building

Virtual learning communities of knowledge building allow members to focus on topics of interest and construct communal databases of information. The two most distinguishable features of virtual learning communities of knowledge building are shared common interest and personal responsibility of contributing to knowledge-building efforts within the greater community while carrying out individual or group work. Computer-supported intentional learning environments (CSILE) are a recent application of virtual learning communities of knowledge building in education (Gilbert & Driscoll, 2002; Scardamalia & Bereiter, 1996). Gilbert and Driscoll (2002) studied a CSILE within a graduate student course in teacher education. Individuals worked independently on group readings followed by group concept mapping activities with others in order to exchange multiple perspectives and negotiate common goals. Key benefits of virtual learning communities of knowledge building include improved workflow and advanced information generation.

Virtual Learning Communities of Inquiry

Virtual learning communities of inquiry emphasizes a goal-based orientation among participants. In virtual learning communities of inquiry, there are definite goals to achieve that require active involvement from community members. Recent application of problem-based learning (PBL) methods in education are a good example of virtual learning communities of inquiry. Participants in problem-based learning work in groups to solve real problems that are often complex and require seeking out a variety of resources to generate possible solutions to a common problem or set of problems. Shared purpose and active solution seeking are primary features of virtual learning communities of inquiry. Recent empirical research on virtual learning communities of inquiry focuses on problem solving in academic contexts (Benbunan-Fich & Star, 1999; Jonassen & Kwon, 2001; Stepich, Ertmer, Lane, & Molly, 2001). Benbunan-Fich and Star (1999) explored how groups of individuals solved case studies through asynchronous learning networks. In a study exploring the use of coaching strategies to facilitate expert problem solving, Stepich et al. (2001) addressed how coaching strategies were associated with incidents of student expert problem solving performance. Jonassen and Kwon (2001) investigated group problem solving of well-defined and ill-defined case studies within a computer conferencing environment with a class of engineering students. Key benefits of virtual learning communities of inquiry include improved problem solving capacity and improved solution quality through collaboration.

Virtual Learning Communities of Practice

Virtual learning communities of practice are based on the notion of learning as co-constitutive processes among persons, their actions, and the world. Knowledge accumulates through the lived practices of the community. The two distinguishable features of virtual learning communities of practice are active engagement and reflection. Often virtual learning communities of practice are apprenticeship-based. For instance, Gold (2001) investigated a 2-week faculty development pedagogical training course aimed at preparing teachers to operate effectively within an online educational environment. Collaborative exercises employed included virtual field trips, online evaluations, interactive essays, and group projects. In a study of online writing development and mentoring, Taylor (2001) explored experiences of participants and facilitators within a virtual writing forum. Hawisher and Pemberton (1997) examined common practices emerging from student experiences within an online writing lab at a large research university. Findings indicated that students judged online writing practices to be extremely helpful in supporting writing development. Key benefits of virtual learning communities of practice include improved workflow and professional skills development.

Virtual Learning Communities of Culture

Virtual learning communities of culture are based on shared history, common sense of ideology, or ritualistic traditions. This is not to be confused with cross-cultural approaches to find ways around cultural factors that sometimes inhibit communication within virtual environments (Gunawardena, Nolla, Wilson, Lopez, Ramirez-Angel, & Megchun-Alpizar, 2001; Ramsoomair, 1997). Religious, political, and ethnic themes constitute a large proportion of virtual learning communities of culture. Strong group identification and sense of tradition distinguish these communities from other categories. The Virtual Center of the Sephardic Jewish Community (www.bsz.org), the African-American Virtual Village (www.kcvirtualvillage.org), and the Greek Village Online (www.greekvillage.com/about/abcell2.htm) are good examples of virtual learning communities of culture. There is a lack of educational research published on virtual learning communities of culture. Key benefits of virtual learning communities of culture include improved culture building and cultural identity preservation.

Virtual Learning Communities of Socialization

Virtual learning communities of socialization are primarily based on connecting individuals with common interests or a common background for social exchange. Learning in virtual learning communities of socialization places emphasis on social interaction and entertainment. There is a seemingly endless supply of virtual learning communities of socialization available on various themes. Central Louisiana's Virtual Community (www.cenla.com), the YMCA Virtual Community (www.ymcacommunity.net/mcgaw/vc.asp), Lava Life (www.free-online-dating-services.com/free-lava-life-dating.htm), and the Young Liberals of Canada (http://www.youngliberals.ca/%20) are examples of virtual learning communities of socialization. There is a paucity of educational research published on virtual learning communities of culture. Key benefits of virtual learning communities of socialization include improved social networking and social identity building.

Virtual Learning Communities of Counseling and Development

Virtual learning communities of counseling and development provide support services and nurture individual growth. There are a number of counseling networks and virtual support groups available online. There are also a variety of virtual communities for personal development. Strong emphasis on empathetic relationship building and concern for human well-being are what distinguishes virtual learning communities of counseling and development from others. Virtual Community for Substance Abuse Training (www.neias.org/SATadneeds.html), the Virtual Health Clinic (www.healthyplace.com/Communities/Addictions/ netaddiction/clinic.htm), E-Social Worker (users.otenet.gr/~lo8lorie/links/index_en.htm), and the Wellness Community (www.thewellnesscommunity.org/programs/frankly/ colorectal/managing/recurrence.htm) are examples of virtual communities for counseling and development. Key benefits of virtual learning communities of counseling and development include personal assistance and growth.

Summary

This discussion presented a topology of six virtual learning communities and cited published research available on virtual learning communities of knowledge building, virtual learning communities of inquiry, and virtual learning communities of practice. There is less published research available and easier online access to virtual learning communities of culture, virtual learning communities of socialization, and virtual learning communities of counseling and development. All six virtual learning communities have distinguishing features and benefits distinguishing them from one another.

DESIGN ELEMENTS FOR VIRTUAL LEARNING COMMUNITIES

What elements are vital in the design and implementation of virtual learning communities? What parameters for designing virtual learning communities are possible? Building on Selznick's (1996) treatment of non-virtual communities, Schwier (2001) presented a list of 10 general elements of virtual communities: historicity, identity, mutuality, plurality, autonomy, participation, technology, future, learning, and integration. This description of general elements of virtual learning communities does not address required elements found within different categories of virtual learning communities. For instance, autonomy is typically an important element in virtual learning communities of knowledge building but not very important within virtual learning communities of culture.

Sharing a sense of common history is typically an important element in virtual learning communities of culture but not a very important element in virtual learning communities of knowledge building or practice. Discerning what elements are vital in the design and implementation of virtual learning communities requires more than an understanding of general elements. Furthermore, knowledge of specific virtual learning community elements could offer valuable insights for designing and implementing different types of virtual learning communities. Therefore, brief descriptions are provided of the six categories of virtual learning communities addressed in this paper (see Table 19.2).

Table 19.2. Design Elements for Categories of Virtual Learning Communities

Categories	Design Elements for Virtual Learning Communities
Virtual learning communities of knowledge building	Moderators are actively involved. There is strong emphasis on individual autonomy and individual expression. Opportunities for integrating new ideas and perspectives from outside the learning community are highlighted. Usually found in formal learning environments.
Virtual learning communities of inquiry	Moderators are actively involved. Opportunities for integrating new ideas and perspectives from outside the learning community are highlighted. Participants are strongly encouraged to invest efforts to understand and collaborate with other participants. Usually found in formal learning environments.
Virtual learning communities of practice	Moderators are actively involved. A strong emphasis on group norms is in place. Participants are encouraged to invest efforts to understand and collaborate with other participants. Usually found in formal learning environments.
Virtual learning communities of culture	A strong emphasis on group norms is in place. Participants are encouraged to invest efforts to understand and cooperate with other participants. There are invested efforts to document and publicize the history and values of the learning community and noteworthy actions of community members. Usually found in informal learning environments.
Virtual learning communities of socialization	There is a moderate emphasis on group norms in place which contributes to a sense of group identity and attachment. Usually found in informal learning environments.
Virtual learning communities of counseling and development	Moderators are actively involved. There is strong emphasis on individual autonomy and individual expression. Participants are encouraged to invest efforts to understand and empathize with other participants. Usually found in formal learning environments.

Elements of Virtual Learning Communities of Knowledge Building

Moderators are actively involved in promoting participation, keeping members focused on learning goals, and reminding members to contribute their input. There is strong emphasis on individual autonomy and individual expression of diverse perspectives. Opportunities for integrating new ideas and perspectives from outside the learning community are highlighted. Participants are sometimes encouraged to invest efforts to understand and collaborate with other participants and to invest efforts to document and publicize the history and values of the learning community and noteworthy actions of community members. This type of virtual learning community is usually found in formal learning environments.

Elements of Virtual Learning Communities of Inquiry

Moderators are actively involved in promoting participation, keeping members focused on learning goals, and reminding members to contribute their input. There is strong emphasis on individual autonomy and individual expression of diverse perspectives. Opportunities for integrating new ideas and perspectives from outside the learning community are highlighted. Participants are strongly encouraged to invest efforts to understand and collaborate with other participants. This type of virtual learning community is usually found in formal learning environments.

Elements of Virtual Learning Communities of Practice

Moderators are actively involved in promoting participation, keeping members focused on learning goals, and reminding members to contribute their input. Future developments within the community and potential applications of acquired learning are actively discussed by participants. A strong emphasis on group norms is highlighted, which contributes to a sense of group identity and attachment. There is moderate emphasis on individual autonomy and individual expression of diverse perspectives. Participants are encouraged to invest efforts to understand and collaborate with other participants. This type of virtual learning community is usually found in formal learning environments.

Elements of Virtual Learning Communities of Culture

There is usually no moderator appointed. A strong emphasis on group norms is in place, which contributes to a sense of group identity and attachment. Participants are encouraged to invest efforts to understand

and cooperate with other participants. There are invested efforts to document and publicize the history and values of the learning community and noteworthy actions of community members. This type of virtual learning community is usually found in informal learning environments.

Elements of Virtual Learning Communities of Socialization

There is usually no moderator appointed. There is a moderate emphasis on group norms in place, which contributes to a sense of group identity and attachment. There is varying emphasis on individual autonomy and individual expression. Participants are often encouraged to invest efforts to understand and cooperate with other participants. Sometimes there are invested efforts to document and publicize the history and values of the learning community and noteworthy actions of community members. This type of virtual learning community is usually found in formal learning environments.

Elements of Virtual Learning Communities of Counseling and Development

Moderators are actively involved in promoting relationship development, providing resource material, and encouraging participants to share their personal experiences. Potential applications of acquired learning are actively discussed by participants. There is strong emphasis on individual autonomy and individual expression. Participants are encouraged to invest efforts to understand and empathize with other participants. There are invested efforts to document and publicize the history and values of the learning community and noteworthy actions of community members. This type of virtual learning community is usually found in formal learning environments.

Summary

In general, active moderator involvement is required in virtual learning communities of knowledge building, virtual learning communities of inquiry, virtual learning communities of practice, and virtual learning communities of counseling and development. Active moderator involvement is not a primary consideration in virtual learning communities of culture and virtual learning communities of socialization. There is a strong emphasis on individual autonomy and individual expression in virtual learning communities of knowledge building and virtual learning communities of counseling and development, but not in virtual learning communities of practice, virtual learning communities of culture, and virtual learning communities of socialization. Instead, a strong emphasis on group norms is highlighted in virtual learning communities of practice, virtual learning communities of culture, and virtual learning communities of socialization. Investing efforts to understand or collaborate with other community members is fundamental to virtual learning communities of culture, virtual learning communities of inquiry, virtual learning communities of practice, and virtual learning communities of counseling and development. Less emphasis on mutual understanding and collaboration is present in virtual learning communities of socialization and virtual learning communities of knowledge building.

FUTURE TRENDS

In addition to virtual community classification, there are other approaches available for guiding the design of virtual learning communities. One particularly noteworthy area revolves around the virtual team classification (Duarte & Snyder, 1999). In an effort to explain the parameters of virtual team organization, Duarte and Snyder (1999) posited seven types of virtual teams: networked teams, parallel teams, project development teams, work teams, service teams, management teams, and action teams. Networked teams collaborate to achieve a common purpose. Parallel teams work on special assignments, outside the regular work of the organization. Project development teams conduct projects for users for a specified period of time. Work teams carry out regular and ongoing work. Service teams carry out service work across time and distance. Management teams perform collaborative work functions on daily management issues. Action teams provide quick responses in emergency situations (Duarte & Snyder, 1999). Similarly, Bell and Kozlowski (2002) created a model of virtual teams, which defined key characteristics to differentiate virtual teams in terms of spatial distance, mode of communication, team lifecycle, and team membership. Wei and Wang (2006) asserted that virtual teams could be defined by a combination of virtual team characteristics and types.

One strength of virtual team classification is that it provides designers with a detailed account of how various types of teams are organized within virtual learning communities. One challenge of virtual team classification is that many virtual communities are not organized into virtual teams with prescribed team functions. Therefore, virtual team classification approaches are better suited for some virtual communities than others.

For instance, virtual communities of practice often involve teamwork and distinct teams for improving practice. For instance, a virtual community for medical practitioners may be divided into doctors, registered nurses, other nurses and nursing assistants, interns, and support staff. Identifying teams for this virtual community would not be difficult. Virtual communities of culture, however, may not be easily divided into virtual teams since there is not typically a set of defined organizational tasks for members to carry out in teams.

Virtual community sustainability is another important consideration for future design work. The sustainability of a virtual community refers to the extent to which a virtual community continues to attract and retain its target members who identify with the mission of the community by taking part in its sponsored activities (Chuang, 2006). Chuang (2006) posited a dynamic process model for enhancing the sustainability of virtual communities governed by a number of key virtual community functions: production functions, member support functions, and well-being functions. The production function creates the outcomes that result in the accomplishment of the virtual community mission. Member support functions attract people to the community while meeting their needs. The well-being function contributes to virtual community through proper governance mechanisms. Under this theoretical framework, chartered missions, governance mechanisms, and members' satisfaction are critical to the sustainability of virtual communities (Chuang, 2006). One strength of this approach to virtual communities it that it provides an explanation for long-term virtual community growth. This offers instructional designers insights into design work applied to long-standing virtual communities. This could become increasingly important in the event that virtual communities become even more entrenched. One challenge of viewing virtual communities from a sustainability perspective is that many virtual communities are short term with changing members and changing virtual community goals. For instance, a virtual community developed in support of a political candidate for election will typically be discontinued after the election.

A number of questions remain that future design work may address, such as: how can various types of virtual teams be managed successfully? What factors related to team design may influence virtual community design? Which virtual community types are most likely to be sustainable for extended period of time? How does the design of virtual communities differ with respect to long term sustainability? From an instructional design perspective, virtual community sustainability and virtual team design are key components of virtual community design. A better understanding of the abovementioned questions could help future designers and trainers to identify the best ways to design and maintain successful virtual communities within education.

CONCLUSION

This chapter posited a topology of virtual learning communities to advance knowledge of educational design: virtual learning communities of knowledge building, virtual learning communities of inquiry, virtual learning communities of practice, virtual learning communities of culture, virtual learning communities of socialization, and virtual learning communities of counseling and development. Building on the descriptions of virtual learning community categories, primary design elements provided rough parameters for the learning community design. Basic design elements of each virtual learning community were identified, including: moderator role, individual autonomy, group norm presence, need for collaboration and understanding, and setting.

Categories of virtual learning communities are not intended to be interpreted as rigid descriptions of independent virtual learning communities. There is a degree of commonality shared by different virtual learning communities. For instance, a virtual learning community of counseling and development interested in rebuilding individual confidence may place a strong emphasis on problem-solving skill development similar to virtual communities of practice. There is also a degree of divergence in purpose within any virtual learning community. For example, the organizers of a virtual community of socialization may attempt to have a long-term vision of their community, with an emphasis similar to virtual learning communities of culture. Virtual learning communities are not appropriate in all learning situations. Other learning strategies are more suitable in situations in which interaction with others in not essential. What is suggested is that categories of virtual learning communities do provide a useful heuristic tool for designing and implementing virtual learning communities.

REFERENCES

Bell, B. S., & Kozlowski, S. W. (2002). A typology of virtual teams: Implications for effective leadership. *Group & Organization Management, 27*(1), 14-49.

Benbunan-Fich, S., & Star, R. (1999). Educational applications of CMC: Solving case studies through asynchronous learning networks. *Journal of Computer Mediated Communication, 4*(3). Retrieved December 1, 2002, from http://www.ascusc.org/jcmc/vol4/issue3/benbunan-fich.html

Brown J., Collins A., & Duguid, P. (1989). Situated cognition and the culture of learning. *Educational Researcher, 18*(1), 32-42.

Chuang, T. (2006). Virtual community sustainability. In S. Dasgupta (Ed.), *Encyclopedia of virtual communities and technologies* (pp. 533-538). London: Idea Group.

Cognition and Technology Group at Vanderbilt. (1990). Anchored instruction and its relationship to situated cognition. *Educational Researcher, 19*(6), 2-10.

Duarte, D. L., & Snyder, N. T. (1999). *Mastering virtual teams: Strategies, tools, and technologies that succeed.* San Francisco: Jossey-Bass.

Gabelnick, F., MacGregor, J., Mattews, R., & Smith, B. (1990). *Learning communities: Creating connections among students, faculty, and disciplines.* San Francisco: Jossey-Bass.

Gilbert, N. J., & Driscoll, M. P. (2002). Collaborative knowledge building: A case study. *Educational Technology Research & Development, 50*(1), 59-79.

Gold, S. (2001). A constructivist approach to online training for online teachers. *Journal of Asynchronous Learning Networks, 5*(1). Retrieved December 1, 2002, from http://www.aln.org/alnweb/journal/Vol5_issue1/Gold/gold.htm

Gunawardena, C., Nolla, P., Wilson, P. Lopez, J., Ramirez-Angel, N., & Megchun-Alpizar, R. (2001). A cross-cultural study of group process and development in online conferences. *Distance Education, 22*(1), 85-110.

Hawisher, G., & Pemberton, M. (1997). Writing across the curriculum encounters asynchronous learning networks or WAC meets up with ALN. *Journal of Asynchronous Learning Networks, 1*(1). Retrieved December 1, 2002, from http://www.aln.org/alnweb/journal/issue1/hawisher.htm

Imel, S. (2001). Learning communities/communities of practice. *Eric Clearinghouse.* Retrieved December 1, 2002, from http//: www.ericacve.org/fulltext.asp

Jonassen, D., & Kwon, H. (2001). Communication patterns in computer mediated versus FTF group problem solving. *Educational Technology Research and Development, 49*(1), 35-51.

Lave, J., & Wenger, E. (1991). *Situated learning: Legitimate peripheral participation.* Cambridge, England: Cambridge University Press.

Lundell, D. (2000). Developing writers, developing professionals: Graduate students bridging theory and practice in basic writing. *Research and Teaching in Developmental Education, 16*(2), 43-53.

Luppicini, R. (2003). Categories of virtual learning communities for educational design. *Quarterly Review of Distance Education, 2*(4), 12-22

Ramsoomair, J. (1997). Internet in the context of cross-cultural management. *Internet Research, 7*(3) 189-194.

Scardamalia, M., & Bereiter, C. (1996). Computer support for knowledge-building communities. In T. Koschmann (Ed.), *CSCL: Theory and practice of an emerging paradigm* (pp. 249-268). Hillsdale, NJ: Erlbaum,

Schwier, R. (2001). Catalysts, emphases, and elements of virtual communities: Implications for research and practice. *Quarterly Review of Distance Education, 2*(1), 5-18.

Selznick, P. (1996). In search of community. In W. Vitel & W. Jackson (Eds.), *Rooted in the land* (pp. 195-203). New Haven, CT: Yale University Press.

Senge, P. (1990). *The fifth discipline: The art and practice of the learning organization*. New York: Doubleday.

Stepich, D., Ertmer, P., & Lane, M. M. (2001). Problem solving in a case-based course: Strategies for facilitating coached expertise. *Educational Technology Research and Development, 49*(3), 53-69.

Taylor, J. (2001). Virtual writing forum with Don Murray and the national writing project in an asynchronous environment. *Journal of Asynchronous Learning Networks, 5*(1). Retrieved December 1, 2006, from http://www.aln.org/alnweb/journal/Vol5_issue1/Taylor/Taylor.htm

Weber, J. (2000). *Learning communities in higher education. A field observation case study*. Unpublished doctoral dissertation, Widener University, Chester, PA.

Wei, K., & Wang, C. (2006). Virtual community sustainability. In S. Dasgupta (Ed.), *Encyclopedia of virtual communities and technologies* (pp. 570-574). London: Idea Group.

CHAPTER 20

CONTRASTING FORCES AFFECTING THE PRACTICE OF DISTANCE EDUCATION

**Brent G. Wilson, Patrick Parrish,
Nathan Balasubramanian, and Scott Switzer**

Our current systems of education are in place for a reason—primarily because they have responded to longstanding societal needs. The rapid rise of distance education can also be explained by its success in addressing important but hitherto unmet needs of convenient access and flexible delivery. In this chapter, we review a number of trends or forces affecting the current practice of distance education. These forces are described as either conservative or progressive in nature. Conservative trends help educators better control processes and outcomes and achieve cost efficiencies in delivery. Progressive trends open up new possibilities in thinking about education and encourage diverse ideas and outcomes. Looking forward, future distance-education practices can be expected to exploit new technologies to further both conservative and progressive ends. The ongoing tension between control and efficiency on the one hand, and creative innovation on the other, is healthy and will continue to shape best practices in the field.

Online Learning Communities
pp. 333–346
Copyright © 2007 by Information Age Publishing

CONTRASTING FORCES AFFECTING
THE PRACTICE OF DISTANCE EDUCATION

How do you get a fix on something that is moving as fast as distance education? In many schools and businesses over the past decade, distance education has moved from a fairly marginal part of a training or outreach program to a central, mission-critical part of the organization. The pace has been relentless in higher education, with other sectors not far behind. In many ways, the rise of distance education is a simple function of new digital technologies applied to the educational domain. Or, more accurately, the cultures surrounding the Web and other technologies have influenced educational practices, leading to transformations as ideas and practices are borrowed and shared.

But that cultural shift has been irregular in its impact. In some ways, distance education, for example, seems more controlled and predictable than traditional classrooms, whose curriculum may not be as fully developed. On the other hand, we are continually seeing examples of innovative learning via distance-learning technologies. This is to be expected, since distance-education practices both mirror and depart from traditional teaching practices.

This chapter provides a broad-stroke overview of many of the forces currently shaping the practice of distance education. These forces both shape and are shaped by practice, since they are aspects of that practice. To bring some order to the analysis, we distinguish conservative trends and forces from progressive ones. Conservative forces help to bring a level of control, efficiency, and accountability to distance education. Ends are not typically questioned, and means are made more efficient and replicable. For example, course management systems like Blackboard are designed to help beginning online teachers develop course resources. The tool helps the teacher do expected course activities quickly, but may not encourage the teacher toward different ends, such as creative learning activities or unique assessments. By contrast, progressive forces open up possibilities for new visions of learning and teaching. Their net impact leads to innovation, creativity, and a departure from status-quo practices. Social networking sites, when discussed among educators, are destabilizing notions of fixed-content courses and teacher-controlled learning activities; hence, their impact may be seen as largely progressive.

Table 20.1 presents forces in two columns according to their projected impact on practice. Note that many of the items are new on the scene, so in that sense they are innovative. But their impact may be essentially conservative, reinforcing established practices or facilitating greater efficiency and control of instruction. We should also note that many of these forces have complex, systemic relations with practices, and that full impacts are never known at early stages—a lesson too seldom acknowledged in the history of instructional technology. The eventual movement toward learning objects, for example, likely will have a variety of impacts, some of which may lead to cost efficiencies, but also to creative changes in content delivery and instructional interactions. We note that a technology often evolves over time, starting out as an innovation, for example, and being co-opted into established practice as people assimilate it into exist-

Table 20.1.   Key Forces Relating to Education, Distance Education, and Learning Technologies

Conservative Forces— *Leading to Greater Efficiency and* *Accountability in Processes and Outcomes*	*Progressive Forces—* *Leading to More Innovative Outcomes* *and Creative Processes*
Technologizing of Instruction • Design curriculum around competencies and standards • Assess outcomes to increase student learning and improve accountability • Align learning outcomes, assessments, and methods • Align resource allocation with performance goals • Regulate processes and methods • De-professionalize the teacher's role • Invest in stable content repositories • Create templated, modular, re-usable learning assets • Digitize everything, making resources archivable, searchable, replicable, linkable, and modelable; also mobile and ubiquitous	**Learner- and User-Centered Philosophies** • Provide convenient, anytime/anywhere access • Give people choices about their learning • Design for active, engaging learning • Respect diversity and unique needs of the learner • Support *digital natives* in their learning styles and preferences • Integrate field-based and informal learning experiences • Encourage social learning through modeling, collaboration, and learning communities • Privilege engagement and activity (learner focus) over instructional strategies (teacher focus), particularly through game and narrative designs
The Educational Marketplace • Let the business side of education predominate • Convert instruction into a commodity • Disaggregate products and services • Leverage efforts into sustainable economies of scale • Encourage free-market participation of commercial interests	**Open Learning and Connectivity** • Acknowledge the Web as a liberating and empowering force • Privilege open source over commercial • Encourage Web-based knowledge production and sharing • Exploit the Long Tail effect • Support communities of practice and social networking • Challenge methods of credentialing • Acknowledge the growing role of the independent pundit • Privilege knowing-who and knowing-where expertise • Offer global education as an alternative to provincial curricula

ing patterns of work. For this reason, our list of forces is presented at a fairly general level, focusing on key paradigms or perspective on education, within which particular technologies must be adapted. We have worded the bullets as prescriptions to reflect the action implications of each perspective.

The remainder of the chapter discusses the content of the table in more detail. We conclude with some reflections on critical ideas that may help shape the direction we go in response to these various forces. Our analysis is based on earlier papers (Wilson, 2002, 2005; see also Albright, Simonson, Smaldino, & Zvacek, 2005; Howell, Williams, & Lindsay, 2003; Moore & Anderson, 2003).

CONSERVATIVE FORCES

Usually, when people talk about trends and futures, the emphasis is on innovation. The future is about the new, almost by definition. In contrast, we begin with established forces that most of us take for granted, but which in large part form the rational underpinning for our current systems of education. Understanding these existing forces can then shed light on the occasional tensions introduced by new technologies and their accompanying cultures.

Technologizing of Instruction

In simple production terms, education is in the business of taking raw material (unskilled, unknowledgeable students), processing those students, and outputting graduates with the knowledge and skill they need. Seen this way, improvements can be made when we are very explicit about the goals of instruction and measures of those desired outcomes. This view of instruction has roots in nineteenth century industrial processes and is sometimes called an efficiency model of curriculum (Kliebard, 1987). Historically this view of instruction has been tied to the integration of learning technologies (Reiser, 2001), partly to avoid the chaotic effects of unpredictable innovations. Or expressed positively, a competency-based approach to instruction and instructional design helps ensure positive impacts of promising innovations, in particular the use of instructional technologies.

Trends within the United States and across most developed nations reveal clear movement toward this efficiency view of instruction. We term this movement a "technologizing" of instruction because the technical aspects of the educational process are emphasized. Curriculum is designed around a fixed set of core standards or competencies. Student achievement of those competencies is assessed at regular intervals. Based on that assessment, adjustments are made at all levels (student, teacher/ classroom, district, etc.) to improve processes and outcomes. Moreover, resources are allocated based on their payoff potential in improving outcomes (Russell, 2006). Instructional methods are similarly aligned to system goals and assessments. Improvement of instruction is defined in terms of effectiveness or efficiency, but rarely in a way that questions the target outcomes themselves.

In this more regulated, controlled mode of instructional delivery, the teacher finds herself or himself in a complex role of having to meet a number of expectations, drawing on available professional knowledge and resources. General learning goals and key assessments are not under teacher control. Typically, teachers do not choose their students and the special needs of those students. They must, however, see that each one of their students achieves the targeted learning goals. To respond to that challenge, teachers make use of a variety of resources, but are often left to their own expertise in finding ways to reach their students and help them progress. Without control over outcomes, assessment or, in many cases, method, there is less room for professional judgment in the teaching process. To some extent, then, teacher roles are deprofessionalized as teachers complete assigned tasks in a more narrowly-framed performance context.

The instructor's role also shifts somewhat in a distance education environment. While many instructors are also the developers of the courses they teach, there are incentives to separate these functions. From a cost-control point of view, online courses should have instructor-facilitators guide the learning of students using carefully designed methods prepared by better-paid design specialists. Similarly, templated course designs, course management systems, and re-usable content assets all are consistent with a technical, efficiency-driven model of instruction. These efficiency aspects of distance education can become essential counterbalances, since in other ways distance education requires more time and labor than traditional face-to-face instruction, particularly on the part of online instructors (Dahl, 2003; Tallent-Runnels et al., 2006).

Educators may feel like the technologizing of instruction is so entrenched in the system that it hardly qualifies as a trend. We acknowledge that the ideas underlying this conservative force are not new. But within the United States at least, the practice has only been very irregularly observed, with longstanding traditions of local control. Moreover, the means and tools to accomplish well-aligned systems are increasingly sophisticated, thanks in large part to information and communication technologies (ICT). The idea of instruction as a coherent system is a formidable metaphor that will continue to impact policy and practice at all levels. This is particularly important when assessing claims of progressive pundits calling for a near-total abandonment of traditional structures of education.

The Educational Marketplace

Education is primarily a service enterprise (as opposed to a product-based industry). It is one of the more labor-intensive forms of work; a typical school district in the United States, for example, spends more than 80% of its budget directly on payroll. Moreover, education has tended to be fairly craft oriented; that is, the strategies and methods that make things really work are developed and fine-tuned at the local level, and are not easily disseminable.

It is the very craft-like nature of education that has led people to look for ways to package and commoditize its offerings. As the global marketplace opens up exchanges, both commercial and social, educational entrepreneurs are seeking ways to turn its services into marketable products, and to find more cost-effective ways of delivering those products.

Enter distance education. Distance-delivered programs must be more carefully developed and packaged than residential programs. Students in a distance-education program may sometimes get certain services separated or "disaggregated" from the overall educational package, and charged for those select services. Gone, for example, are the ivy-covered walls and the maple trees and manicured gardens. The socializing and networking done in a fraternity house is replaced by another form of social networking online. The services sought by online students are primarily the following:

- Credentialing—certifying my expertise in a given area;
- Knowledge acquisition—learning the material, gaining the expertise from those who have it, well enough to take a job or go on with my studies;
- Networking—meeting professionals and other students who may be able to help me with my learning and career; helping me feel like I belong;
- Assessing—assessing my current knowledge, to better guide my learning, and to document, primarily through grades, my performance record; and
- Technical, logistical, and instructional support—helping me with problems that arise in my education.

Each one of these services, in a distance education environment, must be specifically designed for and fine-tuned over time. This is true especially for hard-to-achieve outcomes from a distance, such as the networking, feel-at-home function. And because of their designed nature, these products could be combined in separately priced packages, depending on the unique needs of the learner. A learner who doesn't need the credential, for example, may be offered a curriculum with fewer assessments and prerequisites. More commonly, perhaps, a learner who comes in with prior expertise may pay for a package consisting primarily of the assessment and credentialing services. Indeed, the U.S. Budget Reconciliation Act (passed December 2005) allows federal financial aid to for-profit institutions offering no classes at all, but rather granting degrees based entirely on assessments (Johnstone, 2006). We expect to see more disaggregation of products and services online, to respond to requirements of different markets within the global marketplace.

PROGRESSIVE FORCES

The conservative forces discussed above are formidable and entrenched in their influence. We can expect educational systems to continue their focus on efficiency and profitability. At the same time, a number of forces pointing in more progressive directions are coming on the scene, discussed below.

Learner- and User-Centered Philosophies

For the past 20 years, a learner-centered philosophy of education has become the mainstream pedagogy among teacher preparation institutions in the United State, much of Europe, and to some extent Asia and worldwide. Teachers are taught and encouraged to educate the whole person, to meet the needs of every learner, to engage learners in meaningful, authentic activities that engage and challenge students to take responsibility for their own learning. Many curriculums are designed with constructivist learning theories in mind. While falling under different names—brain-based learning, constructivism, situated learning, inquiry learning, project- and problem-based learning—a learner-centered pedagogy has become the established ideal for most school professionals. Adult educators may use different names, but they too engage students in meaningful, active learning activities that are relevant to their work and professional-growth needs. And as adult educators acknowledge, learning happens outside of class just as well as in class, hence the value attached to informal and field-based learning opportunities such as internships, practicum experiences, action research, and service-learning projects.

A learner-centered pedagogy, by definition, pays attention to the individual learner and that person's unique needs. In today's world, that means increased attention to language needs, cultural/ethnic diversity, and differences in background knowledge, skills, and ability. It also means attention to the "digital native" phenomenon suggesting generational differences toward technology (Prensky, 2001) which, although not well documented empirically, can serve as an important metaphor for understanding learner differences. A distance-delivered course will typically include a wide range of students. For K-12 education, a distance learning population may even be skewed by a higher proportion of students who don't fit into residential schools.

Again, teachers can feel overwhelmed by the expectations to reach out to every learner, and feel a loss of control as students are asked to take more responsibility. And again, as in the case of conservative forces, the desired end of progressive pedagogies can benefit from an infusion of technology. With the aid of technology, teachers can more feasibly manage multiple teams and projects simultaneously, and provide resources and feedback as needed. While not a panacea by any means, technology, particularly distance education technologies, can be put to useful service in addressing the needs of diverse learners (e.g., Balasubramanian, 2006; Jeffs & Morrison, 2005; Solomon, Allen, & Resta, 2003).

Admittedly, pedagogy within distance education courses has not been particularly distinguished as progressive (Rose, 2004). Course management software like Blackboard and WebCT are based on underlying models of traditional course structures—weekly units presently in linear sequence; quizzes and exams, accumulated grade points, and so forth. By their implicit structure these systems tend to reinforce existing practices rather than encourage innovation. Even so, the received tradition that emphasized texts, workbooks, and lectures is being expanded to include an array of strategies such as team projects and collaborative exercises, as well as various forms of online discussion. The quality and variety of strategies continue to be concerns among program leaders, since the quality of the learning experience affects achievement, retention, and overall strength of the program.

There does seem to be some tension between a learner-centered orientation and a community-centered approach to online courses. A true focus on the individual learner, as in the form of self-paced, self-directed instruction, would take a very different shape from a typical course that seeks a level of social cohesion through assigned projects and group interactions. One resolution of this difficulty would acknowledge that learner-centered pedagogy includes attention to learners' active participation in larger groups and communities.

The paradigm shift to a learner-centric service orientation extends beyond pedagogy to include broader issues of delivery and access. Providing increasing choices to prospective students, and making learning resources more convenient and accessible anytime and anywhere, is consistent with corresponding reforms in business practices. The rise of learning management systems (LMS), for example, is part of this greater attention to individual needs and choices.[1] In business environments, providers of products and services have come to understand the need to fully address customer needs and concerns. Distance education thus becomes a critical tool in addressing end-user needs and preferences, not only through any learner-centered strategies that can be integrated into courses, but through convenient and accessible design and delivery of programs.

Open Learning and Connectivity

As noted at the outset, we are still in the beginning stages of the revolution caused by the digital shift and the advent of the World Wide Web. Various labels have been used to describe this fundamental shift—a flattened world, distributed knowledge sharing, networking, globalization, the power of the Web. The core principles relate to how knowledge and participation (and hence learning) are distributed within Web-like systems—and that new structures are emerging in response to that distributed world. Open theorists claim that "webby" systems work better for many kinds of problems than traditional closed, hierarchical systems. Fundamentally, the Web (known also by the current label of Web 2.0) has unleashed tremendous energy and potential, not just in education but in all sectors of society. Our educational future can be envisioned by trying to work out how distributed systems will take shape and do their magic.

Surprisingly, implications for distance education are not very clear. Is distance education part of the new wave, or part of the establishment? Web enthusiasts are drawn to open education as an alternative to conservative, established forces, which in some eyes include course-based distance education (Wiley, 2006). Open education resources are "digitized materials offered freely and openly for educators, students and self-learners to use and re-use for teaching, learning and research" (Wikipedia, 2006). Key elements of the open education movement are free access to digital resources in support of individuals and communities, who draw strength from mutual interaction, sharing, and problem solving. Open educators tend to favor open source tools (like Moodle or Linux) over commercial tools (like Blackboard or Windows). They tend to challenge credentialing institutions by self-directed learning and alternative knowledge demonstration (Anti-credentialism, 2006). They tend to value self-publishing bloggers and pundits over established opinion centers. These pundits are not often sources of new data or news; rather, they are "re-mixers" or interpreters of the news, whose contributions lie primarily in their noticing and highlighting information, and the insights and value given to existing data.

Perhaps the complex relationship between distance education and open resources reflects an underlying complexity in practice generally. In spite of their overall progressive impact, open resources can be put to use supporting the status quo. An example of this is the rise of MySpace.com. At the time of this writing, MySpace has more than 90 million registered participants, with 250,000 new subscribers each day (Norris, 2006), making it the most visited Web site in the United States. Reiss describes My-Space as "part night club, part shopping mall, part 7-11 parking lot." To support his claim that MySpace is "the most disruptive force to hit popular culture since MTV," Reiss points to the powerful word-of-mouth sharing that happens in social networking sites. Word of mouth is the holy grail of advertisers looking for impact. Rupert Murdoch, the owner of MySpace, is now in a position to closely observe word-of-mouth processes as ideas and preferences spread within his system, and adapt product promotion efforts accordingly. So, while MySpace serves progressive ends of distributed sharing and networking, even progressive mechanisms can be co-opted to promote and sell traditional products.

CONCLUDING THOUGHTS

It is possible that our initial move—distinguishing conservative and progressive forces—is fundamentally flawed. Virtually any innovation will be systemically nested within a complex array of practices and inter-depen-dant effects, some fostering change and others reinforcing established practices. Even so, we maintain that a real difference exists in the values underlying the forces noted in our table. These values create tensions that will continue to exist as new technologies enter the scene and enter into conversation with existing practices.

Technological determinists point to the important causative power that new technologies exert on practice. We can observe these powerful effects over the past generation with the cultural changes engendered by the personal computer and the World Wide Web. Technologies do indeed exert a causal impact on practice. At the same time, our analysis highlights the importance of culture and ideology on how technologies are perceived, received, and shared within and among communities. Both the technology and the values within a culture play critical roles in shaping practice.

While technologies have changed dramatically, so have educational ideologies. We have seen in recent years a number of changes in our educational thinking and values, as illustrated below:

- *Acknowledging the breakdown of the established canon of received knowledge.* Conflicts in ideology and value happen at every stage of curriculum and education, from preschool to doctoral research training. Educators must now deal with an increasing number of stable, well-articulated paradigms, each providing an account of educational processes and outcomes.

- *Recognizing the politicized foundation underlying scholarship, science, and technology.* Doing scholarship and advancing knowledge are human activities and, as such, are grounded in human values. Science is sometimes privileged above other forms of inquiry and activity, but this privileging is being increasingly called into question by practitioners and scholars alike.

- *Increasing diversity among learners and communities.* Diversity may not be a core value of every community, but it has become a fact that must be dealt with. As society grows more complex and diverse, values for difference are emerging in importance and prominence.

- *Reversing the centuries-old privilege of abstract theorizing over practical reasoning.* Since Descartes, Western thought has valued abstract, mathematically-based thought over the kind of contingent, practical reasoning common among professionals and problem-solving practitioners (Toulmin, 2004). We are gradually restoring value to the applied forms of reasoning engaged in by practitioners in business, education, politics, and design.

Distance education is a distinctly practical endeavor, combining various forms of reasoning, values, and technologies. The ideological extremes sometimes encountered within the pundit class (both progressive and conservative) are tempered by the bottom-line mandates to stay in business and respond to end-user needs. Acknowledging the significant differences between contrasting perspectives is a first step toward accommodating those perspectives productively into practice. In this chapter, we wish to highlight a point made earlier: the future is not simply determined by the latest and newest technologies; rather, we work out our future by engaging in conversation with these new technologies and accompanying ideas. Conservative and progressive forces will continue to exert influence on practice, over time resulting in new practices and solutions to human needs. Distance education will continue to grow and be a part of that human response.

NOTE

1. While learning management systems have both progressive and conservative qualities, their impact is substantially conservative. Many organizations adopt LMSs for improved monitoring and compliance. LMSs help with the move toward competencies and certifications because they can reliably handle the data-management requirements for competency-based approaches.

REFERENCES

Albright, M., Simonson, M., Smaldino, S., & Zvacek, S. (2005). *Teaching and learning at a distance: Foundations of distance education* (3rd ed.). New York: Prentice Hall.

Anti-credentialism. (2006, May 25). *Anti-credentialism.* Retrieved July 11, 2006, from http://www.p2pfoundation.net/index.php/Anti-Credentialism

Balasubramanian, N. (2006). Increasing student achievement through meaningful, authentic assessment. In C. Crawford et al. (Eds.), *Proceedings of Society for Information Technology and Teacher Education International Conference 2006* (pp. 3-8). Chesapeake, VA: AACE. Retrieved July 20, 2006, from http://www.innathansworld.com/KART/MeaningfulAuthenticAssessment.pdf.

Christensen, C. M. (1997). *The innovator's dilemma: When new technologies cause great firms to fail.* Cambridge MA: Harvard University Press.

Dahl, J. (2003). How much are distance education faculty worth? *Distance Education Report, 7*(14), 5-7.

Howell, S. L., Williams, P. B., & Lindsay, N. K. (2003). Thirty-two trends affecting distance education: An informed foundation for strategic planning. *Online Journal of Distance Learning Administration, 6*(3). Retrieved July 6, 2006, from http://www.westga.edu/~distance/ojdla/fall63/howell63.html.

Jeffs, T., & Morrison, W. F. (2005). Special education technology addressing diversity: A synthesis of the literature. *Journal of Special Education Technology, 20*(4), 19-25.

Jonestone, S. M. (2006, June)). *Issues and trends in American eLearning.* Presented at the Minnesota Online 3rd Annual Summer Conference, Bemidji Minnesota. Retrieved July 6, 2006, from www.mnonline.mnscu.edu/news/Session10a.ppt.

Kliebard, H. M. (1987). *The struggle for the American curriculum 1893-1958.* New York: Routledge.

Moore, M. G., & Anderson W. G. (Eds.). (2003). *Handbook of distance education.* Mahwah NJ: Erlbaum.

Norris, M. (2006, July 12). *The ascendance of MySpace* [interview with Spencer Reiss]. Retrieved July 13, 2006, from http://www.npr.org/templates/story/story.php?storyId=5552587.

Prensky, M. (2001). Digital natives, Digital immigrants. *On the Horizon, 9*(5). Retrieved July 10, 2006, from http://www.marcprensky.com/writing/Prensky%20-%20Digital%20Natives,%20Digital%20Immigrants%20-%20Part1.pdf

Reiser, R. A. (2001). A history of instructional design and technology: Part I: A history of instructional media. *Educational Technology Research and Development, 49*(1), 53-64.

Rose, E. (2004). "Is there a class with this content?" WebCT and the limits of individualization. *Journal of Educational Thought, 38*(1), 43-65.

Russell, M. (2006). *Technology and assessment: The two of two interpretations.* Greenwich CT: Information Age.

Solomon, G., Allen, N., & Resta, P. (2003). *Toward digital equity: Bridging the divide in education.* Boston: Allyn & Bacon.

Tallent-Runnels, M. K., Thomas, J. A., Lan, W. Y., Cooper, S., Ahern, T. C., Shaw, S. M., et al. (2006). Teaching courses online: A review of the research. *Review of Educational Research, 76*(1), 93-135.

Toulmin, S. (2001). *Return to reason.* Cambridge MA: Harvard University Press.

Wikipedia. (2006, June 20). *Open education resources.* Retrieved July 10, 2006, from: http://en.wikipedia.org/wiki/Open_educational_resources

Wiley, D. A. (2006, February 6). My Commission testimony (updated 06 Feb 06). Iterating toward openness. Retrieved July 6, 2006, from: http://opencontent.org/blog/archives/240.

Wilson, B. G. (2002). Trends and futures of education: Implications for distance education. *Quarterly Review of Distance Education, 3*(1), 65-77.

Wilson, B. G. (2005). A survey of progressive and conservative trends in education with implications for distance-education practice. In L. Visser, M. Simonson, & Y. L. Visser (Eds.), *Trends and issues in distance education: An international perspective* (pp. 3-21). Bloomington IN: Association for Educational Communications and Technology.

ABOUT THE AUTHORS

Mary Beth Bianco, PhD, is the director of educational planning at BLaST Intermediate Unit 17, in Williamsport, PA, a regional educational service agency for K-12 schools. She is an adjunct instructor for the Pennsylvania State University's WorldCampus, Instructional Systems Department, and has experience in both online instruction as well as blended learning environments. She can be contacted at mbianco@iu17.org

Alison A. Carr-Chellman, PhD, is a professor of instructional systems in the Department of Learning and Performance Systems, College of Education, at the Pennsylvania State University. She teaches courses in applied qualitative research, educational change and innovation, e-learning in a global society, educational systems design, and research apprenticeship. She recently authored two books, *Global Perspectives on E-Learning: Rhetoric and Reality* published by Sage and *User-Design* published by Erlbaum. Her research focuses on systems theory, e-learning, educational systems design, and identity of the instructional technology field. She can be contacted at aac3@psu.edu

Alice Brown, PhD, is a lecturer in early childhood education and coordinator for the first year students enrolled in the Early Childhood Degrees at the University of Southern Queensland in Australia. She coordinates numerous early childhood courses, including professional experience courses. Her passion is in "Catching a moment to move with young children." She can be contacted at browna@usq.edu.au

Shujen L. Chang, PhD, is an assistant professor of instructional technology at the University of Houston-Clear Lake. Chang has taught and conducted several studies concerning cognition and instruction, instructional systems design, and online learning. She has been an active member and served in positions in three of the most important professional organizations for academics and instructional technologists: the American Educational Research Association, the Association for Educational and Communications Technology, and the National Consortium for Instruction and Cognition. She can be contacted at changs@cl.uh.edu

Joan M. Conway is a lecturer (school pedagogies/on-line pedagogies) in the Faculty of Education at the Toowoomba campus of the University of Southern Queensland in Australia, with research interests in twenty-first century teacher professionals and schools, teachers' knowledge and shared pedagogical meaning, school revitalization as a process, and future schools and communities. She can be contacted at conwayj@usq.edu.au

Stephen Corich is a principal academic staff member at Eastern Institute of Technology, Hawke's Bay, in New Zealand. He is the coordinator of the bachelor of computing systems degree and is involved in teaching Web development and data communications. Corich has a background in commercial computing, having worked for several years at the Defence Computing Bureau in a number of technical positions. He also has more than 15 years experience in tertiary education and is enrolled in a PhD program in information systems at Massey University, Palmerston North, New Zealand. His area of research involves educational technologies and in particular the use of discussion forums in distance education. He has published a number of papers in journals and has presented at international conferences. He can be contacted at Stephenc@eit.ac.nz

P. A. Danaher, PhD, is an associate professor (Education Research) in the Faculty of Education, and member of the Teaching, Learning, and Curriculum Research Cluster in the Centre for Research in Transformative Pedagogies, at the Toowoomba campus of the University of Southern Queensland in Australia, with research interests in the education of mobile communities. He can be contacted at danaher@usq.edu.au

Sir John Daniel, PhD, is president and CEO of the Commonwealth of Learning, a Commonwealth intergovernmental agency headquartered in Vancouver, Canada that helps developing countries apply technology to increase the scale and scope of learning in support of development. A graduate of the universities of Oxford and Paris, he has worked in 10 universities in five jurisdictions. He was president of Laurentian University,

Canada (1984-90); vice-chancellor of the Open University, UK (1990-2001) and assistant director-general for education at UNESCO, Paris (2001-04). Among his 250 publications he is best known for his book *Mega-universities and Knowledge Media: Technology Strategies for Higher Education*, which established his reputation as a leading thinker about how technology can help academics to enhance their effectiveness as teachers and enrich their impact as intellectuals. He has received over 20 honorary doctorates from universities in 12 countries. He can be contacted at jdaniel@col.org

Ugur Demiray, PhD, graduated from the Cinema and TV Department, School of Communication Sciences, Anadolu University, Eskisehir, Turkey, in 1981. He became an associate professor in 1989 and professor in 1995. His studies are focused on the distance education field and scholarly online journalism, especially on distance education. He has many articles that have been published in national and international journals. He has published TOJDE since January 2000. He can be contacted at udemiray@anadolu.edu.tr

Mary E. Engstrom, EdD, is an assistant professor in the Division of Technology for Education and Training at the University of South Dakota. She received her MS degree in Curriculum and Instruction from the University of Wisconsin, Madison, and her EdD in curriculum and instruction from USD. Engstrom coordinated the LOFTI (Learning Organizations for Technology Integration) Technology Innovation Challenge Grant project for the School of Education and chairs the School's Technology Integration Task Force. She teaches both undergraduate and graduate level courses in learning and technology. She can be reached at Mary.Engstrom@usd.edu

Veronica M. Godshalk, PhD, is an associate professor in the Department of Management and Organization at The Pennsylvania State University, Great Valley, School of Graduate Professional Studies. She earned a PhD from Drexel University in organizational behavior and strategic management, and a MS from the University of Pennsylvania. Godshalk teaches courses in organizational behavior, organizational change, strategy, communication skills, and career management. She has been on the faculty at Penn State for 11 years.

Lawrence W. Grimes, PhD, is a professor of experimental statistics. He earned a BS in 1972 and an MS in 1974 from the University of Georgia, and a PhD from The Ohio State University in 1978. Grimes teaches statistical methods and other related courses. He also provides statistical consulting services to faculty and graduate students involved in research in various topics in agriculture, engineering, textiles, and education. He can be contacted at lwgrm@clemson.edu

Seungyeon Han, PhD, received her degree in instructional technology from University of Georgia in 2005. Han has participated in various research and development projects in the field of instructional technology. Her current research focuses on Web-based learning, computer support for collaborative learning, and qualitative inquiry in technology-mediated discourse. She can be contacted at seungyeon.han@gmail.com.

Michael J. Hannafin is professor of instructional technology, Charles H. Wheatley-Georgia Research Alliance Eminent Scholar in Technology-Enhanced Learning, and director of the Learning & Performance Support Laboratory at the University of Georgia. His research interests focus on developing and testing frameworks for the design of technology-enhanced, student-centered learning environments. He can be contacted at hannafin@uga.edu

Douglas Harvey, DEd, is an associate professor of instructional technology at the Richard Stockton College of New Jersey. His academic interests include the effective use of hypermedia, distributed education models, and the practical application of technology in the classroom. He can be reached at harveyd@stockton.edu

Pamela A. Havice, PhD, has more than 25 years of experience in higher education, including developing courses and curriculum using distance and distributed learning models. Havice is an associate professor in counselor education at Clemson University, where she has been an integral part of developing a distributed learning environment for the delivery of the Student Affairs/Counselor Education program. Her primary areas of research include distance and distributed learning applications, multicultural issues, and faculty and student development. She has numerous published articles, book chapters, professional presentations and an edited book on distance and distributed learning. She is currently an associate editor of the *College Student Affairs Journal* and coeditor of the online journal the *Palmetto Practitioner*. She can be contacted at havice@clemson.edu

William L. Havice, PhD, is a professor and associate dean in the College of Health, Education, and Human Development at Clemson University, Clemson, South Carolina. Havice has 26 years of teaching and advising experience at the university. He has taught numerous undergraduate and graduate courses in technology and instructional technology. He has served on the board of directors for the International Technology Education Association and has earned the honor of Distinguished Technology Educator. Recently, he served as a board of examiner for the National Council for Accreditation of Teacher Education. His primary areas of research include Web-based distance and distributed learning applications, multimedia, and hypermedia. Havice has numerous published articles, book chapters, professional presentations, and has edited a book. He can be contacted at whavice@clemson.edu

Andrew Hickey is a lecturer (cultural studies and social theory), and convenor of the Socio-Cultural Studies in Education Academic Working Group, in the Faculty of Education at the Toowoomba campus of the University of Southern Queensland in Australia, with research interests in cultural studies, critical theory, popular culture, and representation politics. He can be contacted at hickeya@usq.edu.au

Janette R. Hill, PhD, is an associate professor of instructional technology in the Department of Educational Psychology and Instructional Technology at the University of Georgia. Hill's research focuses on online, resource based, and informal learning with adults. She is particularly interested in exploring how participants from diverse background make connections and build community in virtual contexts. She can be contacted at janette@uga.edu

David Holder, PhD, is the technology director at Aubrey Independent School District in Denton County, Texas. He is also a teaching fellow for the Department of Technology and Cognition in the College of Education at the University of North Texas. He is interested in the study of cognitive load and its impact on the learning process. He lives in Krum, Texas, with his wife and two children and can be reached at dholder@unt.edu For more about his professional interests, please visit http://www.holdernet.net

Jason B. Huett, PhD, is an assistant professor with the University of West Georgia. He is currently a member of the editorial board for *The Journal of Applied Educational Technology, Information Systems Education Journal*, and serves as cochair on AECT's Distance Education Standards Committee. Huett was a featured researcher at the 2006 AECT International Convention in Dallas, Texas and has published numerous articles relating to distance education—including two award-winning publications. He lives with his wife and three children in Carrollton, Georgia. He can be reached at jhuett@gmail.com

Clint Isbell, EdD, received his doctorate from Texas A&M University in 1980. He has since served on the faculty at Clemson University and California State University, Long Beach. Isbell served as the project director for the Boys & Girls Clubs of America Online Master's in Human Resource Development, one of the first totally online programs at Clemson University. His major research interests are in the areas of distance learning and workforce development. He can be contacted at iclinto@clemson.edu

L. M. Jeffrey, PhD, is a senior lecturer in the Department of International Business and Management. In 1986 she began work in the Business College at Massey University, teaching and conducting research in human resource management, organisational behaviour, computer-based learning, instructional design and psychology, and adult learning. During this time she became involved in the HURDA (Human Resource Development in Aviation) research program in which she developed CALES, a computer-based examination-on-demand system for pilot licensing. Other research interests are human performance, learning strategies and approaches, learning styles, instructional design, online learning, and needs assessment. In addition, she is working on a number of projects, including: learning styles and profiles, methodologies in accident investigation, measuring competence and proficiency, developing an online distance education program, air rage, and online student self-assessment programs.

David Jonassen, PhD, is the Distinguished Professor of Learning Technologies and Educational Psychology at the University of Missouri and director of the Center for the Study of Problem Solving. He can be contacted at Jonassen@missouri.edu

Minchi C. Kim, PhD, is a postdoctoral scholar in the Consortium for Research and Evaluation of Advanced Technologies in Education (CREATE) at New York University. Her research focuses on scaffolding students' scientific problem solving with technology-enhanced learning environments, advancing pedagogical framework for learning and teaching in technology-rich classes, and integrating emergent technologies into K-12 classes. Previously, she worked on several NSF and DOE funded projects as a research assistant at the Learning and Performance Support Laboratory. She can be contacted at minchi.kim@nyu.edu

Kinshuk, PhD, joined Athabasca University in August 2006 as the professor and director of School of Computing and Information Systems. Before moving to Canada, Kinshuk worked at German National Research

Centre for Information Technology as Postgraduate Fellow, and at Massey University, New Zealand as associate professor of information systems and director of Advanced Learning Technology Research Centre. He also holds honorary senior e-learning consultant position with Online Learning Systems Ltd., New Zealand, and docent position with University of Joensuu, Finland. He has been involved in large-scale research projects for exploration-based adaptive educational environments and has published over 185 research papers in international refereed journals, conferences, and book chapters. He is chair of IEEE Technical Committee on Learning Technology and International Forum of Educational Technology & Society. He is also editor of the SSCI indexed *Journal of Educational Technology & Society* (ISSN 1436-4522). He can be contacted at kinshuk@ieee.org

Peter E. Kinyanjui, PhD, taught and administered educational programs in various capacities at the University of Nairobi, Kenya, for over 28 years. He was the founding principal of the College of Education and External Studies, University of Nairobi, and former director of education in the Ministry of Education. He has carried out several consultancy assignments for UNESCO, UNICEF, the World Bank, the Ford Foundation, and USAID. In July 2004, he was made an honorary fellow of the Commonwealth of Learning in recognition of his contribution to the field of distance education, most notably in Africa. He is currently serving as program commissioner and coordinator for NEPAD's e-Africa Commission in charge of Human Development. He can be contacted at pkinyanjui@eafricacommission.org

Badri Koul, PhD, works as a free-lance consultant in distance education, adult education, higher education and teaching of English and Hindi as foreign/second languages. He was director, Distance Education Centre at the University of the West Indies; and held UNESCO Chair (educational technology) from 1999 to 2003. He has published seven books (including a translation of Plato into Hindi) and contributed over 120 articles, etc. on various aspects of distance education and language teaching, besides teaching languages, designing curricula and staff-development programs, training distance educators and being the founding editor of *The Indian Journal of Open Learning* (IJOL). In 2004, he was made an honorary fellow of the Commonwealth of Learning. He can be contacted at bnkoul@yahoo.co.uk

Jennifer V. Lock, PhD, is an assistant professor in the Faculty of Education at the University of Calgary. She teaches in both the undergraduate and graduate programs. Her area of specialization is educational technology. Her doctoral research examined how the concept of community is developed, realized, and sustained within virtual in-service teacher learning environments. Lock's current research interests involve online learning communities, online collaboration, e-learning, building capacity of online educators, and integrating information and communication technology (ICT) in education and teacher education. Lock is the book review editor for the *Canadian Journal of Learning and Technology*. She can be contacted at jvlock@ucalgary.ca

Rocci Luppicini, PhD is a replacement professor in the Department of Communication at the University of Ottawa in Canada. He has published in a number of areas including virtual learning communities and practice (*Quarterly Review Of Distance Education*), research methodology on online instruction (*Journal of Distance Education*), issues in higher education, instructional design (*Canadian Journal of Learning and Technology*), and design research (*International Journal of Technology and Design Education*). His most recent book project is an edited volume titled *Handbook of Conversation Design for Instructional Applications* (Idea Group Global, in progress).

Leslie Moller, PhD, is an associate professor and chair of the Technology for Education and Training Division at the University of South Dakota. He is a graduate of Purdue University's Instructional Research and Development program. He is currently the cochair of the AECT Research Symposium and serves on the editorial boards of the *Quarterly Review of Distance Education, International Journal of Educational Technology*, and *Performance Improvement Quarterly*. Moller is also the former chair of the Instructional Technology Special Interest Group within the American Educational Research Association as well as the Distance Education and Curriculum committees for AECT. He has authored more than three dozen articles and book chapters related to distance education and instructional systems design. He and his wife Mary Ann, two grandchildren, and a houseful of critters, live in Yankton, South Dakota. He can be easily reached at lesmoller@aol.com

Gary R. Morrison is a professor and graduate program director in the Department of Educational Curriculum and Instruction in Old Dominion University's College of Education, where he teaches courses in instructional design. He has worked as instructional designer for three Fortune 500 companies and the University of Mid-America. Previously, he was a professor in the instructional design and technology programs at the University of Memphis and Wayne State University. His research focuses on cognitive load theory, instructional strategies, K-12 technology integration, and distance education. He is the associate editor of the research section of *Educational Technology Research and Development*. Gary is co-author of *Designing Effective Instruction*, 5th ed., with Steven M. Ross and Jerrold E. Kemp. Morrison is also author of more than 20 book chapters, 50 articles, and over 100 conference presentations on topics in instructional technology. He can be contacted at GMorriso@odu.edu

Rena Palloff and Keith Pratt are the authors of the 1999 Frandson Award-winning book *Building Learning Communities in Cyberspace: Effective Strategies for the Online Classroom* (Jossey-Bass, 1999), the second edition of which is currently in publication. They have also written *Lessons from the Cyberspace Classroom* (Jossey-Bass, 2001), *The Virtual Student* (Jossey-Bass, 2003), and *Collaborating Online: Learning Together in Community* (Jossey-Bass, 2005). The books are comprehensive guides to the development of an online environment that helps promote successful learning outcomes while fostering collaboration and building a sense of community among the learners. Palloff and Pratt have been presenting this work across the United States and internationally since 1994 as well as consulting to academic institutions and their faculties regarding the development and delivery of effective distance learning programs. In addition to their consulting work, Palloff is core faculty at the Fielding Graduate University in Santa Barbara, CA, and adjunct faculty at Capella University. Pratt is faculty at Fielding Graduate University, Baker University, and Wayland Baptist University. They can be contacted at rpalloff@mindspring.com and drkpratt@mindspring.com

Arjan Raven, PhD, is an associate professor of management information systems in the Coles College of Business at Kennesaw State University. Raven teaches courses on knowledge management and information systems. His research focuses on instructional and collaborative technologies and knowledge management systems. He can be contacted at araven1@kennesaw.edu

Steven M. Ross received his doctorate in educational psychology from Pennsylvania State University. He is currently a Faudree Professor and executive director of the Center for Research in Educational Policy at the University of Memphis. He is a noted lecturer on school programs and educational evaluation. Ross is the author of six textbooks and more than 120 journal articles in the areas of educational technology and instructional design, at-risk learners, educational reform, computer-based instruction, and individualized instruction. He is the editor of the research section of the journal *Educational Technology Research and Development* and a member of the editorial board for two other professional journals. He has testified on school restructuring research before the U.S. House of Representatives Subcommittee on Early Childhood, Youth, and Families, and is a technical advisor and researcher on current federal and state initiatives.

Richard. A. Schwier, Ed.D., is a professor of educational communications and technology at the University of Saskatchewan, where he coordinates the graduate program in educational communications and technology. He is the principal investigator in the Virtual Learning Communities Research Laboratory, which is currently studying the characteristics of formal online learning communities. His other research interests include instructional design and social change agency. He can be contacted at Richard.Schwier@extfc.usask.ca

Scott H. Switzer, MA, is a freelance learning developer in Colorado Springs, Colorado, and an instructor in the School of Education and Human Development at the University of Colorado at Denver and Health Sciences Center (UCDHSC). Over the past 10 years, he has taught a number of courses in master's programs in instructional technology and has been a presenter at a variety of professional conferences and seminars. His research interests are instructional design and e-learning development and he is also interested in higher education faculty development programs as they relate to creating more effective online and hybrid learning environments. Currently pursuing a PhD in the educational leadership and innovation program at UCDHSC, he has earned a master of arts in education from the University of Colorado at Colorado Springs and a bachelor of science in communication from Ohio University.

Brent G. Wilson, PhD, is professor and coordinator of Information and Learning Technologies at the University of Colorado at Denver and Health Sciences Center. He has published widely on topics in instructional design and learning technologies. His current work seeks to broaden the conceptual foundations for instructional design through greater attention to practitioner knowledge, values, and aesthetic perspectives. Brent is active in a number of organizations including AECT, AERA, TIE, and PIDT, and consults with a number of organizations in corporate and public sectors. Brent participates with the chapter's co-authors in the IDEAL research lab (Innovative Designs of Environments for Adult Learners—see http://thunder1.cudenver.edu/ideal/). He can be contacted at brent.wilson@cudenver.edu